Microfinance India

Thank you for choosing a SAGE product!
If you have any comment, observation or feedback,
I would like to personally hear from you.

Please write to me at **contactceo@sagepub.in**

Vivek Mehra, Managing Director and CEO, SAGE India.

Bulk Sales

SAGE India offers special discounts
for purchase of books in bulk.
We also make available special imprints
and excerpts from our books on demand.

For orders and enquiries, write to us at

Marketing Department
SAGE Publications India Pvt Ltd
B1/I-1, Mohan Cooperative Industrial Area
Mathura Road, Post Bag 7
New Delhi 110044, India

E-mail us at **marketing@sagepub.in**

Subscribe to our mailing list
Write to **marketing@sagepub.in**

This book is also available as an e-book.

Microfinance India
State of the Sector Report 2012

Venugopalan Puhazhendhi

Los Angeles | London | New Delhi
Singapore | Washington DC | Melbourne

First published in 2013 by

 SAGE Publications India Pvt Ltd
B1/I-1 Mohan Cooperative Industrial Area
Mathura Road, New Delhi 110 044, India
www.sagepub.in

SAGE Publications Inc
2455 Teller Road
Thousand Oaks, California 91320, USA

SAGE Publications Ltd
1 Oliver's Yard, 55 City Road
London EC1Y 1SP, United Kingdom

SAGE Publications Asia-Pacific Pte Ltd
33 Pekin Street
#02-01 Far East Square
Singapore 048763

ACCESS Development Services
28, Hauz Khas Village
New Delhi 110 016
www.accessdev.org

Published by Vivek Mehra for SAGE Publications India Pvt Ltd, Phototypeset in 10/12 pt Minion Pro by Diligent Typesetter, Delhi.

Library of Congress Cataloging-in-Publication Data Available

ISBN: 978-81-321-1090-3 (PB)

SAGE Team: Rudra Narayan, Rohini Rangachari Karnik, Rajib Chatterjee and Umesh Kashyap

Disclaimer: The views expressed in this publication are those of the authors and do not necessarily reflect the views and policies of ACCESS Development Services.

Cover photograph courtesy: ACCESS.

Contents

List of Tables, Figures, Boxes, Annexes and Abbreviations

Tables

Figures

Boxes

Annexes

Abbreviations

ABCO	Average Business per Credit Officer
AFSL	Arohan Financial Services Pvt. Ltd.
AML	Anti-Money Laundering
AP	Andhra Pradesh
APDPIP	Andhra Pradesh District Poverty Initiative Project
APGB	Andhra Pragathi Grameen Bank
APL	Above Poverty Line
APMAS	Andhra Pradesh Mahila Abhivruddhi Society
BAIF	Bharatiya Agro Industries Foundation
BC	Business Correspondent
BCNM	Business Correspondent Network Manager
BDS	Business Development Services
BF	Business Facilitator
BIRD	Bankers Institute of Rural Development
BPL	Below Poverty Line
CAB	College of Agricultural Banking
CASHE	Credit and Savings for Household Enterprise
CASHPOR	Credit and Savings for the Hardcore Poor
CBMFIs	Community-Based Microfinance Institutions

CBOs	Community-Based Organizations
CBRM	Community-Based Recovery Mechanism
CDF	Cooperative Development Foundation
CDS	Centre for Development Studies
CGAP	Consultative Group to Assist the Poor
CIBIL	Credit Information Bureau (India) Limited
CMF	Centre for Microfinance
CMR	Centre for Microfinance Research
CMRC	Community Managed resource Centres
COCA	Code of Conduct Compliance Assessment
CRAR	Capital to Risk-weighted Assets Ratio
CSC	Customer Service Centre
CSP	Customer Service Point
DCC	District Consultative Committee
DCCB	District Central Cooperative Bank
DFID	Department of International Development
DIPP	Department of Industrial Policy and Promotion
DoP	Department of Post
DRDA	District Rural development Agency
DWCD	Department of Women and Child Development
EBT	Electronic Benefits Transfer
FIF	Financial Inclusion Fund
FIP	Financial Inclusion Plan
FIPB	Foreign Investment Promotion Board
FITF	Financial Inclusion Technology Fund
FWWB	Friends of Women's World Banking
GCC	General Credit Card
GDP	Gross Domestic Product
GDS	Grameen Development Services
GIZ	Deutsche Gesellschaft fur Internatioale Zusammenarbeit
GoI	Government of India
HDFC	Housing Development Finance Corporation
HDI	Human Development Index
IFAD	International Fund for Agricultural Development
IFC	International Finance Corporation
IFMR	Institute of Financial Management and Research
IGA	Income Generating Activities
IGS	Indian Grameen Services
IKP	Indira Kranti Patham
ILO	International Labour Organization
IMEF	India Microfinance Equity Fund
IMEF	India Micro Equity Fund
INAFI	International Network of Alternative Financial Institutions
IPO	Initial Public Offering
IRDA	Insurance Regulatory and Development Authority
IRDP	Integrated Rural Development Programme
JLG	Joint Liability Group
KBSLAB	Krishna Bhima Samruddhi Local Area Bank
KCCs	Kisan Credit Cards
KDFS	Kalangiam Development and Financial Services
KfW	Kreditanstalt fur Wiederaufbau
KGFS	Kshetriya Gramin Financial Services
KYC	Know Your Customer
LAB	Local Area Bank

LIC	Life Insurance Corporation of India
LWE	Left Wing Extremism
MACS	Mutually Aided Cooperative Society
MBT	Mutual Benefit Trust
MCID	Micro Credit Innovations Department
M-CRIL	Micro-Credit Ratings international Ltd.
MEDP	Micro Enterprise Development Programme
MENA	Middle East and North Africa
MFDC	Micro Finance Development Council
MFDEF	Micro Finance Development and Equity Fund
MFI	Microfinance Institutions
MFIN	Microfinance Institutions Network
MFO	Microfinance Organizations
MGNREGS	The Mahatma Gandhi National Rural Employment Guarantee Scheme
MIA	Micro Insurance Academy
MIS	Management Information System
MIX	Micro Finance Information Exchange
MMS	Mandal Mahila Samakhyas
MPI	Microfinance Penetration Index
MPPI	Microfinance Poverty Penetration Index
MRAP	Micro Finance Researcher's Alliance Programme
MSDF	Michael and Susan Dell Foundation
MSE	Micro and Small Enterprises
MSP	Minimum Support Price
MVDP	Maharashtra Village Development Association
NABARD	National Bank for Agriculture and Rural Development
NABFINS	NABARD Financial Services Ltd.
NAFSCOB	National Federation of State Cooperative Banks
NBFC	Non-Banking Financial Company
NCAER	National Council for Applied Economic Research
NCDs	Non-convertible Debentures
NE	North East
NFAs	No Frill Accounts
NGO	Non-governmental Organization
NHB	National Housing Bank
NOC	No Objection Certificate
NPA	Non-Performing Assets
NPL	National Poverty Line
NPS	New Pension Scheme
NREGA	National Rural Employment Guarantee Act
NREGS	National Rural Employment Guarantee Scheme
NRLM	National Rural Livelihoods Mission
NSSO	National Sample Survey Organization
OER	Operating Expense Ratio
OSS	Operating Self-Sufficiency
PACS	Primary Agricultural Credit Societies
PANI	People's Action for National Integration
PAR	Portfolio Risk
PE	Private Equity
PHC	Public Health Centre
PIL	Public Interest Litigation
PLF	Panchayat Level Federation
PPI	Progress Out of Poverty Index
PPP	Purchasing Power Parity

PRADAN	Professional Assistance for Development Action
PRI	Panchayati Raj Institution
PSL	Priority Sector Lending
QIP	Qualified Institutional Placement
RBI	Reserve Bank of India
RFID	Radio Frequency Identification Device
RFL	Revoving Fund Loan
RGVN	Rashtriya Grameed Vikas Nidhi
RMHC	Rural Micro Health Centre
RMK	Rashtriya Mahila kosh
ROA	Return on Assets
ROE	Return on Equity
ROGLP	Return on Gross Loan Portfolio
ROI	Return on Investment
RPLI	Rural Postal Life Insurance
RRB	Regional Rural Bank
RSETI	Rural Self Employment Training Institute
SBLP	SHG Bank Linkage Programme
SC	Scheduled Caste
SCB	State Cooperative Bank
SERP	Society for Elimination of Rural Poverty
SEWA	Self Employed Women's Association
SGSY	Swarnajayanti Gram Swarozgar Yojana
SHG	Self Help Group
SHPA	Self-help Promotion Agency
SHPI	Self-help Promotion Institution
SIDBI	Small Industries Development Bank of India
SKDRDP	Sri Kshetra Dharmasthala Rural development Project
SLBC	State Level Bankers Committee
SPM	Social Performance Management
SRO	Self Regulatory Organization
ST	Scheduled Tribe
UID	Unique Identification Number
UNDP	United Nations Development Programme
VC	Venture Capital
VFSL	Village Financial Services Ltd.
VHS	Voluntary Health Service
VO	Village Organization
WSHG	Women Self Help Group

Foreword

Just finished reading 'Confessions of a Microfinance Heretic' by Hugh Sinclair. A sordid saga, though exaggerated at places, of a good intent that went haywire. This apparently is a new genre of literature in the sector that is starting to hit the stands. In India, about two years back, Prof. M. S. Sriram of IIM Ahmedabad, wrote a Discussion Paper in a similar gripping narrative titled 'Commercialization of Microfinance in India' that had an insightful description of the boardroom skullduggery within among the most pre-eminent MFIs in the country. The good stories of 'Doing Good and Doing Well' of a model that was touted as a miraculous mechanism of reaching the poor, seemingly have started to dry out and are replaced by scathing details of wrongdoing by MFIs, client abuse, high profiteering, investor greed, manipulations within Board Rooms and are grabbing headlines. While perhaps the Sinclair book is not so well circulated among those that view commercial microfinance with skepticism and suspicion, the Sriram Paper was widely read by a diverse cross-section of stakeholders, more importantly by policy makers and regulators. Among others, the paper then became the *casus belli* that led to the Andhra Pradesh crisis in October 2010. A market that seemed to be sizzling, crashed completely and promoters who featured as among the most influential people by magazines like *Time* and *Newsweek*, disappeared from public sight in the wake of the Andhra Pradesh Ordinance.

Are there any lessons to learn from the Andhra Crisis? For over a quarter century, prodded by a need to sustainably serve the poor, commercial MFIs, as they matured and grew, came to be accepted as a well tested, market-based and scalable model. In India alone, over a period of 15 years they attained an outreach of over 30 million with an outstanding portfolio of over ₹ 200 billion. It was growing at a much faster pace than the more mainstream SHG-Bank linkage programme. Banks were abandoning SHG lending and providing huge bulk loans to MFIs; investors from all across the world were queuing up to invest in these new breed institutions. The regulator turned a blind eye and while one MFI hit the capital markets, several others were dressing up their show for windfall gains through IPOs. The Andhra Pradesh Crisis undid all this as Prof. Sriram titled it in his *Economic and Political Weekly* 'A fairy tale turned into a nightmare'. While there have been some papers and studies on identifying the reasons for the Andhra Pradesh crisis, and both the industry and the regulator are trying to fix the issues, what the sector should learn from the Andhra episode, I guess is more important; since eventually it is the poor who are hit the worst, and perhaps, it can not be business as usual, anymore.

All through 2011, there were efforts at repairing a beleaguered sector; however with little success. There seemed little recovery in sight. The biggest impact of the crisis, apparently was the drying up of capital, both debt and investment. Banks largely adopted a position of wait and watch; waiting for what however was not apparent. While for some time there was a certain uncertainty whether loans to MFIs would be retained in the priority-sector list; and if that were to happen, the liquidity crunch would have only worsened, as MFI lending has been, for some time, among the best risk adjusted lending under the priority sector. Were MFI lending to go out of the priority sector list, there would have been little incentive for banks to continue lending to MFIs. Fortunately, the new priority sector guidelines retained bulk loans to MFIs in the list. Irrespective, fresh lending did not seem to be forthcoming in the last one year, with the list of banks willing to lend to MFIs shrinking down to very few. The severe cash flow crunch resulted in several MFIs folding up, particularly the smaller ones; and both the numbers and outstanding portfolio saw a negative growth. The Reserve

Bank issued a series of policy circulars, created a separate NBFC MFI category, put a cap on spread and issued prudential norms for lending. The composite Microfinance Bill continued to be pending in Parliament for enactment. The industry associations continued their engagement with policy makers, the Regulators and commercial banks announced a unified code of conduct at the ACCESS Microfinance India Summit in December 2011 and undertook social performance ratings in an attempt to keep vigil over practice. An IFC initiative saw the structuring of the Responsible Finance Forum to push the industry towards greater disclosure and transparency. There seemed to be no new breakthrough in the three-way impasse between the Federal and AP State Government and the MFIs. Despite all measures and policy initiatives, at the end of the day, there was no sight of the sector getting back on track some time soon.

The SHG programme too did not remain unscathed, with the pace of growth slowing down, defaults rising, groups breaking and a general sense of ennui being witnessed among both promoters and lenders. While NABARD, which desired to give the movement a fresh impetus through its SHG version 2 of the programme, has not been able to move with the new ideas effectively, the ambitious NRLM (National Rural Livelihoods Mission) has also been slow in rolling out. NRLM, on the ground will enroll 450 crore poor households into SHGs, which will be federated for financial intermediation across 600 districts. However, the fact that the government itself will largely implement the programme, has in fact become the principal reason for its slow start. Across states, there are not enough professionals to hire for implementing a large complex programme like this one. Further, the government too has identified over 100 difficult districts to saturate them with SHGs through MoUs with Self-Help Promoting agencies. All this together should ordinarily have translated into a big new push to the SHG programme, but signs of a re-energized movement are not evident.

Put together, both the MFI and SHG outreach could not cross the 100 million threshold, which should have easily happened if the pace of growth of the previous years had sustained.

The seventh edition of the ACCESS 'State of the Sector' Report seeks to capture the dull and dreary recovery process witnessed over the last one year and the role of different stakeholders in this rebuilding effort. The Report attempts to analyze trends and progress under the two strands of microcredit delivery, identify issues that have enabled but mostly impeded growth. It will highlight new initiatives being taken by the government and the Reserve Bank in pushing the financial inclusion agenda, analyze the enabling environment and policy initiatives that were taken during the year. A special chapter has been dedicated to the important National Rural Livelihoods Mission that seeks to examine its potential impact on the poor, particularly in their effort to access financial services. Another important aspect deals with the issue of customer protection and responsible finance, contextually important since it was the issue of client abuse that precipitated the crisis. Overall the SOS, as always, will represent a major effort in capturing all initiatives, efforts, issues and activities that characterize the progress of the sector witnessed in the last one year.

An important change in this year's SOS has been the author. While over the last four years, the SOS was authored and anchored by N. Srinivasan, who is now so well known within the sector; this year's report has a new author in Dr Venugopalan Puhazhendhi or Puha, as he is nicknamed. Puha came into the country from South Korea, where he taught Economics at Konkuk University in Seoul. Although Puha is a former executive of NABARD, and was among the first to have undertaken studies on the impact of the SHG programme and transaction costs of lending under the programme, several years away from the country perhaps did not help him in keeping abreast with the current state of affairs of the sector. I invited Puha to the Microfinance India Summit last year to assess his inclination to take on the mantle of authoring the *State of the Sector Report*. Despite his handicap, and much to our relief, Puha agreed. He is a keen researcher, and is quick to pick the trends, and a few discussions on the sidelines of the Summit, assured us that he would eventually be able to pull off this task. Soon after our agreeing for him to author the SOS, Puha got onto the job, reading, researching, talking and meeting with key stakeholders and understanding key issues. Fortunately, Srini agreed to free some of his time to continue support to Puha, wherever he required. I am grateful to Puha for having come on board and for bringing out the SOS in time for its annual release.

Bringing out the SOS is indeed a sectoral effort. In addition to a small secretariat within ACCESS that supports the writing of this Report, a whole lot of stakeholders very enthusiastically support this effort. Over the years, the Centre for Micro Finance (CMF), Chennai has been a rock solid support to the SOS. Its research findings from several studies have brought great depth of analysis in the Report. I thank Santa from CMF for the great commitment and contribution from CMF. Graham and Manoj from MicroSave, have equally provided super content to the Report. The data this year from MIX was critical for the MFI chapter and I thank Liz for her willing support. C. S. Reddy from APMAS hugely contributed to the SHG chapter analysis. I profusely thank NABARD for providing all the related information and data for the SHG chapter. I would like to thank Dr Prakash Bakshi, Chairman NABARD, his colleagues Suran and Krishna for their stupendous contribution. The SFMC team at SIDBI, Alok and Priya from MFIN, Greg from CGAP, Titus and Achala from Sa-Dhan, Alok from M-CRIL, Al from NABFINS, Navin from Solutions Exchange and Prema from UNDP have all contributed in equal measure; I thank them all. Support from Sita from the World Bank was critical for the NRLM chapter. Without this overwhelming support, ACCESS by itself could never pull together a document, which traces the variety and vicissitudes in its analysis and content.

Finally, I take great pride in my own teams to have, once again provided anchor support to Puha and the Report. Under the dynamic stewardship of Radhika, Executive Director, ACCESS ASSIST (a specialized affiliate of ACCESS), and duly supported by Nilesh and Juhi at Headquarters, and the exceptional support from Deepak in Lucknow, and Sudipto in Kolkata, the team stood up to provide quality backend support in a timely manner. The team helped in coordination of Puha's meetings with key stakeholders, informing him of important sectoral events, pulling down relevant information. As always, Lalitha was super efficient in organizing Puha's travel and other logistics. This aggregate effort from teams at both ACCESS and ACCESS-ASSIST helped Puha to bring out the Report in time.

I am glad that, with support from all, ACCESS has been able to bring out yet another high quality State of the Sector Report. Increasingly, the SOS has become an important reference document, which has begun to inform as well as influence policy, and policy makers find it useful while taking a view on issues within the sector. While the Malegam Committee used the Report while making its recommendations on the sector, several others in the Parliament reach out to ACCESS for its copies, even if to better understand sectoral issues. The effort, however, is to make the SOS a useful document that can help in anticipating trends and help in improving practice. I am sure the Report serves this meaningful purpose.

Vipin Sharma
CEO
ACCESS Development Services

Preface

When invited to write this year's State of the Sector Report, I accepted with great privilege and pleasure primarily for getting an opportunity to revisit the sector after my involvement in the initial phase of the SHG Bank Linkage Programme. Now I could recognize the vast changes that took place in the sector in its approach, vision and mission as well as the changes among the clients' profile and perspectives. The very high standards set by N. Srinivasan, the author of previous years' reports, made my task both inspiring and challenging. Recognizing the importance and relevance of this document both at national and international levels at a time when the sector is showing signs of recovery from the crisis; I tried to put all my efforts to making this document forward looking and packed with knowledge.

Being a new author of the report, I tried to retain the structure and presentation of the report similar to earlier ones for the sack of continuity. This year's report has 10 chapters broadly similar to the earlier reports, except having a separate chapter on credit plus initiatives by different microfinance institutions. I have also laid greater emphasis on institutional arrangements in SHG mode, focusing on SHG federations. With a view to providing deeper insights, the National Rural Livelihoods Mission (NRLM) has been incorporated as a separate chapter as in the previous years. Financial inclusion has been recognized as a priority goal of the microfinance sector and efforts were made in this report to identify the critical areas of interventions for greater success of the initiatives in the future.

In spite of the huge challenges I faced in getting inputs and information from various institutions and stakeholders, the magnitude and quality of support provided by most of the stakeholders have greatly helped me in bringing out the report on time. I must profusely thank the Centre for Micro Finance (CMF) at the Institute for Financial Management and Research, Chennai, and its Microfinance Researchers Alliance Programme (MRAP), Andhra Pradesh Mahila Abhivruddhi Society (APMAS), MicroSave and the Micro Finance Institutions (MIX) Market for their extraordinary support through sharing their research findings and data. The voluminous data and information provided by MIX Market, the National Bank for Agriculture and Rural Development (NABARD), the Small Industries Development Bank of India (SIDBI), the Micro Finance Institutions Network (MFIN), UNSE Microfinance Community Grameen Foundation and studies by MicroSave and CMF Chennai formed the basis for the report. Santadarshan Sadhu, CMF, Graham Wright, Manoj K. Sharma, MicroSave and C.S. Reddy, APMAS, have shared the burden of preparing this report in time. The study conducted by K.C. Deepti from CMF provided valuable input for the report. Liz Larson and Amarnath Samarapally provided critical data for MFI analysis. C.S. Reddy and Enable network extended valuable support through their research findings on SHG federations.

Aloysius P. Fernandez from NABFINs and Greg Chen of CGAP responded to my request for sharing their views on important issues in the Indian microfinance sector. The generous support extended by Sitaramachandra Machiraju of the World Bank in developing the NRLM chapter deserves special mention here.

Dr Prakash Bakshi, Chairman, NABARD shared his views on the sector performance and related issues. Suran and Krishna from MCID extended all their support, including providing required data. My former colleagues at NABARD—Sathish, Venkatesh Tagat, Jinna, Padmanaban and Chintala—supported me in every possible way in bringing out this report in time. Ashok from NABARD helped me in developing several case studies. Mathew Titus, Achala Savyasaachi from Sa-Dhan, Alok Prasad of MFIN, Kalpana Shankar and Jayaseelan of Hand in Hand, Vasudevan from Equitas, GVS Reddy from SERP, Sampath Kumar from RGMVP and Baskaran in IIBF have assisted me by providing required data and their critical views on the microfinance sector. Radhika, Lalitha, Juhi, Nilesh and Sudipto Saha from Access supported me through the supply of information and in arranging meetings and other logistics in writing this report. Special mention should be made of the excellent support provided by Deepak Goswami, Access Assist, in processing of MIX Market and NABARD data and for his critical editorial assistance in shaping up a few chapters. My thanks are due to R. Balasubramanian, Professor of Agricultural Economics at TNAU, Coimbatore, for reviewing the draft of most of the chapters.

Sridhar from High Mark; Suresh Krishna of Grammen Koota; and Ram of Rang De; Chandi, Jayesh and Gaurav of Grameen Foundation India; Giresh Nair and Devahuti Choudhury from IFC, Atul and Deepak Alok from M2i Consulting, V.S. Reddy from Sthiri Nidhi, Anil Kumar and Rajeev Kaimal from KGFS, Milroy Paul from Habitat for Humanity, Smita Premchander and Chidamabaranathan from Shampark, Arpita Sen from Bandhan extended support by providing critical inputs for the report. Navin Anand's support in bringing out the views of the Microfinance Community Solution Exchange through posting the queries as well as in arranging a round table discussion deserves special thanks. Alok Mishra from M-CRIL extended valuable support by providing inputs in listing out the innovative products of MFIs. Also, excellent support was extended by Rudra Narayan and Rohini Rangachari Karnik from SAGE Publications and the editorial team that contributed to the smooth readability and error free nature of this publication.

All members of the Microfinance Advisory Group at Access, more specifically, Y.C. Nanda, Bridjmohan, Alok Mishra, Jayeshmodi and Vipin Sharma guided me throughout the report preparation with their ideas and feedback for which I am deeply indebted. I thank many other people who have helped me directly or indirectly and whose names I may have missed out. My thanks are due to the sponsors.

I record my sincere and special thanks to N. Srinivasan the author of the State of the Sector (SoS) Reports for the last four years for his wise counsel and his unconditional support and guidance. He critically reviewed most of the chapters which certainly contributed to the qualitative improvement of the report. Finally, my special thanks to Vipin Sharma for entrusting this task with blind faith. I have put in all my efforts to bring out a balanced view on different issues; however, I am the residual claimant for any remaining errors and omissions in the report. I am looking forward to receiving critical feedback for sharpening future efforts.

Venugopalan Puhazhendhi

Overview

GLOBAL ECONOMY

The gloom that engulfed the global economy following the financial crisis in mid-2007 got intensified due to the European debt crisis in the recent period.[1] Most of the advanced economies face deflationary tendencies combined with high unemployment rates. The global economy is projected to grow at 3.5 per cent in 2012, a drop of 0.5 per cent from what was estimated for 2011. The uncertainty surrounding the resolution of the sovereign debt crisis of the Euro zone makes it difficult for the world economy to recover. Concerns over fiscal sustainability in Italy and Spain have also cast a shadow over the Euro zone. However, the recent commitment showed by European Central Banks in providing liquidity to tide over short-term bank rollover risk have signalled the firm resolve of the European leaders to tackle the crisis. While the emerging and developing economies have been able to withstand the crisis to a large extent, they cannot remain immune to the developments. Given the global interlinkages through both trade and finance, these economies have started experiencing the adverse impact of the crisis in a visible manner. The low growth rates in the advanced countries have meant that the export demand emanating from these economies has taken a beating, which is bound to impact the growth of emerging and developing economies. This is apart from the contagion effect that the crisis anyway has. The emerging and developing countries as a group are nevertheless quite diverse, and it would be a fallacy to club them all as a homogenous category and prescribing universal solutions. While some countries need to guard against overheating, others may have to tackle negative output gap.[2] Fiscal consolidation and bank deleveraging are unavoidable, painful remedies, which lead to a contraction in growth rate in the short run.

INDIAN ECONOMY

While the world economy was grappling with its problems, the Indian economy grew at a healthy rate of 8.7 per cent for the five year period 2003–04 to 2007–08. In fact, the average rate of growth for the three year period 2005–06 to 2007–08 was 9.5 per cent. The crisis year (2008–09) saw the growth rate plummeting to 6.7 per cent, which was anyway on expected lines. The economy however bounced back by registering growth of 8.4 per cent for the next two fiscal years.[3] The fairy tale run of the economy seems to have taken a beating with growth plummeting to 6.5 per cent in 2011–12, which incidentally is lower than even the growth recorded in the crisis year 2008–09. The underlying macro economic factors associated with this growth rate appear to indicate that the slowdown is structural in nature rather than cyclical. The slowdown is evidently widespread across the sectors. Barring the two segments, viz., electricity, gas and water supply and community, social and personal services, there was a marked deceleration in the growth rate of output in all other activities. The fall in the growth rate of agriculture, forestry and fishing implies that around 55 per cent of the population dependent on it would be adversely affected and incomes would fall. A reduction in the construction sector growth rate also does not augur well for employment generation as it has one of the highest employment elasticities, across sectors.

The policy debate in India is now firmly focused on the relevant contributory factors such as the interest rate, inflation rate and the exchange rate. Given that the growth rate is forecast to slacken again to 6.5 per cent in 2012–13, there has been a persistent demand for an accommodative monetary policy in order to boost the growth rate. There is a recognition that an investment rate of 36 per cent in order to sustain a growth rate of 9 per cent per annum is not within the realm of reality. The Reserve Bank has downscaled the potential trend growth rate for the economy to 7.5 per cent. The inflation rate continues to remain high despite a bumper crop in foodgrains and large food stocks. Recognizing the possibility of stoking inflationary pressures, the central bank's hesitation to cut interest rates also stems from the high level of fiscal deficit and excessive borrowing by the central government. Furthermore, the perceived policy paralysis at the centre has also undermined the confidence in the India growth story. Highlighting its concern over the fiscal deficit, the international rating agency Standard & Poor's (S&P) cut India's rating by one notch and any further downgrade would mean that India would not have an investment grade rating. A junk rating could dry up capital inflows and make it harder for Indian companies to raise funds overseas.

The pangs of inflation have persisted since the commencement of the decade. During 2011–12, headline WPI inflation rate moderated from a peak of 10.0 per cent in September 2011 to 7.7 per cent in March 2012. However, during 2012–13 so far, provisional data suggest that it inched up from 7.2 per cent in April to 7.6 per cent in May, driven mainly by food and fuel prices, but moderated to 6.9 per cent in June due mainly to base effect. The food inflation, driven mainly by vegetable prices and protein inflation continue to contribute substantially to headline inflation.[4] Predominantly, inflation concerns weigh heavily in policy making as its effects have to be factored in while formulating policies for sustainable economic expansion. Supply-side constraints, a falling rupee, an outsized government budget deficit and a widening current account deficit have added to the economic malaise leaving little policy leeway on both the monetary as well as fiscal fronts. The most serious consequence of inflation is its adverse distributional impact on the poor, people without social security and pensioners. Poor households are unable to maintain consumption levels at current prices and therefore, they are particularly worse off in an inflationary situation.[5] During 2011–12, growth also slowed down, in part because of high inflation. This further reduced the welfare of the common man as firstly, it had an adverse impact on employment and incomes and secondly, with low growth, the trickle down benefits for the poor also reduced. The value of the Rupee against the US dollar witnessed a steep depreciation. From April this financial year, the Indian Rupee has depreciated by 6.6 per cent till July, 2012 on a monthly average

basis, and it was the worst performer among major Asian currencies. Growth of exports (and imports) of both the advanced economies and the emerging and developing economies is projected to halve by 2013 as compared to the growth rate achieved in 2010. Though the conventional view is that a depreciating rupee may aid exports, in the present scenario where demand for Indian exports is dependent on the recovery in advanced economies, pushing exports may not be possible in the short run. India needs to boost exports by evolving an incentive structure and support in a substantial manner if it wants to arrest the further worsening of the current account deficit.

Growth in bank credit has slowed in China and India amid concerns about deteriorating loan quality. Bank credit in India is projected to grow at 17 per cent, against 19.3 per cent in 2011–12. On a year-on-year (y-o-y) basis, non-food bank credit increased by 17 per cent in April as compared with 22.1 per cent a year ago, which improved to 18.6 per cent in June 2012. Credit to agriculture increased by 14.6 per cent in April 2012, up from 12.0 per cent in April 2011, but slackened to 12.8 per cent in June 2012. Credit to industry increased by 19.5 per cent in April 2012 and improved to 20.3 per cent in June 2012 as compared with 25.9 per cent in April 2011. Credit growth to industry in April 2012 was led by infrastructure, metals and metal products, engineering, food processing, gems and jewellery, vehicles, vehicle parts and transport equipment and mining and quarrying. Credit to the services sector increased by 15.8 per cent in April 2012, significantly lower than 24.1 per cent in April 2011, but improved to 19.1 per cent in June 2012. For the Twelfth Plan period the institutional credit for agriculture has been projected in the range of ₹33,000 billion to ₹42,000 billion depending upon the various growth scenarios. The most plausible is the scenario where the institutional agriculture credit flow is estimated at ₹37,000 billion for the five-year period (2012–13 to 2017–18). Achieving this would mean that credit flow has to be doubled between the Eleventh and the Twelfth Plan.

The Twelfth Five Year Plan, which intends to usher in a *faster, sustainable and more inclusive growth*[6] builds and goes beyond the theme of the previous plan. However, the formulation of the Twelfth Five Year Plan, which was supposed to start in 2012, has been delayed by at least one year. The challenge during the Twelfth Plan would be to ensure that the principle of inclusive growth is not sacrificed on account of the lower growth rate of the economy. During the course of the eleventh plan, over 8.3 million central government employees and pensioners benefitted from the implementation of the recommendations of the sixth Central Pay Commission. Their spending ensured that India was a consumption driven growth story. The nationwide rollout of the Mahatma Gandhi National Rural Employment Guarantee Scheme did boost incomes in rural India. These two developments did shield India from the worldwide economic slowdown.

MACROECONOMIC CONDITIONS AND MICROFINANCE INSTITUTIONS[7]

Do the macroeconomic conditions in a country have any bearing on the working and operations of MFI? There are very few studies, which have attempted to explore this relationship. The good news is that this is an area of research, which is increasingly getting the attention of researchers in the field of microfinance. Many impact studies have mentioned the important enabling role that stable macroeconomic conditions play in the development of this sector. A study in Brazil links the relative underperformance of microfinance in the country to high levels of inflation. Another similar study attempts to compare the growth of MFIs in India and Nepal, and comes to the conclusion that the relative success of MFIs in India can be related to the positive macroeconomic conditions whereas the lack of growth of MFIs in Nepal was due to political instability following the Maoist insurgency in 1996. During the crisis period (December 1996 to March 2000) microloan lending and repayment performance of MFIs improved vis-à-vis corporate and retail banking, which were adversely affected. The authors attributed the thriving of microloans to compatibility of cash flows of microloans and small scale business were less import dependent, and hence crisis did not affect them as much as it adversely affected large businesses and thus corporate and retail banking. Moreover, micro finance borrowers repaid promptly even during the crisis to Bank Rakyat as the borrowers feared that defaulting would mean that a critical source of access to finance would be lost. However, a contrasting experience has been presented in a study in the context of Bolivia during the economic crisis period of 1998–2004. The authors assert that adverse macroeconomic conditions led to decline in lending and increase in loan defaults. An important finding of the study was that MFIs that were profit driven (largely concentrated in extending consumer credit) were the ones that were largely hit relative to those, which provided additional services like savings, training, etc., along with loans. The government also bailed out MFIs that had debt problems, which did create moral hazard problems. The two studies, therefore, provide contrasting evidence on the impact of macroeconomic conditions prevailing in a country and MFI performance. A panel data study conducted covering 329 MFIs from 70 countries investigated the macroeconomic determinants of MFI performance and has come up with some interesting findings:

1. Economic growth has a positive influence on MFI performance and gets reflected in a larger MFI loan size to the clients.
2. Higher degree of formalization and industrialization of the economy is associated negatively with MFI performance, specifically with respect to outreach parameters.

The short point that flows out of the empirical evidence emanating from the few studies in this area indicates that macroeconomic conditions can have both positive and negative outcomes with respect to MFI performance.

MICROFINANCE

From a global perspective, it is surmised that in the aftermath of the global financial crisis, microfinance has begun to enter a more mature and sustainable growth phase.[8] Followed by the rapid expansion over the years, the focus of the microfinance sector has turned towards accelerating the improvements in governance, responsible finance practices and regulatory capacity. Further, risk management, which has become a post-crisis priority for all financial institutions, has improved considerably in the microfinance sector, which is essential, given that it is offering an increasingly diversified range of innovative financial services to the poor. Besides taking advantage of new opportunities, microfinance is well positioned to take further advantage of technological and market developments.

Indian microfinance has also been showing mild signs of recovery on account of improving regulatory environment and improvement in governance. The number of savings linked SHGs increased to about ₹7.96 million with the member base[9] of 104 million. The provisional data available from NABARD for the year 2011–12 shows that the number of SHGs provided with bank loans was 4.36 million, which is about 9 per cent less than the previous year's performance.[10] However, the outstanding loan amount recorded an increase of 19 per cent during the above period. In terms of incremental loans outstanding the SBLP added ₹57.23 billion.

The total client outreach of MFIs was recorded at 26.6 million with a gross loan portfolio of ₹209.13 billion. Both the clients outreach and loan portfolio recorded negative growth in this year. The growth rate in client outreach came down by 15.7 per cent in the year 2011–12 as against an increase of 19.1 per cent recorded in the previous year. However, the gross loan portfolio has remained almost stagnant, registering a marginal fall of 3 per cent. Customer outreach has recorded a relatively higher deceleration in growth rate as compared to the loan outstanding, which suggests that MFIs are unable to service existing customers and perhaps not acquiring new customers. This trend could be attributed to the liquidity crisis which affected the MFIs during the second half of the year 2010–11, but remained almost unchanged for the entire year 2011–12. Both SBLP and MFIs put together achieve outreach of 83.4 million clients during 2011–12, which is less by 11.6 per cent of their customer base in the previous year (Figure 1.1). The degree of deceleration was pronounced more among MFIs (–15.7 per cent) than SBLP (–9.5 per cent) (Table 1.1).

The overlapping of customers between MFIs and SBLP is the prevailing phenomenon, which is still continuing. As it was done during the earlier years, while adjusting the overlap,[11] a 10 per cent reduction has been made in respect of the number of members of SHGs and a 35 per cent reduction in respect of customers of MFIs. After the adjustment of overlap, the number of customers of microfinance[12] is estimated to have increased by 12.5 per cent, which is much higher than the growth rate of last year.

Outstanding SHG loans from banks showed an increase of about 19 per cent, whereas the MFIs performance loans decreased 3 per cent when compared to the previous year. Overall, the loans outstanding in the micro finance sector increased by about 9.7 per cent (Figure 1.2). In terms of absolute amounts, the increase was of the order of ₹51 billion. However, a realistic assessment of the portfolio can be made only when the loans that have turned delinquent are taken into account.

As predicted in the last year report, the full impact of the AP events is felt during this year as the

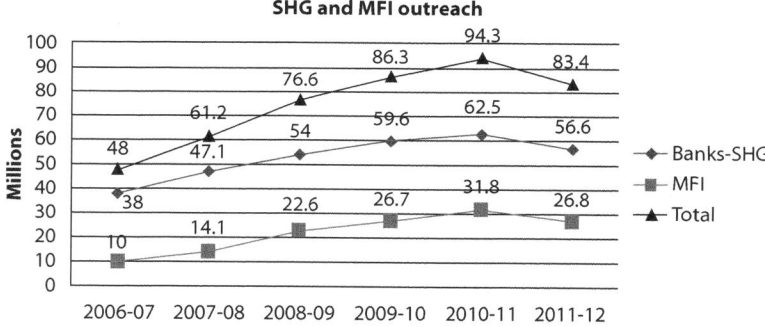

Figure 1.1 Comparison of SHG and MFI client outreach (Customers in millions)

Source: SHG data from provisional data provided by NABARD and MFI data from Sa-Dhan. The Bharat Micro Finance Quick Report 2012 and Mix Market data.

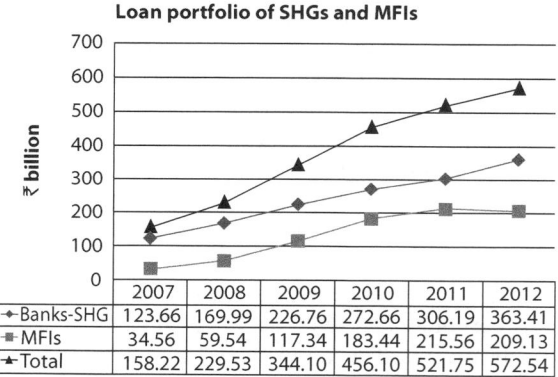

Figure 1.2 Comparison of loan portfolio of SHGs and MFIs (₹ billion)

Source: SHG data from provisional data provided by NABARD and MFI data from Sa-Dhan. The Bharat Micro Finance Quick Report 2012 and Mix Market data.

Table 1.1 Client outreach—borrowers with outstanding accounts (in millions)

	2006–07	2007–08	2008–09	2009–10	2010–11	2011–12	Growth percentage in 2012 (%)
Banks-SHG	38	47.1	54	59.6	62.5	56.6	−9.5
MFI	10	14.1	22.6	26.7	31.8	26.8	−15.7
Total	48	61.2	76.6	86.3	94.3	83.4	−11.6
Adjusted for Overlap	44.9	56	70	71	76.7	68.2	−12.5

Source: SHG data from provisional data provided by NABARD and MFI data from Sa-Dhan. The Bharat Micro Finance Quick report 2012 and Mix Market data.

Table 1.2 Comparison of average loan size

	2008	2009	2010	2011	2012	Extent of increase in 2012
SHG Member	3606	4129	4572	4893	6420	1527
MFI Customer	4223	5192	6870	6779	7803	1024

Source: SHG data from provisional data provided by NABARD and MFI data from Sa-Dhan. The Bharat Micro Finance Quick report 2012 and Mix Market data.

sector had been starved of funds, and many institutions had been forced to scale down operations.

The average loan size of SHGs increased to ₹6,420 representing an increase of ₹1,527 from the previous year (Table 1.2). In the case of MFIs, the average loans per customer increased to ₹7,803 registering 15 per cent more than the previous year with increase of ₹1,024. This increase in average loan size is likely to prove to be beneficial to MFIs in the current context of margin and interest caps that are placed. During the current year, the average loan size would continue to increase in an effort to reduce operating costs and manage the margin.

Broadly, the total number of microfinance sector clients stood at 168.6 million as at the end of March 2011 (Table 1.3). Of this, 43.3 million were customers of commercial banks. This number had declined from the previous year's level of 45.2 million. Overall, like in the previous year, the SHGs and MFIs put together had reached about 8 million clients more than the commercial banks.

The situation in AP during 2011–12 is quite different from earlier years as the MFIs lending has almost stopped, and it is expected that the SBLP have to progress much faster to fill the vacuum. However, reduced coverage of groups during the year 2011–12

Table 1.3 Estimate of microfinance credit clients (millions)

	2008	2009	2010	2011
Commercial banks (including RRBs) small loan accounts	41	39.2	45.2	43.3
PACS borrowers (small, vulnerable)	28.5	28.7	30	31.0
SHG Members	47.1	54	59.6	62.5
MFI Clients	14.1	22.6	26.7	31.8
Total	130.7	144.5	161.5	168.6

Source: SHG data from provisional data provided by NABARD and MFI data from Sa-Dhan. The Bharat Micro Finance Quick report 2012 and Mix Market data

when compared with the previous year in the absence of MFI lending is a concern. The available choices to access loans for the poor in AP are severely shrinking. A recent study conducted by MicroSave brought out a striking finding that with MFIs in Andhra Pradesh drastically reducing new lending, borrowers have been forced to seek out alternative sources for lending.[13] The erstwhile MFI customers in AP are defaulters in the credit bureau records and will find it difficult to access bank loans. Without SHG programmes performing well and the MFI channel resuming operations, client hardship is bound to increase.

Studies on the impact of the SHG movement conducted by various institutions/experts revealed that the programme has indeed helped in the social and economic empowerment of rural poor, especially women, causing significant up-scaling of social capital while at the same time delivering crucial and much-needed financial services at low transaction costs for both banks and poor borrowers. However, slow progress of graduation of SHG members, poor quality of group functioning, dropout of members from groups etc., have also been reported by various study findings in different parts of the country, which need to be taken into account while designing the road map for the next phase of the SHG programme.

The Community Based Microfinance Institutions (CBMFIs) model assumes greater significance, and it provides the possibility for the emergence of a viable option since it is non-exploitative, member-based and member-managed and, more importantly, the members benefit directly from the savings and the profits. SHGs, women's federations and cooperatives are member-owned and managed organizations, thus CBMFI's direct loans from banks and other formal financial organizations are the most benign way of getting financial services to the poor. The percentage of SHGs, which are not having any federation membership was more than 70 per cent, indicating the available potential for forming federations. One of the major benefits of SHG federations was that the federations themselves have become an alternative source of financing for SHGs.

Despite the fact that federations are suited for offering a wide range of services to the rural poor, their capacity to offer these services is limited by the inadequate human resources and experience in innovating and offering a wide array of products and services. However, to ensure their long term financial and economic sustainability, provision of non-credit products and services is essential. Some of the SHGs have already shown the way by entering into marketing arrangements with the corporate sector for supplying raw materials to those companies and/or marketing their products. The limited scope of the federations to act as financial intermediary has been deliberated at length. As such, scaling up of this model is limited due to lack of policy support from NABARD, except providing limited funding support for capacity building and leadership quality of the group members.[14] However, the success stories of the federations being experimented across the country such as SEWA, DHAN Foundation, etc., indicate the scope of this model for wider scaling up. Further, NRLM's focus on federation arrangement will certainly add a new dimension to the federation approaches. Redesigning the federation model in the light of the lessons learnt so far will have a positive impact on this model. Networking will also provide a broader platform for collective action at a larger level and scale so that the demands and requirements of the members and the SHGs at the grassroots level could be effectively taken up with donors and governments.

Financial inclusion is the most important initiative of the Government of India, and the RBI is focusing on providing banking facilities to the poor even in unbanked areas. The financial inclusion survey conducted by the World Bank team in India between April and June 2011 revealed that India lags behind developed and many developing countries in bank account penetration, but is much closer to the global average when it comes to borrowing from formal institutions.[15] In India, 35 per cent of people had formal accounts *versus* the global average of 50 per cent and the average of 41 per cent in developing economies. The survey also points to the slow growth of mobile money in India, where only 4 per cent of adults in the Global Findex sample reported having used a mobile phone in the past 12 months to pay bills or send and/receive money.

With a view to achieving greater financial inclusion, the RBI has advised commercial banks to allocate at least 25 per cent of the total number of branches proposed to be opened during the year in unbanked rural centres.[16] In order to further facilitate financial inclusion, interoperability was permitted at the retail outlets or Customer Service Points of BCs (i.e., at the point of customer interface), subject to certain conditions, provided the technology available with the bank, which has appointed the BC, supported interoperability. However, the BC or its retail outlet or sub-agent at the point of customer interface would continue to represent the bank, which has appointed the BC.

The financial inclusion plan (FIPs) rolled out for three years from 2010 contained self-set targets in respect of opening of rural brick and mortar branches, deployment of business correspondents (BCs), coverage of unbanked villages through various modes, opening of no-frills accounts, Kisan Credit Cards (KCCs) and General Credit Cards (GCCs) to be issued etc. Once banks start leveraging BCs as their extended arms, regular banking products can be channelled through this model. The proposal for implementing social sector schemes through the banking system with the support of Unique Identification (UID) will improve the business case for BCs and increase clients' comfort. Microfinance, being a sector that serves a very large number of small clients distributed over a wider geographical area, could be a highly cost-intensive proposition. The adoption of appropriate technological solutions both in hardware and software platforms has ensured so far that costs remain within the reasonable limits. In the BC space also, there is scope for improved technological solutions, but also for establishing interoperable systems and platforms.

The investment climate in India seems to be more dynamic than ever before. Despite a dearth of debt financing, the equity availability is showing signs of promise. The post-Malegam Committee regulatory initiatives by RBI have brought confidence to investors. In the meantime, the Indian government continues to unfold small-scale programmes designed to help smaller and medium MFIs, including the Indian Microfinance Equity Fund.

The process of bringing the microfinance sector under the regulatory regime has made significant progress during this year. In response to requests from the sector, recently in August 2012, the RBI has come out with a set of modifications in its NBFC (MFI) directions issued in December 2011 in the light of representations received.[17] The timeline provided for MFIs to register as NBFC-MFI has been fixed as end of October 2012. In a move sure to bring relief to the NBFCs functioning in the sector in the country, the RBI has relaxed the criteria regarding the Qualifying Assets to some extent. As per the changes introduced, the assets existing as on January 2012 shall be taken into consideration in calculating the ratio of Qualifying Assets to the net assets. The aggregate amount of loans that an NBFC-MFI may extend for income generation activities may not be less than 70 per cent of the total loans (this was 75 per cent earlier). This relaxation was introduced considering the ground realities of the sector targeting the clientele of microcredit being at subsistence level and that basic consumption requirements of the poor cannot be overlooked. On multiple lending, RBI has clarified that a person who borrows as an individual cannot thereafter borrow from an NBFC-MFI as a member of an SHG or JLG. Again, the same SHG/JLG/individual cannot borrow from more than two MFIs.

NBFC-MFIs have also been directed to be members of at least one credit information company and to provide them with timely and accurate data and use the data available with them to ensure compliance with the conditions regarding membership of SHG/JLG, level of indebtedness and sources of borrowing. All NBFC-MFIs have also been directed to become a member of at least one Self-Regulatory Organization (SRO) recognized[18] by the Reserve Bank of India. Further, these directions introduced flexibility in terms of pricing individual loans. Earlier, the interest rate cap on individual loans given by MFIs was fixed at 26 per cent and the margin at 12 per cent. After these directions, the average interest rate on loans is still limited to the sum of average borrowing costs plus a margin or 26 per cent, whichever is lower, but the interest rate on individual loans given by MFIs may be more than 26 per cent. Also, the caps on margin have been revised to 10 per cent for large MFIs (loans portfolios exceeding ₹1,000 million). The maximum variance permitted for individual loans between the minimum and maximum interest rate cannot exceed 4 per cent.

The directions also recognize the problems faced by MFIs with respect to loans originated in Andhra Pradesh. With regard to the portfolio in Andhra Pradesh, NBFC-MFIs have been directed to ensure that the provisioning made towards the portfolio in Andhra Pradesh should be as per the current provisioning norms. For the purpose of calculation of Capital to Risk-weighted Assets Ratio (CRAR), however, the provisioning made towards the portfolio in Andhra Pradesh shall be notionally reckoned as part of Net Owned Funds, and there shall be progressive reduction in such recognition of the provisions for the AP portfolio equally over a period of five years. There has been a mixed response in the microfinance sector to the directions of the RBI. While the directions relating to reduction in margin cap

for larger MFIs have been criticized, the operational clarifications concerning MFIs being part of at least one Credit Information Company and at least one Self Regulatory Organization (SRO) have been welcomed. Still there are several operational issues on defining the income ceiling of the customers for being eligible for priority sector lending classification, lack of clarity regarding central and state regulatory jurisdiction.

NABARD continues to extend various supports to various stakeholders to facilitate sustained access to financial services for the unreached poor in rural areas through various microfinance innovations in a sustainable manner. During the year 2011–12, refinance of ₹30.73 billion was provided to banks covering their lending to SHGs,[19] which has shown an increase of about 21 per cent over the previous year. As a proportion of NABARD's long term refinance disbursements, the SHG's share increased from 18.9 per cent in 2010–11 to 19.9 per cent in 2011–12. Under the Microfinance Development and Equity Fund, ₹333.1 million was released during 2011–12, of which ₹286.8 million was grant support for promotional activities and ₹46.3 million for Capital Support/Revolving Fund Assistance to Micro Finance Institutions, as against ₹299.5 million and ₹174.3 million, respectively in the previous year. The JLGs fill a critical gap in the rural areas where marginal farmers and tenant farmers find it difficult to individually access bank loans. As capacity building efforts 1,914 Micro Enterprise Development Programmes (MEDP) were conducted during the year for 56,292 members on various location-specific farms, non-farm and service sector activities. So far, 164,948 participants had been covered under the enterprise development programme.

In the revisiting process NABARD brings out several changes in the existing SHG movement strategies. The SHG-2 is going to focus on a few issues such as: creating space for voluntary savings, positioning cash credit as a preferred mode of lending, scope for providing multiple borrowings by SHG members matching with their repaying capacity, creating avenues to meet higher credit requirements for livelihood creation, supporting SHG Federations as non-financial intermediaries, rating and introducing audit of SHGs as part of risk mitigation system, strengthening monitoring mechanisms, etc. The guidelines of SHG-2 have since been issued by NABARD to the concerned stakeholders. During the year 2011–12, NABARD has also formulated a scheme, in association with the Government of India, for promotion of women SHGs in backward and Left Wing Extremism (LWE) affected districts to bring out a viable and self sustainable model for promotion and financing of Women Self Help Groups (WSHGs) by involving an anchor NGO in each of the selected backward districts of the country. It attempts at having NGO-SHPI work not merely as an SHPI for promoting and enabling credit linkage of these groups with banks, but also serving as a banking/business facilitator, tracking, monitoring these groups and also being responsible for loan repayments. To begin with, the scheme is being implemented in 109 selected backward/LWE districts of the country. As instructed by the Government of India, sanctioning Cash Credit Limits to SHGs has been initiated so as to address the issue of delayed/limited or non-approval of repeat loans to SHG, to ensure cost effectiveness to clients and provide greater operational flexibility to SHG clients. The groups in turn are to extend loans to their members as per the extant guidelines of RBI and NABARD.

OTHER DEVELOPMENTS

The Microfinance Institutions (Development and Regulation) Bill, 2012 was tabled in Parliament in May 2012, and the same is currently under examination of the Standing Committee on finance. This Bill views microfinance institutions as 'extended arms of banks and financial services'. Different segments of the sector welcomed the Bill and opined that if this Bill is enacted in its present form, it has the potential to restore order and certainty. Many admit that the crisis reflects the collective inaction, and the Bill is an opportunity to provide remedy and equalize the power relationship between the microlender and the poor. In general, MFIs, especially, smaller and medium ones, who are suffering from liquidity problems, hope for early relief once the bill is approved by the Parliament.

Recognizing the importance of systematic compilation of credit information of clients for effective mentoring and follow-up, RBI has made it mandatory for NBFC-MFIs to register with at least one credit information company. High Mark Credit Information Services has launched the country's first Microfinance Credit Bureau in March 2011, and it already has 119 members. Over the last one year, 74 institutions regularly contribute data to HighMark's bureau database, which now has data on 80 million loan records of 45 million customers. In addition, there was a perceptible and steady increase in the number of enquiries during the last one year, which confirms the greater utility of the credit bureau. All 44 MFIN members have registered with at least one Credit Bureau and are sharing data on a regular basis and are using Credit Bureau reports in their loan approval processes. Further, all MFIN members have recently signed a No Objection Certificate (NOC) that will allow Credit Bureaus to share statistics on credit report usage by MFIs. This will help MFIN monitor and enforce, with greater stringency, the use of Credit Bureau reports for loan processing. In the long run, MFIN is intent to use Credit Bureaus not just as a monitoring and decision making tool for MFIs, but also as a mechanism by which Microfinance borrowers can build credit histories and eventually become integrated with the mainstream financial system. The application of appropriate technological innovations in the credit information management system will significantly contribute to a cost efficient approach with greater efficiency.

As a self-regulatory initiative, Sa-Dhan and MFIN evolved a unified code of conduct for their members, which were released at the Microfinance India Summit 2011 in New Delhi. The unified code of conduct includes integrity and ethical behavior, transparency, client protection, governance, recruitment, client education, data sharing and feedback/grievance redressal mechanisms.[20] Both Sa-Dhan and MFIN have made efforts to ensure that their members are exposed to the underlying principles inherent in their code of conduct. Many prominent lenders to MFIs including SIDBI have started including a Code of Conduct Assessment (COCA) as a covenant in their lending agreements. A critical review of the available 13 COCA of different MFIs spread across the country with different portfolio sizes clearly brings out the emphasis and commitment exerted by the MFIs with a view to have meaningful client contacts and broad attention of code of conduct issues. Further, 55 per cent of the MFIs under review secured higher scores than the average score in the COCA assessment, which was mainly due to staff conduct and loan pricing. On the other hand, the low score among 45 per cent of the MFIs is attributed to less value on client relationship and lack of social responsibilities. While COCA is becoming more and more relevant in the present day context where client protection, governance, transparency and social involvement are the driving principles in the microfinance industry, it needs to be done on an ongoing basis in periodic intervals. Considering the cost burden on MFIs, extensive funding support may provide greater incentives for many MFIs to participate in this monitoring process. Developing appropriate incentive mechanisms for taking this up would go a long way in raising the standards of consumer services and protection.

The governance of MFIs is one thrust area to ensure a balancing act with social and financial goals. Specific issues like the constitution of a quality board with due diligence, ceiling in the financial packages to CEO and the salary structure of the field staff etc. need to have a relook considering the social performance management criteria. Microfinance in India needs to respond positively and bring out changes in its approach towards customers and redesign products and strategies. There is increasing evidence that providing client-responsive financial services can both serve the needs of poor people while maintaining or in fact improving the sustainability and profitability of the MFIs. Similarly, a number of MFIs are providing other products and services such as savings, health and housing loans, loans for water supply and sanitation, etc. Client based innovative financial products will induce greater responses in the market.

On resumption of bulk funding, some of the better MFIs are likely to show higher future growth and consolidation whereas smaller ones are bound to close down or seek sale/merger arrangements.[21] There would be more activity in merger and sale of business by institutions. After passing of the microfinance bill, one can expect the detailed regulation being carried out by SROs with industry associations monitoring code of conduct compliance by MFIs. The efforts of revival of the MFIs will succeed only when the problem of funding is addressed. Convergence of SBLP with NRLM and effective integration of the financial inclusion plan along with regulatory support will ensure greater scope for livelihood financing for the unreached segment of the population.

A critical review of the microfinance sector performance during the year 2011–12 brings out a sense of mixed success. The impact of the crisis has been felt during the year, and a reduction in the client outreach through both SBLP and MFIs certainly indicate that the sector has digested the negative effects. One could afford to be hesitantly optimistic about the future. A greater emphasis on customer focus as well as self-regulatory initiatives by the MFIs is a positive development, which needs to be further strengthened. SBLP and MFIs must be recognized as a contributory institutional arrangement for financial inclusion and recognizing this structure as an effective channel for delivering the government sponsored programmes. Further institutionalizing the voluntary saving initiatives promoted by NABARD will help the customers to access main stream banking progressively. The coming years are very crucial since the microfinance movement is slowly getting back to normal from the crisis situation. The efforts undertaken during the next two years will form the foundation for the next phase of the movement in the country. Policy and regulation have acted with alacrity. Equity investors seem willing to engage with the better parts of the sector. Will the bulk funders—the banks—come forward? Without all stakeholders getting involved, the sector cannot become resurgent. The sector eagerly awaits banks to do a reality check and rerate the risks of engaging with the sector.

ANNEX 1.1
Views of microfinance in India

Responses provided by Greg Chen, Antonique Koning, Alexia Latortue and Kate McKee of CGAP.

1. Status and Progress of the Indian Microfinance Sector in the Context of Global Perspective

India remains one of the largest and most active financial inclusion markets in the world. The Indian government has also recognized its role globally in financial inclusion by joining CGAP as a member during 2012. India is also participating in the G20's Global Partnership on Financial Inclusion. Not only is India expanding its leadership role it also brings into the global dialogue a diverse set of approaches to financial inclusion: SHGs, MFIs, Commercial Banks, Insurance Companies, Pension Funds, Cooperatives and agent-banking through Business Correspondents.

The 2011 Findex data reports that one in three adult Indians has a bank account, a figure higher than many low-income countries though it also indicates how much more work remains to be done. In recent years there is excitement about banks using Business Correspondents (banking agents) an approach with enormous potential. However, the BC approach is still new and unproven in the Indian environment amid the excitement about BCs other efforts are needed to keep other financial inclusion approaches alive and vibrant. For instance, rates of SHG and MFI expansion have slowed in recent years even though they still offer enormous untapped potential.

2. Meeting Client Needs Well with Responsive Products

The diversity of providers and delivery approaches in India is laudable, though debates about the strengths or weaknesses of different delivery models can distract from a more fundamental question—are client needs being met? Unbanked and underserved people need access to a portfolio of financial services to smooth consumption, build assets, and mitigate and manage risk. A single provider or approach will not be able to provide this full suite of services. An ecosystem of providers ranging from insurance companies, MFIs, BCs, commercial banks, and SHGs will be needed in order to offer the payments, savings, credit, insurance and pension services low income people need over their lifetimes. A dynamic Indian financial inclusion landscape will require even more investment in research and development—to creatively source new insights about actual and potential clients, and move to translate this knowledge into a more robust and responsive offering. The efforts of Kshetriya Gramin Financial Services in India is a one positive example of client focused innovation in India and more like this will be critical for the goals of financial inclusion to be fully met http://www.cgap.org/gm/document-1.9.57523/Forum4.pdf .

3. Impact of Regulations for the MFIs in India

The recent regulatory adjustments have rightly brought a clearer focus onto a specialized category of NBFC MFI and highlighted the need for closer regulation. Unfortunately, recent regulations are a mixed bag for clients. The changes do curb some of the most serious excesses that rapid MFI growth brought such as over-selling of loans. At the same time, a narrow restriction on client incomes and the composition of MFI loan portfolios limits innovation. The cap on margins means that it is difficult for MFIs to contemplate new approaches or products, or even to consider doing more for clients—client education, learning more about household needs or offering 'extras' such as access to wider livelihoods opportunities, health care or other valued services.

The regulatory changes are blunt checking the excesses of some MFIs, while at the same time also suppressing client-centred innovation. Future regulatory adjustments might seek to make refinements that establish a more promotional balance that allows for dynamic innovation and growth, while putting in place some buffers or checks that protect clients.

4. Effectiveness of Self-Regulation of MFIs in India

Industry-developed standards, such as those in the Indian Code of Conduct, can play an important role in ensuring that microfinance delivers the intended benefits to clients. There are promising developments along these lines in diverse countries such as the Philippines, Pakistan, Ethiopia and Azerbaijan. Such measures are especially important to ensure that adequate care, client understanding of terms and conditions, and practical grievance redressal mechanisms are in place.

The Indian case is unusual in that the regulator aims to formalize 'self-regulation' and define acceptable standards in some of the areas. Self-regulation of some key points of conduct, establishing standards and norms of practice can contribute to achieving responsible practice. However, self-regulation on its own is not sufficient and some elements of responsible finance require more direct regulation by an independent authority. Moreover, for deposit-taking activities self-regulation is not sufficient and requires prudential regulation and supervision by a qualified independent supervisor.

5. Responsible Financing in Indian Microfinance

There is a strong long-term business case for responsible product features and practices. These should pay off through client trust and loyalty, demand for additional services, and sustainable growth, and the health and reputation of the sector as a whole. In the short run, many MFIs in India are struggling to get back on their feet, raise more capital and comply with new regulations. While some responsible finance measures—such as ensuring sound loan processes and well-designed products—are consistent with putting the house back in order, it is more difficult to implement the full menu of responsible finance measures when revenues are so constrained and the MFI business models are under stress. Regulators, policy makers, investors and other stakeholders should consider appropriate steps to support the sector's recovery as the sector demonstrates good-faith efforts to improve practices and adhere to responsible finance principles.

6. Social Performance Management in Indian Microfinance Sector

Many Indian microfinance providers publicly claim to have a double bottom line and are therefore concerned with both their financial sustainability and achieving their social goals. In recent years providers have been supported by support organizations and investors alike. Many providers have made progress, but more can be done to design and deliver appropriate financial services that meet client needs. While recognizing the challenges faced by the Indian microfinance sector in the short run, the longer-term goal of sustained growth and better outreach can only be achieved if both financial and social goals are balanced. Earlier this year the global microfinance industry agreed upon a set of universal standards for social performance management (www.sptf.info/sp-standards) that set out actionable management practices related to setting strategy, building employee buy-in and putting clients first. We encourage Indian MFIs to apply those standards into their own context.

7. Business Correspondent Role in Indian Financial Inclusion

India recognized early on the potential use of Business Correspondents (bank agents) to extend the reach of the banking system using technology. The RBI introduced guidelines more than six years ago. Over the past two years the government had banks set targets to increase points of service and the government has plans to shift G2P payments to electronic delivery. BC points of presence have increased to over 100,000, but there are large challenges ahead. One is that insufficient investment has gone into the design and compensation the BC delivery channels or to tailor products for end-clients. This has meant relatively low transaction volumes for most BC service points and also low compensation to the agents. Some of these challenges were summarized in a survey the College of Agricultural Banking and CGAP jointly carried out in 2012 (http://www.cgap.org/gm/document-1.9.57911/Survey_Branchless_Banking_India_June_2012_Rev.pdf).

The survey also revealed some bright spots where some states perform better and some pockets where agents are doing much larger business volumes. However, the overall findings show that the BC channel needs focused attention on design and delivery in order to match the underlying needs of end-clients and create stronger incentives for the agents.

NOTES AND REFERENCES

1. The Author gratefully acknowledges the inputs provided by Nirupam Mehrotra and Truti Tapasi, DEAR NABARD for preparing this section.
2. IMF (2012): 'World Economic Outlook Update, April 2012', International Monetary Fund.
3. Government of India, 2012, *Economic Survey 2011–12*, Oxford University Press.
4. Source: *Mid-Quarter Monetary Policy Review*, June 2012, RBI.
5. RBI, *Annual Report 2011–12*, Reserve Bank of India, Mumbai, 2012.
6. Government of India, 2011, 'Faster, Sustainable and more Inclusive Growth—Approach Paper to the 12th Five Year Plan', October, 2011, Planning Commission.
7. This section draws heavily from the article titled, 'The Performance of Microfinance Institutions: Do Macro conditions Matter?' by Niels Hermes and Aljar Meesters, *The Handbook of Microfinance*, World Scientific, 2011.
8. Source: *Global Microscope on the Microfinance Business Environment 2009–2011*, Economic Intelligence Unit Ltd (www.eiu.com).
9. The number of members of SHGs is not based on a count of actual members. As in the case of the last three years, based on a number of field studies, the average number of members of SHGs had been taken at 13. With an increased number of government programmes and the associated time-bound targets, the actual group size might tend to be smaller.
10. The data on SBLP is provisional and is likely to undergo changes at the time of finalization. This data was made available to SOS for the purpose of analyzing trends and comparisons with the past and is incomplete at this point of time. The final data for the year will be published by NABARD by October 2012 as is the normal practice—in its annual publication *Status of Microfinance in India 2011-2012*.
11. The overlap adjustment ratios follow the last year's logic and convention. Refer to the *State of the Sector Report 2011* for more details. This adjustment requires a review in view of reduced multiple lending due to better tracking and appraisal. But the effect of this will fully kick in next year and that would be a time to have a relook at overlap.
12. The numbers assume that every member of a borrowing self-group has taken loans from the SHG. But a small proportion of members of SHGs do not have a loan from their group. For want of reliable information, this has been ignored in estimating the numbers of customers.
13. http://microsave.org/research_paper/what-are-clients-doing-post-the-andhra-pradesh-mfi-crisis
14. Ajay Tankha, *Banking on Self-Help Groups—Twenty Years on*, SAGE Publications, New Delhi, 2012.
15. RBI, *Annual Report 2011–12*, Reserve Bank of India, Mumbai.
16. Unbanked rural centres are Tier 5 and Tier 6 centres that do not have a brick and mortar structure of any SCB for customer-based banking transaction.

17. http://www.ifmr.co.in/blog/2012/08/20/a-summary-of-nbfc-mfi-directions-august-

18. RBI is yet to recognize any SRO so far. Reportedly, the RBI is working on a mechanism for this.

19. Data cited in this section relating to NABARD is sourced from the *Annual Report of NABARD, 2011–12*.

20. http://www.mfinindia.org/sites/default/files/Industry%20Code%20of%20Conduct.pdf

21. Sa-Dhan report on *The Bharat Microfinance Quick Report 2012*.

SHG bank linkage programme—revisit in progress

During the last two decades, the SHG Bank Linkage Programme (SBLP) has passed through various stages like Pilot Testing (1992–96), mainstreaming (1996–98) and expansion (1998 onwards) and has transformed into a microfinance movement in the country. During this period, the efforts of linking SHGs with banks have undergone a series of changes and different models have emerged in this process. With a view to linking the poor in the country with the banking sector for receiving financial services, various approaches were piloted and up-scaled, which are on many occasions, location-specific or client-specific or sometimes stakeholders-specific. While some of the models were successful, a few of them were remaining dormant without any scope for replication. Further, the profile and attitude of the members/clients/customers also has undergone significant changes due to the dynamics of infrastructural advancement, trainings and political/social environments. The SBLP was in accelerated growth trajectory till recently and it has slowed down during the last two years. Last year the programme witnessed early signs of new thrust, and there is a need to revisit the entire set of strategies for greater success of the programme. This chapter attempts to highlight different models/approaches covering the process, progress and issues involved in order to carry forward those experiences, besides providing quantitative perspective of the programme during the year 2011–12.

The growth performance of SBLP during the last two years has reached a stage of a plateau, and it is time for giving it new direction for future expansion. The provisional data available from NABARD for the year 2011–12 shows that the number of SHGs provided with bank loans was ₹4.36 million, which is about 9 per cent less than the previous year performance (Table 2.1). On the other hand, the outstanding loan amount during the reference year has registered an increase of 19 per cent more than the previous year. In terms of incremental loans outstanding, the SBLP added ₹57.23 billion (Annexure 2.1).

Table 2.1 **Growth trends in SBLP**

Particulars	2006	2007	2008	2009	2010	2011	2012
No. of SHGs provided with bank loans	2,238,565	2,924,973	3,625,941	4,224,338	4,587,178	4,813,684	4,354,567
Of which in southern region	1,214,431	1,522,144	1,861,373	2,283,992	2,421,440	2,663,569	2,355,732
Share of southern region (percentage)	54	52	51	54	53	55	54
Average disbursed loan per group (₹)	37,574	44,343	46,800	74,000	115,820	122,744	144,086
Outstanding loans (₹ billion)		123.66	169.99	226.76	272.66	306.19	363.41
Incremental groups (million)		0.69	0.70	0.60	0.36	0.22	(–) 0.05
Incremental loans O/S (₹ billion)		123.66	46.33	56.77	45.90	33.53	57.22

Source: NABARD Provisional data.

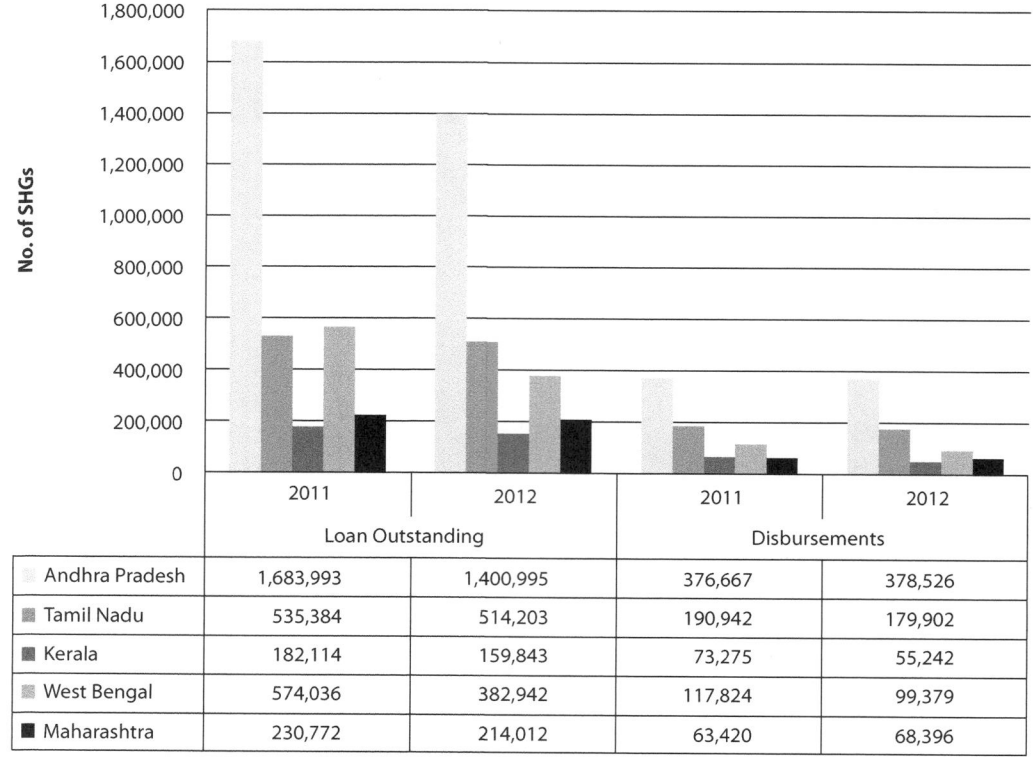

Figure 2.1 SHG with loan outstanding in some states
Source: NABARD Provisional data.

A comparative analysis of the number of groups with loan outstanding among different states revealed that there was significant reduction during the reference year compared to the previous year in most of the major states where the SHG movement is well-established. As could be seen from Figure 2.1, the decreasing trend was quite significant in Andhra Pradesh (17 per cent) and West Bengal (33 per cent) among the groups with loan outstanding. In terms of disbursements, the decrease was more in Kerala (25 per cent) and West Bengal (16 per cent) respectively. Thus the impact of the decreasing trend of the number of groups in the major states resulted in over all decreasing trend for the country as a whole.

In addition to the individual states performance, the performance of the banks also contributes to the progress. The number of groups financed by the State Bank of India, the major bank in SHG lending, registered a decrease of 54 per cent during the year 2012 compared to the previous year (Figure 2.2). Similarly, Andhra Bank and Indian Bank recorded the low performance in terms of groups with loan disbursed during the year 2012. Hence the relatively

poor performance by many of the banks also contributed for the overall reduction in groups finance through SHGs.

Banks disbursed loans amounting to ₹165.15 billion to 1.14 million groups during the year (Annexure 2.3). The average loan disbursed per group amounted to ₹144,086, which is about 17 per cent higher than the previous year's disbursement. Overall, the SBLP had underperformed in terms of outreach of groups, even though the quantum of loan per group has increased. Further, the growth of loan outstanding is more on account of the large base and the long term nature of loans. Though the increase in the outstanding loan amount is a healthy sign and has been increasing at a healthy rate year after year in nominal terms, the growth rate had been very moderate in real terms (Figure 2.3). There was about 12 per cent growth in loans in real terms (2005 prices) between the year 2011 and 2012. The average disbursed loan per SHG had increased to 10 per cent from ₹82,604 in 2011 to ₹92,024 during 2012. The marginal increase in real terms raises the question of its sustainability and ability to manage livelihood activities.

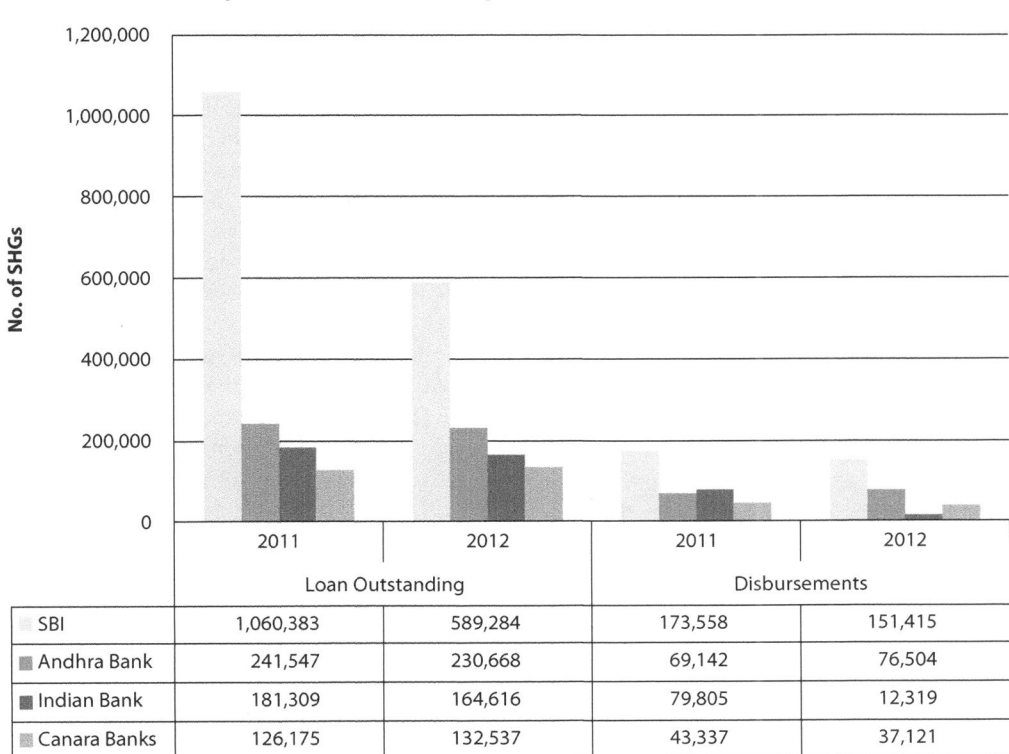

Major Banks' Loan Outstanding and Disbursements

	Loan Outstanding		Disbursements	
	2011	2012	2011	2012
SBI	1,060,383	589,284	173,558	151,415
Andhra Bank	241,547	230,668	69,142	76,504
Indian Bank	181,309	164,616	79,805	12,319
Canara Banks	126,175	132,537	43,337	37,121

Figure 2.2 SHG with loan outstanding for major banks

Source: NABARD Provisional data.

The impact of the AP crisis must be one of the major factors where banks are cautious in financing groups. Yet another reason for the decrease in the number of groups with loan outstanding was presumably the change in the attitude of the banks towards microfinance lending. While the banks almost stopped lending to MFIs, considering the impact of the crisis, the banks might have adopted the go slow or wait and watch strategy. It is evident from the fact that the State Bank of India, the leading microfinance lender in the country had almost reduced its participation to half of its level. Some of the bankers opined that the change in the reporting system of the SHG accounts data might be responsible for a reduced number of groups. NABARD has already initiated dialogue with the major bank on these issues and is in the process of preparing potential mapping for SHGs in all the states, and efforts are in the process to discuss these plans in the SLBC for appropriate action. An in-depth probe must be done by NABARD on a priority basis to assess the causes for slow progress of the SBLP for taking forward the SBLP to the next stage.

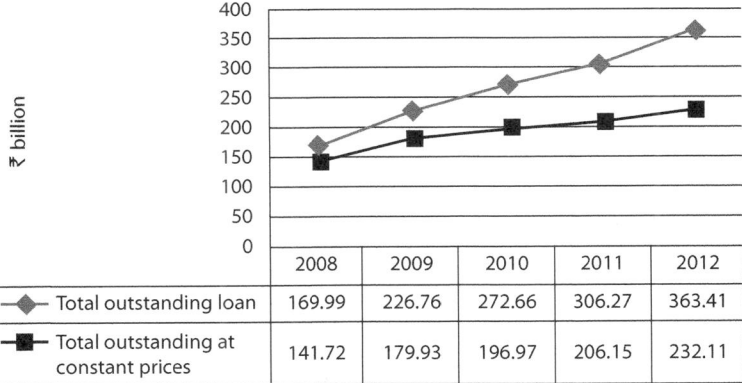

	2008	2009	2010	2011	2012
Total outstanding loan	169.99	226.76	272.66	306.27	363.41
Total outstanding at constant prices	141.72	179.93	196.97	206.15	232.11

Figure 2.3 Outstanding SHG loans—nominal and real terms

Source: NABARD Provisional data.

SAVINGS PERFORMANCE

As at the end of March 2012, as much as 7.96 million groups were savings-linked with the banking system, which is 5.4 per cent higher than the previous year's performance. However, there was a deceleration in terms of savings amount during this year when compared to previous years. The savings amount during 2011–12 was ₹65.51 billion, which was ₹3.74 billion lesser than the previous year's savings amount (Figure 2.4). At this level, it constitutes about 18

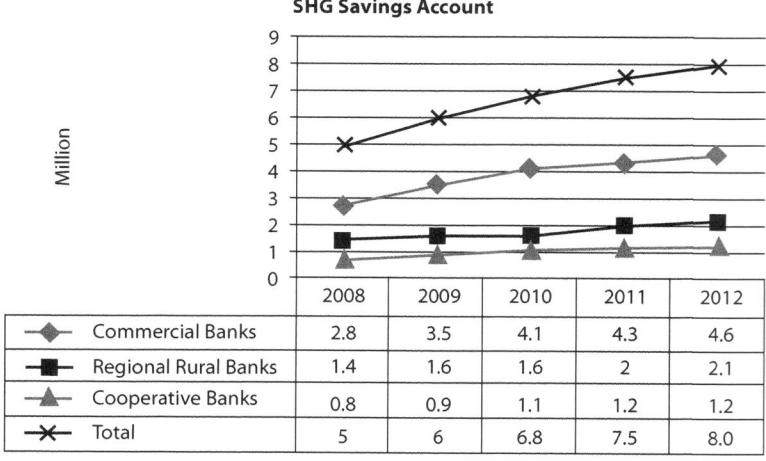

SHG Savings Account

	2008	2009	2010	2011	2012
Commercial Banks	2.8	3.5	4.1	4.3	4.6
Regional Rural Banks	1.4	1.6	1.6	2	2.1
Cooperative Banks	0.8	0.9	1.1	1.2	1.2
Total	5	6	6.8	7.5	8.0

Figure 2.4 Number of SHGs holding savings accounts, 2008–12 (millions)
Source: NABARD Provisional data.

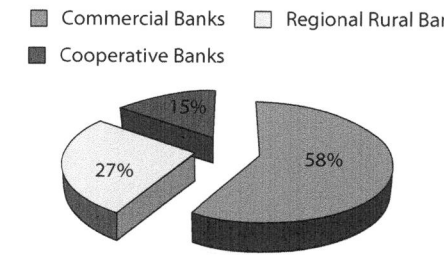

Figure 2.5 SHG with savings accounts—FY 2011–12
Source: NABARD Provisional data.

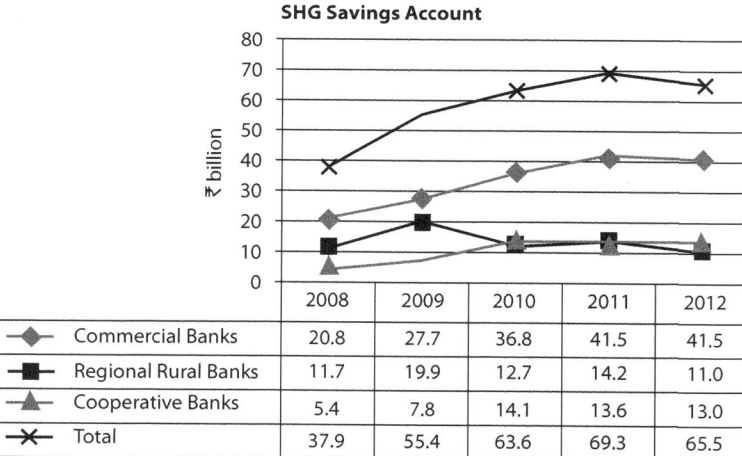

SHG Savings Account

	2008	2009	2010	2011	2012
Commercial Banks	20.8	27.7	36.8	41.5	41.5
Regional Rural Banks	11.7	19.9	12.7	14.2	11.0
Cooperative Banks	5.4	7.8	14.1	13.6	13.0
Total	37.9	55.4	63.6	69.3	65.5

Figure 2.6 Savings growth by SHGs, 2008–12 (₹ billion)
Source: NABARD Provisional data.

per cent of outstanding loans, which implies that the funding from the group accounts for more than one fifth of the lending to the members. The fact remains that these savings amount are parked with the banks available for its business and not necessarily lending to the members. It is also reported that these savings are being used as collateral for lending to group members.

Commercial banks had 58 per cent of all groups that are savings-linked, followed by regional rural banks with a share of 27 per cent (Figure 2.5). The share of cooperative banks remained at 15 per cent. Overall the share of different banks having savings-linked groups remains the same as in the previous year. The progress of savings-linked groups over the period of five years presented is in Figure 2.6.

In terms of saving amount, commercial banks are the most preferred one by the group members, where about ₹41.5 billion (63 per cent) of the savings are deposited, followed by cooperative banks at ₹13 billion (20 per cent) and regional rural banks at ₹11 Billion (17 per cent) (Figure 2.7).

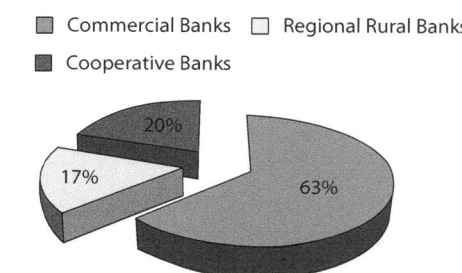

Figure 2.7 SHG saving amount with banks—FY 2011–12
Source: NABARD Provisional data.

In absolute terms, the amount saved with commercial banks remained the same as in the previous year. The share of cooperatives in outstanding savings has declined by 3 per cent, as compared to last year. Commercial banks increased their share of savings by 3 per cent.

Contrary to the trends in loan outstanding, the number of groups saved as well as amount of savings has registered an increasing trend in Andhra Pradesh. Average savings per group were the highest in the cooperative banks at ₹9,040 followed by commercial banks at ₹8,993. The state-wise distribution of savings performance of SHGs is presented in Annexure 2.4

While the improved savings performance is the positive impact of the SHG movement, still there are several issues, which need to be addressed for evolving future strategies. The common attitude of the groups is to divide the savings and corpus funds at the end of the year rather than accumulate the same into equity over a longer time. Other issues such as lack of mutual trust, rigidity in withdrawing savings and excessive build-up of corpus in older groups etc., have greater negative impact on the saving attitude of the members. Banks as collateral for loans insist on SHGs retaining their savings in bank accounts rather than using the same for intra-group lending. While some banks are willing to take fixed deposits from SHGs at higher rates of interest, there are banks that retain the money in savings accounts of SHGs at low rates of interest, thereby indirectly increasing the cost of borrowing for groups. The strength of SHGs used to be their focus on savings; but in recent times, the groups are focused on bank loans and do the necessary minimum savings to qualify for the loan. In the case of government programmes, the focus is on subsidies and revolving funds, and the group effort is directed at fulfilling the requirements there for. Hence, there is a need for new ideas and products that would contribute for enhanced savings behaviour among the members.

REGIONAL SPREAD OF THE LENDING PROGRAMME

During the financial year ending March 2012, the percentage share of groups linked with loans in the southern region has shown a marginal decrease to 54.1 per cent from 55.3 per cent in the previous year (Table 2.2). The eastern region also decreased its share in the number of groups from 24.3 per cent to 22.6 per cent. The northern region increased its share to 4.9 per cent from 3.1 per cent. Similarly, the North Eastern region and the Central region registered

increased share whereas the share of western region remained almost the same between the years 2011 and 2012.

Like in the past, Andhra Pradesh topped the list of states with the maximum number of groups with a share of 32 per cent, Tamil Nadu with 11.8 per cent stood in the second place. While West Bengal ranked third with 8.8 per cent share, Odisha, with a share of 7.22 per cent, ranked fourth and Karnataka, with a share of 6.1 per cent, ranked fifth. In terms of loans outstanding, Andhra Pradesh had a 42 per cent share with Tamil Nadu following as a distant second with a 12 per cent share. Karnataka with 9.5 per cent share was in the third place and UP with a 5.6 per cent share was in the fourth place.

A study on delinquencies of SHGs conducted in the North Eastern region highlighted that within the North East Region, the growth in SBLP is concentrated in the plains of Assam and Tripura.[1] The RRBs have been spearheading the growth of the movement in most of the major states like Assam, Tripura and in states where this has not been done, it has been languishing. The SGSY Programme has been dominating the SHG movement in NER unlike other parts of India where the SBLP leads.

Compared to the last year, some states have recorded a weak performance in SBLP. Sixteen states had a lower number of groups with outstanding loans by the end of March 2012 compared to the previous year. Larger states such as Maharashtra, Tamil Nadu, Odisha, and Madhya Pradesh have recorded a decline in terms of the number of groups with loan outstanding. A table showing comparative picture is provided in Annexure 2.1. Loan disbursements in 2011–12 were higher than the previous year by about ₹17.46 billion. The number of groups that availed loans during the year has declined drastically by 56,727 as compared to the previous year. A state-wise comparison of loan disbursements

Table 2.2 Regional share in linkages—SHGs with outstanding loans

	2009		2010		2011		2012	
	Groups	% Share	Groups	% Share	Groups	% Share	Groups	% Share
Northern	166,511	3.9	158,829	3.9	151,260	3.1	212,041	4.9
Northeastern	117,812	2.8	85,276	2.8	151,280	3.1	159,541	3.7
Eastern	933,489	22.1	985,094	22.1	1,171,840	24.3	985,329	22.6
Central	332,116	7.9	497,340	7.9	361,822	7.5	352,452	8.1
Western	393,499	9.3	439,199	9.3	313,913	6.5	289,472	6.6
Southern	2,280,911	54	2,421,440	54	2,663,569	55.3	2,355,732	54.1
All	4,224,338	100	2,165,738	100	4,813,684	100	4,354,567	100

Source: NABARD Provisional data.

and number of SHGs availing loans for the last two years is provided in Annexure 2.2. While there is no change in the performance in Andhra Pradesh, there was declining performance in states like Tamil Nadu, West Bengal and Kerala. The reasons for this decline in performance in such a large number of states need to be analyzed in depth so as to improve the performance. NABARD would study these developments while launching SHG II during the coming years.

PERFORMANCE OF BANKS IN LENDING

The commercial banks had a share of 60 per cent (showing a decrease of four per cent) of all groups with outstanding loans followed by Regional Rural Banks with a 30 per cent (increased by four per cent) share (Figure 2.3). The cooperative banks' share of the number of groups had remained the same at 10 per cent as in the previous year.

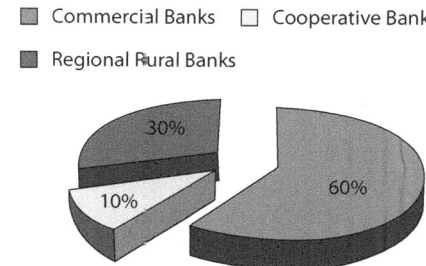

Figure 2.8 No. of SHGs with outstanding loans
Source: NABARD Provisional data.

Commercial banks had 71 per cent of all loans outstanding with SHGs, followed by regional rural banks with a 23.7 per cent share. The share of cooperative banks in loans was at a measly 5.3 per cent. The average loan disbursed per groups was almost the same in the case of commercial banks and Regional Rural Banks at ₹165,000 (Figure 2.9). While there has been an increase in disbursement of ₹20,000 per SHG in case of commercial banks, RRBs' disbursement per SHG has increased by ₹55,000. Cooperative banks disbursed less than half the average of commercial banks at ₹64,300 per group, which is significantly lower than their own figures for the last year.

The average outstanding loan per group was the highest in the case of commercial banks ₹98,600 followed by RRBs at ₹66,500. In the case of cooperative banks, the average outstanding loan was only

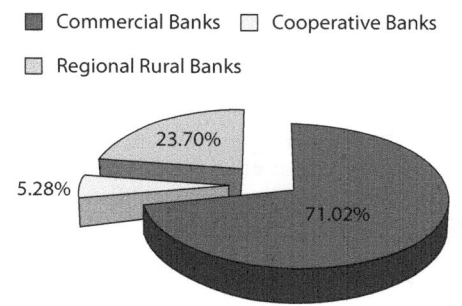

Figure 2.9 Banks' outstanding loan amount with SHGs
Source: NABARD Provisional data.

₹43,232, which is less than 50 per cent of that of commercial banks (Table 2.3).

Table 2.3 Bank loans outstanding against SHGs, 2011–12

	No. of SHGs	Loan outstanding (₹ million)
Commercial Bank	2,617,199	258,102.89
Cooperative Bank	443,559	19,176.08
Regional Rural Bank	1,293,809	86,135.78
Total	**4,354,567**	**363,414.75**

Source: NABARD Provisional data.

SBLP in Andhra Pradesh

Andhra Pradesh is in the forefront of the SHG movement in India and has drawn worldwide attention due to the introduction of the Andhra Pradesh Micro Finance Institutions (Regulation of Money Lending) Act, 2010, and subsequent developments. The situation in AP during 2011–12 is quite different from earlier as the MFIs lending has almost stopped, and it is expected that the SBLP has to progress much faster to compensate the sluggish growth caused by fledgling MFIs during the last year. The analysis of SBLP in AP reveals that the progress of SBLP has increased in terms of bank loans, whereas there was a reduction in the coverage of groups (Table 2.4). During the financial year ending March 2012, ₹78.66 billion worth of bank loans were disbursed to 346,682 groups and under Pavala Vaddi Incentive ₹8.79 billion was given to 1,948,384 SHG groups during the reference year with the cumulative loan of ₹19.67 billion since inception of the scheme.

Table 2.4 SHG bank linkages in Andhra Pradesh[2]

Year	No. of groups covered	Loan amount (₹ in billions)	Number of branches	Loan amount per group (₹)	Groups per branch
2004–05	261,254	10.18	3,853	38,954	68
2005–06	288,711	20.01	3,853	69,322	75
2006–07	366,489	30.64	3,950	83,601	93
2007–08	431,515	58.83	4,000	136,329	108
2008–09	483,601	66.84	4,150	137,498	118
2009–10	413,625	65.01	4,274	157,180	97
2010–11	389,444	70.93	4,286	182,123	91
2011–12	346,682	78.66	4,324	226,901	81

Source: NABARD Provisional data.

The reduced coverage of groups during the year 2011–12 when compared to the previous year is a matter of concern issues in the situation where MFI lending has almost stopped. This might have led to a liquidity problem among the poor in AP, which needs to be analyzed in depth for developing future strategies. Indira Kranthi Patham (IKP) being implemented by the Society for Elimination of Rural Poverty (SERP) in all the 22 rural districts in the state is the major institutional arrangement for SHG movement in the State. The project has made significant progress over a period of time; however, its role in the present day context assumes greater significance in the absence of MFI lending.[3]

With a view to encourage the poor, including disadvantaged groups and communities to access the credit-related services seamlessly, Community Investment Fund (CIF) from project side, and linkages from bank side are provided to the poor women SHG members to improve their livelihoods. CIF supports the poor in prioritizing livelihood needs by investments in sub-projects proposed and implemented by the Community-Based Organizations (CBOs). The cumulative CIF expenditure up to March 2012 is ₹10.88 billon, and the total number of beneficiaries stood at around 3 million. The Government provides incentives in the form of reimbursement of interest above 3 per cent per annum on the loans taken by the self help groups under this scheme. During the year 2011–12, ₹8.79 million were reimbursed to 1,948,384 SHGs, with the cumulative disbursement of ₹19.67 billion since the inception of the scheme. The Government of AP has announced an improved incentive scheme for the SHGs repaying instalment promptly from the present Pavala vaddi to 0 per cent interest (Vaddi Leni Runalu) effective from January 2012 for all the SHGs whose borrowings do not exceed ₹0.50 million. Mandal Mahila Samakhyas (MMS) of SHGs in association with Government of Andhra Pradesh have promoted 'Sthree Nidhi' Credit Cooperative Federation Ltd to address the issues relating to inadequate finance and to ensure timely availability of credit. Till March 2012, ₹862.6 million were disbursed to 74,187 members of 24,087 SHGs in 7,600 Village officers in 824 mandals. Of the above, an amount of ₹278.5 million was disbursed to 20141 groups under a special program to finance the poorest of the poor to take up livelihood activities identified for this purpose under the Sthree Nidhi livelihood program.

Despite the positive initiatives undertaken by the state government, the issue of meeting the financial needs of the poor is not fully addressed yet. A recent study conducted by MicroSave brought out a striking finding that with MFIs in Andhra Pradesh drastically reducing new lending, borrowers have been forced to seek alternative sources for lending.[4] This situation calls for an urgent need to revisit the SHG movements' vision and mission, in addition to utilizing the successful elements of different models for further up-scaling.

Impact of SBLP on living standards of poor[5]

Beyond outreach and scaling up, there is a need to understand the impact of the programme on the targeted members in terms of achieving the mission objectives. Studies conducted by various institutions/experts revealed that the programme has indeed helped social and economic empowerment of rural poor, especially the women, causing significant up-scaling of social capital, while at the same time delivering crucial and much-needed financial services at low transaction costs for both banks and poor borrowers.[6] However, slow progress of graduation of SHG members, the poor quality of group functioning, dropout of members from groups etc., have also been reported by various scholars in different parts of the country, which need to be taken into account while designing the road map for the next phase of the SHG programme.[7]

SAVINGS AND BANK LOAN THROUGH SHGs

A study carried out by APMAS covering 1942 self-help groups and about 23800 members across eight states spread throughout the country sheds light on social composition of SHG members, SHG federations, dropout rates, saving and borrowings from banks. The social composition of sample SHGs revealed that the share of SC/ST members was more than 40 per cent in states such as Rajasthan, West Bengal and Gujarat. In West Bengal and Gujarat the share was more than 50 per cent, indicating that the SHGs in these states are highly concentrated among SC/ST categories. The SC/ST composition was lower in Bihar, Andhra Pradesh and Karnataka. The composition of minorities is more than one-fifth in Assam and Maharashtra. For all the sample states put together, the composition of SC/ST to the total SHG members was one-third of total members, while another one-third was constituted by backward communities. Minorities accounted for about 13 per cent of SHG membership, while other communities accounted for close to one-fifth of total SHG members.

The study findings further confirmed the importance of savings shown by the members. In all the states except Andhra Pradesh' and Karnataka, the average savings was less than ₹25,000 in about 50 per cent or more number of SHGs, while more than

70 per cent of the SHGs in high-poverty states such as Rajasthan and Bihar had less than ₹25,000 as average savings per SHG. In all the states put together, more than 50 per cent of the SHGs had a savings of less than ₹25,000 (Table 2.5). Andhra Pradesh had about 80 per cent of the SHGs with an average savings of more than ₹25,000. In Karnataka, more than one-fourth of the SHGs had an average savings of more than ₹75,000, while in Andhra Pradesh the percentage of SHGs having average savings of more than ₹75,000 was about 15 per cent. In terms of the overall savings per SHG in the state as a whole, Karnataka topped the list with an average saving per SHG of about ₹59,500, followed by Andhra Pradesh with an average saving of about ₹47,000. The high-poverty states such as Bihar and Rajasthan had an average savings of ₹20,700 and ₹22,000 respectively. The average savings per SHG for all the states was ₹33,000.

The details on percentage of SHGs currently (at the time of the survey) having a bank loan and average loan size reveal that Andhra Pradesh topped the list in terms of both the percentage of SHGs having a bank loan (90 per cent) as well as in terms of average loan size (about ₹0.3 million). The percentage of SHGs having a current loan from bank was the lowest in Gujarat (18 per cent) and Rajasthan (27 per cent). The average loan size was also the lowest in Gujarat with ₹24,000 (Table 2.6). Karnataka had about 50 per cent of its SHGs with a current bank loan with an average loan size of ₹0.15 million. In all states put together, there were close to 50 per cent of the SHGs with a current bank loan, and their average loan size was about ₹0.14 million.

Similar to this observation, a study[8] of 800 households spread over four districts in Odisha state on

Table 2.5 **State wise total savings of SHG members as of March 2011**

(in percentages)

Amount in ₹000	RJN	ASM	BHR	WB	GJR	MHR	AP	KNT	Total
<25	72.80	52.65	78.78	45.81	55.41	58.33	20.08	37.55	52.63
26–50	17.62	39.18	16.73	48.90	34.39	25.79	41.80	18.59	29.74
51–75	5.75	6.12	3.27	4.41	6.37	9.92	22.95	17.84	9.84
>75	3.83	2.04	1.22	0.88	3.82	5.95	15.16	26.02	7.79
Total	100.00	100.00	100.00	100.00	100.00	100.00	100.00	100.00	100.00
Average savings per SHG	22,021	27,288	20,695	29,777	27,276	28,456	46,826	59,378	33,148

Source: APMAS Hyderabad.

Table 2.6 State-wise percentage of SHGs currently having bank loan and average loan size

Particulars	RJN	ASM	BHR	WB	GJR	MHR	AP	KNT	Total
SHGs having bank loan (%)	26.69	41.20	43.25	69.29	18.13	43.48	90.00	50.37	48.92
Average loan size (₹)	101,845	60,128	52,243	46,634	24,034	125,182	299,347	145,145	135,228

Source: APMAS Hyderabad.

the impact of microfinance on rural household savings revealed that the average annual savings of microfinance beneficiary households was about 53 per cent higher than that of control group. However, a disaggregated analysis of source-wise savings indicated that commercial banks are the major destination for savings rather than SHGs themselves both for beneficiary and control group households. The average savings with SHGs by the microfinance beneficiaries was only ₹130, whereas the beneficiary households saved about ₹2,100 with commercial banks.

A study was carried out among 1,000 households spread over four states viz., Gujarat, Rajasthan, Himachal Pradesh and Madhya Pradesh to assess the economic and social impact of SBLP on its members with focus on poverty.[9] The findings indicate that consumption (26.72 per cent), farm activities (14.59 per cent), medical exigencies (11.32 per cent), house repair (10.74 per cent) and income generating activity (9.92 per cent) were the five main purposes for which loans were availed by the members. Consumption was found to be the top most reason for joining SHGs in all the four states. The study concluded that the SHG financing has reduced the dependency of its members on moneylenders and the income level of members has also gone up on account of their becoming members of SHGs.

WOMEN EMPOWERMENT

The role of microcredit spearheaded by the SHG movement in women empowerment is by now a well-established fact. Liberating rural women from their traditional confinements to homesteads, participation in microfinance programmes contributes to social change as well as empowering women by strengthening their economic roles. In many MFIs, women have become preferred clients as their income benefits their families through improved nutrition, health, education and well-being; because they have higher repayment rates; and because women work better in the group lending programmes that

makes reaching the poor efficient.[10] Access to the basic financial products such as savings and loans enable women to set up new economic activities or expand the existing ones for higher income. The control over this increased income and assets can be used directly for her own well-being and that of her children/family. Moreover, the control over income and assets strengthens women's ability to negotiate change in gender relations within the household and wider community. Thus, besides a popular poverty alleviation strategy, the empowerment of women has become a key rationale for SHG expansion and replication. A study[11] of 1,000 households spread over four states on the role of microfinance in social and economic empowerment of women in four states revealed that animal husbandry was the primary occupation for about 20 per cent of women in both SHG and non-SHG categories. A higher percentage of SHG women were engaged in petty business/services compared to control group women, possibly because of access to credit through SHGs. The results of the study suggest that micro finance creates an enabling environment for empowerment. It is found that participation in microfinance programmes not only enhances women's economic security but also empowers them socially, psychologically and politically as compared to non-participants.

Access to credit enables women to negotiate gender barriers, increase their control over economic resources and improve their relative positions within and outside their households. A majority of the women involved in these programmes maintain a significant control over their incomes. Although the magnitude of their income is small, its effect on women's empowerment is substantial. This is visible from participant's view on their significant improvement of spending on household consumption needs, children's education and personal things as well as their involvement and bargaining power in household decision making.

A study[12] on the impact of microfinance on women empowerment in Punjab found that participation in microfinance programmes has not only significantly increased income, but has also developed regular saving habits among women. As a consequence of their economic empowerment, women could actively participate in household decision making, besides enhancing their social and psychological empowerment. Similar results were reported from study[13] conducted in West Bengal. In spite of the improvements in savings and banking habits due to the participation in microfinance programmes, the problem of default is an important issue, affecting the sustainability of the SHGs.[14]

DEFAULT AND DROPOUTS IN SHG

Several studies in the past quantified the excellent repayment performance of above 90 per cent, which was one of the driving factors which influence banks to actively participate in the programme. However, with fast expansion in terms of numbers and geographies, delinquencies are creeping into SBLP. As per NABARD's data the Non-Performing Assets of banks against loans to SHGs has gone up from ₹14.74 billion (4.74 per cent) as on 31 March 2011 to ₹16.55 billion (6.38 per cent) as on 31 March 2012. The trend of increasing NPAs is observed across all regions of the country. The trend of increasing NPAs in this programme may force bankers to go slow on SHG lending, which in turn may affect the financial inclusion drive as SBLP is one of the important tools for financial inclusion. The higher level of NPAs against the SHGs in central and northern regions needs to be addressed as these are the states where the financial inclusion are at the lowest levels. There is an urgent need to probe the causes for delinquencies in SHG lending for redesigning the strategies of the SHG movement.

In this background, the CMF, IFMR Chennai launched three studies on delinquencies by SHGs in different regions of the country, viz., (a) Rajasthan, (b) North Eastern Region, and (c) Odisha and Madhya Pradesh states. The Rajasthan study highlights several reasons for default: improper process of group formation is the foremost reason for default as accepted norms for area selection, selection of members, concept seeding, etc., were not followed in any of the defaulted groups, while the other set of 18 sample groups with 100 per cent repayment have gone through some locally established process. Further, it was observed that there was progressive decline in record maintenance and updating, and regularity of meetings among the defaulting SHGs. One of the important findings of the study was that the prime objective of about two-thirds of members

in the defaulting groups was to get bank credit only and for another 13 per cent of them, subsidy was the main driving force. On the other hand, for 84 per cent of the members from groups with 100 per cent loan repayment both savings and credit were the main reasons for joining the SHGs, and they started with savings and then graduated to credit.

Savings behaviour of these groups revealed that after the third year, there has been a decline in average savings per member, and it is one of the main characteristics of defaulting groups, and it starts after bigger loan amount are sanctioned to groups, which in turn reflects that groups were formed only to avail credit. Almost 44 per cent of the defaulting groups were in the age bracket of three to five years and 35 per cent in the age group of six to eight years. It is precisely during three to five years of age the groups get bigger loans or activity-based loan from banks. This implies that groups need special attention/input when they are three-five years old. In other words, perfect credit planning, hand holding and business development services at a group-level are required to manage the bigger loan amount. In many SHGs, there is manipulative intermediation by the President or Secretary, who takes the lion's share of the loan and distributes the rest among the members. This is further aggravated by multiple group membership of leaders. Permanent leaders, often the ones with power and resources, form groups of their convenience and use it to source bank loans for themselves. As far as external factors are concerned, continuous drought situation, low levels of economic activity and poor income were found to be the major triggering factors that accelerated the process of group degeneration and eventual default. About a fifth of the groups cited poor economic status of members as the major reason for their defaulting repayment.

The study on delinquencies in the North Eastern Region,[15] revealed that the quality of the SHGs in the region has been affected primarily because of non-adherence to some basic tenets of SHG management such as regularity of meeting, attendance of members in the meeting, regularity of savings and maintenance of records with delinquency rates. Non-adherence to the basic rules is due to the role played by different agencies involved in the SHG movement. It was also found that there has been a significant underreporting of delinquency rates by banks as compared to the actual field-level delinquencies, which calls for urgent steps to correct the problem. The study on loan defaults by SHGs in Odisha and Madhya Pradesh[16] also confirmed that flawed formation of SHGs without adhering to the basic principles of SHG functioning was the root cause for defaults. Many of the groups were not fully aware of the basic function of SHGs including purpose of savings mobilisation and inter-loaning. It was disheartening to note that more than one half of the SHGs in the sample had already stopped collecting mandatory savings from members once the bank loans were disbursed and the groups were disbanded. This is in line with the earlier finding that the main purpose of a large number of groups was only to avail credit with subsidy. Irregularity and/or discontinuation of group meetings were also characteristics of these defaulting groups. However, one of the interesting findings of the study is that the average repayment of SHGs who had attended/participated in either income generating activity related or capacity building training programmes was more than that of groups who were not part of any such programmes. The percentage of active groups increased with the age of SHGs suggesting that most SHGs pass through a critical stage when they are within five years old. Thus, if a group survives for five years, there is a higher chance of it to sustain.

An important observation in the field is that grading is not done properly by banks as well as DRDA/block officials. Had there been proper grading, most of the sample SHGs would have not been eligible for availing loans from banks and, to that extent, default could have been avoided. Another factor observed (more in Odisha) was that post 2006 when the division between BPL and APL members got more accentuated, some members suddenly became ineligible for government subsidy. In many of the SHGs, APL members were denied subsidy. Although loan component was equally shared among all members, the subsidy component was equally divided exclusively among BPL members only. Many also quoted that this was the main reason for group conflicts and hence default by the new APL members. In few cases, it is also observed that the APL members had taken internal loan equivalent to subsidy amount and did

not repay to the group. In such cases this too has led to internal conflict and adversely affected repayment behaviour of the members. Expectation of debt relief, failure or low income from IGA at the group/individual level, death or migration of member(s) who had outstanding loan, non-receipt of insurance claim for dead animals purchased through loan, internal conflict, utilization of loan on household expenditure were some of the other important reasons reported by groups/members for their non-repayment of loans. To conclude, the studies have identified certain features of the groups such as ad hoc formation of groups, lack of emphasis on group development, widespread laxity in writing and absence of basic books of record, lack of attention to member savings, low incidence of inter-loaning appropriation of benefits by the leaders/office bearers and credit to group without estimating credit needs of members as the reasons for default.

Dropout from groups is one of the major concerns being debated while discussing the sustainability of the groups. The study conducted by APMAS addressed this issue and critically evaluated the performance of SHGs in the dropout context. The details on dropout rates from SHG membership revealed that the dropout rate was the lowest in Rajasthan, Maharashtra, Gujarat and Bihar, where more than two-thirds of SHGs did not report even a single member dropout. The dropout rate was the highest in Andhra Pradesh where the percentage of SHGs reporting no dropout was only 43 per cent, implying that about 57 per cent of the SHGs have lost at least one member (Table 2.7). All the states put together, the percentage of SHGs reporting no dropout was more than 60 per cent. Overall, about one-fourth of the SHGs reported a dropout rate of at least one to two members, while less than five per cent of the SHGs have lost more than five members. This implies that there is a need to look at the reasons for dropouts and to take steps to prevent the dropouts.

Table 2.7 Percentage of dropouts in SHGs

No. of members	RJN	ASM	BHR	WB	GJR	MHR	AP	KNT	Total
No dropouts	74.81	63.60	67.46	57.26	69.38	73.12	43.20	51.48	62.26
1–2 members	17.67	18.80	26.98	28.22	13.75	20.95	37.60	27.41	24.36
3–4 members	4.89	9.20	4.37	9.13	10.63	3.56	12.80	14.44	8.55
5 & above	2.63	8.40	1.19	5.39	6.25	2.37	6.40	6.67	4.84
Total	100.00	100.00	100.00	100.00	100.00	100.00	100.00	100.00	100.00

Source: APMAS Hyderabad.

COMMUNITY-BASED MICROFINANCE INSTITUTIONS

The Community-based Microfinance Institutions (CBMFIs) model assumes greater significance, creating possibilities for emergence of a viable option since such organizations are non-exploitative, member-based and member-managed and more importantly, the members benefit directly from the savings and the profits. SHGs, women's federations and cooperatives are member-owned and managed organizations, thus CBMFI's direct loans from banks and other formal financial organizations as the most benign way of getting financial services to the poor.

The SHG federation has emerged as a critical institutional mechanism to ensure sustainability of SHGs besides providing them both financial and non-financial support. The main objective of federating the Self-Help Groups is to make them stronger and ensure their organizational, operational and financial sustainability. More often than not, federations were formed by the initiatives of the State Governments and NGOs or other Self-help Promoting Institutions (SHPI) rather than the initiatives of the SHGs themselves. The SHPIs took the lead in establishing federations, mainly as an exit strategy for themselves. In addition to making the SHG members perceive a sense of solidarity as members of a larger organization, the formation of federations has substantially increased the bargaining power of the SHGs in taking up issues with local bodies, banks and other government departments and institutions and accessing the government programs. Some of the government departments are involving these federations in implementing pro-poor welfare programmes. In addition to reducing the default rates and increasing the financial discipline among the SHGs, the federations also help in resolving conflicts among SHG members, between SHGs, and between SHGs and banks. Besides strengthening existing SHGs, these federations themselves have become the promoters of new SHGs in remote areas where other SHPIs have not reached. They have also facilitated the SHG-Bank linkage program. Many government departments, corporate sector and civil society organizations co-opted the federations in implementing their activities like watersheds, PDS, NREGS, Mid-day meals, awareness about HIV/ AIDS, health camps, microinsurance, etc. Such cooption benefited both federations and concerned organizations. Some banks started using federations as the business facilitators on payment basis, which proved to be beneficial to both banks and federations.

There is also potential for the SHG federations to become business correspondent of banks.[17]

The earliest SHG federation was formed by the then PRADAN (presently Dhan Foundation) in Tirupati in 1992 and a later in Madurai, soon followed by CDS, Alappuzha in 1993 and MYRADA in 1996. Rapid expansion in the number of SHG federations took place in South India in the late 1990s, particularly with the introduction of several externally funded projects through DRDAs. The Southern region had more than 95 per cent of the total number of federations in India, even by the year 2007. Only after 2007 a large number of federations were formed in the Eastern region. The main purpose of forming SHG federations was to ensure sustainability of SHGs by providing them with the necessary support in the areas of bookkeeping, auditing, conflict resolution and linkages with banks. The federations also provide certain financial services, forward and backward linkages to SHGs, promote new SHGs, act as special purpose vehicles for mobilizing funds from SHGs and act as a withdrawal strategy for SHG promoters.

The number of primary, secondary and tertiary federations of SHGs in different regions of the country as of March 2012 is presented in Table 2.8. There are more than 0.16 million primary federations, and 6,358 secondary federations and 98 tertiary federations in the country. Southern and eastern regions account for more than 90 per cent of the total number of federations in the country.

The SHG federations are predominant in West Bengal, Andhra Pradesh, Kerala and Tamil Nadu states. In Andhra Pradesh the federations are registered under the Mutually Aided Cooperative Societies Act, thus providing substantial autonomy for the federations with reduced government domination. In Kerala, the federations are promoted through the Kudumbashree program, while the Tamil Nadu Government promotes the federations under its Vazhndhu Kaatuvom and Mahalir Thittam projects. PRADAN, MYRADA, DHAN and CARE are the prominent NGOs that promote SHG federations in large scale. Financial federations provide finance-related services such as saving, credit, insurance and money transfer, while non-financial federations provide sector development, livelihood development and social development services. There is, however, a third category called multi-purpose federations, which undertake at least one financial and one non-financial function. Most of the federations in the country belong to the multi-purpose category as they provide a range of products and services thus following a 'credit plus' approach rather

Table 2.8 Regional spread of SHG federations in India in 2007 and 2012[18]

Region	No. of primary federations		No. of secondary federations		No. of tertiary federations		Total	
	2007	2012	2007	2012	2007	2012	2007	2012
Northern	126	371	21	24	–	14	147	409
North Eastern	122	369	10	18	–	0	132	387
Eastern	5,745	62,189	105	2,940	–	56	5,852	65,185
Central	487	5,459	334	180	–	2	821	5,641
Western	663	8,629	1	11	–	1	664	8,641
Southern	59,172	83,268	2,093	3,185	22	25	61,287	86,478
Union Territories	–	1	–	0	–	0	–	1
All India	66,310	160,286	2,571	6,358	22	98	68,903	166,742

Source: APMAS Hyderabad.

than 'credit only' approach. The federations usually have a three-tier structure with primary level federations at village level, secondary level federations at the cluster level and apex-level federations at the district or state level. The size of federations ranges widely across the country, with the number of SHGs in each of the federations ranging from 10 to 1,000. The federations perform four broad categories of functions viz., financial functions, business development/livelihood services, strengthening or supporting services for SHGs, and social or developmental initiatives.

A study conducted by APMAS focusing on the extent of SHGs membership in federations revealed that the percentage of SHGs having federation membership was the highest at 100 per cent in Andhra Pradesh, followed by about 37 to 38 per cent in Karnataka and Bihar[19] (Table 2.9). In Maharashtra and Gujarat, the federated SHGs accounted for about 16–18 per cent of the total number of SHGs in these states. The percentage of federated SHGs was negligible in West Bengal (~1 per cent), Rajasthan (~3 per cent) and Assam (7.60 per cent). In all the states put together, the percentage of SHGs, which are not having any federation membership was more than 70 per cent, indicating a large scope for forming federations.

A study on SHG federations covering six states found that the structure, functioning, and the style of functioning were influenced very much by the Self-help Group Promoting Agencies (SHPA). It was found that most of the sample federations have good linkages with government departments, programs and projects; private sector companies, insurance companies, corporate hospitals, NGOs, etc. It was also observed that the performance of the federations was closely related to the SHPA's vision of institution building for the poor, as well as on the quality, adequacy and appropriateness of the services provided to the members. A study[20] was conducted in Uttar Pradesh to determine the contribution of SHG federations to economic, political and social empowerment of SHG members. These federations were of two different types promoted by two NGOs viz., People's Action for National Integration (PANI) and Grameen Development Services (GDS). The findings of the study have been mixed, and are strongly dependent on the structure and service provided by the SHG federations. The financial and organizational sustainability are strongly interlinked and highly dependent on the structure and range of services provided by the federations. The federation concept of PANI is simple and less complex than that of GDS. There are no separate committees or

Table 2.9 SHG memberships in federations

Membership	RJN	ASM	BHR	WB	GJR	MHR	AP	KNT	Total
Having	3.38	7.60	38.49	1.24	18.13	15.81	100.00	36.67	28.12
Not Having	96.62	92.40	61.51	98.76	81.88	84.19	0.00	63.33	71.88
Total	100.00	100.00	100.00	100.00	100.00	100.00	100.00	100.00	100.00

Source: APMAS Hyderabad.

specific services delivered to the SHGs, but there is a strong focus on collective social action and linkages to government services are made, a system that contributes (at least to some extent) to political and social empowerment of SHG members. This leads to a very cost effective system where operational self-sufficiency can be quite easily obtained. GDS implements a more complex federation concept where the federation has various committees. GDS federations offer a broader range of services to their SHGs leading to different findings regarding financial and operational sustainability. A major benefit from the federations in the perception of the SHG members is the agricultural support offered by the federations, leading to a sense of entrepreneurship amongst the SHG members and economic empowerment (Box 2.1). However, the structure of various committees of the federations leads to several complications, such as confusion about roles and responsibilities and a large time investment of federation leaders. Benefits of these committees are not always clear in the perception of SHG members.

Although operating Self-Sufficiency (OSS) seems to be achievable in this model, it will be a complex and time-consuming process, and it will be very difficult to achieve OSS without collecting membership fees for the services offered by federations. However, these federations have considerable impact on those activities in which economies of scale are significant. For example, in agricultural input production and/or supply and machinery hiring there are substantial economies of scale whenever the federations took up these tasks at a larger scale.[21] Another study[22] supported by the World Bank also revealed that federations could help SHGs to become institutionally and financially sustainable as they provide economies of scale that reduce transaction costs and make the provision of these services viable. However, their sustainability is constrained by several factors—both internal, related to the federations themselves, and external, related to the other stakeholders.

One of the major benefits of SHG federations was that the federations themselves have become an alternative source of financing for the SHGs. Though credit is the predominant product offered by most of the SHG federations, non-credit services such as agricultural input supply and output marketing are also important. In spite of the fact that the federations are best suited for offering a wide range of services to the rural poor, their capacity to offer these services is limited by the inadequate human resources and experience in innovating and offering a wide array of products and services. However, to ensure their long term financial and economic sustainability, provision of non-credit products and services is essential. Some of the SHGs have already shown the way by entering into marketing arrangements with the corporate sector for supplying raw materials to those companies and/or marketing their products. Provision of microinsurance products covering life and health insurance, livestock insurance, and agricultural extension advisory services including small-scale inputs production activities such as bio-fertilizers and bio-pesticides would enhance the financial viability of the federations.

Box 2.1 MicroGraam's Micro Ventures

Micro Venture investment model, which is a dramatic departure from traditional microcredit lending promoted by MicroGraam aims to bring an array of diverse financial tools for India's underprivileged rural poor. In Micro Ventures, a micro-entrepreneur and a micro venture capitalist enter into a revenue sharing agreement, which enables the two partners to create a micro to small enterprise (MSE). Although traditional microcredit provides the essential service of access to credit, entrepreneurs who are willing and able to undertake larger business ventures are unable to do so under the current paradigm. MicroGraam has created Micro Ventures to address this underserved niche market of entrepreneurs who require a larger loan size but cannot obtain them from commercial financing. Micro Ventures provide flexibility and cost savings, which can only arise from long term financing.

In this model, the micro venture capitalist provides the full upfront cost to starting the business, and the two parties agree to share a percentage of the profits or losses. The two parties agree upon how to share the profits or losses (50-50, 60-40, etc.) and the number of years the micro venture capitalist will be involved. MicroGraam acts as the facilitator in the transaction and helps the entrepreneur with their business model.

The first micro venture facilitated by MicroGraam was a Dairy Farm in Kolar district of Karnataka. MicroGraam facilitated equity capital of ₹300,000 from six micro venture capitalists in July 2010. The dairy farm was set by the members of the Self-Help Group and the group members jointly managed the dairy farm. Micro Venture Capitalist hold 40 per cent stake in the dairy farm and 60 per cent is held by the SHG group. In two years, micro venture capitalist have been able to exit fully with an annual ROI of 11 per cent. The latest Micro Venture initiative supported by MicroGraam is a 'water shop' in northern Karnataka. The micro-entrepreneur, Sikander, received financing from three micro venture capitalists to the tune of ₹300,000. He recently opened shop to provide clean drinking water to the surrounding area with 500+ households. This social business leverages sustainable business practices to address the public health need for safe water. Access to clean water and sanitation facilitates are pressing conditions in rural India and Micro Ventures has enabled this social cause to become a viable social business. In order to achieve long term, sustainable development in rural India, financial models beyond traditional loans and saving are essential. MicroGraam continues to develop innovating financings for the needs of its borrowers, and it is looking forward to helping

Source: Primary information collected from MicroGraam.

The quality of financial management was found to be better among federated SHGs than non-federated SHGs, while in general management both federated and non-federated SHGs were on par with each other, and in terms of governance and accounts maintenance, non-federated SHGs were better placed than federated SHGs. One of the serious challenges faced by the SHG federations is their financial sustainability. A study[23] based on 10 SHG federations spread over five states, found that 50 per cent of the sample federations was having very poor levels of financial sustainability, 20 per cent of them had a moderate level of financial sustainability, while 30 per cent of the federations had high levels of financial sustainability.

In spite of their positive role and contributions towards strengthening the self-help movement in the country, SHG federations are facing a number of problems/constraints. Another study found that almost all the federations studied had limited financial resources, though there are variations across different federation structures. Most of the services provided by the federations are inadequate due to external constraints such as low investments in capacity building, bankers' non-cooperation in SHG Bank linkage, restrictions imposed by the promoting agencies, etc. Limitations of promoting agencies also became limitations of the federations. However, it is possible to overcome these problems and make the federations

sustainable in the long run through regular capacity building programs such as training and workshops and by undertaking financially more remunerative support services and collecting reasonable fees and user charges for the various services provided.[24] In this scenario, Sampark has been able to get limited funding support from donor organizations to invest in capacity building of women and build viable cooperatives, else it would not have been possible to have the lessons it offers for community-based microfinance and women's empowerment. Sampark's work with women over the past decade shows that they benefit much more if they retain control over their financial resources and organizations.

Limited scope of the federations to act as financial intermediary has been deliberated at length.[25] As such, scaling up of this model is limited due to lack of policy support from NABARD, except providing limited funding support for capacity building and leadership quality enhancement of the group members.[26] However, the success stories of the federations being experimented across the country such as SEWA, DHAN Foundation, etc., indicate the scope of this model for wider scaling up (Box 2.2).

As such there are many CBMFIs, which are characterized by smaller operation scales, being larger in number, dispersed, less organized and less documented. However, their experiences are not effectively deliberated among policy circles despite the recent emphasis on re-vitalizing the cooperative sector. Even though SHGs have come of age, and most rural women are now familiar with them, microfinance cooperatives of women are still not so common. Traditionally, agricultural and multi-purpose cooperatives have been the preserve of men, and microfinance models were heavily biased in favour of commercial MFIs.[27] To access external funds, these cooperatives have to conform to high standards of credit-worthiness, and need data and monitoring systems. Women, who are poor and illiterate, need to build their capacities to manage SHGs and cooperatives on their own. These capacity building requirements are time- and cost-intensive, and need the full attention of a promoting organization.

Further, National Rural Livelihood Mission's focus on federation arrangement will certainly bring the new dimension in federation approaches. Redesigning the federation model in light of the lessons learnt so far will have a positive impact on this model. Networking will also provide a broader platform for collective action at a larger level and scale so that the demands and requirements of the members and the SHGs at a grassroots level could be effectively taken up with donors and governments.

Box 2.2 Kalamandir Saksham SHG federation—a case study for success

Like other villages of Jharkhand, Janumdih was a small village of the Bhumij tribes in the remote corner of Potka block in East Singhbhum. Out of 158 families, 136 families were below the poverty line. In the year 1999, *kalamandir* initiated a programme on revival of the Firkaal dance. Soon it was found that the one and only source of income in their village was from rain fed agriculture, that too a single crop. Due to scarcity of water and inadequate irrigation facility in the hilly terrains, the Bhumij agriculturists used to work as contract labour in road construction and brick kilns. In the year 2005–06 the scenario started changing in favour of a silent revolution in the villages. SHG members from *munda* tribes who were farming grass in the wasteland were given training by NABARD support but no credit linkage was possible as bankers were not taken into confidence.

Two SHGs that were weaving Grass Mat unit at Janumdih started growing from strength to strength. They took loans of ₹0.5 million from the Union Bank of India, Khairpal under SGSY and started production in full swing. More artisan groups were formed at nearby potential villages after the success of the SHG run micro enterprise. The community was keen to support such an initiative. The situation of Janumdih started changing totally. It was getting converted into a fully developed art and craft village. *Kalamandir*—CCAF initiated formation of a Federation of Self Help Groups of Farmers, weavers and artisans from among 40 SHGs. A proper business plan was developed in consultation with all stake holders and loan was applied after a bankable project was prepared in the process. The efforts for hand-holding of SHG Federation for successfully running the Rural Mart were a unique story. The entire responsibilities on account of Rural Mart rested on the *Kalamandir*-CCAF, and the expenses towards proper management of the Rural Mart i.e., right from procurement of finished products from the SHG members (on cost basis and also in some cases, on buy-back arrangements), maintaining stock, advertising and selling of the products, maintenance of accounts, etc. were being incurred by the NGO.

For more than two years, the members of the SHGs (within the Federation) were under constant guidance and support from the management of *Kalamandir*-CCAF for procurement, processing, packaging and marketing. But for the past one and a half years, they are procuring raw materials independently for making the finished products from West Bengal and from other local villages. Besides increased turnover in business, their quality of life also has improved because of the increase in income, and the women of the village have stopped working as bonded labor in the brick kln, and now they have additional income generating activities such as procurement of raw material, weaving, stitching, maintaining the records and few are also involved in the farming of grass. The SHG Federation is now capable of running and managing the Rural Mart.

Source: Primary information collected from Kalamandir.

IDENTIFYING CRITICAL STAGES OF SBLP

The SBLP has already completed two decades of its implementation and attempts are being made to launch the second phase of SHG in order to speed up the process of social and economic development in the country. A study on the life cycle of SHGs conducted in three states namely, Andhra Pradesh, Tamil Nadu and West Bengal[28] suggests that the key elements to ensure long-term sustainability of SHGs are: systematic and scientific approach in the formation of SHGs including clear goal of SHGs, homogeneity and solidarity among members, existence, evolution and enforcement of bye-laws, and participation of members in decision making and transparency in the operations and functions of the groups. The study also reports that the assistance provided by various SHPIs and NGOs in overcoming the difficulties faced by the groups starting from the group formation to further graduating to micro enterprises/producer groups/individual borrowers, were very critical in the development process of the groups. More than 90 per cent of SHGs reported getting a second loan, i.e., entering into growth and expansion phase of their life cycle, and more than three-fourth (78 per cent), one-half and (52 per cent) and about one-third (30 per cent) of sample SHGs reported getting third, fourth and fifth bank loans respectively. It was observed that with the increase in loan linkages, SHG members utilised the loans either for initiating new economic activities or for diversifying their existing activities. This helped not only in increasing the members' income but also in generating asset base and further reflected on members' ability to directly borrow from the bank without the group support. The study recommended the following measures to be taken into consideration while preparing suitable policies for further improving the functioning and long-run sustainability of the SHGs in the states or regions where the performance is poor:

1. Ensure better bookkeeping, effective training programmes and helping the SHGs to devise viable incentives for participation in the system.
2. Further strengthen the capacity building and skills of the self-help promoting institutions (SHPIs) on various aspects of group management practices.
3. While preparing the strategies for graduating SHG members from micro-borrower to micro-enterprises or diversifying their economic activities, the package has to be designed taking into consideration the investment capacity, indigenous knowledge, skill of SHG members and availability of local raw materials and market demand for the produce.
4. In the context of training on income generation activities, there is an urgent need to give prior attention to the specific requirement of group members related to their economic activities before organising any such training programmes.
5. In order to encourage banks to take interest in furthering the SHG movement—there is an urgent need to develop a scheme of performance-linked incentive for banks, like credit disbursed under the SHG-Bank linkage programme.
6. Though NABARD has already taken initiatives in setting up rural marts exclusively for SHG products, there is a need to further strengthen this initiative particularly in areas/regions where no such initiatives have been taken up so far.

SHGs—NABARD's ROLE AND PERFORMANCE[29]

NABARD has been extending various supports to various stakeholders to facilitate sustained access to financial services for the unreached poor in rural areas through various microfinance innovations in a sustainable manner (Box 2.3). NABARD continued its refinancing and promotional role to support stakeholders including banks. During the year 2011–12, refinance of ₹30.73 billion was provided to banks covering their lending to SHGs. This was an increase from ₹25.45 billion disbursed in 2010–11. As a proportion of NABARD's total refinance disbursements SHG share increased from 18.9 per cent in 2010–11 to 19.9 per cent in 2011–12. The Microfinance Development and Equity Fund has been created with the corpus ₹4.00 billion to facilitate and support various promotional activities like grant assistance to Self-Help Promoting Institutions, funding of training and capacity building of microfinance clients and stakeholders of the SHG Bank Linkage Programme, support to MFIs, for supporting introduction of Management Information System (MIS) for the sector, for helping research and publications concerning microfinance related issues. Under this fund, ₹333.1 million was released during 2011–12, of which ₹286.8 million was grant support for promotional activities and ₹46.3 million for Capital Support/Revolving Fund Assistance to Micro Finance Institutions, as against ₹299.5 million and ₹174.3 million, respectively in the previous year.

During the year 2011–12, grant assistance of ₹379.5 million was sanctioned to various agencies for promoting and credit linking of 94,482 groups thus taking the cumulative assistance sanctioned

---

Box 2.3 Women SHG in Union Budget speech

The Government has also announced ₹100 billion to NABARD (National Bank for Agriculture and Rural Development) for refinancing rural banks and help better for free flow funding. Much has been concentrated towards rural upliftment where interest subsidy for women Self-help Groups (SHGs) is announced up to ₹0.3 million at the rate of seven per cent and an additional three per cent more to allow the SHGs to repay the amount promptly on the said time. The Hon'ble Finance Minister stated,

Last year I had announced the creation of 'Women SHGs Development Fund' which had been set up by NABARD. In 2012–13 I have proposed to increase the sum of ₹2,000 million to ₹3,000 million. This Fund will also support the objectives of Aajeevika i.e., the National Rural Livelihood Mission. It will empower women SHGs to access bank credit. The initiative, in the first phase, would focus on selected 600 blocks of 150 districts, including the Left Wing Extremism affected districts.

Source: Union Budget, Ministry of Finance, Government of India, New Delhi.

Table 2.10 NABARD support to SHPIs and their performance

Agency	Sanctions during the year 2011–12			Total groups formed so far
	No.	Amount (₹ million)	No. of Groups	
DCCB	7	11.85	4,740	71,695
RRB	3	9.68	3,810	53,145
NGO	166	357.38	85,571	499,909
FC	4	0.07	61	7,689
IRV	1	0.52	300	43,223
Total	181	379.50	94,482	675,661

Source: Provisional Data from NABARD Head Office Mumbai.

to ₹1,841.7 million to nearly 0.68 million groups (Table 2.10). As on 31 March 2012, an amount of ₹552.8 million was released resulting in formation of 0.42 million groups. The number of groups credit linked till March 2012 was nearly 0.27 million. But this constituted a small proportion (less than 10 per cent) of total groups credit linked and 5.6 per cent of groups savings linked. Given the ambitious target of linking one million groups in each of the next five years, the nature and extent of this assistance should undergo a radical change. The effective cost of promoting and nurturing groups of reasonable quality by SHPIs has been estimated to be between ₹7,000 and 10,000 by different studies. The average cost[30] granted so far under the MFDEF to SHPIs is around ₹2,708. Unless reasonable costs are allowed, it might be difficult to attract competent institutions to act as SHPIs.

Box 2.4 Are SHGs and JLGs working at cross purposes?

Shri Alosiusp Fernandez who conceptualized the SHG concept reacted to this question—

There is confusion regarding the difference between SHGs and JLGs even across NABARD. After discussing with the Chairman NABARD, I understand the following as regards SHGs and JLGs:

SHGs are for the poor and for those who have no assets or very low productive assets (dryland, etc.). The SHGs need to have proper institutional capacity building, which takes time and money; the members need to acquire confidence, skills to decide, negotiate, establish linkages with other institutions (for financial and technical support), lobby for change at home and in society, etc. The management of savings and credit helps

---

to build these organizational and financial management skills.

JLGs are for the 'not so poor' who have assets, which are productive but who cannot get loans because they have no papers (like small farmers with irrigation who take lands on lease) or have problems with accessing banks. They already have some linkages with markets since they have surpluses. In this connection it may be useful to stress those second level institutions, which aggregate, add value and provide marketing support including risk coverage—like producers companies and coops have a major role to play. Credit is a strong trigger here; but different types of credit are required—production, term, soft, working capital and technology (NCDEX) including storage. This package is required if surpluses of small farmers are to fetch a fair and sustained price. Unfortunately these support services are highly fragmented and inadequate. The country does not have organizational and financial scaffolding provided by one agency taking the lead to support these second level institutions. NABFINS is making a small attempt to set up this integrated support system.

The JLGs also need some Institutional Capacity Building (including practice of regular savings—placed in a group common fund, the meaning of joint liability and its implications etc). This reduces the time for training compared to SHGs. The JLG should have a group account…as one basis for the 'jointness', Further the Bank loan should be given to the JLG group account, and then it goes to the individual (this strengthens the jointness)…the size and purpose of loans is decided in advance before the loan is given…unlike in the SHGs where the loan is given in bulk and the members decide later on purpose etc.

Unfortunately the way the JLG program is being implemented—it appears to be working at cross purposes with the SHG program.

Source: Interview by author.

NABARD continued with its initiative of promoting Joint Liability Groups (JLGs) with a view to promoting access to credit for small and marginal farmers and tenant cultivators (Box 2.4). The JLGs fill a critical gap in the rural areas where marginal farmers and tenant farmers find it difficult to access bank loans. The JLGs typically consist of such farmers to facilitate them in availing loans for farming. Reportedly, banks are more keen on JLGs on account of a larger loan size and lower monitoring/handholding requirements. A grant of ₹366.8 million was sanctioned for promoting 194,000 JLGs across the country till March 2012, as against ₹247 million for promoting 125,000 JLGs last year.

In the international realm, governments, non-profit organizations, and community and development agencies have targeted microenterprise development by viewing it as one of the most sustainable paths of local economic growth, employment creation and poverty reduction.[31] Microfinance is widely recognized for its benefits towards opening the doors for small business ownership around the world.[32] Microenterprise development helps micro-entrepreneurs combine their knowledge and determination with microfinance services to attain standards of living and generate income through business (Box 2.5).

In 2005–06, NABARD had initiated a pilot project 'MicroEnterprise Development Programme' (MEDP) to motivate and assist members of matured SHGs to take up income generating activities on a sustainable basis, in nine districts in nine states, involving 14 NGOs. Since then the sphere of MEDP has grown tremendously. During the year 2011–12, 1,914 Micro Enterprise Development Programmes (MEDPs) were conducted for 56,292 members on various location-specific farms, non-farm and service sector activities. So far, 164,948 participants had been covered under the enterprise development programme. The reported numbers are small in comparison with the requirements. Scaling up the MEDP so as to serve at least 15 per cent of all mature groups (of four years vintage or more) might make a discernible impact.

A study on the scope for promoting microenterprise activities through SHGs in select districts of Bihar and Uttar Pradesh covering 456 respondents[33] covered under the Priyadarshini Programme revealed that more than 90 per cent of the respondents were matured SHG members who had undergone MEDP/REDP training, 3.95 per cent respondents were NGOs who had conducted MEDP/REDP trainings and 5.70 per cent respondents were NABARD and Bank officials. The study highlighted that hardly 15 per cent of the matured SHG members in U.P. and Bihar had graduated to microenterprises and that too at a lower level business. Difficulties in getting adequate credit, low level of awareness and lack of skills were the main reasons for not graduating to microenterprises. Even the 15 per cent of the matured SHG members, who had graduated to microenterprises, were still at the nascent stage and their business size was not economically viable. The study suggested that the value chain for

raw materials, and packaging and marketing would help in microenterprise development and should be established through assistance from Microfinance Innovation Fund. Common service centre for packaging and use of latest technology for packaging will help in marketing of the produce. Making available technologies/tools to micro-entrepreneurs, transfer of technology, regular technical support and linking of micro-enterprises with related research organizations would help in microenterprise development. The incremental income from the units established after attending the MEPD was found to vary from activity to activity and location to location depending upon the availability of raw materials and the market for the product. The study also highlighted that the coverage of SHG members under microenterprise development programme had a definite and positive impact on their income generation level.

The pilot project of SHG-Post Office Linkage Programme was launched in 2006 in five districts of Tamil Nadu, with the objectives of (*a*) examining the feasibility of utilizing a vast network of post offices in rural areas in disbursement of credit to rural poor, and (*b*) to test the efficacy of Department of Posts (DoP) in providing microfinance services to rural clients. NABARD had sanctioned refinance assistance of ₹30 million for on-lending to SHGs on an interest sharing basis and released an amount of ₹3.72 million till March 2012. A total of 2,189 SHGs have opened saving accounts, of which 1,259 SHGs have been credit linked by various post offices, with cumulative loan disbursements amounting to ₹36.5 million as on 31 March 2012. Though the pilot project is able to show the scope for greater financial inclusion through the existing well-established network of post offices, the success of the model primarily depended on the involvement of the DoP staff at the field-level. There are evidences that wherever DoP staff is involved enthusiastically in the project, the successes are assured. Hence, further up-scaling of this model heavily depends on the training and follow-up to the implementing staff. However, from members' perspective this model is worth replication due to the proximity of post offices to them.

Box 2.5 Employment generation through microfinance initiatives

An enterprise survey conducted by M-CRIL in June 2012 to find out the jobs created with the support of Hand in Hand's MF programme covering the sample of 2,558 respondents from 330

SHGs revealed that Hand in Hand has created/supported 1.16 million jobs out of its microfinance programme as of March 2012. The study findings quantified that 94.9 per cent of members used the loan for productive purposes and 90.1 per cent of the loan amount from the groups is used for Productive purposes where as 76.4 per cent of Bank loan amount is used for productive purposes. Further it is assessed that one family based enterprise (investment up to ₹50,000) creates 1.67 jobs and one micro enterprise (investment above ₹50,000) creates 2.61 jobs. Hand in Hand's focus on capacity building of clients and handholding support for enterprise promotion leads to this high level of loan usage for productive purposes and creation of jobs at the bottom-of-the-pyramid, which adds to the vibrancy of the local economy and prosperity at the household level.

Source: Study conducted by M-CRIL for Hand in Hand unpublished findings provided by Hand in Hand.

The skewed growth of SHGs in certain regions of the country had narrowed the growth process of the programme. In this background, during the year 2011–12, NABARD revisited the SBLP for identifying the shortcomings and incorporating suitable changes to give the programme a renewed thrust and direction in the form of SHG-2. The objective of SHG-2 is to focus on a few key issues like creating space for voluntary savings, positioning cash credit as the preferred mode of lending, scope for providing multiple borrowings by SHG members matching with their repaying capacity, creating avenues to meet higher credit requirements for livelihood creation, supporting SHG federations as non-financial intermediaries, credit rating and auditing of SHGs as a part of the risk mitigation system, strengthening monitoring mechanisms, etc. The guidelines of SHG-2 have since been issued by NABARD to the concerned stakeholders. The proposed initiatives by NABARD focusing on savings and related products is a positive step forward in strengthening the SHG movement. Validating the proposed strategies through piloted experiment would certainly help in evolving client-oriented products. SHG movement was initiated with the basic presumption that the poor can save, and they require a safe place to protect the same. Compulsory savings was in-built in the model when the poor had less social and economic empowerment. Now over two decades, it is expected that the graduation of SHG members in an economic perspective would expand the scope

of greater savings. Experience shows that the graduation process is restricted mainly to enterprising members and not uniform to all. Hence, there is a need to have different saving products. In this context, voluntary savings may emerge as an additional product for graduated SHG members. Already several such savings products are being offered by several SHPIs and even at group-level. Since the voluntary savings products are expected to be required by a section of group members, it needs to be treated separately, without burdening SHGs with more financial responsibilities. Further, SHGs may not be a safe or protected place for parking more of savings in view of voluntary nature without legal backing. Introducing voluntary savings at the group-level may also influence inequality among equals. Hence, the appropriate strategy would be strengthening the federal structures or Community Banking with legal support to undertake such activities. Evolving specific saving products by banks with flexible terms in liquidity and operation processes will be a better option. These efforts will pave the way for greater financial inclusion and financial literacy among the poor. Considering the diversity in profile and the demand of microfinance clients, the voluntary savings products may be experimented and piloted across regions before including in the main stream business of SHG bank linkage programme.

During the year 2011–12, NABARD, in association with the Government of India, has formulated a scheme for the promotion of women SHGs in backward and Left Wing Extremism (LWE) affected districts. The main objective of this scheme is to bring out a viable and self-sustainable model for promotion and financing of Women Self Help Groups (WSHGs) by involving an anchor NGO in each of the selected backward districts of the country. It attempts at having NGO-SHPI to work not merely as an SHPI for promoting and enabling credit linkage of these groups with banks, but also serving as a banking/business facilitator, tracking, monitoring these groups and also being responsible for loan repayments. To begin with, the scheme is being implemented in 109 selected backward/LWE districts of the country.

As instructed by the Government of India, sanctioning Cash Credit Limits to SHGs has been initiated so as to address the issue of delayed/limited or non-approval of repeat loans to SHG, to ensure cost effectiveness to clients and to provide greater operational flexibility to SHG clients. The groups, in turn, are to extend loans to their members as per the extant guidelines of RBI and NABARD. The SHGs are to ensure payments of interest on a monthly basis on the cash credit availed by them. Earlier, the SHGs were being sanctioned term loans by banks depending on the quantum of savings made by the group. The tenure of such loans was up to a period of three years. However, often, the groups tended to prepay such loan leading to a situation where the groups were not sanctioned fresh loans/repeat loans. Therefore, even for their emergent needs these SHGs were depending on various alternate options like MFIs, etc. The introduction of cash credit is thus aimed at smoothing the consumption and working capital needs of the SHGs during the initial years as well as, to a certain extent, in subsequent years.

PROVIDING LIVELIHOODS—LOCAL AREA BANK MODEL

The concept of local area banks (LABs), which was introduced in the year 1996 with a view to providing institutional mechanisms for promoting rural savings as well as for the provision of credit for viable economic activities in local areas has not been able to establish itself due to various operational issues. Out of 227 licences applied for, only six banks were licensed. Of these, the licence of one was withdrawn, and one was merged with the Bank of Baroda and four are now functioning. The number of banks is too small to make a comment on the success of the LAB model. A review group set up in 2002 recommended not to issues licenses to new LABs till the existing ones were placed on a sound footing. It also recommended that LABs attain a net worth level of ₹250 million and CRAR of 15 per cent. Two of the four LABs, viz. Coastal Local Area Bank and Capital Local Area Bank operate in prosperous regions in the country. While Capital LAB, the largest amongst the LABs, operates in the rich Doaba belt in Punjab, Coastal LAB operates in Krishna, Guntur and West Godavari districts, which is one of the most prosperous regions in India. Capital LAB has advances of over ₹5 billion with a net profit of ₹106.3 million as on March 2012. While the advances of Coastal Bank are around ₹1,250 million, both Coastal LAB and Capital LAB yield a return on equity of 17 to 18 per cent. Both of these banks offer services to all segments of customers in the same manner as SCBs. Subhadra Local Area Bank operates in Kolhapur, Sangli districts of Maharashtra and Belgaum in Karnataka. It is the smallest in terms of business in the four LABs. The operating area of this LAB also is quite a prosperous region. KB Samruddhi LAB has the unique model of financing the bottom-of-the-pyramid. As such its operating costs are higher due to low ticket size of accounts and doorstep delivery.

In spite of this, it had an ROE of over 12 per cent in March 2011, which came down to 7.45 per cent as at the end of March 2012 due to exceptional reasons—mainly the effects of the microfinance ordinance of the AP government. It is yet to reach the net worth level of ₹250 million. It may be added that besides the mission of serving the underserved, KB Samruddhi LAB is the only LAB, which operates mainly in underdeveloped areas. It may, therefore, be assumed as a model of its own within the LAB model.

KRISHNA BHIMA SAMRUDDHI LOCAL AREA BANK

Krishna Bhima Samruddhi Local Area Bank (KBSLAB),[34] which was promoted by BASIX as a local area bank is operating in Mahbubnagar district in Andhra Pradesh (AP) and Gulbarga and Raichur districts in Karnataka since 2001. Besides being a local area bank, another distinguishing feature of the Bank is that it chose to operate only in the underserved segment of the population with microfinance as the business model to pursue its mission. Being a bank, it not only provides credit but also provides services for savings, insurance and technical services, wherever needed, to agriculturists and dairy farmers through other group entities. The Bank at present operates through 14 branches, including a mobile van. However, the network through which it provides services to its customers is not restricted to these branches. It has appointed Indian Grameen Services, a not-for-profit company, as its Business Correspondent. Through the use of the Business Correspondent (BC) model, it has expanded its reach by setting up 59 BC locations including 19 hubs and 40 spokes. The Bank effectively exploits the features of modern technology to serve its customers. It has moved to a Core Banking System platform with centralized database since 2011. The transactions through hand-held devices used by its customer service representatives in the field get updated online in the centralized database through the use of mobile technology. Customers get a printed receipt from the hand-held device for the amount tendered by them.

Business model

With its mission to reach the underserved and to provide livelihoods, the bank's lending is mainly concentrated at the bottom-of-the-pyramid. The Bank lends mainly to small farmers, dairy farmers, small retailers and entrepreneurs, roadside vendors and hawkers, village artisans, service providers, etc. Most of the loans are in the non-farm sector with over 56 per cent of the lending for microenterprises in this sector. About 26 per cent of the loans are for animal husbandry including dairy farming, sheep and goat rearing etc. The average size of a loan outstanding is below ₹14,000, and most of the loans of the Bank are below ₹50,000. Of late, the Bank has also started promoting loans of a higher value mostly in the segment from ₹50,000 to ₹200,000. These customers are retailers and kirana shops, distributors of commodities such as fertilisers/cement etc., dealers in garments and ladies wear etc. besides dairy farmers or agriculturists. Wherever the Bank does not have a branch, it extends services through the BC network. Since the BC also provides both credit and deposit services, the model has proved to be sustainable.

In spite of the limited area of operation and the small size of accounts, the Bank has been able to cross a deposit base of ₹1 billion by March 2012. The advances were at a level of around ₹840 million. The number of deposit accounts was 276,000 as at the end of March 2012 while loan accounts were over 59,000. The number of customers it reached was close to 182,000. The ordinance of the Andhra Pradesh government regulating the operations of microfinance organizations also affected the Bank to some extent, due to the similarity of operations and the customer segment served, though the ordinance was not applicable to banks. Due to its status as a Bank, it could contain the adverse effects of the ordinance and managed to clock a net profit of ₹11.8 million for the year ended 2011–12. The Bank went slow on disbursements to consolidate its portfolio and improve recovery. As the effects of the ordinance have now been crystallized, profitability and advances will only show an upward trend.

KBS LAB commenced its operations with a capital base of ₹50 million in the year 2001. Over the years, the entire profits have been ploughed back and additional capital has been brought in, thus increasing its net worth to ₹164.4 million as on March 2012. The initial years saw a dependence on borrowings for financing its operations. The credit deposit ratio was over 100 due to reliance on borrowings for supplementing its financial requirements. However, as years passed by, the dependence on borrowings was reduced and by March 2011, the Bank could bring down its CD ratio below 100 for the first time to 95. The borrowings, which are now being replaced almost entirely by deposits to finance operations, stood at ₹145 million as on March 2012 as against ₹245 million as on March 2011.

KBS LAB is yet to reach out to a large population in its customer segment even within its limited area of operation. It will have to expand its network, augment its capital base, strengthen its team both in terms of numbers and capabilities, intensify its efforts for increased penetration and optimum use of resources to achieve its goal of reaching out to half a million customers. For this, it intends to focus on increasing its capital base, intensifying deposit mobilisation efforts, expanding its branch and BC network, using technology to provide further services and reducing operating costs, diversifying its loan portfolio by increasing component of high value loans while continuing to reach the underserved and gain visibility in customer segments where it does not have a large presence at present, especially for deposits. The key to future growth will be the ability to mobilise deposits at reasonable cost. To achieve this, it will have to reach out to the affluent segments and win their trust.

THE LAB MODEL—HOW CAN IT BE MORE EFFECTIVE?

LABs, being a bank, are licensed and regulated effectively by RBI, which ensures soundness of operations and prudent financial management. As Banks, LABs can accept deposits and thus provide the entire gamut of financial services to its customers. It can be claimed that the existing LABs are on a sound financial footing and have reached a stage at which their growth can get accelerated. In that sense, the experiment has succeeded. It is, therefore, time for a review of the model and also, perhaps, to examine the scope of expanding the model.

The suggestion of MFIs taking to the LAB model is also quite relevant. However, they will have to operate within the limited geographical area, which may be a constraint for growth. It is generally observed that geographical expansion is a faster route to growth. Besides allowing the LABs to expand their area of operation, they may also be made eligible to draw financial support in the form of refinance, etc., from institutions like NABARD, which would facilitate increasing their resource base. Moreover, with an increasing role for RBI in the oversight of NBFC-MFIs, and if deposit acceptance by NBFC-MFIs is permitted subject to certain conditions, it should also be considered if becoming a bank offers substantial advantages to an organization over the NBFC model.

NABARD FINANCIAL SERVICES Ltd (NABFINS)

In an environment where microfinance largely lost its stardom, where future policy was still unfolding and uncertainty reigned, where investors were concerned with re-scheduling loans rather than increasing exposure, and where potential clients were faced with reduced choices, NABFINS managed to grow in terms of outstandings from ₹527 million in 2010–11 to ₹2,160 million in 2011–12. It was able to achieve this progress due to the support of its partners including 67 Business Correspondents/ Facilitators, three Producer collectives and 8,969 SHGs. The growth during 2011–12 was partly due to the staff and infrastructure setup in late 2010, which became operational during 2011–12. As on March 2012, NABFINS has established offices in 31 Districts in three States, with 87 staff. It availed a refinance of ₹2,000 million from NABARD during the year; the average cost of funds in 2011–12 was 8.08 per cent and its net owned funds stood at ₹484.7 million. NABFINS approach is emerging as a unique model of an NBFC-MFI with greater attention on appropriate governance leading to transparency in accounting, remuneration and disclosure, reasonable rates of interest and other costs, which earn a profit but do not maximize profits or profiteer at the expense of the clients at the bottom-of-the-pyramid. Investment in activities that generate income in the short, medium and long term and increase capital with the poor family is essential. Since these activities chosen by the group members are not only diverse in terms of sectors/categories but also in purpose, size, and repayment periods within a sector/category, they require a business model, which is able to customize loans and repayment schedules in order to respond to the diversity of livelihood situations. Standardization, therefore, cannot be the main driver even though it results in higher profits for the NBFC-MFI. It is necessary to ensure fair practices so that there is no over/multiple lending or coercion in collection which, experience has shown, results from business models driven by speed and scale to maximize profits and in many cases led to quick exit of investors. Keeping in mind these guiding norms, NABFINS decided in 2010 to promote a culture, organizational and financial systems and software which would 'balance business with inclusion in growth'. Inclusion here focuses on the poor and marginalized. To maintain this balance is the prime responsibility of the Governing Board. As a for-profit entity, it endeavours to earn enough income to cover all costs related to management and expansion, design and absorption of appropriate technology support systems, training and reasonable incentives to staff and management, and to cover its risks arising from investment in second level institutions like producer collectives. All these are well accepted in the for-profit sector.

Box 2. 6 Has the intention of SHGs deviated during the last two decades from what was envisaged?

Shri Alosiusp Fernandez opined—

The SHGs were never intended to be financial (intermediation) institutions only...they were empowering institutions which included building self confidence, social values, management skills, confidence to lobby for change in the family and in local society, to build linkages (with banks and markets) etc...the habit of savings gave the members a degree of independence from large farmers (who are the money lenders) which got strengthened by Bank loans...It was the management of savings and loans which was empowering—not provision of credit per se. This was based on an analysis that 'power relations' in the local situation played a major role in preventing access to resources (credit, natural as well as work/labour at fair wages etc) by the poor. As I wrote years ago: 'Myrada discovered that it was not enough to teach people to fish when they could not reach the river; and when they reach the river they find that fishing rights have already been captured by the powerful'. Unfortunately the SHGs have been reduced to financial intermediaries...I hope SHG-2 addresses this... as this clear direction can only come in a major way from NABARD.

Source: Interview by author.

But, NABFINS also seeks to promote inclusion of the poor and marginalized in growth—not only financial inclusion which has been reduced to opening 'no frill accounts'. Inclusion of the poor and marginalized in the growth sector in a sustained way requires support from a variety of institutions involved in building confidence and management skills of the poor and their ability to lobby for change and build linkages with others; it also requires technical, organizational and infrastructure support in production, aggregation and marketing of products; these in turn require financial support like grants, term loans, cash credit, working capital, revolving funds and appropriate infrastructure. In the field of dry land agriculture—a high risk operation—where a large part of the loans of SHGs/JLGs are invested, support is required to reduce the clients' risks and make their investments productive and sustainable. They need to be insured against crop failure—but even more, the production risk has to be reduced. Hence, NABFINS loans to groups involved in dry land agriculture are focused on areas where watershed management programs are being implemented by NABARD, the Government and NGOs. This reduces the risk of investment in this sector. To build confidence and management skills, NABFINS provides grants sourced from NABARD for institutional capacity building and to improve the organizational and financial management of SHGs, JLGs and producer collectives. Likewise where investment is in livestock, it partners with an institution that has the expertise and outreach to provide animal healthcare. All these interventions require extra investment and a longer period of gestation, thus reducing profits to NABFINS; but they also help to develop a network and support system for the poor client to build a sustainable livelihood base and to be 'included' in the growth sector.

NABFINS tries to keep the balance between 'market forces geared entirely to earn profits' and 'development finance', which attempts to open more opportunities to the marginalized. As a business model, which promotes development finance, it levies interest at reasonable rates but also ensures that the overall cost to the client remains low by providing door step services and quick turnaround. Up to March 2012 the rate of interest to SHGs/JLGs was 13.5 per cent; to second level institutions, like producer collectives, it was 11.5 per cent; the margin cap was 4.66 per cent—both well below the RBI norms of 26 per cent (interest) and 12 per cent (margin cap) respectively. The average cost of funds was reasonably low at the rate of 8.08 per cent due to funding support from NABARD. Considering the scope and speed of the business expansion, the need of funding support from other sources has become inevitable. Efforts are on in this direction and there is greater scope for participation of different institutions in view of its focus on social enhancement with appropriate profit level.

SUMMING UP

The SHG Bank linkage programme implemented during the last two decades has significantly contributed in terms of outreach of financial services to unreached people thus far. The review of the performance of the programme reveals that there has been a significant improvement in terms of socio-economic empowerment of rural poor, particularly of women, across states in India. However, certain challenges/issues remain to be addressed fully. Some of these are: (a) Outreach challenges—whether all very poor or hard core poor identified and included financially under SBLP? (b) Quality and sustainability of Self-help Groups as a grassroots level institutions for financial inclusion; (c) Convergence of SBLP with NRLM approach to take advantage of the strengths of both may be given a serious thought for efficient and effective outcome; (d) Graduation of groups from consumption to production to investment credit or in other words, graduation to microenterprise level poses severe challenges relating to entrepreneurship development, appropriate technology and product design and marketing of rural products. Some of these concerns hopefully will be taken care of in SHG-2 and NRLM; (e) Even after 20 years of SBLP, bankers are yet to own SHGs as their valued customers whether it is through SBLP or government supported programmes like SGSY; and (f) The declining trend in the disbursement of loan to SHGs by financial institutions should also be viewed seriously and attempt should be made to reverse this trend by some policy or non-policy interventions including that of providing some incentives to the bankers engaged directly/indirectly in promoting and financing of SHGs. A discussion at a Round Table organized by Access Development Services in collaboration with NRLM on the next phase of development of the SHG Model in September 2011 suggested that SHG were in need of investment in institutional capacity building and phased expansion. The need for SBLP align with NRLM, greater emphasis on capacity building, expanding the role of federations as BC etc., were the other priority areas identified for future considerations.

Prof. Malcolm Harper reiterated that, being the leader of the SHG movement, NABARD has a greater role in taking the movement to the next phase with a reengineered vision of the original SHG model emphasizing savings as well as credit, with features such as smaller joint liability groups for larger borrowers, cash credit limit to replace term loans and offering SHG members a 'ladder' to genuine financial inclusion through individual full service bank accounts.[35]

Considering financial inclusion as a major agenda, the need for redesigning the long tested strategies of the SHG movement need not be over emphasized. Scope for active participation of community oriented organizations in the institutional arrangement for financial products' delivery to the poor seems to be bright. The experiences and lessons learnt during the last two decades are very valuable based on which future road map of the SHG movement may be drawn. Let the coordinated efforts by all the stakeholders with genuine focus on the poor and their active participation contribute for the livelihood development of the poor in the country.

ANNEX 2.1[1]
Women's cooperatives promoted by Sampark

Sampark is implementing the women's empowerment programme since 1998 in 38 villages in Koppal by organising poor women into small associations on the basis of self-help and collective responsibility. These SHGs were initially grouped as clusters (15–50 SHGs) to further align their efforts and organize their functions so as to deliver better and sustainable performance, which was registered as co-operatives under the Karnataka Souharda Sahakari Act, 1997.[36] As on May 2012, Sampark's SHG programme covers 38 villages in Koppal and a total of 5,350 women. These women have been grouped into 351 SHGs with the average membership of an SHG being 15 women. These groups are organized under eight cooperatives, of which one (Eshwara) is located in Koppal town and the other seven are in the rural areas. The purpose behind forming cooperatives is to organize the women into formal and democratically run institutions, which are owned and managed by the women themselves.

Each cooperative is managed by a well defined administrative set up with due representation and clearly earmarked responsibilities to manage efficiently. The core activities of a cooperative are to provide financial services (savings and loan facilities), social services and capacity building to SHGs and its members. Sampark has conducted a series of capacity building trainings for SHGs, cooperative committee leaders and their staff so that they are empowered and able to manage their organizations and meet the demands of the people. While the cooperative gets linkages with external agencies, Sampark has organized a Revolving Loan Fund (RLF) from various sources and has provided bridge loans to the cooperatives to meet their groups' credit needs.

Sampark formed the Eshwara cluster since 2006 to support the groups in meeting their unmet demands and also to bring external credit capital to the clusters. The clusters used conduct meetings in a public park on the 1st of every month. They have started building their capital for credit supply by issuing shares in 2007 to each member of the SHG (each share is ₹100, and a woman can buy maximum of five). The women members were not fully convinced to buy the shares as they are new to the cluster structure and fully understood about the shares. Slowly members started purchasing and by end of 2008, there were 37 shares (amounting ₹3,700), and collected share fee of ₹25 per share (for covering expenses of giving share certificate) that come to ₹925. The cooperative also charged a one-time registration fee of ₹100 from each group to be associated with the cluster for accessing benefits. Another ₹1,000 got added from the 10 groups. With this money (₹5,625), the cluster gave its first loan of ₹5,000 to one group at the end of 2008 (which reflects under the financial year 2008–09). As the demand rose, in the same year Sampark started giving loans to the cluster as the group was prompt in their repayments and never defaulted. In the same year in 2008 Sampark helped the Eshwara cluster to register as a Souharda Cooperative to get appropriate legal structure so that they can mobilise external resources to meet their credit needs. Sampark helped them in establishing a clear structure with a Board of Directors, Working Committees for various activities, and a full-time cooperative staff to work with the SHGs and strengthen them. The cooperative staff worked very hard to educate the members about the cooperative structure, the share capitals and form three more groups (13 groups by the end of 2009). This enabled the entire member to buy shares, and the share capital has increased to ₹45,200 by 2009. She trained all of the groups on seven SHG modules. This helped the groups to maintain very high standards whereby the banks gave them repeat loans.

The Cooperative shows concerns not only for the members' livelihood needs by providing them with loans but also addresses other social livelihood concerns by facilitating the groups and members to access social services from external agencies and government. For example, Eshwara had working committees for education and health from 2007 to 2010 (which are merged now as a social development committee) which worked with Sampark to support children's education (143 children from class 1–10), skill training of youth (15 boys and girls) and for creating awareness on health issues among the community. The committees, particularly the health committee has helped 110 families in Koppal region to access health care facilities, especially for women and children from government hospitals. In recent times (April 2012) the social development committee has been trained to mobilize resources from public and private sources; to address various social development issues including girl children's education, housing, health issues and to facilitate their members to access various schemes.

---

[1] The author gratefully acknowledges the support extended by M. Chidambaranathan and Smita Premchander, Sampark in preparing this Annexure.

Table 2.11 Financial overview of Eshwara Cooperative (as on May 2012)

Out Reach	
No. of SHGs	57
No. of members	982
No. of shares by members	1,366
Financial Operations	
SHG members own capital (in ₹)	1,966,432
Cooperative's own capital (in ₹)	547,770
Cumulative loans borrowed from NABFINS (in ₹)	3,488,000
Cumulative loans borrowed from Sampark (in ₹)	6,222,000
Cumulative external loans borrowed (in ₹)	9,710,000
Cumulative loan disbursed (in ₹)	10,647,000
Grass portfolio (loan outstanding) (in ₹)	3,635,080
Total income during last FY (in ₹)	618,448
Total expenses during last FY (in ₹)	452,234
Net profit during last FY (in ₹)	166,214
Financial Benefits to SHGs and Members	
Total no. of groups received loans	24
Total no. of women received loans	463
Average loan amount accessed per group (in ₹)	443,625
Average loan amount per loanee member (in ₹)	22,996
Average income earned per group from loans supplied by coop (in ₹)	26,618
Profit dividend per share In the last FY (1 share value = ₹100) (in ₹)	150
Performance Ratios	
Portfolio at Risk (PAR): arrears >30 days (%)	0
Repayment rate (from group to cooperative) (%)	100
Repayment rate (from cooperative to NABFINS), Sampark (%)	100
Administrative cost ratio (%)	6
Financial cost ratio (%)	14
Operating cost ratio (%)	21
Capital adequacy ratio (%)	11
Operational self-sufficiency (%)	108

Source: Primary information provided by Sampark.

A combination of service charges, earning from credit business and external contributions ensured financial sustainability of the cooperative model.[37] Since most of the cooperative members are engaged in business activities, they understand the business logic well and apply those skills in the microfinance activity of their cooperative. They ask for service charges from the members who request loan, and this includes like loan application fee (₹20 per member), grading fee (₹50), loan processing fee (₹80/₹10,000). The interest earned from lending and the service charges have helped in meeting their organizational costs.

A strong team and sound governance practices ensure institutional sustainability of the cooperative model. The cooperative is operationally self sustainable, and managerially the team is strong to take the organization forward. The Board of Directors who are part of the three working committees (admin, micro credit and social development) are reasonably educated (at least up to 10th, some of them 12th and one graduate). Six out the 10 are old members who have been working since the inception of the cooperative, and had received adequate training and gained a lot of experience over the years. The governance aspect is important because it affects the managerial sustainability and smooth functioning of the routine affairs of the organization.

The slow expansion and low level of information in the public domain about people's collective microfinance organizations have resulted in lack of advocacy, and therefore less policy attention to them. CBMFIs have therefore lacked the kind of donor and government attention that has been given to externally held and managed MFIs. The donors and investors need to treat the 'community-based approach' as a major and recognized form of organization compared to other organizational forms that are externally owned and where the profits go to external stakeholders and not members/clients. When an MFI is 'community owned and community managed' it has greater potential to be more sustainable, long lasting and less dependent on outsiders. It also strengthens grassroots democracy, brings social cohesion and leads to empowerment. All these values are very critical for the sovereignty of this country.

The cooperative model has shown a great success in terms of creating strong community-based MFIs as they have made significant progress in terms of: governance; slowly moving towards scale; ownership and control over their organization by way of women planning and taking their decisions; handling both soft and technical aspects of operations; gaining capacity to handle their staff; managing to handle external linkages for accessing credit capital as well for grant mobilizations; achieving good recovery of loans considering AP MFI effected everywhere; being able to cover their costs through small margins of interest and service charges; and most importantly addressing needs of the clients, and to a great extent retaining their trust with them.

However, achieving similar kinds of results is not guaranteed in all cases. There are several factors that contribute towards such success and also factors that hinder progress or even lead to failure in creating such organizations. Sampark has experienced both, out of eight cooperatives promoted, four have developed well and four are very slow and still weak. The understanding of what contributed or hindered the successful or advanced level of community-based organization will be of great help for any organization, which is keen to replicate this model.

Comparison of groups with outstanding loans and loan amounts—state-wise

State	Year 2010–11		Year 2011–12		Growth	
	No. of SHGs	Loans O/S	No. of SHGs	Loans O/S (₹ million)	No. of SHGs	Loans O/S (₹ million)
A&N Islands (UT)			1,349	61.05	1,349	61.05
Andhra Pradesh	1,683,993	128,694	1,400,995	153,417.23	−282,998	24,723.23
Arunachal Pradesh	3,910	83	486	43.84	−3,424	−39.16
Assam	111,589	5,146	117,809	6,302.16	6,220	1,156.16
Bihar	190,341	7,784	223,033	10,407.13	32,692	2,623.13
Chhattisgarh	62,740	1,930	53,285	2,025.96	−9,455	95.96
Goa	9,446	360	2,965	249.11	−6,481	−110.89
Gujarat	73,695	1,554	72,495	1,763.32	−1,200	209.32
Haryana	18,704	1,909	21,433	2,057.50	2,729	148.50
Himachal Pradesh	25,116	1,599	35,872	1,409.03	10,756	−189.97
Jammu & Kashmir	2,163	116	3,138	164.71	975	48.71
Jharkhand	72,422	3,220	63,336	3,595.59	−9,086	375.59
Karnataka	252,129	22,748	266,978	34,698.82	14,849	11,950.82
Kerala	182,114	15,904	159,843	17,792.26	−22,271	1,888.26
Lakshadweep			35	1.21	35	1.21
Madhya Pradesh	64,350	3,924	60,815	4,140.81	−3,535	216.81
Maharashtra	230,772	9,659	214,012	11,625.40	−16,760	1,966.40
Manipur	4,561	201	5,807	230.02	1,246	29.02
Meghalaya	3,412	148	2,569	139.46	−843	−8.54
Mizoram	311	62	2,383	400.34	2,072	338.34
Nagaland	3,930	163	2,752	178.98	−1,178	15.98
New Delhi	657	62	1,120	142.00	463	80.00
Odisha	335,041	15,779	314,669	16,533.87	−20,372	754.87
Puducherry	7,393	943	13,678	1,643.66	6,285	700.66
Punjab	11,343	960	15,517	860.48	4,174	−99.52
Rajasthan	93,068	4,491	134,961	7,149.03	41,893	2,658.03
Sikkim	5,466	70	2,561	120.83	−2,905	50.83
Tamil Nadu	535,384	43,173	514,203	46,392.68	−21,181	3,219.68
Tripura	18,101	785	25,174	2,531.78	7,073	1,746.78
Uttar Pradesh	216,879	16,999	212,922	20,317.70	−3,957	3,318.70
Uttarakhand	17,853	1,469	25,430	1,318.44	7,577	−150.56
West Bengal	574,036	16,255	382,942	15,700.34	−191,094	−554.66
Total	**4,810,919**	**306,190**	**4,354,567**	**363,414.75**	**−456,352**	**57,224.74**

Source: Provisional Data from NABARD Head Office Mumbai.

ANNEX 2.3
Comparison of disbursements in SHG loans—state-wise

State	Year 2010–11		Year 2011–12		Growth	
	No. of SHGs	Loans disbursed (₹ million)	No. of SHGs	Loans disbursed (₹ million)	No. of SHGs	Loans disbursed (₹ million)
A&N Islands (UT)	NA	NA	710	57	710	57
Andhra Pradesh	376,667	63,542	378,526	81,714	1,859	18,172
Arunachal Pradesh	956	45	63	12	−893	−33
Assam	29,094	2,272	28,012	1,875	−1,082	−397
Bihar	31,495	3,160	39,241	3,986	7,746	826
Chhattisgarh	8,979	596	10,087	926	1,108	330
Goa	3,058	236	2,312	199	−746	−37
Gujarat	25,767	901	30,336	1,312	4,569	411
Haryana	4,628	607	3,865	620	−763	13
Himachal Pradesh	5,293	733	4,269	532	−1,024	−201
Jammu & Kashmir	622	68	1,013	80	391	12
Jharkhand	11,286	1,433	12,040	1,274	754	−159
Karnataka	89,259	13,668	87,943	16,295	−1,316	2,627
Kerala	73,275	7,836	55,242	8,542	−18,033	706
Lakshadweep	NA	NA	8	0	8	0
Madhya Pradesh	9,408	2,215	8,751	954	−657	−1261
Maharashtra	63,420	4,607	68,396	6,018	4,976	1,411
Manipur	721	35	1,308	86	587	51
Meghalaya	1,113	76	689	49	−424	−27
Mizoram	420	29	575	69	155	40
Nagaland	321	27	862	62	541	35
New Delhi	344	38	511	51	167	13
Odisha	71,343	5,750	49,831	5,410	−21,512	−340
Puducherry	4,016	788	3,798	738	−218	−50
Punjab	2,686	328	2,231	244	−455	−84
Rajasthan	40,766	2,762	18,862	1,827	−21,904	−935
Sikkim	331	17	396	42	65	25
Tamil Nadu	190,942	25,486	179,902	19,329	−11,040	−6,157
Tripura	4,391	489	17,405	2,120	13,014	1,631
Uttar Pradesh	30,328	4,178	34,497	4,454	4,169	276
Uttarakhand	4,159	481	5,125	759	966	278
West Bengal	117,824	5,284	99,379	5,514	−18,445	230
Total	**1,202,912**	**147,687**	**1,146,185**	**165,149**	**−56,727**	**17,462**

Source: Provisional Data from NABARD Head Office Mumbai.

ANNEX 2.4
Comparative performance of savings of SHGs

State	Year 2011–12		Year 2011–12		Growth	
	No. of SHGs	Savings amount	No. of SHGs	Savings amount (million)	No. of SHGs	Savings amount (million)
A&N Islands (UT)	4,750	11.60	5,521	13.13	771	1.53
Andhra Pradesh	1,351,330	10,891.60	1,495,904	14,901.56	144,574	4,009.96
Arunachal Pradesh	7,079	18.60	8,149	17.29	1,070	−1.31
Assam	245,120	813.80	276,565	984.60	31,445	170.80
Bihar	243,407	1,061.80	305,113	1,404.24	61,706	342.44
Chhattisgarh	119,684	852.60	129,854	739.45	10,170	−113.15
Goa	7,926	81.90	8,414	86.87	488	4.97
Gujarat	192,421	1,716.10	226,626	1,396.32	34,205	−319.78
Haryana	34,227	983.00	44,184	367.84	9,957	−615.16
Himachal Pradesh	53,021	369.70	65,641	328.86	12,620	−40.84
Jammu & Kashmir	5,569	38.70	6,349	43.31	780	4.61
Jharkhand	87,189	1,419.60	89,603	672.17	2,414	−747.43
Karnataka	671,032	11,351.20	628,643	10,021.29	−42,389	−1,329.91
Kerala	500,599	4,219.80	615,714	4,137.11	115,115	−82.69
Lakshadweep	164	1.00	171	1.25	7	0.25
Madhya Pradesh	166,447	1,445.80	163,588	1,122.91	−2,859	−322.89
Maharashtra	826,934	6,481.40	827,047	7,236.18	113	754.78
Manipur	10,306	24.00	12,711	21.94	2,405	−2.06
Meghalaya	10,653	37.60	14,091	41.47	3,438	3.87
Mizoram	4,592	17.80	4,976	57.29	384	39.49
Nagaland	9,866	36.30	10,711	37.45	845	1.15
New Delhi	3,042	31.80	3,536	32.50	494	0.70
Odisha	520,388	3,535.50	540,029	3,613.64	19,641	78.14
Puducherry	20,335	241.80	17,913	168.29	−2,422	−73.51
Punjab	40,274	437.40	37,962	476.47	−2,312	39.07
Rajasthan	302,743	1,710.40	251,654	1,278.71	−51,089	−431.69
Sikkim	2,811	16.90	5,280	26.00	2,469	9.10
Tamil Nadu	938,390	9,814.10	925,392	7,903.98	−12,998	−1,910.12
Tripura	34,312	339.50	34,021	337.80	−291	−1.71
Uttar Pradesh	457,475	3,501.40	471,184	3,682.14	13,709	180.74
Uttarakhand	44,870	418.40	48,141	591.33	3,271	172.93
West Bengal	630,313	7,329.70	685,448	3,769.44	55,135	−3,560.26
Total	**7,547,269**	**69,250.80**	**7,960,135**	**65,512.80**	**412,866**	**−3,738.00**

Source: Provisional Data from NABARD Head Office Mumbai.

ANNEX 2.5
Credit to savings ratio across states—2012

State	Average loan outstanding per SHG (₹)	Average savings per SHG (₹)	Loans to savings ratio (Mutiples)
A&N Islands (UT)	45,257	2,377.83	19
Andhra Pradesh	109,506	9,961.57	11
Arunachal Pradesh	90,206	2,121.36	43
Assam	53,495	3,560.10	15
Bihar	46,662	4,602.35	10
Chhattisgarh	38,021	5,694.44	7
Goa	84,018	10,324.46	8
Gujarat	24,323	6,161.35	4
Haryana	95,997	8,325.08	12
Himachal Pradesh	39,279	5,010.01	8
Jammu & Kashmir	52,489	6,821.23	8
Jharkhand	56,770	7,501.70	8
Karnataka	129,969	15,941.14	8
Kerala	111,311	6,719.21	17
Lakshadweep	34,571	7,298.25	5
Madhya Pradesh	68,089	6,864.23	10
Maharashtra	54,321	8,749.41	6
Manipur	39,610	1,725.91	23
Meghalaya	54,287	2,943.30	18
Mizoram	167,997	11,513.46	15
Nagaland	65,036	3,496.17	19
New Delhi	126,785	9,191.73	14
Odisha	52,544	6,691.57	8
Puducherry	120,168	9,394.91	13
Punjab	55,454	12,551.26	4
Rajasthan	52,971	5,081.22	10
Sikkim	47,180	4,924.17	10
Tamil Nadu	90,223	8,541.22	11
Tripura	100,571	9,929.01	10
Uttar Pradesh	95,423	7,814.66	12
Uttarakhand	51,846	12,283.23	4
West Bengal	40,999	5,499.24	7

Source: Provisional Data from NABARD Head Office Mumbai.

Support extended by Krishna, MCID, NABARD in providing data and Deepak Goswami, Access Assist in data processing is gratefully acknowledged.

NOTES AND REFERENCES

1. Sharma, Abhijit. 2011. 'Delinquencies by SHGs in North East', IIBM, Guwahati, Sub-centre of Centre for Microfinance Research, BIRD, Lucknow.

2. Source Agenda Notes, SLBC, Hyderabad, Andhra Pradesh.

3. Data collected from the SERP website.

4. http://microsave.org/research_paper/what-are-clients-doing-post-the-andhra-pradesh-mfi-crisis

5. Inputs and support received from Dr Gyanendra Mani from NABARD for this section are greatly appreciated.

6. Gyanendra Mani and T. Sudheer. 2012. 'Two Decades of SHG-Bank Linkage Programme: Different Facets', The Microfinance Review, IV(1): 137–56.

7. Kumar, Pankaj and Ramesh Golait. 2009. 'Bank Penetration and SHG Bank Linkage Programme: A Critique', Reserve Bank of India Occasional Papers, 29(3): 119–38.

8. Panda, D.K. and H. Atibudhi. 2009. 'Impact of Group Based Microfinance on Rural Household Savings: Empirical Findings from India', The Microfinance Review, 1(1): 54–68.

9. Singh, Surjit and Gagan Bihari Sahu. 2011. 'SHG Bank Linkages in North West India-Experiences and Challenges in Financial Access and Poverty Alleviation', IDS, Jaipur, Sub-centre of Centre for Microfinance Research, BIRD, Lucknow.

10. Cheston, Susy. 2006. 'Just the Facts, Ma'am: Gender Stories from Unexpected Sources with Morals for Microfinance', Micro-credit Summit Campaign, Washington DC. (www.microcreditsummit.org/papers/workshops/28_Cheston.pdf) Accessed on July 2012.

11. Centre for Micro Finance, 'Microfinance and Gender: Social and Economic Empowerment', IDS, Jaipur Sub Centre of Centre for Microfinance Research, BIRD, Lucknow, 2011.

12. Mahajan, R.K. and D. Bansal. 2009. 'Microfinance and Women Empowerment: A Case Study of Punjab', The Microfinance Review, 1(1): 84–104.

13. De, Sudipta and D. Sarker. 2010. 'Impact of Micro-credit Programmes on Women Empowerment: An Empirical Study in West Bengal', The Microfinance Review, 2(1): 46–67.

14. Dhanya, M.B. and P. Sivakumar. 2010. 'Microfinance, Women Empowerment and Banking Habit: Perspectives on Kerala', The Microfinance Review, 2(1): 97–109.

15. Sharma, Abhijit. 2011. 'Delinquencies by SHGs in North East', IIBM, Guwahati Sub-centre of Centre for Microfinance Research, BIRD, Lucknow.

16. Sahu, Gagan Bihari. 2012. 'Loan Defaults by SHGs in Odisha and Madhya Pradesh', IDS, Jaipur Sub-centre of Centre for Microfinance Research, BIRD, Lucknow.

17. National Conference on SHG Federations: An Effective Instrument for Poverty Reduction & Women Empowerment, 21–23 February 2008, NIMSME, Hyderabad.

18. APMAS, 2007, SHG Federations in India, Available online at apmas.org

19. ENABLE Network, 2011–12, 'The Quality and Sustainability of Self Help Groups in India', study conducted by ENABLE Network, and the report is at the final stage. Inputs provided by C.S. Reddy, Raja Reddy and Rama Lakshmi APMAS are gratefully acknowledged.

20. Heijden, Jael van der. 2006, Sustainability and Empowerment through SHG federations—A study in East Uttar Pradesh, India. Thesis submitted for the Masters Program in International Development Studies (IDS), University of Amsterdam, The Hague, Netherlands.

21. Reddy, C.S., SHG Federation, an Institutional Innovation to Sustain SHGs, The Microfinance Review, Vol. IV(1) January–June 2012.

22. Nair, A. 2005. 'Sustainability of Microfinance Self Help Groups in India: Would Federating Help?' World Bank Policy Research Working Paper 3516, Washington DC: The World Bank.

23. Kumar, S. 2010. Study on SHG Federations—Challenges and Opportunities, Centre for Microfinance Research, Bankers' Institute for Rural Development, Lucknow.

24. Kumar, S. 2010. Study on SHG Federations—Challenges and Opportunities, Centre for Microfinance Research, Bankers' Institute for Rural Development, Lucknow.

25. Girija Srinivasan and Ajay Tankha, 2012. SHG Federations—Development Costs and Sustainability, Access Development Services, New Delhi.

26. Ajay Tankha. Banking on Self-Help Groups—Twenty years on, New Delhi, SAGE Publications, 2012.

27. Premchander, Smita and Jaipal Singh. 2011. Community-Based Micro Finance Institutions: The Direct Route to Better Regulation and Accountability in Indian Microfinance, ftp://ftp.solutionexchange.net.in/public/mf/resource/res_info_02121001.pdf

28. Tripathi, Ashutosh. 2012. 'Life Cycle of SHGs—What are the Critical Interventions Required in the Life Cycle of a SHG?' Centre for Microfinance Research, Lucknow, BIRD (on-going study).

29. Data cited in this section relating to NABARD is sourced from the Annual Report of NABARD 2011–12.

30. This average comprises both historical and current costs as it is worked out cumulative number of groups.

31. Eversole, Robyn. 2003. 'Help, Risk, and Deceit: Micro-entrepreneurs Talk about Microfinance', *Journal of International Development*, 15(2): 179–88.

32. Edgcomb, Elaine L., and Joyee A. Klein 2005. 'Opening Opportunities, Building Ownership: Fulfilling the Promise of Micro-enterprise in the United States', Fund for Innovation, Effectiveness, Learning and Dissemination, 1–140.

33. Chowbey, Manesh and Babu Lal Mishra. 2011. 'Scope of Promoting Micro-enterprises through SHGs—A Study in Select Districts of Uttar Pradesh and Bihar', CIM, Patna Sub-centre of Centre for Microfinance Research Centre.

34. Contribution made by Mr Vijay Nadkarni, Managing Director Krishna Bhima Samruddhi Local Area Bank, by providing the necessary input is gratefully acknowledged.

35. Malcolm Harper, 2012. 'Self Help Group 2 Vs MFIs—Competing to Serve the Poor', The Micro Finance Review, *Journal of the Centre for Microfinance Research*, 4(1): 33–43.

36. The Karnataka Souharda Sahakari Act 1997 is the new Cooperative Act started parallel to the existing old Cooperative Society Act in the state to make provisions for the members to have full power, more member participation and control over their organizations rather than intervention of government and external agencies. It makes provisions for many SHGs together to register as a cooperative under this act.

37. Srinivasan, Girija and Ajay Tankha. 2010. *SHG Federations: Development Costs and Sustainability*. New Delhi: Access Development Services.

Microfinance institutions—signs of recovery

Microfinance institutions in India have made significant progress during the last two decades in terms of outreach and penetration in unbanked areas through several innovations in credit delivery and terms of lending, thereby emerging as a structural addition to the financial system. However, high growth MFIs have encountered serious setbacks in their development due to adverse consequences of the Andhra Pradesh crisis and its dark shadow over the entire sector across the country. The negative growth in terms of outreach and loan portfolio from the second half of the crisis year 2010–11 continued into 2011–12. Despite the stagnating top line, the sector has been cautiously optimistic on account of strong regulatory initiatives, greater emphasis on client protection and improving governance with a social focus. There are several issues of concern over the sustainability of smaller MFIs in the new environment, which should be addressed seriously. The issues concerning performance of larger MFIs with specific reference to shrinking client outreach, liquidity constraints etc., also need to be tackled effectively.

The Indian MFIs that began the journey essentially as a single credit product programme have now moved onto a different realm with MFIs trying to understand their clients' financial needs in a more meaningful way and designing products to suit these needs within the scope of regulatory restrictions. While the initial phase consisted of a standard, one-year joint liability loan, during the course of time many institutions broadened the service range with innovative products, offered directly or through their sister organizations. Microfinance was supposed to move the product paradigm from single products to a basket of customized products based on client needs (more on this in Chapter 5). The journey on this front has however not been without bumps. The period 2005–10 witnessed intense growth at the cost of innovation as it was easier to increase outreach with a standard product. Further, the regulatory framework did not permit broadening the range to savings and other services like remittances. The relative position of the Indian microfinance sector in the global context (Table 3.1) has shown a significant downfall during the last three years, which needs to be taken note of. This chapter attempts to discuss aspects of the current performance of MFIs.

PROGRESS AND PERFORMANCE OF MFIs

The progress and performance of the MFIs have been analyzed using data from multiple sources. The overall industry outreach was analyzed using the data collected from 'The Bharat Microfinance Quick Report—2012' published by Sa-Dhan comprising information from 167 MFIs. The individual MFI data were sourced from the MIX Market that included a data set of 61 MFIs.[1]

Table: 3.1 **Relative position of Indian microfinance sector**

Particulars	2009		2010		2011	
	Score	Rank	Score	Rank	Score	Rank
Overall MF business Environment	62.1	4	59.1	8	43.1	27
Regulatory frame work and Practices	62.5	13	62.5	14	50.0	22
Institutional Development/ Supporting framework	66.7	3	58.3	7	40.0	20
Investment Climate	51.9	14	53.9	14	–	–
Stability	–	–	–	–	62.5	40

Source: Global Microscope on the Microfinance Business Environment 2009–11, Economic Intelligence Unit Ltd., 2012 (www.eiu.com).

Table 3.2 Progress of MFIs

	2010	2011	Growth rate (%)	2012	Growth rate (%)
No. of MFIs Reporting	264	170		167	
Customer Outreach (Million)	26.7	31.8	19.1	26.8	–15.7
Outstanding Loans (₹ Billion)	183.44	215.56	17.5	209.13	–3.0

Source: Data from Sa-Dhan's 'The Bharat Microfinance Quick Report-2012'.

While the year 2011–12 was the year when a number of developments took place to pull the MFI sector out of the crisis, it tested the MFIs' ability to survive in the worst times. The impact of the crisis on MFIs' performance was more prominent in the year 2011–12 as compared to the previous year. As against 264 MFIs that reported information during the year 2010, only 167 MFIs (two thirds of the 264 that reported in 2010) shared information with Sa-Dhan, which at best indicated the lack of motivation among MFIs and at worst the closure/dormancy of the rest. Though the regulatory environment is becoming clear, the lack of funding to the MFIs has resulted in a negative growth of the MFIs. As per the data made available by Sa-Dhan, the total client outreach of MFIs was recorded at 26.8 million with a gross loan portfolio of ₹209.13 billion (Table 3.2). Both the client outreach and loan portfolio registered negative growth in this year. There was negative growth in client outreach; the number of clients declining by 15.7 per cent in the year 2011–12. However, the gross loan portfolio fared marginally better with a smaller decline of 3 per cent. Customer outreach has recorded a relatively higher deceleration in growth rate as compared to the loan outstanding. The MFIs have been unable to retain their customers on account of the liquidity crisis, which affected the MFIs during the second half of the year 2010–11, but remained almost unchanged for the entire year 2011–12. A further problem is the loss of clients in AP who cannot be substituted easily by the MFIs. This can also be an indication that MFIs are adhering to 'the maximum two loans per borrower guideline'. This might have resulted in a lesser number of loans per borrower and thus a steeper decline in the industry outreach since the consolidation of clients reduces the overlap of clients i.e., since the client being counted as an active borrower from multiple MFIs. This could also be considered a healthy sign in the direction of reducing multiple lending within the sector.

Among the MFIs operating in India, the list of top ten MFIs according to client outreach is provided in Table 3.3. The MFIs in the 10 ranking remained unchanged but for the new entrant CASHPOR into the list (Table 3.3) SKS retained first place in terms of client outreach, and Bandhan moved up to second place. However, in terms of gross loan portfolio Bandhan has emerged as the largest MFI in India. BASIX that occupied fifth place last year has dropped down to ninth place in the list. Both Equitas and Ujjivan have moved up by three places and stood at fifth and seventh place respectively. The outreach and portfolio data reported by AP based MFIs have to be adjusted with the default numbers so as to arrive at a truly comparable national position of MFIs.

Amongst the top 10 MFIs, only Bandhan and CASHPOR could achieve a positive growth in outreach (Figure 3.1). All the other MFIs have shown a negative growth in outreach. BASIX recorded the steepest decline of 63 per cent in clients outreach followed by SKS with 32 per cent. BASIX and SKS have also recorded the steepest decline in gross loan portfolio with negative growth figures of 77 per cent and 59 per cent respectively. Only four amongst the top ten MFIs could achieve an increase in their portfolio. Bandhan achieved the largest growth in loan portfolio with an increase of 49 per cent followed by

Table 3.3 Top 10 MFIs by outreach

Year	Outreach (million)		Outreach growth %	Loans o/s (₹ billion)		Loans growth %
	2011	2012		2011	2012	
SKS	6.24	4.26	–32	41.11	16.69	–59
Bandhan	3.25	3.62	11	25.07	37.30	49
Spandana	4.19	3.44	–18	34.58	27.15	–21
SHARE	2.84	2.16	–24	20.65	21.10	2
Equitas	1.53	1.19	–22	7.94	7.24	–9
SKDRDP	1.38	1.02	–26	9.58	6.01	–37
Ujjivan	0.84	0.82	–2	6.25	7.03	13
Grama Vidiyal	0.93	0.82	–12	5.2	5.20	0
BASIX	1.53	0.57	–53	12.49	2.92	–77
CASHPOR	0.43	0.46	7	2.38	3.23	36

Source: Data from MIX.org

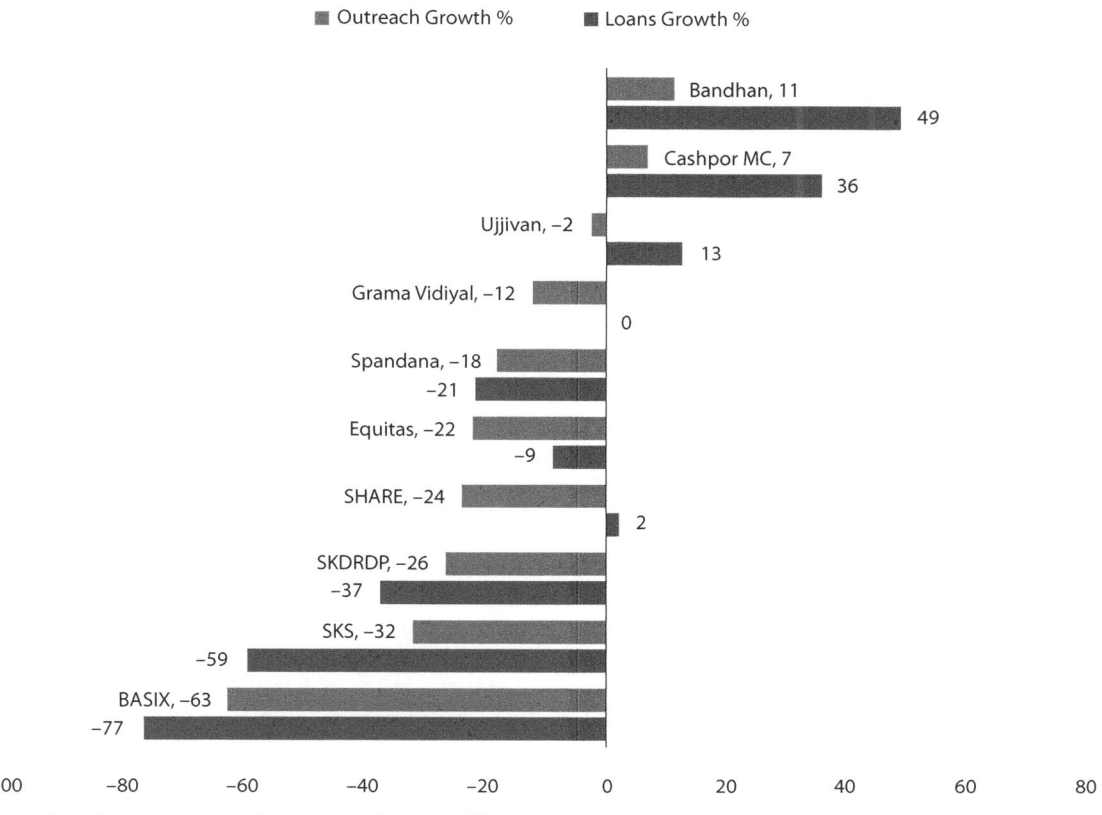

Figure 3.1 Comparative performance of top 10 MFIs

Source: MIX market.

CASHPOR with an increase of 36 per cent. Ujjivan, though had a slight decline in outreach, increased its loan portfolio by 13 per cent. However, while Bandhan, CASHPOR and Ujjivan did not have any portfolio exposure in Andhra Pradesh, the rest of the MFIs had a significant portfolio exposure in Andhra Pradesh.

The outreach scenario for a larger number of MFIs is very much contrary to that of the last year. During the previous year, a greater number of MFIs recorded growth in outreach, however, during the year 2011–12 a majority of MFIs has shown decrease in the outreach. Figure 3.2 presents a frequency distribution of growth in client outreach for 61 MFIs that reported to MIX. While in the previous year 75 per cent of the MFIs reported an increase in their outreach, only 35 per cent of MFIs in the data set have reported an increase in the client outreach during the year 2011–12. The client outreach for 21 MFIs has declined by zero to 25 per cent. Another 14 MFIs' outreach has declined by 26 to 50 per cent (Figure 3.2). Such reduction in outreach by MFIs during this year may be due to voluntarily reduced exposure by some MFIs as

they were not clear about the risks. Some other MFIs had to appraise clients rigorously for debt level and drop a number of clients who had other loans elsewhere. Small and medium MFIs had to reduce their staff and branches as they did not get

Growth Range (%)	No. of MFIs
Increase	21
More than 100	2
51–100	3
26–50	5
0–25	11
Decrease	39
0–25	21
26–50	14
More than 50	4

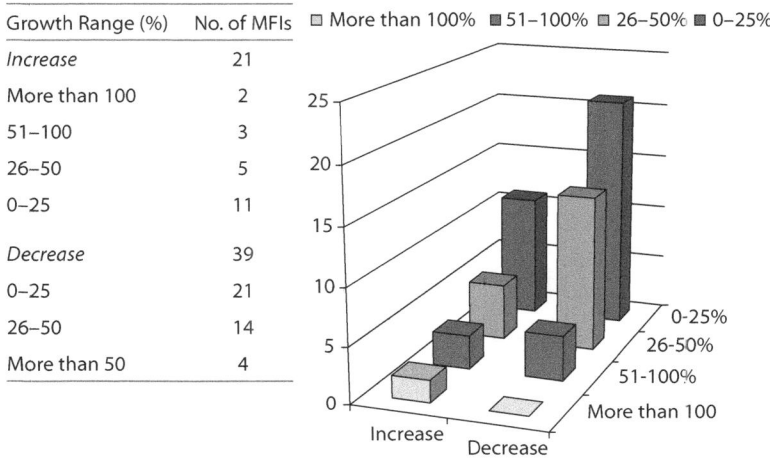

Figure 3.2 Growth in client outreach: A frequency distribution

Source: MIX market.

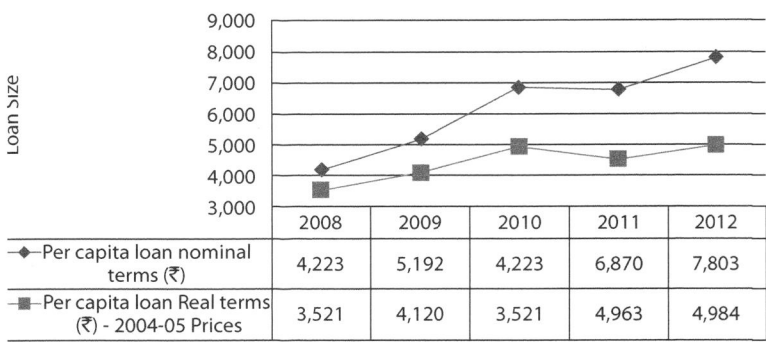

Figure 3.3 Per capita loan size

Source: MIX market.

	2008	2009	2010	2011	2012
Per capita loan nominal terms (₹)	4,223	5,192	4,223	6,870	7,803
Per capita loan Real terms (₹) - 2004-05 Prices	3,521	4,120	3,521	4,963	4,984

bank loans. The AP crisis has taken many clients out of the system.

The average per capita loan size during the reference year was ₹7,803 which was about 15 per cent higher than the previous year (Figure 3.3). However, the loan size is still smaller compared to the demand for livelihood development. While the loan size in nominal terms is increasing, in real terms after factoring the effect of inflation, the growth size is modest only. A sharp decline of 16 per cent in the client outreach (compared to the loan portfolio, 3 per cent) has also resulted in a higher level of per capita loan amount. Besides increased individual loans of larger size, what happened during the year was that loans of ₹15,000 and above were given two years of loan period as per RBI norms. This led to the outstanding balance at the end of the year increasing for the level of disbursement. This is especially

true of Bandhan, which contributes more than 25 per cent of portfolio value in top ten MFIs.

To understand the outreach distribution based on the size of the MFIs, the MFIs have been classified into four categories based on portfolio size as (*a*) Mega (more than ₹1,000 million), (*b*) Large (₹500–1,000 million), (*c*) Medium (₹100–500 million), and (*d*) Small (less than 100 million). Out of 61 MFIs, 24 fall in mega size category, 13 in large category, 12 in medium category and 12 in small category (Figure 3.4). The outreach and portfolio by the size of MFI, follows a trend similar to previous year's distribution. Mega MFIs continue to account for over 90 per cent of client outreach and loan portfolio. Medium MFIs market share has declined and there was a slight increase in the share of large MFIs. Small MFIs' outreach and loan portfolio remained almost unchanged at less than 1 per cent.

It is interesting to observe that the share of both mega—and small-sized MFIs remained the same when compared to previous years both in terms of outreach and portfolio (Figure 3.5). On the other hand, the share of large MFIs has increased and consequently the medium size MFIs share has been reduced. This trend in distribution may provide an indication that medium-sized MFIs are being displaced on account of crisis and the prevailing uncertain situation in the sector.

Out of 61 MFIs reported, 40 were typically Non-Banking financial companies (NBFCs) (Table 3.4). The other form of MFIs included societies (10 in number) and section 25 companies (five in number) cooperatives, trust and local area bank. In terms of

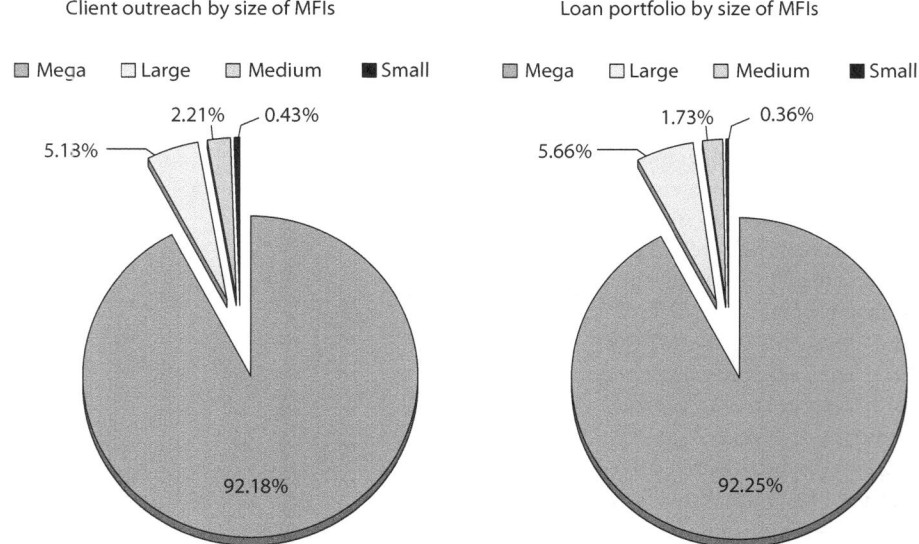

Figure 3.4 Client outreach and loan portfolio by size of the MFIs

Source: MIX market.

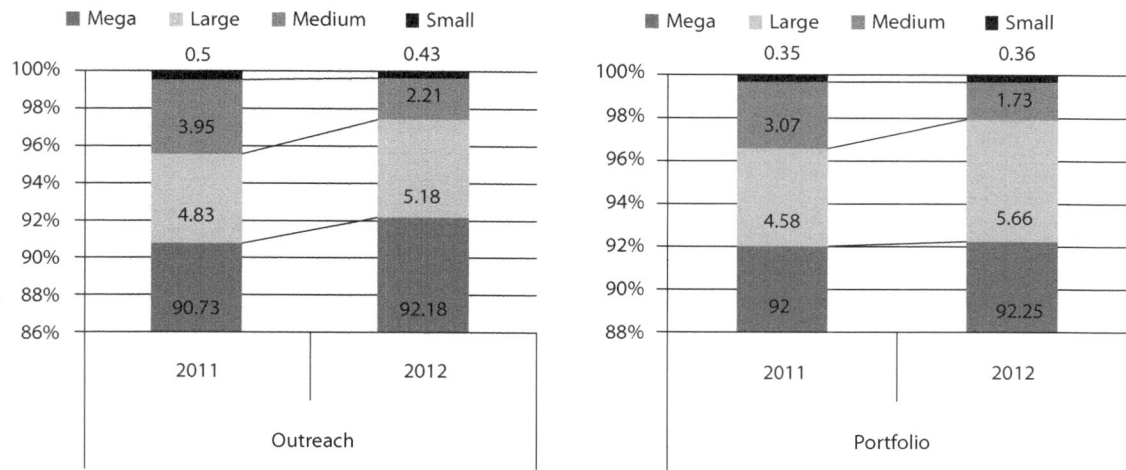

Figure 3.5 Change in outreach and portfolio by size of MFIs

Source: MIX market.

loan portfolio, almost 90 per cent of the market share remains with the NBFCs (Fig. 3.6).

Table 3.4 Distribution of loan portfolio by the legal form

Legal form	No. of MFI	GLP ₹ (billion)
NBFC	40	157.25
Trust	2	6.06
Section 25 Cos	5	5.20
Society	10	4.60
Cooperatives	3	1.70
Local Area Bank	1	0.84
Total	61	175.64

Source: MIX market.

REGIONAL DISTRIBUTION

The regional distribution of outreach and loan portfolio estimates based on the Sa-Dhan Bharat Microfinance Quick Report-2012, revealed that the dominance of the southern region still continues. The Southern region accounts for almost 50 per cent in both outreach and portfolio followed by the Eastern region (25 per cent). The outreach share of the Northern region remains below 5 per cent. (Figure 3.7).

When compared to the previous year the Southern region registered an increased share both in terms of client outreach as well as loan portfolio

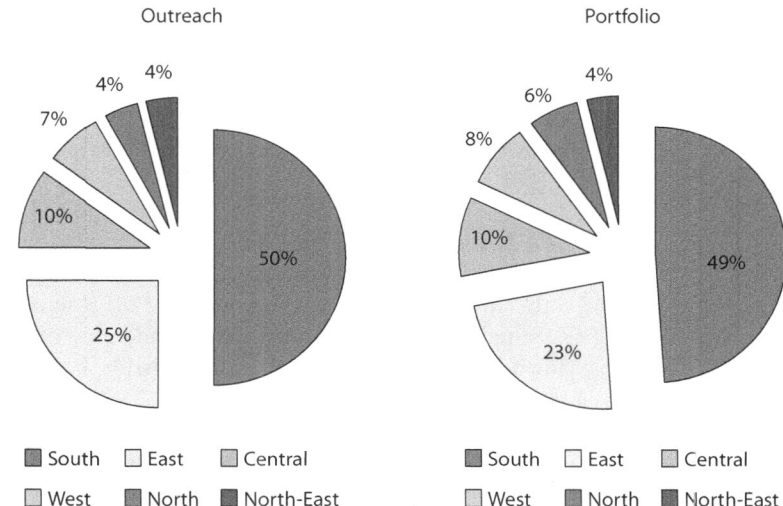

Figure 3.6 Loan portfolio by legal form of MFIs

Source: Sa-Dhan Bharat Microfinance Quick Report 2012.

Figure 3.7 Regional distribution of outreach and loan portfolio

Source: Sa-Dhan Bharat Microfinance Quick Report 2012.

Table 3.5 Comparison of market share of different regions

Region	Share of clients 2010–11%	Share of clients 2011–12%	Share of loans 2010–11%	Share of loans 2011–12%
North	4.8	4.2	3.7	4.2
North East	3.2	4.2	3.6	6.1
East	17.9	25.1	18.1	23.3
Central	16.7	9.6	14.3	9.7
West	12.1	7.2	11.4	7.6
South	45.3	49.7	48.9	49.1

Source: Mix market.

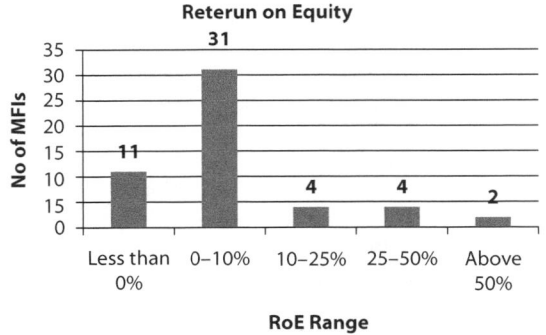

Figure 3.9 RoE range-wise distribution of MFIs

Source: Sa-Dhan Bharat Microfinance Quick Report 2012.

(Table 3.5). The share of the North East and Eastern regions has registered impressive growth while the Western region lost its share significantly.

COSTS AND PROFITABILITY

Out of 61 MFIs, 11 MFIs had negative Return on Assets (RoA) while seven of them had RoA between 0 to –10 per cent, four MFIs had RoA below the level of –10 per cent (Figure 3.8). The number of MFIs with RoA above one per cent has also declined. The majority of MFIs (21) had the RoA in the range of 0–1 per cent.

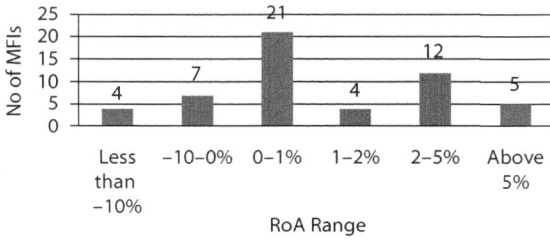

Figure 3.8 RoA range-wise distribution of MFIs

Source: SaDhan Bharat Microfinance Quick Report 2012.

In terms of Return on Equity, half of the MFI sample (31) has RoE in the range of 0–10 per cent. Unlike the previous year, the number of MFIs with RoE higher than 10 per cent has considerably declined this year (Figure 3.9). Eleven MFIs had a negative Return on Equity this year.

Figure 3.10 presents the trend (median figures) of operating cost and Yield on portfolio. Yield on portfolio has come down below the level of 24 per cent in 2012 from the level of 26.63 per cent in the previous year. On the cost front, the operating cost has increased in 2012. The median figure of operating cost of MFIs remained at 13.36. Though exact data was not available, provisioning expenses for loan loss have considerably increased for MFIs. Though RBI has removed the interest rate cap, the margin cap of 10 and 12 per cent above the financial cost remain in vogue. The revenue net of operating costs is 13.52 per cent, which is lower than the cost of funds, indicating that MFIs are unable to cover their total costs in hardening interest rate scenario. The margin cap of 12 per cent is not sufficient to cover operating costs, let alone the provisioning costs. Overall the profitability of the MFIs during the year 2011–12 has been eroded due to after effect of crisis, liquidity constraint and reduced client outreach. While MFIs will have to achieve a higher level of efficiency, without increased funds flow, the idle capacity in MFIs cannot be utilized to bring down the operating costs.

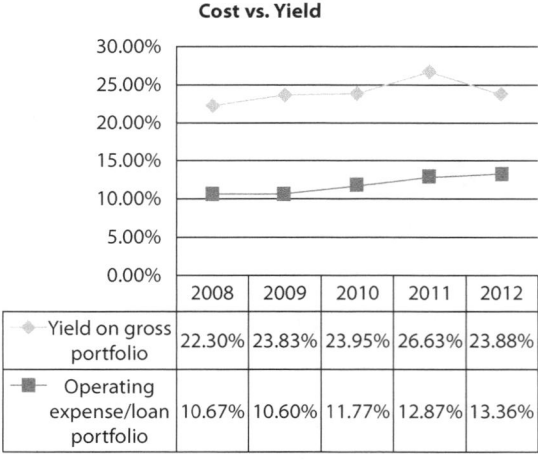

Figure 3.10 Cost and portfolio yield over the years

Source: Mix Market.

FLOW OF FUND

There have been some positive developments in equity flow to Indian MFIs. The regulatory interventions by RBI during this year have helped in improving the investor confidence in the sector, which was evident through the resumed equity investments in the sector. The equity flow to Indian MFIs in 2012[2] has increased to ₹5.03 billion as compared to ₹1.94 billion in the previous year. The top ten MFIs in terms of equity investment are shown in Table 3.6.

Table 3.6 Top 10 MFIs in terms of equity flow in 2011–12

MFI	Amount (₹ million)
Bandhan	1,350
Ujjivan	1,280
Janalakshmi	540
SVCL	400
Trident	340
RGVN	300
Jagaran	280
Swadhaar	150
Anjali	60
NERFL	50

Source: Data from Sa-Dhan's 'The Bharat Microfinance Quick Report-2012'.

SIDBI, with the support from the Government of India, has launched India Micro Equity Fund (IMEF) for extending equity or any other form of capital for quasi-equity or subordinated debt to Tier-II (having borrowers between 50,000 and 250,000) and Tier-III NBFC MFIs (having less than 50,000 borrowers) and all non-NBFC MFIs. It is a ₹1,000 million revolving fund. SIDBI is very keen on ensuring that the equity funds under IMEF are released to MFIs very soon.

The majority of debt to MFIs come from banks. Though the banks have stopped lending to MFIs after the AP crisis, the bank lending to MFIs has restarted slowly during the financial year 2011–12. However, the majority of the MFIs receiving the bank loan are those with very small or no exposure in Andhra Pradesh. Out of the total debt of ₹72.87 billion received by MFIs in year 2011–12, the banks have disbursed around ₹67.78 billion[3] to MFIs. Out of the total debt outstanding with MFIs of around ₹161 billion in 2011–12, the total bank outstanding

stood at around 116 billion accounting for more than 70 per cent. As noted in the Sa-Dhan report, NGO MFIs (society and trusts) have received bank loans of around ₹104 billion in year 2011–12, which is 32 per cent higher than that in the previous year. However, the NBFCs bank loan receipts have declined by 34 per cent. Table 3.7 presents a list of MFIs receiving bank loans above ₹500 millon.

Table 3.7 MFIs receiving bank loans above ₹500 million

MFI	Amount (₹ million)
Bandhan	24,960
SKDRDP	8,670
SKS	5,480
Ujjivan	3,830
S E Investment	2,840
Equitas	2,760
Janalakshmi	2,360
Grama Vidiyal	2,310
Grameen Financial Services	1,970
Satin Credit Care Network Ltd	1,750
CASPOR	1,710
ESAF	1,310
Suryoday	1,100
Smile	850
BSS Microfinance	830
SVCL	770
Madura Microfinance Ltd	720
RGVN	670
NERFL	540
Village Financial Services Ltd	530

Source: Sa-Dhan Bharat Microfinance Quick Report 2012.

POST-CRISIS PERFORMANCE OF MFIs IN ANDHRA PRADESH

The state law enforced by the Andhra Pradesh government on microfinance during the year 2012 has almost halted the MFI activities in the state.[4] The well-indented law has had many unintended consequences, which in turn had serious adverse impacts on clients, MFIs, banks and the microfinance sector in general. As a result, the credit discipline of MFI clients got vitiated resulting in mass default. The very existence of many of the smaller MFIs' existence has become a big challenge. The MFIs have been forced to adopt several austerity measures to reduce the operational cost, besides they have to honour their repayment commitment to the banks. Stoppage of operation of MFIs in the State due to the stringent government norm led to repayment default from the clients and non-availability of bank fund. As a result, many of the MFIs downsized the work force and also either closed down and/or merged branches to reduce the cost of operation. For example, PWMACS reduced the staff strength to one third of the original strength and has merged their branches to have only four branches post crisis.[5] Similarly CRESA staff strength got reduced to 42 from 206 and the MFIs closed 12 branches besides slashing the staff salaries by 25 per cent for all employees. Another example is Saadhana where the staff strength has been reduced to 19 now from 258 earlier. The financing banks, besides stopping the credit support, initiated legal action against MFIs for recovery of loans. The 2012 Quick Data collected by Sa-Dhan from AP-based MFIs reveal the adverse impact of crisis on the operational and financial performance of MFIs during 2011–12. Overall the AP-based MFIs had reduced their branch infrastructure, and client and portfolio base resulting in a lower yield and profit (Table 3.8).

Table 3.8 AP–MFIs operational and financial performance

AP based MFIs	2001	2012	Decline (%)
No. of Branch	6,426	5,227	19
No. of Staff	55,512	39,067	30
Active Clients (million)	16	12	25
Loan Portfolio(₹ million)	139,430	79,120	43
Disbursement (₹ million)	191,800	62,900	67
PAR 60 (%)	30	31	
Total Asset (₹ million)	135,210	91,730	32
Net Owned Fund (NoF) ₹ million	31,490	25,380	19
Yield (%)	22	10	
Operating Expense (%)	10	6	
Operational Sufficiency—OSS (%)	111	55	
Return on Asset (RoA)—(%)	2	-8	
Return on Equity (RoE)–(%)	2	-35	

Source: Sa-Dhan Bharat Microfinance Quick Report 2012.

In the mean time, a few banks have come forward to take over the debt owed by SHGs to MFIs by offering fresh loans to SHGs to repay their MFI loans. The Debt Swapping attempt was adopted by an Indian Bank branch where the bank branch disbursed ₹10 million to nearly 20 SHG's to the maximum of ₹0.5 million for each group. The field officers of the branch are recovering through weekly instalments on an experimental basis, which seems to be working well, and there is scope for greater expansion in the near future.

A quick study conducted by Sa-Dhan to understand the impact of AP crisis on clients brought out that many of the MFI clients have stopped micro enterprise activities and have started doing wage labour for their livelihoods. Some are managing their liquidity problem through selling their valuables like gold, cattle, etc. since they were not able to borrow from any sources. Further, this situation is forcing the MFI clients to revert back to informal sources with very high interest rate. In the same line the study conducted by MicroSave has brought out a similar observation of overdependence on informal sources of credit in the absence of MFI loan. About 56 per cent of the respondents had either postponed their expansion or reduced their operations due to the reason that access to credit had become difficult and 90 per cent of the clients expressed their willingness to repay the loan if MFI's start disbursing them fresh loan.

CMF IFMR Chennai has commissioned a study to assess how the MFI clients of Andhra Pradesh are managing their portfolio in the near absence of access to MFI loans, for follow-up surveys on the cohort of MFI clients.[6] For the purpose of the study, 197 households who had MFI loan outstanding during 2009–10 were revisited. Table 3.9 presents the summary of key findings from the survey with a comparison of 2009 and 2012 data.

A comparison of the client households' loan portfolio between 2009 and 2012 showed a large fall in proportion of households with MFI loan outstanding, which signifies the large scale reduction in MFI operations across eight districts of AP. The comparison also indicated that there is a significant fall in the proportion of households' indebtedness to the friends and relatives who charge interest to extend loans. Overall, the analysis revealed that even though a smaller proportion of the households are now borrowing from the MFIs and friends, there is no evidence of substitution of MFI loans by other formal or informal sources leading to a fall in proportion of households with loan outstanding. The outstanding amount comparison showed that median total outstanding has increased by around 25 per cent, which seems to be contributed by the increase in median loan size of banks, SHGs, and moneylenders. Comparing the proportion indebted and median size, it seems

Table 3.9 Comparison of household loan portfolios, 2009 vs. 2012 in AP

| Particulars | Households with +ve loan outstanding (%) | | Median outstanding in ₹ | | |
	2009	2012	2009	2012 (Nominal)	2012** (Real)
Banks	29	29	17,350	25000	20,955
SHG	65	62	5,000	9000	7,544
MFI	94	44*	8,200	5000	4,191
Moneylender	24	30	20,000	25000	20,955
Friends (with interest)	54	41*	30,000	33000	27,660
Friends (no interest)	10	6	5,000	5000	4,191
Employer/Landlord	24	25	21,000	20000	16,764
All informal sources	83	81	30,000	35000	29,337
Any Loan source	99	93*	37,891	47500	39,814

* *Indicates difference between 2012 and 2009 is statistically significant.*
** *Inflation adjusted to 2009 prices.*
Source: Study on 'Access to Finance in Rural Andhra Pradesh—Revisiting the MFI Clients 2012' conducted by Centre for Micro Finance, IFMR, Chennai with funding support from IFMR Capital Private Ltd. Forthcoming report.

that the loan size for existing clients increased significantly for bank, SHG and moneylenders, and thus it seems that the share of contribution of MFIs has been filled by these sources. Overall, a smaller fraction of the client households are now availing credit with increased median loan size. The savings comparison showed that a smaller fraction of households are now able to generate saving with the around 25 per cent increase in nominal value of savings, and a moderate (10 per cent) increase in inflation adjusted value of savings.

The surveys collected information of household expenditure for a 30-day period prior to the survey (Table 3.10). Both rounds of survey were conducted almost in the same time of the year, so the expenditure figures are free from seasonal fluctuations. The survey data indicated that the consumption expenditure of client households decreased by around 11 per cent during the reference period, which possibly indicates a worsening of the standard of living of households in 2012 as compared to 2009.

Thus, the analysis of MFI clients revisit survey data indicated that after the AP crisis that resulted in a large scale fall in availability of loans from MFI, there is no evidence that other sources fill in the vacuum created by the withdrawal of MFIs and that existing clients of banks and SHGs secured more loans, while some clients remain excluded from the market. The revisit survey also documented evidence of fall in household expenditure after the crisis. Post-crisis, the government ordinance in 2010

Table 3.10 Comparison of household consumption expenditures, 2009 vs. 2012 in AP

Variable	Year	Observations	Mean	Std. Dev.	Median
Total Monthly expenditure (Reference period: 30 days prior to the survey)	2009	193	3703	1718	3400
	2012	192	3272	1863	3000

Source: Study on 'Access to Finance in Rural Andhra Pradesh—Revisiting the MFI Clients 2012' conducted by Centre for Micro Finance, IFMR, Chennai with funding support from IFMR Capital Private Ltd. Forthcoming report.

severely restricted MFI operations in the state, contributing to an environment that resulted in mass non-repayment to MFIs and a reduction in available microcredit.

ADHERENCE TO REGULATORY NORMS

The Centre for Micro Finance (CMF), at IFMR, Chennai, conducted a study to understand whether the RBI guidelines regarding the eligibility of microfinance institutions for priority sector lending align with the profiles of microfinance clients.[7] A total of 928 urban and semi-urban MFI clients were interviewed in the states of Karnataka, Maharashtra, Tamil Nadu, Uttar Pradesh and West Bengal between January and March 2012. One of the RBI guidelines stipulates that 75 per cent of the loan should go to income generating activities. However, the study found that only about half of the clients (49 per cent) reported that investment in the current business was one of the reasons for them to borrow from MFIs, while 17 per cent of the client-households utilized the loan for consumption purposes. Clients with pre-existing entrepreneurial activity had a high propensity to invest MFI loans in their enterprise. As high as 84 per cent of those clients running at least one form of enterprise reported that they used the MFI loan for business purposes, while only around 8 per cent of clients with an enterprise used MFI loan for household consumption.

Although a majority of MFI clients had access to a formal banking system, it was not a primary source of credit. It was found that 62 per cent of client households had at least one bank account. Despite the prevalence of formal banking amongst the clients, only 11 per cent had ever taken loans from banks. Primary reasons reported for not taking loans from banks were: (*a*) the respondents did not require type of credit that banks provide (30 per cent); (*b*) documentation and application procedures too complicated (25 per cent); and (*c*) lack of knowledge about the products and services provided by the banks (11 per cent). Among those who did not have any bank account, 20 per cent reported that they did not open bank accounts due to their low savings and/or low income, 19 per cent reported that they had no idea about credit availability from banks or their financial products, and 13 per cent reported that their loan applications had been rejected.

Borrowing from multiple MFIs was not prevalent at the time of the survey. The study also finds that RBI's recommendation that not more than two MFIs should lend to the same borrower is largely followed throughout the target regions. It was found that even though several MFIs are operating within the given study areas, only four per cent of the sample population had outstanding loans from more than two MFIs. A total of 1,143 MFI loans were taken by 928 clients, suggesting an average of 1.2 loans per household.

The study revealed that the Self Help Group model was not a predominant source of credit among the clients from urban and semi-urban centres in the study areas as 76 per cent of clients reported that none of their household members had any SHG account. Close to one half of the clients (47 per cent) without any SHG account reported that they had no idea of the functioning of SHG, and 15 per cent reported that they did not know any SHG member.

This was predominantly found in semi-urban areas of UP, where 99 per cent of the sample respondents were not part of SHGs. Likewise in urban areas of West Bengal and Tamil Nadu, more than 70 per cent of clients reported that none of the household members were SHG members.

Clients perceived aggressive loan recovery methods to be inappropriate. The series of unprecedented number of among suicides among microfinance clients reported by the media in Andhra Pradesh ushered in a wide spread criticism of MFIs in India. The line of critique was on the exorbitantly high profits earned by MFIs and coercive money collection practices. This prompted the Andhra Pradesh Government to bring in the Andhra Pradesh Microfinance Ordinance 2010. The incident eventually resulted in the RBI releasing recommendations for the MFI sector, and these recommendations strive to address the primary customer complaints that led to the crisis, including coercive collection practices, usurious interest rates, and selling practices that resulted in overindebtedness. The survey found that even though 83 per cent of these clients mentioned that they feel obligated to pay somebody else's instalment, a majority of them reported that the coercive collection practices—especially through confiscation of assets and extension of meeting time till the loan is recovered were inappropriate. A majority of respondents (56 per cent) had admitted the practice of charging a fine for late payment.

UNIFIED CODE OF CONDUCT

As the Self-Regulatory Organizations for the sector, microfinance institutions are required to deal with compliance and enforcement of Industry Code of Conduct and other regulations, as prescribed by the RBI/State Governments/other Regulatory bodies, for the microfinance industry. In 2011, the two industry associations, Sa-Dhan and MFIN evolved a unified code of conduct for their members. The Code of Conduct was released at the Microfinance India Summit 2011 in New Delhi. The Code of Conduct seeks to ensure that microfinance services are provided in a manner that is ethical and transparent and benefits clients in a holistic manner. The unified code of conduct includes integrity and ethical behaviour, transparency, client protection, governance, recruitment, client education, data sharing and feedback/grievance redressal mechanisms.[8] Both Sa-Dhan and MFIN have made efforts to ensure that their members are to understand and are exposed to the underlying principles inherent in their code of conduct.

There was a closer scrutiny on the operational practices of MFIs in 2011–12. SIDBI,[9] which had initiated the development of a methodology for assessment of these practices in 2010 had several MFIs assessed on their adherence to the code of conduct. Several agencies have participated in performing these assessments, M2i Consulting[10] (Box 3.1), Access Development Services, ICRA Management Consulting Services, SMERA and MCRIL. SIDBI has put many of these assessments in the public domain. Many prominent lenders to MFIs including SIDBI have started including Code of Conduct Assessment (COCA) as a covenant in their lending agreements. A critical review of the available 13 COCA of different MFIs spread across the country with different portfolio size clearly brings out the emphasis and commitment exerted by the MFIs with a view to have meaningful client contacts and broad attention of code of conduct issues. Further, 55 per cent of the MFIs under review secured higher scores than the average score in the COCA assessment, which was mainly due to staff conduct and loan pricing. On the other hand, the low score among 45 per cent of the MFIs is attributed to weaker client relationship and lack of social responsibilities. The process of developing the Common Code of Conduct was supported by the International Finance Corporation, World Bank, Michael and Susan Dell Foundation, SIDBI, and ACCESS Development Services, under the auspices of the Responsible Finance Forum developed by the IFC.

Based on the RBI Directions of 2nd December 2011, both Sa Dhan and MFIN further tightened their enforcement mechanisms and instituted separate processes to deal with complaints received on Code of Conduct Compliance and complaints received on Regulatory Compliance by having well-defined peer monitoring mechanisms for effective monitoring of CoC compliance issues. While COCA is becoming more and more relevant in the present day context where client protection, governance, transparency and social involvement are the driving principles in the MF sector, it needs to be done on an ongoing basis in periodic intervals. Considering the cost burden on MFIs, extensive funding support may provide greater incentives for many MFIs to participate in this monitoring process. Developing appropriate incentive mechanisms for taking this up would go a long way in raising the standards of consumer services and protection.

Box 3.1 M2i's code of conduct assessment

M2i performs its assessments along six dimensions:

1. Client origination and targeting
2. Loan pricing
3. Loan appraisal
4. Client data security
5. Staff conduct encompassing
   - Communication with clients
   - Loan collection and recovery process
6. Relationship management and feedback mechanism

M2i has drawn from a review of the norms prescribed for MFIs including Sadhan's and MFIN's code of conduct, fair practices guidelines from the Reserve bank of India and CGAP's client protection principles (Smart Campaign). M2i measures the adherence to these principles on four parameters (called ADDO in short):

- Approval at the policy level from the board
- Documentation of the guidelines and procedures that emerge from the policy
- Dissemination of the guidelines and procedures across the organization
- Observance in practice of these guidelines and procedures.

Source: SIDBI web page.

PRODUCT INNOVATION

During the formative years the earliest Indian MFIs lent to groups of 5–20 women, extending uniform credit products. Between 1997 and 2005, product development activities centred on tweaking of interest rates, loan tenure, group structure and lending processes. With a view to achieving low costs and rapid scalability, most Indian MFIs settled on the most convenient product structure—group-guarantee loans in calibrated slabs, paid back through equated weekly instalments over 45–52 weeks. Some of the leading MFIs of the time did experiment with consumer durable loans, and loans for purchase of solar lamps and smokeless cook-stoves or construction of toilets. However, these loans remained at the periphery of the main business which constituted plain vanilla loans designated for income generation activities. Several constraints curbed the success of innovative loans: (*a*) MFIs placed caps on the number of loans they extended to each client, so clients who could access higher loan amounts on standardized credit products, did not want to access smaller loans for specific purposes instead. Money being fungible, clients realized that they could take income generation loans and use these partially or wholly for consumption needs. (*b*) Loan officers who were often incentivized on the basis of outstanding portfolio did not want to push small loans, even if they were specifically customized for client needs. (*c*) MFIs became wary of partnerships with suppliers of cook-stoves, water filters, etc., as problems with these products resulted in defaults and souring of relationships with their clients as they were blamed for promoting inferior or faulty products.

With vintage clients demanding new products on the one hand and severe competition in the Southern and Eastern states on the other, MFIs dedicated more resources to product design. With a view to bringing out the genuine efforts put in by MFIs to reach the clients' requirements, a list of innovative financial products evolved by different MFIs are presented in Annexure 3.1. In addition to the above, among a wave of new MFIs there were a few institutions, which entered the market with well thought out strategies for serving hitherto ignored segments such as the urban poor. While these MFIs focused on meeting the credit needs of their target segment through standardized group products, they spent considerable effort to understand the other financial needs of these segments. Swadhaar FinAccess, Arohan, Ujjivan Financial Services and Janalakshmi Financial Services were some of those MFIs that focused on the urban poor and developed unique processes and loan products to suit the urban context better.

MFIs themselves have recently begun to realize that micro-credit is not a silver bullet or panacea for all ills. Even well-intentioned loans for health, sanitation and other non-productive but inevitable consumption purposes have limitation in improving the quality of life. Since MFIs have to find ways to reduce operational costs, having built a robust distribution system for financial services delivery to the last mile, they should view the current situation as an opportunity to capitalize on this network by adding products and services deemed necessary by their clients. The mix would vary from place to place, depending on local needs and existing infrastructure. MFIs would do well to add products and services one at a time to avoid confusion and complications in their information systems, staff incentives and internal processes. However, in the long run, it would appear that benefits of a multi-service approach far outweigh the risks and costs.

MICRO-ENTERPRISE FINANCING BY MFIs

Micro, small and medium enterprises (MSMEs) contribute 8 per cent of India's GDP, 45 per cent of the manufactured output and 40 per cent of its exports. Among MSMEs, microenterprises display a high degree of heterogeneity. India is estimated to have more than 26 million MSMEs. While a few of the MSMEs operate as registered entities (with at least minimal registration required as per the taxation laws), a large majority (94 per cent) of them operate as very small unregistered proprietary concerns owned by microentrepreneurs (Box 3.2). Borrowing from informal lenders is not a viable option for MSMEs because of the cost of borrowing and limited turnaround of capital due to shorter-term credit lines.

Box 3.2 Loan product for trading and vending enterprises

Arohan offers weekly group lending products, but identified the need to support micro and small vending enterprises in Kolkata. Arohan developed a small-group, individual liability lending product based on market research to assess demand through client need assessment, product attribute ranking, financial sector trend analysis, and a supply side scoping study to examine current product offerings, key challenges and financing gaps. Arohan then developed and pilot-tested detailed product guidelines, policies, processes and business projections for MSE financing. This product is known as the *bazaar* (market) loan as it caters to individuals who are involved in trading and vending at authorized *bazaars* (markets) and have a proper legal authorization to undertake their business. The key design features (in alignment with client demand) were, no collateral, lower interest rate as compared to the *bazaar samiti* (market traders' association), doorstep collection of instalments, free insurance, weekly repayment mechanism and faster turnaround from loan application to disbursement.

Source: Primary information from Arohan.

Enabling access to finance for underserved entrepreneurial segments can significantly impact the development of microenterprises and promote decentralized job creation. Thus MFIs need to be supported to develop and implement microenterprise financing loan products based on market research into the dominant microenterprise segments. Development and implementation of microenterprise financing programmes by MFIs needs a coordinated plan of action. The key actions include institutional readiness assessment, strategic planning, market research and dominant cluster mapping. Once MFIs have laid down a roadmap they might need support for capacity building for the institution and staff, support for pilot testing and perhaps onsite implementation support[11] (Box 3.3).

Box 3.3 MicroVentures

MicroGraam is the first organization of its kind in India to introduce a new MicroVenture investment model, which is a dramatic departure from traditional microcredit lending. MicroGraam aims to bring an array of diverse financial tools for India's underprivileged rural poor. In MicroVentures, a micro-entrepreneur and a micro-venture capitalist enter into a revenue sharing agreement, which enables the two partners to create a micro and small enterprises (MSE). Although traditional microcredit provides the essential service of access to credit, entrepreneurs who are willing and able to undertake larger business ventures are unable to do so under the current paradigm. MicroGraam has created MicroVentures to address this underserved niche market of entrepreneurs who require a larger loan size but cannot obtain them from commercial financing. MicroVentures provides flexibility and cost savings, which can only arise from long term financing.

MicroGraam facilitates the connection between competent micro-entrepreneurs and micro-venture capitalist interested in investing in small to medium sized businesses. In this model, the micro-venture capitalist provides the full upfront cost to starting the business and the two parties agree to share a percentage of the profits or losses. The two parties agree upon how to share the profits or losses (50-50, 60-40 etc.) and the number of years the micro-venture capitalist will be involved. MicroGraam acts as the facilitator in the transaction and helps the entrepreneur with their business model.

The first MicroVenture was a Dairy Farm in Kolar district of Karnataka. MicroGraam facilitated equity capital of ₹300,000 from six micro-venture capitalists in July 2010. The dairy farm was set by the members of the Self-Help Group, and the group members jointly managed the dairy farm. MicroVenture Capitalist hold 40 per cent stake in the dairy farm and 60 per cent is held by the SHG group. In two years, micro-venture capitalists have been able to exit fully with an ROI of 11 per cent p.a.

MicroGraam's latest MicroVenture initiative is a 'water shop' in northern Karnataka. The micro-entrepreneur, Sikander, received financing from three micro-venture capitalists to the tune of ₹300,000. He recently opened the shop to provide clean drinking water to the surrounding areas with more than 500 households. This social business leverages sustainable business practices to address the public health need for safe water. Access to clean water and sanitation facilitates are pressing conditions in rural India and MicroVentures has enabled this social cause to become a viable social business. In order to achieve sustainable development in rural India, financial models beyond traditional loans and saving are essential and MicroGraam continues to develop innovating financial products to meet the needs of its borrowers.

Source: Primary information from MicroGraam.

POVERTY TRACKING THROUGH PPI

The Progress Out of Poverty Index (PPI)[12] is increasingly used as an effective and accurate tool that measures poverty levels of groups and individuals. Using the PPI, MFIs are able to determine their clients' needs, whose programmes are most effective, how quickly clients leave poverty, and what helps them to move out of poverty faster.[13] As of now 18 MFIs are using the PPI, and Grameen Koota (GK) is the first fully certified PPI user in all stages of its customer related processes. With the help of the information gathered through PPI, GK has been able to discern the progress made by the customer and the possible contribution of microfinance to their lives.

An analysis of data relating to 0.272 million customers of GK revealed that the proportion of customers below the poverty level declined over the period of the last three years (Figure 3.11). The proportion of customers with income below US$1.25 a day decreased from 35.8 per cent in FY 2011 to 32.6 per cent in FY 2012 (Figure 3.15). The improvement of income levels for a significant proportion of customers is a matter of satisfaction to the MFI. Even though one cannot attribute the entire progress to microfinance loans, the fact that customers have been able progress even when they have contracted the 'high-cost' loans is worth noting.

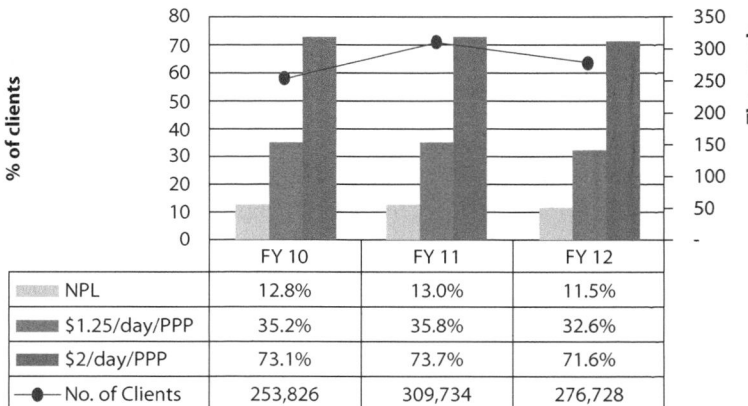

	FY 10	FY 11	FY 12
NPL	12.8%	13.0%	11.5%
$1.25/day/PPP	35.2%	35.8%	32.6%
$2/day/PPP	73.1%	73.7%	71.6%
No. of Clients	253,826	309,734	276,728

Figure 3.11 Poverty profile of clients over the last three years

Source: The PPI®, developed by Grameen Foundation, is a poverty measurement tool that is a unique composite of ten easy-to-collect, country-specific, non-financial indicators such as family size, the number of children attending school, the type of housing and ownership of certain assets. It is a simple, practical, easy to use tool yet statistically accurate.

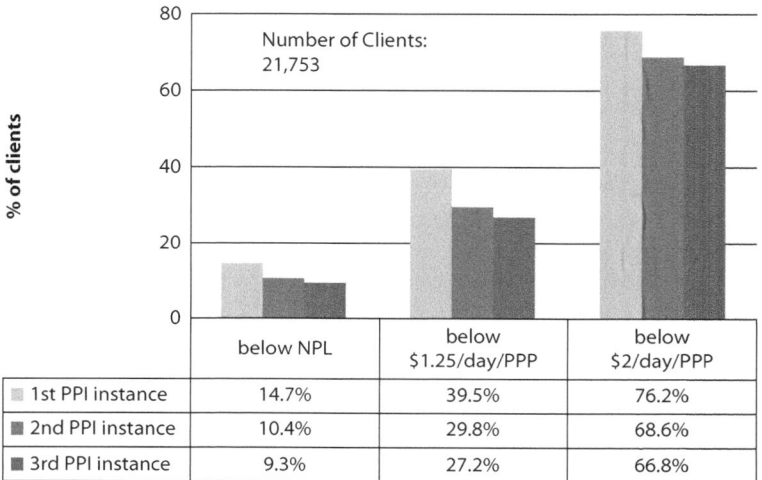

Poverty Likelihood of Grameen Koota Clients, March 12

Number of Clients: 21,753

	below NPL	below $1.25/day/PPP	below $2/day/PPP
1st PPI instance	14.7%	39.5%	76.2%
2nd PPI instance	10.4%	29.8%	68.6%
3rd PPI instance	9.3%	27.2%	66.8%

Figure 3.12 PPI report—poverty livelihood of grameen koota clients

Source: Study on 'Access to Finance in Rural Andhra Pradesh—Revisiting the MFI Clients 2012' conducted by Centre for Micro Finance, IFMR, Chennai with funding support from IFMR Capital Private Ltd. Forthcoming report.

Table: 3.11   Status of poverty level of GK clients

Portfolio	Clients (Nos)	Below NPL (%)	Below US $1.25/day/ PPP (%)	Below US $2/day/ PPP (%)
Dropouts	155,387	13.7	37.2	74.7
Active Clients	276,728	11.5	32.6	71.6

Source: Study on 'Access to Finance in Rural Andhra Pradesh—Revisiting the MFI Clients 2012' conducted by Centre for Micro Finance, IFMR, Chennai with funding support from IFMR Capital Private Ltd. Forthcoming report.

A similar trend was also observed for 21,753 clients of GK for whom GK has three PPI data points across time (as on March 2012). The progress out of poverty is more evident in this case as 31 per cent of the clients who were below the US$1.25/day/PPP line, and 12 per cent of the clients who were below the US$2/day/PPP line during the first PPI dataset have moved above their respective poverty lines in the duration of two loan cycles from GK (Figure 3.12). While the average period of these clients since joining GK is 42 months, the average period between 1st PPI Instance and 3rd PPI instance is 26 months.

The details of the poverty status of the dropout clients as of March 12 revealed that the status of the poverty likelihood of dropouts is worse-off than the current set of active clients (Table 3.11). The increased incidence of poverty level among the dropouts clearly establishes the positive impact of the MFI lending.

However, it would be interesting to know what poverty levels they stood at during their 1st PPI instance. There are 50,567 such dropouts whose scores can be analyzed; comparing the poverty levels of dropouts during the 1st PPI instance and the last PPI instance, significant proportion of people move out of the absolute poverty line (US$1.25 a day) (Figure 3.13).

FACTORS INFLUENCING THE POVERTY LEVEL OF MF CLIENTS

Grameen Foundation made an attempt to identify the factors that are influencing the poverty level using PPI® data with demographic information of clients collected from 470,548 respondents from 14 MFIs operating in 16 States in India.[14] The PPI® data collected shows that the poverty profiles of the 14 MFIs we examine range widely, from MFIs with 6.44 per cent of clients under the National Poverty Line (NPL) to one MFI that has 38.40 per cent of clients under the NPL (Figure 3.14). It is important to remember that every MFI has different poverty outreach goals, and therefore the comparison is not straightforward. The average poverty concentration under the NPL is 19.16 per cent. The analysis further quantified that many MFIs are unable to achieve a poverty concentration greater than the national poverty rate at each of the poverty lines. Only six MFIs have poverty concentrations exceeding 74.9 per cent under the US$2/day line.

The purpose for which the client availed the loan and the relative demand for this purpose can be informative for MFIs looking to adjust product design in order to attract more poor people. The study findings revealed that almost 50 per cent of clients are taking out loans for agriculture suggesting that MFIs could better serve their clients by offering loan products specifically tailored for agriculture. The primary occupation of the client in relation to their poverty level can help MFIs get to know their clients better and inform business decisions regarding targeting, potential demand for new products, and cross-selling.

Further the study findings establish that poverty rates are less for microfinance clients who have progressed to higher loan cycles. There is an inverse relationship between the client's poverty rates and the number of loan cycle. There could be various reasons for this finding and further analysis of the data is necessary to establish causality. Some plausible reasons for this result include:

1. Clients benefitted from participation in GK's credit programme and have improved their economic well-being.
2. Higher loan amounts for each consecutive loan cycle enabled MFIs to attract and retain better off clients.
3. Dropout of poorer clients at the end of each loan cycle, which could be due to a variety of reasons.

A similar relationship is observed between education and poverty level (Figure 3.15). Knowing the client's demographic information is imperative in order to deliver appropriate services to the client.

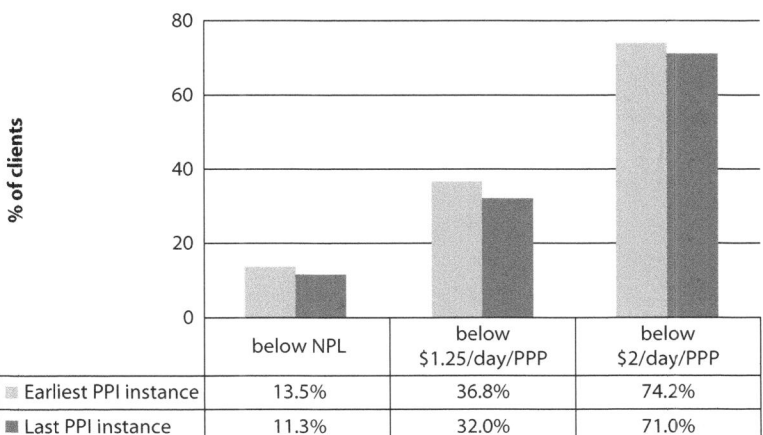

	below NPL	below $1.25/day/PPP	below $2/day/PPP
Earliest PPI instance	13.5%	36.8%	74.2%
Last PPI instance	11.3%	32.0%	71.0%

Figure 3.13 Poverty profile of Grameen Koota dropouts at different instances

Source: Study on 'Access to Finance in Rural Andhra Pradesh—Revisiting the MFI Clients 2012' conducted by Centre for Micro Finance, IFMR, Chennai with funding support from IFMR Capital Private Ltd. Forthcoming report.

The poor are not a homogenous group, and those with no education or those coming from disadvantaged caste groups may require specialized products and services that can empower them to become more effective economic players. Clients with some college education have only a 4 per cent likelihood of falling under the National Poverty Line whereas clients with no education have an 18 per cent likelihood of falling under the same poverty line (Figure 3.16).

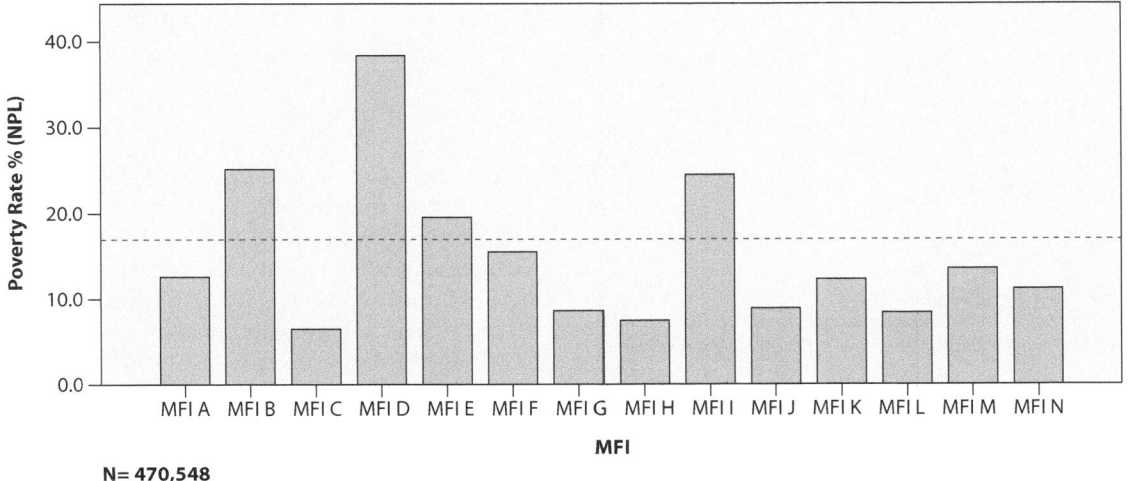

N= 470,548

Figure 3.14 Poverty concentration of MFIs under NPL

Source: Study on 'Access to Finance in Rural Andhra Pradesh—Revisiting the MFI Clients 2012' conducted by Centre for Micro Finance, IFMR, Chennai with funding support from IFMR Capital Private Ltd. Forthcoming report.

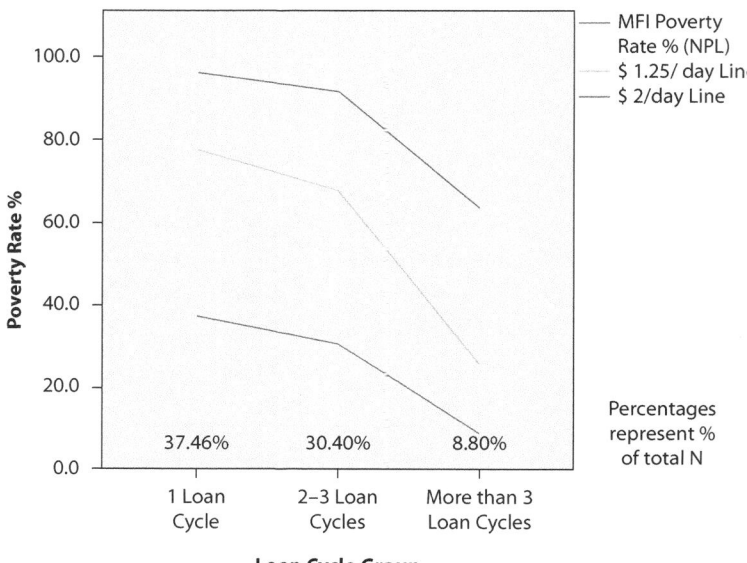

N= 152,841

Figure 3.15 Loan cycle group and poverty rates

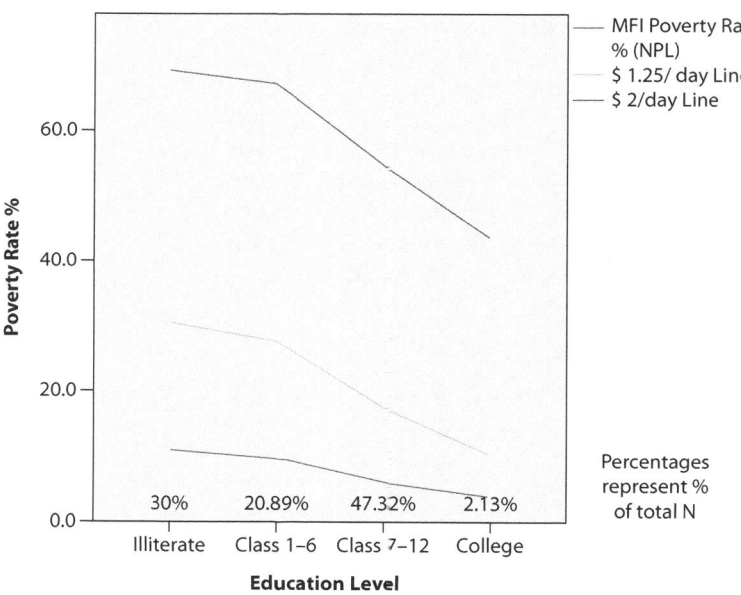

N= 3,806

Figure 3.16 Education and poverty level

Source for both Figures 3.15 and 3.16: Study on 'Access to Finance in Rural Andhra Pradesh—Revisiting the MFI Clients 2012' conducted by Centre for Micro Finance, IFMR, Chennai with funding support from IFMR Capital Private Ltd. Forthcoming report.

With the likelihood of being under the National Poverty Line as the dependent variable, and religion, rural or urban, caste, education level, age and state included as independent variables analyzed using multivariate linear regression method, it is observed that for a selected sample of 326 respondents and for US$2 poverty line, when all else is held constant, the client's education level, age, religion and caste are significantly related to poverty. This suggests that understanding the client's level of education, age and segmentation based on religion/caste would help to have an estimation of probability of clients falling below/above US$2 poverty line. One interesting finding is that as we change poverty line to US$1.25/day or national poverty line, the factors significant to the level of poverty also changes. Hence if an MFI is targeting clients under the NPL, factors the institution should focus on are different than the factors that should be considered under the US$2/day line where education, age and religion/caste play a role in explaining poverty.

SOCIAL PERFORMANCE AND CONSUMER PROTECTION

Microfinance primarily evolved as a social movement, however the focus and strategies have deviated over the period of time and commercial considerations have taken over by the new generation MFIs. The initial goal was to help individuals and families save for the future, build small businesses, meet emergent consumption needs, cope with unexpected setbacks such as illness or poor crops, thereby assuring social security with an improved quality of life for the poor. This is especially important for the vulnerable, low-income populations that make up the bulk of microfinance clients. These clients are always vulnerable for misinformation and misleading initiatives and hence require greater protection. Several initiatives are being undertaken by the MFIs across the country through which, vulnerable and poor households had benefitted to a greater extent (Box 3.4). As a case in point, the experience of Bandhan is worth noting.

Recognizing the need for supporting the poorest of the poor who are normally neglected by the society under the microfinance initiatives, Bandhan is implementing the Targeting Hardcore Poor (THP) programme in West Bengal state. The eligible hardcore poor, mostly women, are identified based on well laid criteria, and a weekly/subsistence allowance of ₹140 is given during the first 13 to 40 weeks, which is complemented with appropriate trainings on social behaviour and economic activities depending on the enterprise activity selected by the members. As most of the ultra-poor households do not have prior experience with formal financial institutions like banks or MFIs, Bandhan conducts a three-day microcredit orientation course for THP programme beneficiaries, attendance at which is required to be considered for a microloan. The training addresses a number of social, health and community issues and explains the functioning of a microcredit group, its rules and regulations, group solidarity and the role of savings in one's financial life.

The results of the internal study conducted for Bandhan indicate that this intervention succeeds in elevating the economic condition of the poorest. It is found that the program results in a 15 per cent increase in household consumption and has positive impacts on other measures of household wealth and welfare, such as assets and emotional well-being. These results are consistent with the notion that the wealth transfer, in the form of asset distribution, directly increased consumption among beneficiary households through the liquidation of assets, but other sources of income, notably from small enterprises, appear to have contributed to the overall increase in consumption as well. The key issues and challenges for the THP includes providing for adequate levels of handholding and training support, individual

---

Box 3.4 Sanghamithra—lending for livelihoods

Sanghamitra is not just a financial intermediary but believes in 'investing to create value'. Each region was identified to focus on certain key areas, which are crucial to livelihoods during the previous year. It is committed to undertake livelihood promotion for poverty alleviation among SHG members. The livelihood approach considers the 'household' as an economic unit. It also takes into account that families have a livelihood strategy, which differs from family to family and which comprises several smaller activities. Sustainable poverty reduction can be achieved through the promotion of livelihood strategies. Myrada, the promoting organization has taken many initiatives to upgrade the skills of SHG members to enable them to undertake livelihood activities. Myrada's sample study of 2,978 SHGs shows that they used loans mobilized from banks, Sanghamithra as well from their group common funds amounting to 830 million for various institutional capacity building and inclusive growth purposes. During the year 2011–12, the outstanding grew from ₹795. 4 million to ₹922.4 million, registering a growth of 15.95 per cent over the previous year, despite the MFI crisis in the country.

Well laid down systems and procedures, good governance and transparent practices are the strengths of Sanghamithra. It reaches unreached areas where formal financial institutions are not able to reach and provides credit to the SHGs at affordable rate of interest with flexible repayment periods, depending on the cash flow of the group/members. The cost of operations is low as it deals with the group and not the individual, besides keeping the staff cost low as compared to the industry level. Sanghamitra has been able to raise resources from banks/financial institutions even during the Andhra Pradesh crisis, because of the established credibility and confidence reposed by the lenders. It is interesting to observe that the recovery in Andhra Pradesh (Ananthapur district) was almost 100 per cent during the crisis due to the practices of following transparency in dealing with clients (SHGs) in terms of moderate interest rate, mode of recovery no coercive method of recovery as envisaged in the Andhra Pradesh Act.

The clients of Sanghamitra are groups, which are formed by NGOs, Government etc., where they do not have control over the quality of groups in terms of utilization and repayment of loans. In view of the ongoing MFI crisis, which eroded the credibility of NBFC/MFIs, the Government of India and others are seriously considering to revive/reinvent the SHGs for which the Government of India has earmarked 5,000 million towards strengthening of SHGs. Thus, there exist greater opportunities to expand its operation. The MFI Bill when implemented will facilitate and encourage MFIs to reach out to the unreached SHGs. The threat of unhealthy competition and breaking up of groups has come down considerably after the Andhra Pradesh Act and after implementation of recommendations of the Malegam Committee report by RBI.

Source: Primary information from Sanghamithra.

---

monitoring, constant guidance to encourage livelihoods diversification.

The Smart Campaign argues that financial institutions that protect clients will create a responsible and loyal clientele, while protecting themselves from the reputation risk that can come with bad practices.[15] The MFIs recognize the need for the client protection and initiated several strategies in recent times. Regulatory measures also focussing on the social performance and consumer protections as priority agenda (Box 3.5).

Box 3.5 Ujjivan effort in client protection

Facing a growing incidence of multiple borrowing (clients taking simultaneous loans from different providers) and ghost borrowing (clients taking out loans on behalf of others, in return for a commission), Ujjivan developed an educational video highlighting the risks of these practices. Featuring the characters Sushila and Revati, rural women who represent typical microfinance borrowers in India, the video narrates the acceptable practices through examples. In the first segment, a respected relative of Sushila and her husband meets and convinces them to take out a large loan in Sushila's name and hand him the proceeds, which he promises to repay punctually. Soon after, he vanishes, leaving Sushila burdened with a repayment commitment she cannot meet.

The second sketch shows Revati, a microfinance client who is bullied by her husband into taking out a second loan so that he can buy a motorbike, and a third loan to make the repayments. Soon after, they find themselves being unable to repay. The two vignettes are simple, but Ujjivan reports that clients watch the videos with unusual focus, and follow them with highly animated discussions. Clients appear to identify themselves readily with Sushila and Revati, whose dealings with overbearing husbands and relatives closely reflect the family dynamics they see in their own homes. The film also introduces clients to the concept of a credit bureau and educates them on the importance of building a positive credit history.

Within a year, Ujjivan showed the film to more than one million families, through local television channels as well as during its own client meetings, where it follows up with a guided discussion. The video is now mandatory for all new Ujjivan clients and staff, and represents a notable contribution towards avoiding the types of issues that have plagued Indian microfinance in the recent years.

Source: Primary information from Ujjivan.

CREDIT BUREAU[16]

'Credit Information' reporting and referencing has been proven world over to bring about a vast change in lending practices through improved transparency and speed of decision making, ultimately lowering the cost of lending and most importantly by keeping a check on NPAs.

Box 3.6: Web-based microfinance

Rang De is a pioneering web-based social initiative that supports rural entrepreneurs with cost effective microcredit for business and education. Through an online portal, which is also India's first, Rang De enables individuals to become social investors and lend small sums of money to borrowers from low income households listed on the website. The social investors get back their money with a nominal financial return and a tangible social return. The rationale behind Rang De is to the leverage the internet to deliver low cost microcredit to individuals from low income households. By raising social investments from individuals Rang De is able to deliver microcredit at interest rates ranging from 9 per cent APR to 15 per cent APR. Rang De currently operates in the following states: Maharashtra, Madhya Pradesh, West Bengal, Odisha, Karnataka, Kerala, Tamil Nadu, Gujarat, Bihar, Jharkhand and Manipur. The organization is in advanced stages of due diligence of field partners in states such as Rajasthan and Chhattisgarh. Rang De has significantly expanded its operations and has had some fantastic field partnerships including Bhagini Nivedita Gramin Vigyan Niketan (BNGVN)—which is run by Magsaysay Awardee Ms Nileema Mishra. Many field partners are setting up dedicated branches for Rang De's social capital. For three of Rang De's field partners, the total disbursal has crossed ₹10 million. Rang De's disbursals have increased from ₹0.30 million per month in January 2012 to ₹ 5 million. The organization aims to cross monthly disbursal of ₹10 million by November 2012. Rang De will thus be crossing ₹100 million of annual disbursals by the end of the financial year. In terms of outreach, Rang De covered 12,789 borrowers across India till 2012 with the addition of 72 per cent than the previous year. Rang De has tested some new models of engagement for social investors. Rang De's Education loans for primary, secondary and professional skill development have all been well received by social investors. The organization hopes to disburse more than ₹10 million for education loans during this financial year. Many foundations and corporate houses have come forward to participate in Rang De as part of their CSR initiatives.

Source: Primary information from Rang De.

A robust credit bureau infrastructure, in the long-run, can cause a large-scale mobilization of quality credit, thus in turn triggering financial literacy, availability of more financial products and ultimately, a healthier financial ecosystem.

The need of a Microfinance Credit Bureau Infrastructure in India was triggered mainly by two factors—

1. Regulatory changes brought in by RBI allowing MFIs to register as NBFC-MFIs, and making it mandatory for NBFC-MFIs to register with at least one credit information company (CIC),
2. The strong need in the industry to know about the other liabilities of its borrowers and their performance on those.

In this backdrop, High Mark Credit Information Services (High Mark) launched the country's first Microfinance Credit Bureau in March 2011.

High Mark today has 119 Microfinance institutions as its members. High Mark has provided its proprietary tool—*MFI Connect™* to enable easy Data Mapping, Validation and Submission. The recent members to join this bureau platform include several NGOs and Societies that are beginning to participate actively and are working with High Mark to identify fields that need to be captured accurately, digitized and mapped for bureau submission. The data captured in High Mark's database is of individuals who have been given credit through—JLG, SHG or direct lending. As on date, 74 institutions regularly contribute data to High Mark's bureau database, which now has data on 80 million loan records (active and closed) of 45 million customers, making it the world's largest Microfinance data base. In addition, there was a perceptible and steady increase in the number of enquiries during the last one year which confirms the greater utility of the credit bureau (Figure 3.17).

High Mark has also, in an attempt to simplify and promote bureau usage amongst its members, provided over 1500 installations of *Credit Assist™*, a proprietary report consumption platform for branches to view summaries of the reports, based on their conformance to the RBI/Industry/Institution's guidelines. Of the 74 data contributors, 57 are regularly using High Mark for their credit report referencing, as a key input in their loan sanctioning process. In the last 16 months, 12.8 million credit references have been made with High Mark. About 37 per cent of the inquired cases have been found to have one or more loans with another institution.

In line with global experience of the benefits accrued by using credit bureaus, the MFI industry in India has begun to see a positive impact. MFIs have reported an increase in accountability among

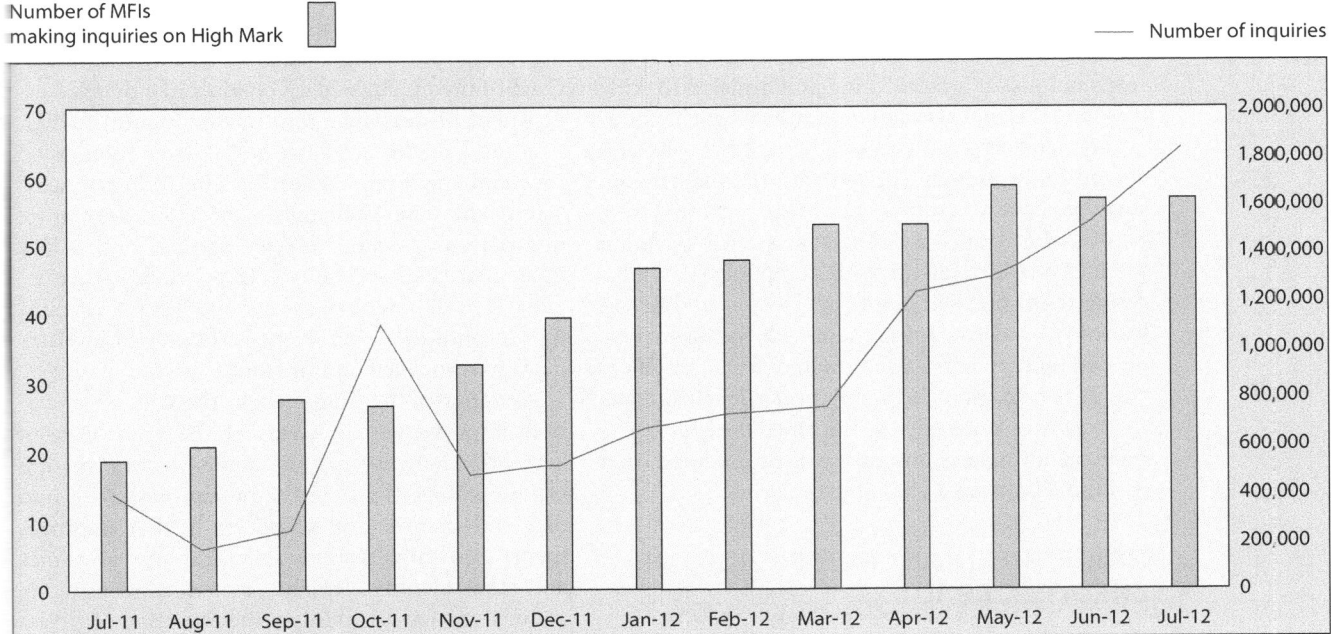

Figure 3.17 Number of enquiries with High Mark during 2011–12

Source: Data from High Mark bureau data base.

MFI borrowers because of credit referencing with a bureau. Some institutions have reported that since adopting High Mark Credit reports, wilful defaults have reduced amongst MFI borrowers; as they are clearing off their outstanding to get a clean credit history, building the foundation for a sound credit culture among borrowers. Although some MFIs may be using the bureau from regulatory perspective, it has been amply proven that bureau usage results in better originations/risk management. Since the database now contains most of the MFI lending information from across the country, new member institutions can immediately benefit with bureau referencing, as soon as they join and begin sharing data.

MFIN is advocating the use of credit bureau among member MFIs and others since June 2012, MFIN has made it mandatory for all members to use credit bureau reports as part of their loan approval processes. As of now, all 44 MFIN members have registered with at least one credit bureau and are sharing data on a regular basis and are using credit bureau reports in their loan approval processes. Forty-three of these have signed up with two bureaus—High Mark and Equifax, the other bureau that also caters to this industry. Further, all MFIN members have recently signed a No Objection Certificate (NOC) that will allow credit bureaus to share statistics on credit report usage by MFIs. This will help MFIN monitor and enforce, with greater stringency, the use of credit bureau reports for loan processing.

In the long run, MFIN intends to use credit bureaus not just as a monitoring and decision making tool for MFIs, but also as a mechanism by which microfinance borrowers can build credit histories and eventually become integrated with the mainstream financial system. To this end, MFIN and IFC have partnered to launch a financial awareness program for microfinance clients with components of educating them on their rights and responsibilities as borrowers and equipping them with the basic tools needed for managing cash flow and debt. The objective of the program is to empower clients to make financially responsible and informed decisions. The financial awareness program will be executed on a pan India basis, in a phased manner.

GRAMEEN FINANCIAL SERVICES IN CREDIT BUREAU

Grameen Financial Services (GFSPL or GK), which is operating in 42 districts across the states of Karnataka, Maharashtra and Tamil Nadu is currently serving more than 0.4 million clients with financial and non-financial services. This is one among the first set of MFIs to join credit bureau initiatives and initiate data quality improvements. Basic information of the Key Customer Data relation to identification particulars with KYC, active and default loan particulars are provided with credit bureaus (CBs) on a weekly basis since April 2012 (earlier monthly basis).

The experience by Grameen Financial services reiterates the simple and effortless data submission through web portal with feedback of error and warning on the quality of data submission. At present data, quality has improved significantly and current acceptance rate is 99.94 per cent. A small percentage of data is rejected due to the absence of a usable borrower's name and address.

With referencing of bureau reports, the quality of lending has seen significant improvement and no fresh income generation loan gets sanctioned without CB inquiry and no new members joined without verifying with CB. More than 0.49 million CB inquiries have been made during the year and there is positive feedback from field staff with the increased confidence levels. As a case example, Grameen Financial Services reports that during the first inquiry in January 2012, a customer had borrowed from two MFIs and her loan was rejected by GFSPL. She cleared her loan with one MFI in February 2012 and brought loan clearance certificate from the MFI. Based on the second bureau inquiry in April 2012, loan is given to the customer by GK.

During the design stage of the Microfinance Credit Bureau, High Mark conducted a detailed assessment of customer information captured, digitized and readily available for Bureau submission (September–December 2010). The industry faced significant data challenges—very low degrees of digitization, incomplete data capture, and a lack of standardization. Figure 3.18 provides a 'then vs. 'now' view of how 16 of the top 20 MFIs in the country (accounting for 60–65 per cent of MFI industry data) have evolved on this front.

As reported by High Mark, there is a perceptible improvement in terms of the availability of key KYC elements and the quality of information captured since the time the bureau has come into play, but there is still scope for further improvement, especially around better capture of names and other identity elements, as well as in bringing about a greater discipline in the reporting of closed accounts. Further, most State bodies and banks that do SHG lending do not capture individual level data for the SHG accounts, and therefore are unable to monitor or update this information on a periodic

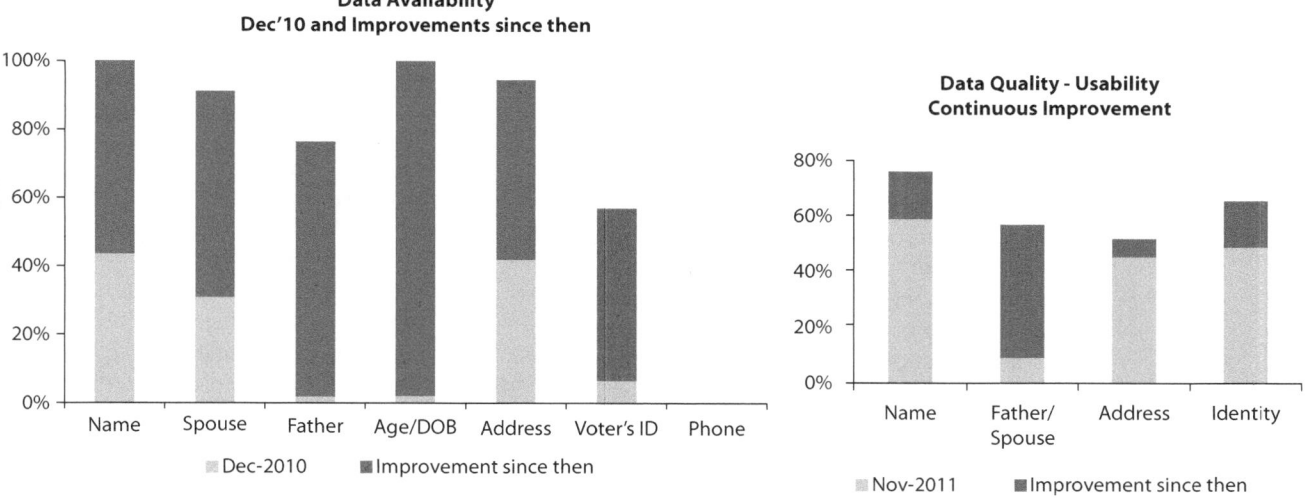

Figure 3.18 Improvement in data availability and quality
Source: Data from High Mark bureau data base.

basis. A further improvement in data quality (not just from a bureau perspective but overall) and effective use of bureau referencing will certainly help improve the sector's confidence level among investors and lenders alike.

There is an urgent need to impress upon the MFIs and other stakeholders in microfinance sector about the need for active participation in the credit bureau activities, and adequate funding support is needed at least in the initial stage of development, till the credit bureau stabilizes. The integration of appropriate technology support with coordinated efforts by all the players in the industry will go a long way to achieve comprehensive capture of credit information and needs to be addressed on a priority basis for active use of the credit bureau, and in fostering a healthy microfinance ecosystem in the country.

GOVERNANCE

The governance of MFIs is one of the relevant issues being debated in the context of the crisis situation. MFI boards have often been blamed for not steering the growth of the institutions with due care and for not balancing the social and financial goals of the MFIs.[17] The role of MFI governance is quite different from the mainstream financial institutions since the fact that MFI clients are vulnerable and often uneducated about finance is sinking into the boards of MFIs. Constitution of quality boards and establishing good governance practices has become very important in dealing with the external scrutiny of for-profit organizations. With a view to ensuring

good governance some of the MFIs have already inducted qualified professionals with required skill sets into their boards who have the capacity to focus on social and financial goals. MFIs are having a relook at CEO compensation, since high pay packets are largely paid out of the interest paid by poor clients, and there has been a concern that board should fix reasonable compensation. Investors reported paying more attention to the quality of governance in due diligence, agreements and reporting frameworks. Investor board representatives have largely been supportive of the balanced returns and fund allocation for non-financial welfare activities. While, in general, directors nominated to fill board seats for investors bring useful expertise and perspectives, their duty of loyalty and their willingness and ability to balance social and financial goals and targets have been an area of concern. A recent development in a few boards is the appointment of a subcommittee for social performance management or appointing an SPM director to monitor the social performance and responsible financing practices. While boards are largely monitoring the compliance of regulatory norms and code of conduct requirements, a few boards are setting social goals in terms of outreach with segmentation, product usage and even setting targets for movement clients out of poverty.

TRANSPARENCY

Microfinance industry in the changing environment requires a new level of understanding and openness about the costs of lending in small units and transparent communication of the prices charged to cover those costs. An industry born to displace the moneylenders by providing low-cost credit to the working poor needs to ensure that its clients have clear information about the cost of the money they borrow. Till now there is no single market rate and there was a tendency of confused pricing under the unregulated environment. Practicing pricing transparency will certainly contribute to building a healthy and vibrant market for microcredit products by providing a valuable component necessary for free and competitive markets to develop open communication about the actual pricing. Transparency is extremely critical for MFIs to build trust with clients and all other stakeholders in today's environment. This would include: (a) Educating (not just informing) low-income clients on all product terms, as per the contract (including interest to be paid or received); (b) Enabling clients to understand all other policies of the institution (such as penalties for repayment, recovery processes, etc.) and the working model; and (c) Ensuring that the product terms, policies and models are not distorted during implementation through appropriate controls. Only this will enable clients to make informed and knowledgeable purchase choices and MFIs must strive to facilitate this. The interest rate issue is critical and clients need to know the interest rates they are paying or receiving and MFIs must clearly indicate the nominal and effective interest rates as well as total cost to client under normal and delinquent situations. The RBI has also issued its pricing guidelines and has specified the components of pricing that can be charged on microcredit loans and has also recommended the MFIs to communicate the effective interest rates to the clients. These prices were comparable as they were calculated uniformly for all the participating MFIs using the standard APR and EIR methodology. However, the industry needs such initiatives on an ongoing basis. The proposed India MIX type information platform (being set up by SIDBI) will hopefully take up the transparency agenda further.

SUMMING UP

Ever since the process of bringing the sector under a regulatory regime and tabling the Microfinance Bill in May 2012, MFIs have been reasonably assured of future stability. As a result, the path that many leading MFIs may take under the regulated environment is likely to earn them lower margins than before. This needs to be viewed as an opportunity for MFIs to reinvent themselves and search for new avenues to serve customers. Although MFIs have been reluctant to move away from their specialization of financial services delivery to the unbanked, it would be useful to explore the provision of other services, which are crucial to their operational area, especially to their key client segments. Not only will this build loyalty and a lasting relationship with their clients, it may also positively impact repayment rates as the quality of life of clients and their families improves. In doing so, MFIs would also protect themselves from being viewed as moneylenders and opportunists by political forces and societal sceptics.

With severe controls and restrictions on uncollateralized lending, MFIs have begun to explore other routes for extending loans such as gold loans, SME sector loans, asset loans and loans without group guarantee. MFIs, which had evolved from NGOs and Section 25 Companies, have explored possibilities of their parent institutions partnering with banks as BCs to make use of the human resources which were lying idle during the fund crunch. During the crisis-induced lull in operations, operational processes and products have been re-engineered to ensure highest levels of responsibility to clients. The way forward in product development is likely to be highly client-centric, as MFIs strive to avoid future crises. MFIs need to actively engage themselves as partners in the financial inclusion programme and integrate their vision and mission with the state and central government to achieve a prosperous future for the customers. In achieving a higher standard of excellence of customer centric services, MFIs need all possible support, not only from policy and regulation, but also from the other stakeholders.

ANNEX—3.1[1]
Innovative products by Indian microfinance institutions

Details of different categories of innovative products, highlighting some of the best practices by MFIs in the industry, and illustrating innovative product features and processes are presented in this annexure. *While many MFIs have fine-tuned their product features to the requirements of their clients and their institutional priorities and constraints, only a few products and services have been featured here, as an indication of the variety of options available for developing a meaningful association with clients.*

LOANS TO GRADUATED CLIENTS

Some MFIs recognized that a significant proportion of their clients had outgrown the group systems and constraints of group meetings and co-guaranteeing. Products for graduated borrowers and new, middle-income level clients were structured with monthly repayments for some and daily repayments for others, based on the nature of business cash flows.

GENERAL PRODUCT FEATURES: Available to clients after they have completed a specified number of loan cycles or years with the MFI, or have reached the maximum borrowing limit on group loans. This product is offered only to clients with a perfect repayment record.

SOME OF THE MFIs IN THIS SPACE: **Satin Credit Care** was one of the pioneers of individual lending to businesses in Delhi. The product entailed daily collections at the client's shop and was very popular with traders. Other MFIs such as **Spandana, Future Financial Services Ltd,** and **SHARE** designated separate branches for 'daily collection loans'. **CASHPOR's** Bada Loan was developed to cater to clients who had successfully repaid the highest group loan size of ₹18,000.

BEST PRACTICES: (*a*) Administered by a separate set of staff; (*b*) Detailed appraisal of client businesses to ensure that business volume can support repayments; (*c*) Ensures that client has a savings route also by disbursing the loan only in a savings bank account.

ADVANTAGES: Group clients have an aspirational target to reach, which acts as a good repayment incentive.

DISADVANTAGES: Loan size and repayment period are constrained by regulatory restrictions leaving a very limited scope for flexibility in product design.

> **CASHPOR** offered its Bada Loan to clients of three cycles over a minimum period of two years with a perfect repayment record. The loan size ranged from ₹15,000–25,000, and clients had to have a savings bank into which the loan amount was credited. Guarantee by a family member was compulsory and both client and guarantor were insured. Repayments were in 46 weekly instalments over a period of 52 weeks, leaving scope for flexibility in low-turnover periods of the business. The product was discontinued because of RBI guidelines, but will be reintroduced in the near future.

Source: Primary information from CASHPOR.

EMERGENCY LOANS

It was discovered that many clients were still approaching moneylenders to borrow small sums of money during emergencies, as MFI loans were not always accessible on demand. This resulted in the design of 'emergency loan' products.

GENERAL PRODUCT FEATURES: Usually available to clients in the 2nd loan cycle onwards; the amount equivalent to 4–10 instalments of the regular loan. Sometimes this is also called a seasonal/festival loan and can be used for seasonal expenditure incurred on unavoidable religious and social practices.

BEST PRACTICES:

1. The client should have a record of perfect repayment for at least a year;
2. For festival/seasonal loans, disbursement is restricted to certain times of the year;
3. May require special guarantee by a group member or leader to substitute detailed appraisal;
4. For health emergencies, disbursements should be made within 24 hours of demand;
5. Some MFIs offer such loans free of interest;
6. **Mahasemam Trust** offers a wedding loan of ₹15,000 which has a 10 day tenure.

[1]Valuable inputs and support provided by Dr Alok Mishra CEO, M-CRIL for preparing the Annexure is gratefully acknowledged.

It is usually repaid from cash gifts received at the wedding.

ADVANTAGES:

1. Enables the client to meet her exigency without approaching a moneylender;
2. Allows the MFI to fulfil the client's need and strengthen its relationship.

DISADVANTAGES:

1. Often misused to cover up overdues for two to three weeks;
2. Festival loan is viewed as encouragement to indulge in wasteful expenditure;
3. Loan amounts are usually too small to cover more than a fraction of costs in a serious health emergency.

MFIs began to understand that insisting that clients use loans only for income generation purposes was unrealistic. Clients would invariably use part of the loan for business and the rest to pay off earlier debts, childrens' school fees or other pressing needs. The first few 'consumption loans' for school fees, water filters, etc., were designed around these needs.

OTHER CONSUMPTION LOANS

GENERAL PRODUCT FEATURES: Available to clients after they have completed at least one-two loan cycles with the MFI, with perfect repayment. Given for purposes, which would improve quality of life for customers—water connection, water purifying equipment, toilet construction, solar lighting, payment for institutional delivery (pregnancy loan), and childrens' school fees. Sometimes these are given for purchase of small assets, which would indirectly enhance productivity, such as bicycle or mobile phone.

BEST PRACTICES:

1. MFIs which leverage on in-house or external technical expertise in water, sanitation, health, etc., may perform better in ensuring proper utilization of such loans, by ensuring purchase of good material and good construction quality. **Guardian** leverages on its parent NGO **Gramalaya's** experience in water and sanitation to provide loans exclusively for a variety of health and sanitation purposes. **Grameen Financial Services** provides technical support for water connection and toilet installations through its spin-off, **NavyaDisha Trust**.
2. Tie-in with an institution's overall mission is important. **Hand in Hand**, whose focus is on women's empowerment offered a pregnancy loan to cover expectant women's institutional delivery costs from a combination of own savings and an HIH loan.
3. Sometimes these loans are offered in tie-ups with providers to ensure lower prices and proper quality. **SKS** has tied up with Nokia for supplying handsets to borrowers at a lower price, paid over 25 easy instalments. Leveraging on SKS's outreach, Nokia has sold over 0.32 million handsets to SKS customers, spelling a win-win for SKS, Nokia and the clients. Similarly, Sonata's tie up with Hero for cycles has removed the distributor's margin thereby reducing the price for clients, as well as saving their time and opportunity cost of buying from a dealer. Tie-ups should be made with well-known and popular brands, with a history of excellent after-sales service.
4. Ensuring proper utilization is important: **Ujjivan** requires documentary proof for its education loans such as the child's report card or fee receipts. **Guardian** also has strict operational guidelines for checks on loan utilization.

ADVANTAGES:

1. Such products give a competitive advantage and ensure client retention even if competitors offer lower interest rates on regular loans.
2. These products also enable MFIs to meet the actual needs of their clients and to track utilization effectively.
3. Tie-ups with technical/material providers increase the efficacy of these loans several-fold.

DISADVANTAGES

1. Usually these loans face shortfalls as income-generating loans are prioritized especially in fund-crunch periods.

2. Being low ticket size products, they usually need to be offered as add-ons to regular loans to make them cost effective.
3. A risk of tie-ups is that problems with product quality could result in default on the loan.
4. As product offering is such that it is not required repeatedly, MFIs incur higher costs in acquiring new clients.

Some MFIs feel that it is not necessary to structure separate consumption purpose loans, as money is fungible and clients invariably use a small part of their income generation loans for consumption anyway. Others MFIs are wary of emergency loans because they can be frittered away on impulsive expenses. Suresh Krishna, MD of Grameen Financial Services takes a different view, saying:

> We are too caught up in ensuring that clients use every rupee productively to generate income. This is unrealistic. Clients also live normal lives and have needs that revolve around family and social events. If an emergency loan is used for a family celebration it is something we have to factor in while designing the loan. Stipulating that all loans must be used for productive purposes only encourages clients to lie or misuse the loan. This is why GFS has structured a separate loan for each of the important consumption needs in addition to income generation loans.

Source: Discussion with different MFIs.

MFIs that had broken even went a step further to offer non-financial services to their clients in order to retain their loyalty. Some of these MFIs sought to plough back some of their profits in the form of support to destitute and ultra-poor, who needed more than just financial support to rise above poverty. MFIs see this as providing a crucial service to the poorest in their operational areas, while also investing in a potential future market segment. Others offered their clients scholarships for their children, subsidized treatment in designated hospitals, organized health camps and distributed gifts to vintage clients and centre leaders as a gesture of goodwill. Some MFIs have also designed financial literacy programmes, which are undertaken in-house or by partner tie-ups. Financial awareness is seen to be a critical factor for avoiding over-borrowing and bad credit decisions.

NON-FINANCIAL SERVICES

GENERAL PRODUCT FEATURES: Differ in target segment: Some non-financial services are undertaken for ultra-poor beneficiaries who are not yet eligible for loans, but require grants and other support (ultra-poor programmes, vocational training, income-generating asset distribution, schools for poorest children). Some MFIs provide non-financial services to existing clients and their families or community in the operational area at large (health camps, financial education). Others provide these services to the best borrowers as an incentive to the others (business development training, sustainable farming practices). These services may be provided by the MFI directly, or through its parent/sister NGO.

Bandhan Konnagar focuses on poverty alleviation through livelihoods, health and education interventions, funded from a portion of surplus from the microfinance activities of **Bandhan Financial Services**.

1. The hard core poor programme (THP) identifies ultra-poor families and gives them productive assets and know-how to help them emerge from poverty in two years.
2. Health programme (BHP) creates health awareness amongst mothers and girls and improves accessibility to health services through community volunteers.
3. Education programme (BEP) supports 'out of school' children and dropouts for enrolment in secondary schools.
4. Employment programme (EUP) trains, guides and links youth to decent job opportunities.

SKS funds a similar ultra-poor programme, which is run by **SKS Foundation** and involves the beneficiary being given an asset, training and health inputs to begin a sustainable income generating enterprise. **Ujjivan**, in association with **Parinaam Foundation** has provided financial literacy training to its clients as well as the larger community through (*a*) a film on perils of indebtedness and pipelining and the necessity of a good credit record, screened at all Ujjivan branches and viewed by 0.35 million people on cable TV and (*b*) module-based training on comprehensive financial services for a pilot of 372 customers. Parinaam also provides services in healthcare, education, and community development to Ujjivan's clients and the broader community, thereby fostering good relations in Ujjivan's operational area.

Grameen Financial Services has piloted 18 education centres in rural Karnataka with learning programmes for pre-school, primary and high school children. The centres have been set up in partnership with Hippocampus Learning Centres. GFS has also undertaken a client education initiative, covering health, sanitation, gender issues, alcoholism and many other relevant topics through a weekly letter written from a fictional client 'Jagriti', read by field staff at the centre meetings. Jagriti's letters are scripted by Phicus, a development consultancy firm promoted by GFS and Cocoon Consulting.

IDF Financial Services through its parent NGO, **IDF Foundation**, has implemented an innovative project called Sujeevan on financial inclusion for livelihood security of small and marginal farmers, landless labourers and tenants. The project aims at financial inclusion of farm families through a BC tie-up with SBI, and promotion of sustainable livelihoods through participatory, group-based training of farmers in improved agricultural practices.

Equitas conducts training in candle making, dressmaking, embroidery, food processing and other income generating activities through its training centre **Equitas Gyaan Kendra**. Market linkages have been forged with ITC, Lijjat etc., for sale of the products. Equitas also conducts health camps (general, eye and dental), and covers the cost of spectacles, cataract operations and cancer screening.

Programmes integrated in microfinance activities

CASHPOR in partnership with **Healing Fields Foundation (HFF)** has trained 90 women among its clients for six months to become a full-fledged Community Health Leaders (CHLs). Each of such 90 CHLs provides health intermediary services to 300 client households, thereby reaching a population of around 135,000. CASHPOR hopes to improve health seeking behaviour, hygiene and dietary habits, and increase awareness of healthcare programmes offered by the government, to reduce incidence of preventable diseases over two to four years.

Centre Managers in 12 branches across three provide 15 minutes of health education for clients in each centre meeting after conducting their normal loan transactions. Fifty-seven per cent clients have been covered till date. CMs have been trained by CASHPOR's training department with inputs from **Freedom from Hunger** and the **Micro Credit Summit Campaign**.

Samhita realized the benefits of financial literacy training from a pilot program and integrated this with its Pre-Enrolment training to nascent groups. To ensure that operational costs did not rise, redundant material from the training was replaced with modules on various financial services and how to choose the best providers. Customized and durable, low-cost flipcharts are used to keep costs low. Samhita has tied up with the NPS Lite pension product, after customers became aware of the benefits of pension and began demanding the service.

Mahasemam Trust has a unique 'goat donation programme', which is funded by donations from its staff and external well-wishers. Poor families are identified within Mahasemam's operational villages. A pregnant goat is donated to these families. Once the goat gives birth, the family donates one of the kids to another poor family. Community involvement ensures that appropriate beneficiaries are selected. Families prefer goats as these are low-maintenance animals, which can be sold profitably or bred further.

BEST PRACTICES:

1. MFIs either apportion a part of the year's profits for non-financial activities or raise grants independently.
2. The activities may be undertaken by the parent NGO or sister concern of the MFI, or by a separate set of staff, so as not to mix roles of field staff.
3. Some MFIs have successfully mixed non-financial services with microfinance activities to enhance the involvement of field staff and ensure client attendance (CASHPOR, GFS's Jagriti and Samhita).
4. Activities should be prioritized based on community needs, within the MFI's funding constraints.

ADVANTAGES: Non-financial services help to cement the relationship between the community and the MFI as the local people identify the MFI with its social mission rather than just as a financial service provider.

DISADVANTAGES: Field staff may be over-burdened if they undertake the provision of both financial and non-financial services.

> Praseeda Kunam of Samhita says, '*Financial literacy is absolutely essential for microfinance clients. Our agenda as MFIs should be to empower the poor with awareness to secure and build on the little money they have, not just to lend to them*'.

Source: Discussion by author,

LOANS FOR SPECIFIC ENTERPRISES OR BUSINESS SEGMENTS

GENERAL PRODUCT FEATURES: Usually available to a segment, which is completely distinct from the group lending target segment. Comprises middle-level businesses with high working capital requirements but may lack documentation and awareness to approach banks. These loans require extensive appraisal of customer credentials as well as business performance and its future prospects. These loans may conform to RBI guidelines for priority sector lending in terms of loan size, collateral requirements and pricing, or not; this would determine the extent of portfolio they constitute, as non-compliant loans require to be capped at 15 per cent of portfolio. These loans are offered to both men and women entrepreneurs as individuals, or in small groups of five to six.

Swadhaar FinServe has identified segments, which required credit over and above the group lending limits:

1. Semi-mobile businesses;
2. Small businesses at fixed location—food businesses, traders or service providers;
3. Wholesalers/large retailers;
4. Home-based manufacturing businesses.

A separate vertical was created to cater to these businesses with loan sizes ranging from ₹20,000 to ₹0.10 million at 36 per cent p.a. interest and three per cent processing fee for 12 months. Swadhaar recruited a separate line of Loan Officers who were familiar with business appraisal, street-smart and presentable. Swadhaar marketed its loans to businesses, which had run from the same location for 10–15 years. Despite having no collateral requirement, the product was very popular and constituted 30 per cent of portfolio and 20 per cent of clients, before the RBI guidelines came into force, resulting in a deliberate effort to run down this portfolio by not disbursing loans to new clients.

Arohan has designed two types of loans to cater to segments other than low-income women. (*a*) *Pragati loans* are offered to individuals involved in manufacturing businesses and employing at least three wage labourers. Loans range from ₹40,000 to 0.20 million at 30 per cent p.a. interest and four per cent loan processing fee for 12–36 months and monthly repayment is made through PDCs. (*b*) Bazaar loans are offered to groups of traders undertaking a common type of business within a small area of a recognized permanent marketplace. These are typically vegetable, fruit and flower vendors, fishmongers, etc., who operate in close proximity in municipal markets. Arohan first builds a good rapport with the Market Committee and after getting permission to operate there sends in its team of staff to mobilize trader groups. Loan sizes are small at ₹6,000 to 18,000, with weekly repayments over 45 weeks at 26 per cent p.a. interest with 1 per cent processing fee. By offering two products, Arohan has catered to manufacturing and trading businesses with appropriate offerings. Bazaar loan conforms with RBI guidelines while Pragati loan is outside the priority sector lending norms.

SKS has designed a Sangam Store Loan to serve its large base of kirana shop (Sangam store) customers ~10 per cent of its seven million clients. SKS has targeted clients with good attendance and perfect repayment over at least one completed group cycle. The product serves store owners with a credit line to source products cheaply from a reliable wholesaler, Metro Cash and Carry (India) Pvt Ltd. The credit limit is based on evaluation of the business, daily average sales, and weekly purchase costs. The product is a non-cash loan, with no group guarantee, thereby posing very little risk to SKS. The SKS Loan officer who visits the store conveys the real time information in terms of product availability and pricing from a list of 250 products. The order is taken according to the store's credit limit and is consolidated weekly for the city, and delivered to Metro, which delivers the goods to the client's store directly within 24 hours. SKS has also developed a mobile based MIS system to collect and consolidate orders and track the loan portfolio. For SKS, the product serves as a customer retention and portfolio diversification strategy, with short-term credit and good end-use monitoring. For Metro, it signifies a broad and readily available customer base to leverage, using SKS's trained manpower and mobile-based technology platform at no additional cost. For the clients, the partnership is a one-stop-solution for all stocking needs, with the combined benefit of doorstep delivery, credit period of seven days and delivery within 24 hours. Having succeed in Hyderabad, SKS is now expanding this programme to Bengaluru and Kolkata as well as to non-members. While SKS's earnings from Metro's margin currently do not cover costs, this program is the first step in creating distribution channels for a wide range of other non-financial products.

Janalakshmi Financial Services has a separate vertical for Enterprise Loans—Target businesses have > three years vintage and loan sizes range from ₹0.2 million to ₹1 million. Loan tenure is 12–36 months; repayment is through EMIs collected through post-dated cheques. A Fraud Control Unit investigates all applications. Loans are priced at 22 per cent p.a. and carry a 3 per cent processing charge, plus separate charges to cover credit bureau checks and appraisal costs. Guarantors are required for all loans, and are also appraised separately.

Utkarsh's Micro Enterprise Loan has been recently introduced and offers loans of ₹25,000 to ₹0.3 million. Guarantors are required for all loans and collateral for loans above ₹60,000. Repayments are made fortnightly or monthly at the convenience of the client over a term of 6–36 months. Interest charged is 29 per cent p.a. with a one per cent processing fee and insurance charge of one per cent. Utkarsh's aim is to serve a completely neglected segment, while diversifying its portfolio.

PFSPL (KGFS) offers Retailer loans, which are collateral free loans of relatively larger size (up to ₹50,000), for shop owners. A personal guarantee is required. Loans are repaid monthly at 27 per cent p.a. interest and processing fee of 0.5–1 per cent, depending on loan size.

BEST PRACTICES:

1. Janalakshmi has developed stringent processes for borrower and business appraisal.
2. SKS has catered to a specialized segment of member traders, whilst building a potential market of non-members who own kirana shops in SKS's operational areas. SKS has created a win-win for all parties, where Metro gains business volumes at no extra cost to itself; distributor margins of 7 per cent are now distributed between clients (5 per cent) and SKS (2 per cent). Clients also gain from special offers from Metro, while the credit line is interest free.
3. Swadhaar has identified its market with extensive research.
4. Arohan has segmented its market, balancing compliance with RBI guidelines.

ADVANTAGES:

1. Serving such markets poses a good risk diversification opportunity to MFIs.
2. Higher ticket sizes balance high appraisal costs.
3. Tie-up arrangements can cover costs without any additional charges to clients.

DISADVANTAGES:

1. These loans are invariably outside the scope of RBI guidelines with respect to loan size, as well as household income, interest charged (to cover high appraisal costs), etc.
2. If market research and client appraisal is not done very thoroughly, this segment can prove highly risky.

ASSET CREATION LOANS

GENERAL PRODUCT FEATURES: Usually available to clients of a certain vintage and good repayment record, sometimes non-members may also be eligible. Home loan appraisals usually revolve around land title documents of the borrower, repayment capacity of the family and imminent risks in the medium-long term. Asset creation loans are long term and require strong knowledge of the asset itself in terms of cost, market value, productivity, riskiness, etc.

Home loans and housing loans

Shalom Trust offers a housing loan product to its clients—they must be residents of the area with a monthly income of ₹3,000–5,000, living in substandard housing conditions for at least 10 years and having no liabilities. The loan is given only on the guarantee of fellow group members, and the client must be willing to render not less than 50 hrs of labour to his/her counter parts, in construction of other Shalom houses. Loans are given for new house construction, renovation and repairs and sanitation/ electrification. Loans range from ₹50,000 to ₹0.10 million based on plot dimensions. Disbursements are made in stages—

1. on completion of foundation;
2. on completion of walls;
3. completion of roofing; and
4. completion of plastering, fittings, etc. Loan term is 10 years, with monthly instalments and moratorium for six months. Loans are extended by Shalom Trust at three per cent above its cost of funds, with a 3 per cent processing fee.

Shalom Trust also offers a 'Save and Build' product, which aims at helping people save for building their own house. Applicants must be a member of an SHG at least for one year, with a good credit record and a guarantee from the group. The applicant should have saved ₹15,000 towards purchase of land and should be living in a dilapidated home or rented home currently. Credible NGOs are invited to mobilize eligible members to form a 'Save and Build' group of 15–25 members. The members have to save an amount of ₹1,200 to 2,000 per month until the construction is complete, after which they have to increase the savings in tune with their EMI. After six months of group formation, the Trust, jointly with group members identifies the land suitable for construction of houses and purchases the same in the Trust's name. The cost of land comes from accumulated beneficiary savings. Each home owner partner signs an Allottee agreement with the Trust. The houses constructed on the project site are uniform in nature and homeowners are not allowed to deviate from the approved plan. It is mandatory that every homeowner of Shalom house has to contribute stipulated manual labour for construction of their house and also 40 hours to a neighbour, thereby building a stake in the home and the overall project. The actual cost of the material, funding cost and technical inputs provided to the beneficiary is taken as the loan principal (expenses are divided on a pro-rata basis per house unit). The project is completed in six to nine months from the date of mortgage. On completion, the repayment of loan commences and continues for a period of 15 to 20 years. The homeowner is not entitled to transfer or rent the property, or make any alterations till the loan is fully repaid. The property is transferred to the homeowner on completion of repayment. Shalom Trust has a sister construction company, which has experience in low cost housing schemes and which undertakes the construction and provides technical inputs for the 'Save and Build' projects.

BSFL introduced the GrahSamruddhi product, which was developed mainly for rural clients, with a maximum loan size ₹0.15 million, seven year tenure and 18 per cent p.a. interest. However, it did not perform well as many rural clients lacked land titles. BSFL then piloted its RahenSahen Samruddhi product, developed in association with **Micro Home Loan Solutions (MHLS)**, in Mangolpuri and Sultanpuri colonies in Delhi. Forty-five clients having cash flows of ₹20,000–30,000 and the original land allotment slips from Municipal Corporation of Delhi were chosen. Though the allotment slips constitute a non-enforceable guarantee as the property is non-transferable, people fear losing it as it signifies their title to the land. BSFL collaborated with ACC cement to conduct workshops on building structure norms. BSFL also tied up with **Baliga Trust**, which had been working in the area for 30 years, to promote the product. Loan sizes were ₹50,000 to ₹0.30 million. Technical assistance was provided by MHLS, including the building plan, and construction norms. Clients were charged a 3 per cent technical assistance fee and a three per cent processing fee and are paying 27 per cent interest p.a. A 2 per cent interest rebate for timely loan closure has been offered. Loan tenure was fixed at five years, with monthly repayment. Following the AP crisis, BSFL has stopped these loans.

One of the key observations of the NABARD Committee on Rural Habitat is that there is a need to cater to the housing requirements of the very poor, who prefer to undertake house construction in incremental stages for which appropriate financing products need to be designed. The Committee has recommended that short duration incremental housing loans for different components such as laying foundation, tiled roofing, flooring, fixtures, etc., should be provided in a modular funding model at different points of time. **Swarna Pragati** has introduced such incremental housing to ensure that progressive upgradation/ construction of a house is financed in modules of ₹10,000 to ₹20,000. Loan amounts average ₹40,000— ₹80,000 released in small modules, with average loan terms of 36–48 months. Borrowers complete the construction of their homes through a series of loans.

Source: NABARD.

Janalakshmi Social Services (parent institution of Janalakshmi Financial Services), has invested in Janadhar Constructions Pvt. Ltd (JCPL), a construction company exclusively for low cost housing. JCPL tied up with builders having core competencies in low cost design, to build low cost apartments half of which are sold exclusively to families with monthly income of ₹15,000–25,000 (need not be existing JFS customers). The loans extended by JFS are up to 80 per cent of the cost of the apartment (₹0.6–0.7 million), at 12.5 per cent interest p.a., while the customer pays 20 per cent of the cost as a margin money. Loan tenure is 15–20 years with monthly repayments. The remaining apartments are sold at market value in the open market, for cross subsidization. JFS and JCPL faced some challenge in converting demand into sales because of rigorous screening of applicants, lack of applicant's cash surplus for margin money, and rising construction costs. However, the project is being scaled up, and JFS is in talks with National Housing Bank for funding.

Other asset loans

Margdarshak has recently piloted a '2nd cattle financing' loan of ₹25,000 for its clients who have completed a year of good repayment and already own one milch animal. Client eligibility norms include residence in permanent accommodation in a rural area. The product aims to compensate loss of milk yield during the lean period of the first animal. Loans are extended to groups of five members and are given jointly to husband and wife as both are intended to participate in the livestock upkeep and milk sale. Technical training is provided by Margdarshak's expert livestock officer. Loans are compliant with RBI guidelines and livestock are insured at ₹1,700 for the two-year repayment period.

Bhartiya Micro Credit with support from America India Foundation started the *Rickshaw Sangh* programme in Uttar Pradesh. This is an innovative social business venture that enables pullers of rented rickshaws to acquire their own vehicle. Through partnership with banks and grass root NGOs, it enables rickshaw drivers to take loans that are repaid in easy daily/weekly instalments. The central idea of the programme is to promote asset ownership among urban poor and rural migrants. Apart from enabling the rickshaw pullers to become the owner, the programme ensures that they are organized into a *Rickshaw Sangh*. Rickshaw Bank enabled a large number of rickshaw pullers to invest in efficiency-enhancing rickshaws, so that they could own the vehicle in 18 months instead of making daily rental payments to owners. Rickshaw pullers were also able to enhance their income as the superior design of the re-engineered rickshaws increased their efficiency and speed, enabling them to fit more trips into a day.

BEST PRACTICES:

1. Such loans should be administered by a completely separate set of staff who are trained in evaluation of both client and underlying documentation/asset quality.
2. Tie-ups with construction companies/technical service providers are essential. If the MFI can ensure that the client is getting a high quality asset, then it can be surer of the repayment rate as well.
3. A significant monetary stake in the asset must come from the client. Encouraging client/family participation in home construction can build a stake in the home as well.
4. It is essential to insure the asset as well as the key breadwinners of the family against death and accidents.
5. All family income sources and risks need to be factored in to the client appraisal.

ADVANTAGES: Such loans offer aspirational value to existing group clients and also act as a good selling point for attracting new members. Asset financing can be provided far cheaper by MFIs than by other non-bank providers.

DISADVANTAGES:

1. Loan sizes are constrained by the RBI guidelines, so home loans will fall out of the priority sector lending norms.
2. Such loans may be at high risk if underlying asset quality is not good. In situations where fake titles to land are produced, MFIs may face risks later.
3. Sudden loss of income source for the client or key breadwinners in the family may severely affect the repayment rate.

LOANS TO SPECIFIC SEGMENTS

GENERAL PRODUCT FEATURES: THE client segment is defined by socio-economic characteristics, location, etc.

Mahasemam Trust/SMILE offers a loan product to destitute persons, of ₹1,000 payable without interest in instalments decided at the time of the disbursement by the beneficiaries.

BSFL PIONEERED EXTENSION OF CROP LOANS AND LIVESTOCK LOANS EXCLUSIVELY TO FARMERS, SCHEDULING THE REPAYMENTS AS PER THEIR CASH FLOWS. SIMILAR loans were structured for sheep rearing and purchase of agriculture inputs at interest rate of 24 per cent p.a. Farmers formed JLGs of four to six members and repaid loans in bullet repayments after three to six months, or enjoyed a moratorium of four to six months, making monthly payments thereafter. These loans performed very well, even during loan waivers and political campaigns until the AP crisis. BSFL also extended loans to ROSCAs so that they could access funds in excess of their own savings.

Many poor families who migrate out of the Tamia block of Chhindwara as seasonal labour, take credit from contractors to meet their migration related expenses. The contractors in turn force them to work for meagre wages. To address this situation, and MFI in the area, **MahilaSmriddhi Bank-PararthSamiti**, is pilot testing a four-month migration loan with a bullet repayment, to enable migrants to earn 60–80 per cent more.

BEST PRACTICES: Such loans need to be structured after carefully observing the borrower group—evaluating cash flows is vital, but it is also necessary to evaluate business risk or inherent traits of the group itself.

ADVANTAGES: MFIs can reach out to different socio-economic categories and expand their market.

DISADVANTAGES: May prove risky if adequate study of the group's behaviour and underlying risk profile is not undertaken.

Many Muslims hail from low income groups across India and typically lack access to bank credit, as documented in the Sachar committee report (2006). Islamic microfinance through Shari'a compliant products may spell an end to the exclusion of the low-income Muslims and may reduce incidents like the Kolar crisis in Karnataka in 2009.

Source: SOS, 2009.

MARKET LINKAGES

GENERAL PRODUCT FEATURES: Comprises backward linkages—sourcing high quality inputs for client businesses or forward linkages—marketing produce manufactured by clients.

ESAF Retail Ltd, a specialized supermarket set up by **ESAF Microfinance (EMFIL)**, markets locally produced food and consumables, manufactured by its group members under the *Swasraya Bazar* brand through six stores in Thrissur. Products are sourced from primary producers; price benefit is passed on to consumers. ESAF's team inspects product quality and also provides training in packing, branding, grading, etc., thereby ensuring that locally sourced products are made saleable in mainstream retail stores. Group members who are successfully linked are trained to increase production capacity for economies of scale.

IDF Foundation supports SHG members and rural artisans for market linkage of their products through a tie-up with its sister concern, **GramyaPvt. Ltd**, which undertakes product branding, marketing and sales of these products.

Madura Micro Finance Ltd (MMFL) has a 'Micro marketing' effort—a free ads magazine is published and circulated to all member SHGs which informs them about products manufactured and traded by MMFL's members across Tamil Nadu. MMFL coordinates marketing of these products across its groups by aggregating demand and organizing the transport of produce across its operational area. MMFL's team also helps clients market their produce in the open market by building a supply chain, and giving entrepreneurs business training to improve their capacity for doing business profitably.

BEST PRACTICES: Tie-ups are essential for linkages and MFIs need to devise low cost aggregation of produce as well as timely aggregation of demand and link these. Demand assessment and deep study of intermediaries is crucial.

ADVANTAGES: Linkage activities encourage retention and good repayment rates by ensuring that clients do not fail in their business activity.

DISADVANTAGES: Marketing activities may pose a strain on microfinance staff and dilute their efficiency. Despite the best efforts, if marketing does not result in sales, both clients and MFI will be at a loss.

OTHER FINANCIAL SERVICES

GENERAL PRODUCT FEATURES: These include savings through banking correspondent arrangements; Pensions and Insurance through tie-ups; and Remittances.

SAVINGS—**Janalakshmi** has leveraged its parent organization JSS to enter into a BC arrangement with Axis Bank. JSS has so far overachieved on its target accounts per month. Clients can save weekly, fortnightly, monthly or even on demand. JSS staff operate from JFS branches at marginal incremental cost. Staff are equipped with Axis Bank's POS terminals to do real time reporting of collections, directly synced to Axis Bank's CBS, thereby preventing any fraud. Eighty per cent accounts are active with an average balance of ₹450–500. Only 20–25 per cent of savings customers are existing JFS clients, which opens up a huge potential pool of new relationships for JFS.

INSURANCE—**PFSPL (KGFS)**: PFSPL provides its clients tie-up products for Personal Accident Insurance, Term-Life Insurance and Livestock insurance at reasonable rates. What sets PFSPL apart from other MFIs is that its insurance tie-up products are entirely voluntary and that its compulsory credit-life insurance for loan clients is not charged to the clients, but paid by PFSPL itself. All PFSPL unsecured loan borrowers aging 18–60 are protected through a loan-cover tie up between PFSPL and Kotak Life Insurance (premium paid by PFSPL, outstanding loan covered). Health insurance and weather insurance tie-ups are being explored.

Janalakshmi has launched its new initiative JanaOne, a one-stop shop providing a bouquet of customized financial advisory services with appropriate, customized products to Janalakshmi customers of two-year vintage, and successful repayment record over minimum two-group loan cycles. The services included are individual loans of ₹50,000-0.2 million, medium term savings through endowment products and insurance and micro pension services through tie-ups.

Source: Primary data from Janalakshmi.

National Insurance VimoSEWA Cooperative Ltd. (VimoSEWA) is registered under the Multi State Co-operative Societies Act 2002. At present, the insurance services are carried through three variants (*a*) under VimoSEWA (*b*) under SEWA and (*c*) under mutual model. VimoSEWA's legal form as microinsurance agent allows it to retail insurance products of only one life insurer and one non-life insurer and also prohibits it from carrying underwriting risk. While operating under SEWA allows it to have a tie-up with more than one insurer, under the mutual model it also carries part of the underwriting risk.

As under the present regulatory arrangement, VimoSEWA can only act as a microinsurance agent, it negates its ability to design products suitable for its target market. Insurance companies offering these products lack market understanding, which has resulted in a mismatch between needs and standard products on offer. VimoSEWA has engaged with insurance companies to influence their product design to suit low-income members. Since inception in 1992 the product range has become comprehensive, covering credit-life, life, endowment, hospitalization, health and assets. Considering the preference of the poor for bundled products, combination products covering health, life and asset are also being offered through the mutual model. As per extant IRDA guidelines, agents like VimoSEWA cannot charge any additional premium while distributing insurance products and have to cover their costs through commission received from insurance company. For a stand-alone microinsurance agent like VimoSEWA, these regulations make it unviable.

PENSIONS—**Janalakshmi** through a tie-up with UTI IIMPS, JFS has offered its group loan clients the option of investing ₹100, 200 or 500 per month in a micro pension scheme with minimal exit charges depending on time of redemption. The product has 40 per cent uptake among JFS's loan clients, with 70–80 per cent uptake in the southern and western states. Clients can call a 24-hour toll free number to seek clarification on product terms, balances, returns, etc.

BEST PRACTICES: MFIs have to bargain with the best service providers for the most beneficial deals for their clients. MFIs which have extensive outreach will be able to bargain hard on product pricing.

ADVANTAGES: Providing such tie-ups builds several links between the clients and MFI, forging a deep relationship and ensuring client retention.

DISADVANTAGES: Explanation of product terms and conditions has to be done very carefully, as misunderstanding may lead to default on loans, which remain the primary driver of earnings for MFIs.

NOTES AND REFERENCES

Support provided by Deepak Goswami, Access Assist in data processing is gratefully acknowledged.

1. The data from 61 MFIs from MIX market source may be treated as representative since almost all the major players in the sector covering more than 90 per cent of the client outreach and loan portfolio reported by Sa-Dhan were included in the MIX market data source.

2. Data from Sa-Dhan's *The Bharat Microfinance Quick Report-2012.*

3. Data from Sa-Dhan's *The Bharat Microfinance Quick Report-2012.*

4. The Andhra Pradesh crisis has been discussed in detail in the *State of the Sector Report 2011.*

5. 'Microfinance—Growing Against All Odds', 2012. *The Bharat Microfinance, Quick Report 2012.* Sa-Dhan, New Delhi.

6. Study on 'Access to Finance in Rural Andhra Pradesh—Revisiting the MFI Clients 2012' conducted by Centre for Micro Finance, IFMR, Chennai with funding support from IFMR Capital Private Ltd. Forthcoming report.

7. Deepti, K.C. 2012. 'Rethinking Reserve Bank of India (RBI) Regulations for MFIs' Center for Microfinance IFMR, Chennai.

8. http://www.mfinindia.org/sites/default/files/Industry%20Code%20of%20Conduct.pdf. Accessed on July 2012.

9. http://www.sidbi.in/micro/codeofconduct.html. Accessed on July 2012.

10. http://m2iconsulting.com/coca-reports.html. Accessed on July 2012.

11. See *MicroSave's* Briefing Notes # 84 'Individual Lending for MFIs Strategic Issues to Consider First'; # 85 'Managing Individual Lending'; # 86 'Product Features of Individual Lending Part 1'; # 87 'Product Features of Individual Lending Part 2'; and # 88 'Breaking the Barriers: Market Expansion Through Individual Lending'. Accessed on July 2012.

12. The PPI®, developed by Grameen Foundation, is a poverty measurement tool that is a unique composite of ten easy-to-collect, country-specific, non-financial indicators such as family size, the number of children attending school, the type of housing and ownership of certain assets. It is a simple, practical, easy to use tool yet statistically accurate.

13. The PPI is endorsed/supported by many social investors, funders and other stakeholders such as CGAP, Ford Foundation, MSDF, Dia Vikas, Plan International among others as an effective tool for serving the poor by getting more client level data, poverty assessment, and measuring movement out of poverty.

14. Excerpt from *draft* PPI data analytics document shared by Grameen Foundation India. The author gratefully acknowledges the support and inputs provided by Chandni, Jayesh and Gaurav, Grameen Foundation India.

15. Daniel Rozas, *The State of the Practice, 2011.* A Report from the Smart Campaign, Center for Financial Inclusion Publication No. 14.

16. Information provided by Mr K. Sridhar (High Mark) and Mr Suresh Krishna (Grameen Financial Services) in preparing this section are gratefully acknowledged.

17. Girija Srinivasan, 2012. *Microfinance Social Performance Report 2012.* Access Development Services, New Delhi: SAGE Publications.

Financial inclusion—process and progress

Financial inclusion is both a cause and consequence of economic growth. Financial inclusion has become a buzzword in development policy, and has come to be regarded as an important and inevitable milestone in achieving inclusive growth. The process of economic growth, especially when it is on a high growth trajectory, must strive to encompass participation from all sections of society. Lack of access to finance for vulnerable and weaker sections of the society has been recognized as a serious threat to economic progress especially in developing countries. Moreover, prolonged and persistent deprivation of banking services to a large segment of the population leads to a decline in investment and has the potential to fuel social tensions causing social exclusion. Access to finance, especially by the poor and vulnerable groups is a prerequisite for employment, economic growth, poverty reduction and social cohesion.

While the Financial Inclusion Committee defined financial inclusion as the process of ensuring access to financial services and timely and adequate credit where needed by vulnerable groups such as weaker sections and low-income groups at an affordable cost, financial sector reform committee refers to it as the universal access to a wide range of financial services at a reasonable cost. These include not only banking products but also other financial services such as insurance and equity investment products. However, what matters most is not just the access to financial services, but its actual usage. Among the non-users of formal financial services a clear distinction needs to be made between voluntary and involuntary exclusion. The problem of financial inclusion addresses the 'involuntarily excluded' as they are the ones who, despite needing financial services, do not have access to them.[1] Based on its experience as a rating agency for microfinance

institutions, M-CRIL's perspective on financial inclusion is that financial inclusion is not just a matter of providing various financial products and services to the excluded population but doing so in a responsible manner.[2]

FINANCIAL INCLUSION—A GLOBAL PERSPECTIVE

Globally the importance of an inclusive financial system is widely recognized in policy circles. Several countries now look at financial inclusion as the means of a more comprehensive growth, wherein each citizen of the country is able to use his/her earning as a financial resource that he/she can put to work to improve their future financial status, adding to the nation's progress. In advanced markets, it is mostly a demand side issue. Initiatives for financial inclusion have come from the financial regulators, the governments and the banking industry. The banking sector has taken a lead role in promoting financial inclusion. Legislative measures have been initiated in some countries. For example, in the United States, the Community Reinvestment Act (1997) requires banks to offer credit throughout their entire area of operation and prohibits them from targeting only the rich neighbourhoods. In France, the law on exclusion (1998) emphasizes an individual's right to have a bank account. The German Bankers' Association introduced a voluntary code in 1996 providing for an 'everyman' current banking account that facilitates basic banking transactions. In 2004 the South African Banking Association launched a low cost bank account for financially excluded people. In the United Kingdom, the government set up a 'Financial Inclusion Task Force' in 2005 in order to monitor the progress of financial inclusion. The

'Principles for Innovative Financial Inclusion' adopted in the G20 Leadership Summit in Toronto (2010) serve as a guide for policy and regulatory approaches with the objectives of fostering safe and sound adoption of innovative, adequate, low-cost financial delivery models, helping provide conditions for fair competition and a framework of incentives for the various bank, insurance, and non-bank actors involved and delivery of the full range of affordable, quality financial services. Though several initiatives were undertaken for deepening and widening the process of providing financial services to the poor and vulnerable groups in recent periods, still there exists greater exclusion, which emphasizes the need for qualitative and quantitative additions in ongoing efforts.

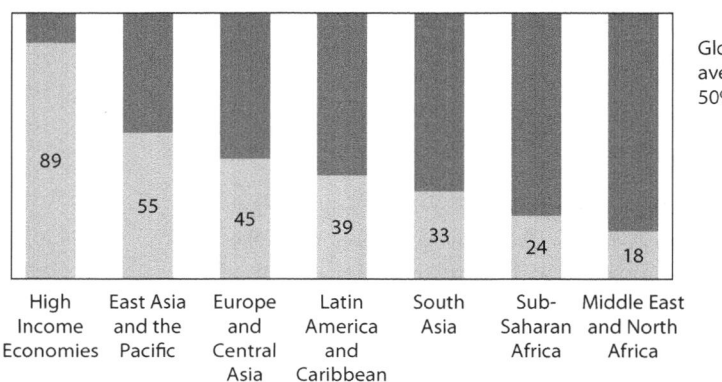

Figure 4.1   Account penetration

Source: Demirguc-Kunt and Klapper, 2012.

Launching of the Global Findex dataset, based on nationally representative surveys of more than 150,000 adults in 148 economies, provides fresh and robust answer to the question of the extent of financial inclusion across the countries.[3] The database quantified that globally approximately 2.5 billion adults lack a formal bank account, and most of these people are concentrated in developing economies. Those without an account are deprived of a secure way to save and transfer money, both basic abilities that support multiple dimensions of human well-being. However, studies on portfolios of the poor have shown that the poor are often quite ingenious at overcoming this lack of access. While the stereotype may be of cash hidden under a mattress, the poor often manage a complex set of financial relationships with their family, friends and the wider community to manage risk, save for large purchases, and invest in their children or in small businesses.

The Findex data show sharp disparities in the use of financial services between high-income and developing economies as indicated by the percentage of adults holding an account at a formal financial institution (Figure 4.1). National income was found to explain much of the variation in account penetration across most countries. There is a strong positive correlation between economic development of nations and the extent of financial inclusion, with more than 80 per cent of adults in high income economies having an account in a formal financial institution, while in poorer economies such as sub-Saharan Africa and MENA countries less than 25 per cent of the adult population has a bank account. Rural poor, illiterate, women and the workers in unorganized sectors are those who are severely deprived of financial services from formal financial institutions. However, there is a positive message from the Global Findex data. Many hurdles that hamper account holding in banks such as time and travel costs, distance/physical access and documentation requirements and bank charges for opening an account may be overcome by technology and policy changes. Public policy can tackle many of the barriers to access and thus pave the way for improving financial access. For example, regulation and promotional policies can help reduce the cost of opening an account, improve access in rural areas (e.g., through mobile money), and reduce documentation requirements.

The financial portfolios of most poor people contain a blend of formal and informal services. For example, Findex data suggest that while 30 per cent of adults have borrowed in the last 12 months, informal sources of finance are dominant among the poor. In countries such as Bangladesh, Bolivia, Sri Lanka and Thailand, the numbers of consumers using formal loans range only from 23 per cent to 15 per cent. The emerging evidence from Kenya and Malawi suggests that the choice of what source of finance to use at any given moment is a function of why it is needed, what is available, and the sequence of transactions that precedes it. Research shows that for low-income populations, 'life is one long risk' and managing shocks is a complicated process. Therefore, the most frequent use of credit and savings is for emergencies. This calls for a favourable policy environment and regulatory system as well as sustained efforts on the part of all stakeholders on both demand and supply-sides.

FINANCIAL INCLUSION—THE INDIAN SCENARIO

Inclusive economic growth has been one of the priority agendas of the Government of India (GoI) over the past decade. It is widely acknowledged that inclusive economic growth cannot be accomplished without achieving financial inclusion for the nearly two-thirds of India's population who are unbanked. The committee on financial inclusion[4] was set up to suggest strategies to extend financial services to small and marginal farmers and other vulnerable groups. In the following year, a High Level Committee on Financial Sector Reforms[5] was set up with the focus on identifying emerging challenges in meeting the financing needs of the Indian economy.

Earlier, the focus of financial inclusion was primarily confined to ensuring a bare minimum access to a savings bank account without frills to all. However, recently in August 2012, RBI has redesigned the NFA with the inclusion of additional common banking facilities. In the first-ever Index of Financial Inclusion conducted to find out the extent of the reach of banking services across the world, India was ranked 50th out of a total of a 100 countries. A comparative perspective on the status of financial inclusion in India and China are presented in Table 4.1. The data reveal that the level of financial inclusion in India is much lower compared to that in China, except in the case of credit. As per the Findex data, the number of adults having accounts with formal financial institutions in India was little more than 40 per cent for male and about one-third for female, which is much lower than the Sri Lankan case where almost 70 per cent of the people have bank accounts (Figure 4.2). However, in terms of usage of the accounts for saving and/or borrowing the Indian scenario was abysmally low with only about 10 per cent of the adults with saving or borrowings from a formal institution (Figure 4.3). This underscores the strong need for widening and deepening of financial services to the unbanked people.

The microfinance sector in India is considered to be one of the main contributors to financial inclusion in the country. There are two major models for delivery of microfinance services—the SHG Bank Linkage Programme (SBLP) and the MFI model.

Table 4.1 Status of financial inclusion in India, 2012[6]

	India	China
Account at a formal financial institution		
All adults (%, age 15+)	35.2	63.8
Adults living in a rural area (%, age 15+)	33.1	58.0
Adults living in an urban area (%, age 15+)	41.0	82.1
Savings (%, age 15+)		
Savings any money in the past year	22.4	38.4
Saved at a formal financial institution in the past year	11.6	32.1
Credit (%, age 15+)		
Loan from a formal financial institution in the past year	7.7	7.3
Loan from family or friends in the past year	19.7	25.0
Loan from an informal private lender in the past year	6.6	1.1
Insurance (%, age 15+)		
Personally paid for health insurance	6.8	47.2

Source: The Little Data Book on Financial Inclusion. 2012. The World Bank, p. 74.

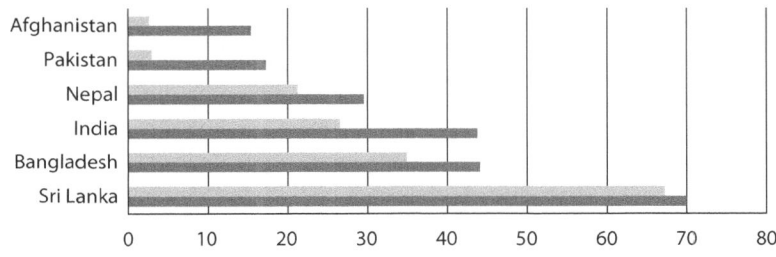

Figure 4.2 Adults with accounts at a formal financial institution

Source: Demirguc-Kunt, Asli, and LeoraKlapper. 2012. 'Measuring Financial Inclusion: The Global Findex Database.' Policy Research Working Paper 6025, Washington: World Bank.

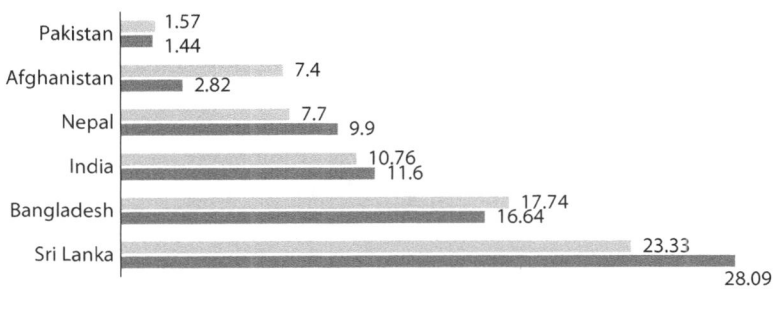

Figure 4.3 Saving at and borrowing from formal financial institution

Source: Demirguc-Kunt, Asli, and LeoraKlapper. 2012. 'Measuring Financial Inclusion: The Global Findex Database.' Policy Research Working Paper 6025, Washington: World Bank.

Under the SBLP model, NABARD has been refinancing bank loans to SHGs through commercial banks, but the credit risk is carried by the banks. The MFI model uses a variety of methodologies ranging from the very popular SHG methodology traditionally pursued in the country to Grameen and Joint Liability Groups (JLG), as well as individual banking arrangements. The MFIs use their own equity and external borrowings from commercial sources (apex financial institutions including NABARD and SIDBI, commercial banks and other financial institutions) for on-lending to their micro-borrowers.

FINANCIAL INCLUSION—RBI INTERVENTIONS

The conventional view is that financial inclusion cannot be achieved without active support from policy makers and regulators. The Government of India has made several rounds of efforts at several points over the past few decades to promote inclusive financial growth. Keeping in mind the aim to achieve sustainable and equitable growth, the RBI has taken several initiatives to increase access to banking services, credit markets and financial education. These included the lead bank scheme of the commercial banks and the promotion of self-help groups (SHGs), a program promoted by NABARD and facilitated by the RBI's acceptance of unregistered groups of low income individuals as an entity for banking purposes.[7] To strengthen the financial inclusion drive, RBI asked banks to cover all villages with a population of more than 2,000 with at least one banking outlet by March 2012. As much as 74,499 such villages were identified as unbanked, and were allocated to various banks, including regional rural banks (RRBs) for providing banking services by March 2012. In the Monetary Policy 2012–13,[8] RBI has proposed that State Level Banker's Committees (SLBCs) prepare a roadmap for coverage of unbanked villages with a population below 2,000 for providing banking services in a time-bound manner.

The current round of initiatives for the promotion of financial inclusion includes:

1. Appointment of the Business Correspondent (BC)/Business Facilitator (BF) for outreach to low income families/individuals.
2. Introduction of the concept of no-frills accounts and encouraging banks to open such accounts for low income families.
3. Encouragement to RRBs/Cooperative banks to sell insurance and other financial products.
4. Creation of special funds for financial inclusion.
5. Revival of the cooperative credit structure involving PACS, District Central Cooperative Banks (DCCBs) and State Cooperative Banks (SCBs).
6. Liberalization of KYC norms for small accounts and KCC/GCC Guidelines
7. Introduction of technology products and services such as prepaid cards, mobile banking.
8. Liberalization of branch expansion.
9. Promotion of financial literacy and strengthen consumer protection.

Initially, the RBI specified that those who could act as BCs were 'not-for-profit' entities who could conduct banking business as agents of the banks at places other than the bank's premises. The activities they could conduct were borrower's identification, collections, preliminary processing and submission of loan applications, creating awareness about savings and opening of account (though KYC compliances were the bank's responsibility), promoting SHGs and JLGs, collection of small value deposits, disbursal of small value loans, follow-up on recovery of principal/interest, sale of microinsurance, and receipt and delivery of small value remittances. The hesitation of the RBI in mainstreaming agent-banking model was reflected not only in its restriction of the model to not-for-profit entities (though later the engagement of some types for-profits was also permitted), but also by the restrictions imposed on pricing. BCs were to be paid from the bank's margin, and no charges could be imposed on the customer either by the bank or the BC. This limited the viability of the model since the margins of banks are of the order of 4 per cent, and it is well known that any form of micro banking activity incurs a cost of 6–10 per cent of the money value of the transaction. Soon concerned about allowing the links between BCs and bank branches to become too tenuous (leading to a 'lack of supervision'), the RBI limited the distance from the branch within which the BC had to operate. While this was widely seen as a limited step, these provisions led to some experimentation with leading commercial banks establishing pilot programmes with various not-for-profit entities to determine the feasibility of enabling financial inclusion within the strait jacket then imposed by the rules. Essentially, BCs were employed in opening NFA, providing payment services under government welfare programmes and to a lesser extent in mobilizing deposits.

While a few, such as FINO, A Little World (ALW) and Eko Aspire Foundation, reached numbers in the tens of thousands over the next three years, in a country with perhaps 120 million financially excluded families, these numbers are too small to attract attention. However, FINO has reportedly done better in outreach through collaborations with state governments in the facilitation of payments under government welfare programs, reaching a customer base of 22 million.

FINANCIAL INCLUSION PLAN

The elements of financial inclusion focused in the recent initiatives by RBI include saving-cum-overdraft account, remittance facility, and access to credit through instruments like general credit cards. Performance of providing these services depends on the institutional network coverage of bank branches in the remote areas. The RBI had pursued the financial inclusion agenda more closely and now the banks have prepared plans in each and every State targeting 72,800 villages with the population of more than 2000 that are not covered by main stream financial institutions.

The number of no-frills savings account with an overdraft facility has increased from 1.3 million in 2010 to 1.52 million in 2012 (Table 4.2). As part of the financial inclusion process, banks have opened 3,226 rural branches in the last two years. To encourage banks to open branches in the rural areas, they are permitted to freely open branches in tier III to tier VI centres, subject to reporting to the RBI. Further, to increase the reach of banking services, the number of business correspondents (BCs) or BC agents deployed by banks jumped nearly three-fold to 96,828 in 2012 from 33,042 in 2010. The number of electronic beneficiary transfer (EBT) accounts

opened through BCs rose from 7.48 million 2010 to 21.76 million in 2012. Banks are opening EBT accounts so that social benefits can be transferred electronically to the bank account of the beneficiary. Similarly the number of KCC issued has increased from 17.63 million in 2010 to 22.34 million in 2012 where as GCC growth was three-fold during this period. The data shows that in the last two years banks done much more compared to the preceding five years when the concept of BC/BF was introduced. The FIP mooted by RBI has been a clear reason for this recent expansion of network of BCs.

NO-FRILLS ACCOUNTS

Taking the view that access to a bank account can be considered a public good, in 2005, RBI directed all banks to offer at all branches the facility of 'No-Frill Accounts' (NFA) to any person desirous of opening such an account. These accounts have nil or low minimum balances and charges, and have limited facilities. As at the end of the year 2011–12, 103.21 million NFAs had been opened by the banking system, which was doubled when compared to the previous year performance. The impressive performance in terms of growth in the number of NFA is overshadowed by the low usage and high dormancy in these accounts. At the ground level, it was observed that most of the NFAs were non-operative, and clients were not even aware of the terms of use of these accounts, though these accounts were designed keeping in mind the needs of vulnerable groups. There are barriers that inhibit the active operation of NFAs such as the time and

Table 4.2 **Financial inclusion plans of banks for three years—achievements**[9]

Particulars	Year ended March 2010	Year ended March 2012	Progress April 2010—March 2012
No. of BCs/BC Agents Deployed	33,042	96,828	63,786
Banking Outlets through Branches	21,475	24,701	3,226
Banking Outlets through BCs	32,684	120,355	87,671
Banking Outlets-through other Modes	99	2,478	2,379
Total Banking Outlets	**54,258**	**147,534**	**93,276**
No Frill A/Cs (no. in millions)	49.33	103.21	53.88
Overdraft-No Frill A/Cs (no. in millions)	0.13	1.52	1.39
BC- ICT based A/Cs (no. in millions)	12.54	52.07	39.53
EBT A/Cs-through BCs (no. in millions)	7.48	21.76	14.28
KCC (no. in millions)	17.63	22.34	4.71
GCC (no. in millions)	0.45	1.27	0.82

Source: Reddy, D.R.K. 2012. 'Financial Inclusion: Road Ahead, Bankquest', *The Journal of Indian Institute of Banking & Finance*, 83(2): 40–46.

cost involved in reaching the nearest branch where the accounts have been opened. Concerted efforts by the implementing authorities by providing appropriate financial literacy with the innovations in use of technology will certainly improve the impact of these efforts to a greater extent.

One of the main constraints to the operation of NFAs is physical access to banks. The costs of conveyance, and the opportunity cost of the time required to reach the bank consumes a significant proportion of the savings of low-income households and thus becomes an economically unviable option for them. Keeping this in mind, the committee on financial inclusion stressed the provision of banking services physically close to the account holders through channels such as mobile banking, formation of SHGs, and provision of banking services through BCs. Information about NFAs is publicized either through the print media or websites. Mostly illiterate or semi-literate individuals living in remote areas are unable to obtain the information necessary to take advantage of the facility. Though the RBI has introduced the concept of financial literacy centres for providing counselling to the target clients, the efficacy of such centres in reaching a large number of target clients is still untested. The low-income households for whom the NFAs are designed tend to have an irregular and uncertain flow of income; the frequency and amount of savings undertaken by such account holders is low and infrequent as well. Recently RBI redesigned the NFA criteria and converted them into full bank accounts with debit cards and all the trimmings. This forward looking direction will certainly enhance the utility of NFA to a greater extent and accelerate the financial inclusion process.

BUSINESS CORRESPONDENTS (BCs)

Concerted efforts are being made by the financial institutions, under the direction and supervision of the Reserve Bank of India (RBI) and the Ministry of Finance (MoF), in using the Business Correspondent model as an effective linkage between the banking net work and the unreached clients. In 2010–12, the Swabhimaan campaign was launched by the government to extend a helping hand to improve banking facilities through Business Correspondents' to habitations, which are having a population exceeding 2000. In his budget speech 2012, the Union Finance Minister announced that out of 73,000 identified habitations that were covered in March 2012, about 70,000 have been provided with banking facilities.[10] With this number over 25.5 million beneficiary

accounts will be operating soon, the remaining will be covered by 31 March 2012. He further added that Ultra Small Branches will be set up at these habitations where the business correspondents would deal with cash transactions. In the year 2012–13, the 'Swabhimaan' campaign will be extended to habitations with a population of more than 1,000 in the North Eastern state, hilly states and to other habitations whose population has crossed over 2,000 as per the 2011 Census.

Banks have taken partnership with their BCs to new levels over the past year. Future strategies for improving the effectiveness of the BC model will have to address innovations in attracting new customer segments especially low income customers, enhanced product portfolio including providing client oriented transaction accounts, remittance/payment services and suitable credit products. Once banks start leveraging BCs as their extended arms, regular banking products can be channeled through this model. The proposal of implementing the social sector schemes through the banking system with the support of Unique Identification (UID) provides enormous scope for being BC as intermediary between banks and clients.

Over a period of time, the implementation of BC model has made significant progress in terms of coverage as well as value addition at grass root level. A number of participants have emerged and several innovations were adopted in the banking system for facilitating the banking system to accept the BC model. However, there exists greater potential in terms of outreach and usage. Still, the sustainability of the model is one of the major concerns for both banks and BCs, which calls for in-depth understanding on the clients' preference to BC model. Branch-based banking is extremely expensive, and therefore not an optimal option for serving customers at the bottom-of-the-pyramid—thus agent-based banking is an obvious opportunity. However, BC's acceptance as a low-cost alternative channel is only just beginning to gain recognition, for genuine, long-term players. While revenue will take time to reach meaningful levels, the cost side of the equation cannot be ignored.[11] Further outreach through BCs seems the only credible alternative on the horizon, therefore serious efforts to relook at the financials and to make adjustments for them to work are in order.

A BC is truly an extension of the bank with an outside arrangement for expanding the area of operation. It is a new approach, therefore needing time, efforts and experience to stabilize and become seamless. The current exclusive focus on quantity of targets achieved, ignoring quality in this endeavour, are not allowing enough opportunity for the bank–BC partnership to flourish and to grant the much-warranted legitimacy to this relationship. Furthermore, it is essential that the relationship moves from BCs as vendors of a service that must be sourced as cheaply as possible, to that of BCs as partners with whom banks can work to deliver quality financial services. A change of perspective is desirable on two counts. Firstly, the focus needs to shift from compliance with RBI directives on accounts opened to viewing them as another customer segment that can be profitably served through the BCs. Secondly banks need to recognize BCs as an alternate channel to service the wider low-income segment (not just unbanked), that otherwise is unviable to service through traditional banking and is usually denied access, convenience and quality service. Once banks recognize BCs as their extended arms and better mutual trust is established, efforts to ensure win-win in the true spirit of partnership will gain ground. This will inevitably lead to segmenting customers, offering them suitable products addressing their needs, servicing them through the most efficient channels and investing in awareness building and targeted marketing.

Options such as migration of existing bank customers to the BC channel for door-step services can then be explored, giving banks the opportunity to decongest branches and to provide improved service to their preferred customers. BCs will, in turn, get an assured incremental revenue stream to motivate them to offer superior service levels and to address customer expectations better. However, still business correspondent network managers (BCNMs) are struggling to get recognition at the ground level, and the viability of this channel is still a question of debate (Annexure 4.1). The BCNM selection process has been adopted by banks under the direction of the Ministry of Finance. The recently introduced reverse-auction approach for the selection of common BC across an entire State/cluster (for handling government benefit payments) is leading to price-wars and bottom-less price-quotes.[12] Since this will create a parallel BC network to compete with the nascent BC network created under the FIPs, there is a possibility that both sets of BCs will suffer from unviability. This approach puts the survival of the existing players at risk and could lead to destabilization of the sector. For banks, the current remittance business of over ₹300 billion can grow 20 per cent by enabling BCNMs to acquire inter-bank transactions. Together with the opportunity that arises with CBS integration of RRBs, the market potential for

the banks is estimated to be three-fold their current business of money transfer. If the regulator were to selectively enhance transaction limits for transfers, BCNMs can tap into a significant opportunity of better-off individuals and micro businesses. This is estimated to be almost six times the current business being serviced through BCNMs. A collaborative approach between banks and State Governments can aid considerable synergistic benefits for all.

There are several evidences to support how BCNMs have been effectively leveraged by several Government departments to bring about transformation in delivery of welfare payments or even for regular wage pay-outs. On channeling MGNREGS payments in several districts electronically through BCNMs, the Andhra Pradesh Government has seen utilization of funds increase by as much as 25 per cent. Its daily irregularity reports mention less than 0.9 per cent deviations from close to two-thirds of works inspected. It has gone a step further leveraging its superior IT infrastructure and connectivity, enabling online availability of information for each work sanctioned, its location, and status of completion, status of payment, disbursement delays and ageing. This is an extraordinary method to bring about access to information, generate awareness and to create transparency. BCNM has been successfully piloted in several states to deliver and track welfare benefits using biometric smart cards and mobile phones. There are several other isolated but distinct examples of Government departments riding on electronic payment methods for improved delivery. Even in States like Uttar Pradesh (one amongst the four under-developed States of Bihar, Madhya Pradesh, Rajasthan and UP, referred to as BIMARU, or unwell), progressive departments like the UP Forest Corporation are extensively and effectively using electronic/mobile banking channels to tackle inefficiencies and leakages to *Tendu* leaf collectors.[13] Another illustration is a model of wage payment to health workers (ASHA) being pilot-tested by the Government of Bihar in collaboration with the State Bank of India.[14]

There are ample field-level studies being conducted by different stakeholders and researchers on the viability and sustainability of BC modes across the country. A study conducted by Sa-Dhan on the efficacy of Banking Correspondent model (2012) has identified that commercial viability is the greatest challenge as a consequence of compensation too meager to sustain the model.[15] Another study by MicroSave conducted in Tamil Nadu, Uttar Pradesh and Rajasthan states reveals that over 80 per cent of India's rural unbanked population is willing to pay for the convenience of banking at their doorstep through a banking correspondent. Saving in time and money spent on walking or travelling to and from the bank, waiting in the queue, improved security in cash handling, and the flexibility and convenience of banking correspondent model. Almost half of the survey respondents said they prefer a percentage model of 1–2 per cent of the transaction total as the service fee, while close to 30 per cent opted for a flat fee. Attracting the poor towards financial products such as recurring deposits, insurance premiums and mobile loan payments is a time-consuming process requiring patience and persuasive skills on the part of the bank staff/correspondents.

Lack of Customer Service Points, least staying power, poor morale and high expectations, infirmity in selection process of BCs, over emphasis on quantity, inadequate financial literacy support, and lack of customer grievance mechanism and business continuity plan are the constraining factors in BC model implementation. Among different models, Kiosk based model takes three-and-a-half years to break even under the best of circumstances whereas biometric GPRS mobile based model and SMS based remittance model takes about two years and less than two years respectively. The following strategies are identified for improving viability:

1. Viability gap funding and assured minimum fixed income to the CSP-Banks to provide viability gap funding for BCs for the initial three years.
2. RBI/IBA to prescribe uniform minimum rates to BCs to ensure fair return on investments to BCs.
3. SHG Federations, CBOs and MFIs including NBFC-MFIs as BCs-NBFC-MFIs to offer saving products as BC.
4. Routing all Government to Persons (G2P) payments through BCs. All payments to beneficiaries under state sponsored programmes to be routed through BCs through the No Frill Accounts. Pay two per cent administration costs to Banks
5. Convergence of BC Model with National e-governance plan- Kiosk model of BCs to act as Common Service Centre (CSC).
6. Weed out non-serious players-replace with SHG Federations from MFI.
7. Financial literacy programme to be given equal emphasis to derive benefits from building, financial infrastructure in rural areas-literacy programme should run hand-in-hand.
8. Dedicated Customer Grievance Mechanism for clients of BCs.

CAB and CGAP have jointly undertaken an All India Survey to study the operational aspects of the BC arrangement at an early stage of implementation of FIP covering 860 sample Consumer Service Points (CSPs) in 11 states across the country.[16] The study findings concluded that CSPs are yet to establish the economic sustainability with present remuneration level and mainly social relevance and enhanced reputation are motivating the CSOs to continue in the business. While product diversification and quality services are the influencing factor for better revenue, liquidity problem and technology failure are some of the constraints experienced by CSPs. The survey identifies certain action possibilities that can remedy some current weaknesses and improve the CSP operations over time.

1. Improving the remuneration of CSPs should be a priority. This is not just a question of increasing the compensation rates, but a strategic reorientation of the business both by CSPs/BCs and banks.
2. One key driver of viability of a CSP is increased transaction volume. Banks should provide marketing support to increase both the number and value of transactions.
3. Attention to technology issues (especially biometric and smart cards) to reduce failures in the field will improve transaction levels and credibility of the CSP.
4. Banks should clearly delineate where CSPs are to be full extensions of the banks and where they are to remain minimalist remote tellers. This would help in planning services and optimizing costs of CSPs.
5. With several CSPs exclusively carrying out banking services (and not as an add-on to other business), the regulatory and business model underlying the original logic of BCs requires a review.
6. A robust monitoring system that brings feedback and data from the field on the reliability, efficiency and effectiveness aspects of the BC arrangement for ongoing policy review has to be set up.
7. Banks should take steps to introduce appropriate CSP hiring and training practices, offer a basket of demanded products through CSP and make agent-banking a part of banks' business strategies.

While the business case of CSP network remains to be proved at CSP and bank levels, the motivation to continue remains high on the part of CSPs. The strong reported desire on the part of CSPs to continue for a long time will possibly contain the attrition rates in the short run. In the near future solutions should be found. The solutions for the most part are with the banks; they would be able to make the investments in the solutions only if they make financial inclusion a part of their core business. The guidelines in place do not seem to have been fully utilized to get the best business models on the ground. Overall the nascent BC network needs more attention, and RBI needs to consider fixing its problems of viability, before expand the same to smaller villages.

KYC NORMS

KYC norms introduced by the RBI are meant for the purpose of customer identification, monitoring of accounts and reporting of suspicious transactions to the appropriate authorities. Among the key elements of the KYC procedure, customer identification was believed to be a major challenge to achieving financial inclusion. Since most excluded people belong to low income households and do not have identity or address documents, it was difficult to insist on these documents as part of the KYC norms. RBI norms clearly prescribe documents both for individual identification and permanent residence proof, and lists the acceptable ID proof documents. But, for first time banking clients, these are more often unusual and strange documents and even if they have one, it is often a challenge to get their names correctly spelled to the satisfaction of the cautious banker. The issue is even more nightmarish when these first timers are women members. For group-based savings units like Self-Help Groups (SHGs) the issue gets even more complex to get a KYC approved. Assessments have shown that 60 per cent of the cases where SHG women desirous of opening accounts have faced challenges in complying with KYC norms. Paradoxically, it is more prevalent in resource poor areas, which have also shown slow progress in SHG movement. However, the banks still needed to ensure the integrity of the customer before opening of a bank account for any financial transaction. Considering these issues the latest RBI circular allows flexibility in the requirement of identity and address documents for small deposit accounts. In this context, the introduction of the Aadhar project is expected to address the KYC problem in the near future by providing a Unique Identification Number for each citizen of India. The speed with which UIDs are provided to residents will further facilitate banks' penetration and therefore boost financial inclusion.

TECHNOLOGY AND FINANCIAL INCLUSION

Technology and financial inclusion are the popular coinage in banking parleys in the country. While technological upgradation and mobile banking are catching up so fast, financial inclusion is relatively tardy in progress. Given the reach of the mobile phone connectivity and associated communication technologies in the country, mobile banking has the potential to emerge as a positive strategy in terms of costs, convenience, and speed of reach. Mobile banking is used in many parts of the world with little or no infrastructure, especially remote and rural areas. This aspect of mobile technology is also popular in countries where most of their population is unbanked. In most of these places, banks can only be found in big cities, and customers have to travel long distances to the nearest bank. By 2012, it is estimated that there will be 1.7 billion people with a mobile phone but not a bank account and as many as 364 million unbanked people could be reached by agent-networked banking through mobile phones. Kenya's M-PESA mobile banking service, for example, allows customers of the mobile phone operator Safaricom to hold cash balances, which are recorded on their SIM cards. Cash may be deposited or withdrawn from M-PESA accounts at Safaricom retail outlets located throughout the country, and may be transferred electronically from person to person as well as used to pay bills to companies. One of the most innovative applications of mobile banking technology is Zidisha, a US-based non-profit microlending platform that allows residents of developing countries to raise small business loans from web users worldwide. Zidisha uses mobile banking for loan disbursements and repayments, transferring funds from lenders in the United States to the borrowers in rural Africa using nothing but the internet and mobile phones.

Mobile banking is just one of the reasons India is a place to watch for innovations in financial inclusion. Eko Financial Services Ltd., which had created the software programme five years ago, and which allows migrant workers in cities across India to send money to their families using a mobile phone is now working with two major banks, the State Bank of India and ICICI Bank, to offer financial services to poor and low income customers using local corner stores, pharmacies and airtime resellers as agents. By harnessing the huge potential of domestic remittances as an anchor product, Eko hopes to tap a huge potential market in India, where three quarters of the 1.25 billion people live on less than US$2 a day. Eko was the first company dedicated to a mobile phone-based basic savings account and payment service for the unbanked in India.[17] Launched in 2007, Eko has developed a mobile-based service usable even on the most basic handsets and continually revised and re-fashioned its approach. At first, Eko experimented with a basic deposit and payment service from one Eko account to another. But by the second half of 2011 Eko had struck on a revised formula that appeared to work as a business—providing a highly efficient and simple payment directly into the account of a bank anywhere in India (Box 4.1).

Mobile banking in India is yet to overcome several constraints relating to operational, regulatory and security issues. Agent networks are the major issue that mobile operators and banks need to get right if they are to turn branchless banking into a sustainable business.[20] The Reserve Bank of India recently removed restrictions on agent exclusivity, and hence customers can now transact at customer service points of one bank even if their accounts are held at another bank. Such interoperability means greater efficiency and lower costs across the system. Recently the Government of India released a taskforce report[21] on a unified payments infrastructure linked to the biometric Aadhar number[22] that proposes electronic payments for government-to-people payments as a means to cut costs for the government and bring added convenience to welfare recipients (Box 4.2).

Box 4.1 Eko—easy way of remittance

Leveraging a strong base of agents in Delhi,[18] Eko offers users a simple way to send money anywhere in India. Users can come to Eko's agents to make a deposit into any bank account held by the SBI. By presenting the mobile number of the sender and receiver to the Eko agent, plus the account number of the receiver, the agent can make a payment into the account securely simply by dialing a short sequence of numbers. Each transaction is then verified by an SMS to both sender and receiver with a time and date stamp, the fees levied and a transaction ID. The success of this *tatkal* payment service is predicated on two basic features.[19] The first is that Eko's service ties into the core banking system of SBI on a real-time basis. Thus, clients send and receive transactions instantly giving them confidence. The power of the service is persuasive to clients as the receivers simply withdraw the funds from any SBI channel across India. This includes a national network of interoperable ATMs which charge no fee on most withdrawals. The second important feature is simplicity. Clients only need to know the correct account number and the sending and (optionally) receiving phone numbers. And they only need to go to an authorized agent to complete the transaction. This is more convenient than getting to branches, which may be further away and often require longer waits. The big difference for Eko has been the irrefutable legitimacy that *tatkal* transactions bring to the SBI-Eko outlets. The fact that the client's relative thousands of kilometres away can instantly withdraw cash at an ATM just a few seconds after the transaction completes is a definite success of technology in financial inclusion.

Source: Primary information from Eko (http://technology. cgap.org/2012/02/09/an-optimistic-picture-of-branchless-banking-from-india-interview-with-microsave/).

Box 4.2 There is a human story behind branchless banking[23]

In the north Indian hill town of Almora, 35-year-old Sangeeta Joshi rises most mornings at 4.30 a.m. to complete her household chores before heading out for a day's work on foot. A member of the SEWA, a legendary labor union established for workers in the informal economy, Sangeeta works on commission as a customer service point for the State Bank of India.

Using technology provided by A Little World, Sangeeta has for the last two years opened nearly 500 accounts and now delivers regular pension payments to many people living along the hillsides in Almora. The work is physically demanding as Sangeeta has to travel by foot to deliver and authenticate payments. The fingerprint-based POS machine that Sangeeta wields provides her with a means of transacting securely, giving the bank and the government confidence that the right person has received their payment.

Sangeeta is one story among many thousands of new customer service point operators across India. But it is her effort that will make or break branchless banking. Despite the difficulties of being a CSP, it is a source of livelihood for Sangeeta. She also says that the job has given her respect in the community.

In the coming years we can expect Sangeeta's story to be repeated hundreds of thousands of time across India. Building a mutually fulfilling relationship with the Sangeetas across India will be the key to the success of branchless banking.

Source: CGAP.

MICROFINANCE PENETRATION INDEX

As in the previous years the penetration of microfinance in different states has been computed[24] (Box 4.3). The analysis shows Manipur has taken the top position for the second consecutive year with a score of 4.13 in MPI and 7.06 in MPPI. AP, the top ranking state in penetration in the previous years is now placed third. Puducheri (Pondicherry) has improved its ranking and moved to second place. The ranking of the last five ranks remain the same as the previous year except that there was some increase in the values. The population data has been sourced from the latest Census 2011 and this might be one of the reasons for some changes among states in terms of MPI. The changes in the spread of SHG linkage and MFIs customer base as the result of the crisis have caused some changes to the MMPI rankings of states (Table 4.3).

Table 4.3 Ranking of select states based on MPI and MPPI

Top 5			
State	**MPI**	**State**	**MPPI**
Manipur	4.13	Manipur	7.06
Pondicherry	3.46	Andhra Pradesh	6.24
Andhra Pradesh	3.34	Pondicherry	4.67
Tamil Nadu	2.32	Tamil Nadu	2.76
Odisha	2.19	Sikkim	3.28
Last 5			
State	**MPI**	**State**	**MPPI**
Jammu & Kashmir	0.07	Mizoram	0.23
Mizoram	0.32	Jammu & Kashmir	0.46
New Delhi	0.24	New Delhi	0.45
Punjab	0.27	Bihar	0.42
Meghalaya	0.21	Uttar Pradesh	0.38

Source: Calculation by author.

Box 4.3 Calculation of MPI and MPPI

The number of credit clients of MFIs and members of SHGs with outstanding loans to banks were computed and each state's share to the country's total microfinance clients was worked out. The intensity of penetration of microfinance (MPI) was computed by dividing the Share of the State in microfinance clients with its share of population. The Intensity of Penetration of Microfinance among Poor (MPPI) was derived by dividing the share of the state in microfinance clients by share of the state in population of the poor. Since the microfinance clients are in the numerator, a value of more than one indicates that clients acquired were more than proportional to the population. The higher the score is above one, the better the performance. The lower the score from one, which is the par value, the poorer is the performance in the state.

Source: Methodology adopted by author.

The low MPPI ratio in states like Bihar and UP with a large proportion of households under poverty line indicates that considerable work has to be done in these states both by SBLP and MFIs.

REMITTANCE

Globally, the process of reinventing how low-income people send and receive money in remote locations; how they pay bills and loans; and how they save and insure against emergencies; thus for increasing numbers of people, how they enjoy greater freedom and control over their financial future is gaining great attention. MicroSave[25] research clearly indicates that they are willing to pay for these services, and hence there is evidence of a business case for banks to do this on a profitable basis. Indeed several banks in India are already thinking along these lines. But banks are more comfortable with their traditional business models of low volumes of high value transactions—and, of course, India's burgeoning middle class offers plenty of opportunity for growth and profitability using this model.

NABARD and Deutsche Gesellschaft für Internationale Zusammenarbeit (GIZ) together conducted a study on Remittance Needs and Opportunities in India. The study addresses the issues of improving financial services for domestic migrants by improving delivery channels, especially through Business Correspondents upgrading payment systems for small value money transfer and strengthening financial institutions for providing adequate remittance facilities as well as other financial services through enhanced financial education. The study covered four specific remittance corridors: Gujarat-Southern Rajasthan, Eastern UP-Mumbai, Odisha-Hyderabad/AP and intra-state migration and remittance in Maharashtra. The study concluded that sending remittances could be faster, easier and more secure, when the significant problems of sending money through the formal banking system over long distances—which migrants and the recipients in India are currently facing is removed. The component IV of the RFIP aims at involving more number of service providers for remittances. The identification of area/institution for launching the pilot project is in progress. Further, earmark a core team of its officers for increasing the outreach and acceptance of Aadhar Payments Bridge (APB) and AEPS (Aadhar Enabled Payments System), which promise to bring the much required transparency, speed and ease of operations into last mile banking and has set up CERFI (Centre of Excellence for Rural Financial Institutions) with its basic responsibilities being the propagation of APB and AEPS among rural financial institutions for all kinds of cashless transactions and new KCC operations. It will also document and disseminate the benefits, procedure, financial implications and time frame for adoption of AEPS by rural financial institutions. RRBs will be targeted in the first phase while CCBs with CBS platform will be covered in the second. An MOU is being signed among NABARD, UIDAI and NPCI to provide a formal outline to this collaborative effort.

Box 4.4 IIBF in financial inclusion

Indian Institute of Bank Management (IIBF) is playing an active role in financial inclusion as a provider of education and certification agency. The institute is offering an innovative training cum examination oriented certificate course for the employees of BC companies and individual BC/BF certificate course for BC/BF focusing on financial inclusion. IIBF has trained about 14,900 BC/BF of various banks during the year ended March 2012 through the accredited training institutes.

Source: IIBF website.

FINANCIAL INCLUSION—NABARD INITIATIVES

NABARD focuses its initiatives towards technology upgradation, capacity building and financial literacy for greater financial inclusion. The 'Financial Inclusion Fund' (FIF) managed by NABARD supports developmental and promotional interventions leading to financial inclusion and 'Financial Inclusion Technology Fund' (FITF) supports investments in meeting the cost of technology adoption aimed at promoting financial inclusion. As on 31 March 2012, the contribution to these Funds stood at ₹793.2 million (FIF) and ₹1,304.9 million (FITF), the cumulative sanctions under FIF and FITF were

₹1,146.2 million and ₹3,434.8 million respectively, and disbursements were ₹364.6 million and ₹1,841.6 million, respectively.

In addition to the above, NABARD had initiated the following policy initiatives during 2011–12:

1. Sanctioned a project on implementing ICT through Application Service Provider (ASP) Model to RRBs, with a grant support of ₹1,077 million to 53 RRBs and disbursed ₹405.2 million during 2011–12.
2. Support for CBS to weak RRBs from FITF—It has been decided to support the identified weak RRBs for CBS implementation through ASP Model. Under the scheme of support to 28 identified weak RRBs for CBS installation, proposals were received from 27 RRBs as on 31 March 2012, against which assistance was sanctioned to 26 RRBs for ₹2,165.2 million with disbursements amounting to ₹1,395.4 million.
3. Establishment of Financial Literacy and Credit Counselling Centre (FLCC) by Lead Banks: Under the scheme, support is being provided from FIF for establishment of FLCCs by Lead Banks in 256 excluded districts and 10 disturbed districts. As on 31 March 2012, ₹107.1 million has been sanctioned to Lead Banks in 128 districts of 12 States viz., Assam, Bihar, Manipur, Meghalaya, Rajasthan, West Bengal, Uttar Pradesh, Jharkhand, Madhya Pradesh, Maharashtra, Odisha and Gujarat for setting up FLCCs.
4. Financial Literacy through Audio Visual medium—Doordarshan: Grant assistance of ₹32.8 million was provided from FIF to Doordarshan for producing and directing a half-an-hour financial literacy programme in Hindi, to be telecast in six centres.
5. NABARD extended support to the extent of ₹22.5 million from the FIF to Invest India Micro Pension Services to pilot test a micro pension model among SHG members in eight districts of four States, viz., Odisha, Uttar Pradesh, Bihar and Tamil Nadu. The project aims at covering 40,000 rural poor under the old-age pension scheme. So far, ₹17.4 million has been released covering 16,395 persons.
6. Engaging Farmers' Club as BF by RRBs: Financial support is being extended by NABARD for Farmers' Clubs acting as Business Facilitators of RRBs in villages having 2,000+ population in their command areas. As on 31 March 2012, ₹20.8 million sanctioned to 22 RRBs in 12 States from FIF. Support was made available from the FIF to RRBs for engaging 'Authorized functionaries of well

run SHGs linked to Banks to act as BC/BF', with the purpose of extending financial services in semi-urban and rural areas in their command area. As on 31 March 2012, eight RRBs were sanctioned ₹4.381 million for training of authorized functionaries of well-run SHGs in six States. NABARD has sanctioned and released ₹2.171 million to National Informatics Centre for development of web-based GIS Application for assessing the reach and the extent of banking in India and also development of a web-based MIS for capturing the banking facility.

NABARD has recently launched a pilot project m-KCC in Villupuram district in Tamil Nadu (Box 4.5) enabling farmers having KCC accounts with Pallavan Grama Bank to transact their loan accounts without visiting the bank branch by using their mobiles as the interface. The objective of the project is to provide banking facilities to the KCC holders at their door step in a safe, secure, quick and reliable method through mobile phones thereby ensuring anywhere and anytime banking and reducing the transaction costs of the farmers in terms of time and travel. The technology introduced in the project enables farmers to do their transactions like the purchase of agricultural inputs without cash as the merchants with their bank accounts are also registered with the service provider. Cash withdrawals and cash deposits are also possible where the registered merchants are also engaged by the bank as BCs.

Box 4.5 m-KCC by NABARD

A pilot project, m-KCC, was launched in Villupuram district in Tamil Nadu on 2 October 2011 enabling farmers having KCC to conduct transactions on their loan accounts without visiting the bank branches by using their mobiles as the interface. The technology introduced in the project enables farmers to do their transactions like purchase of agricultural inputs without cash as the merchants with their bank accounts are also registered with the service provider. Cash withdrawals and cash deposits are also possible where the registered merchants are also engaged by the bank as BCs.

The key features of the project are:

- Enables enquiry about required agricultural inputs over the mobile including negotiation of prices and placing orders linked to assured payment against the sanctioned KCC limit.
- Allows cash withdrawals through BC up to amounts permitted by RBI.
- Facilitates withdrawals of funds or payments for purchases as per requirement in small chunks at convenient times and locations, thus saving interest cost to the farmers.
- Real time status of account balance as also last five transactions—Secure PIN & IVR/SMS based transactions.
- Works on all handsets. No GPRS or Smart phone required.
- No need to visit the bank with a passbook each time.
- No need to handle cash, saving on risks and costs for the farmers, input dealers, as well as banks.

The essential requirements are:

- The merchant should have a bank account with the bank and his mobile number should be registered with the bank for transactions through mobile.
- The farmer should have a KCC limit sanctioned with the bank and his mobile number should be registered with the bank for transactions through mobile.
- The Pay Mate platform should be given access to the CBS platform of the banks.

Source: NABARD Head Office Mumbai.

MICROINSURANCE

The government's concern about the inadequate emphasis on covering the disadvantaged, low-income population, especially those living in rural areas that led to the nationalization of life insurance in 1956 and general insurance in 1973. Post-liberalization in the late 1990s, the IRDA regulations declared in 2002 made it necessary for new private insurance companies to procure insurance business on a quota basis from pre-defined rural areas and social sectors, failing which they could be penalized. Specific regulations for microinsurance were announced in 2005 to enable the design and easier distribution of products appropriate to the needs of low-income families. Until recently, it was these, rural and social sector obligations that motivated insurance companies to go down-market and provide services to the financially excluded. Innovative products in microinsurance and related issues are discussed in Chapter 5.

COMPLETE FINANCIAL INCLUSION BY KGFS MODEL

The Kshetriya Gramin Financial Services (KGFS) model is promoted by IFMR Trust with the mission of ensuring access of financial services for every individual and every enterprise. IFMR Trust provided the initial capital of US$10 million to launch the first three KGFS institutions, targeting a return on its equity of 20 per cent annually. The KGFS institutions are Non-Banking financial companies (NBFC) licensed and supervised by India's central bank; it is not permitted to take deposits. Although all KGFS institutions have a common parent company that provides equity capital to each KGFS, each KGFS institution is designed to be an autonomous, self-contained regional operation with its own management team hired locally. KGFS institutions were set up in very distinct regions of the country with a view to understanding the design implications of the model in diverse regional contexts.[26] The KGFS serves at Thanjavur districts of Tamil Nadu, which are fertile agrarian economies whereas the other in Odisha serves Ganjam and Khurda districts, which are economies characterized by subsistence agriculture supplemented by domestic migration. The KGFS in Uttarakhand serves five hilly districts that are sparsely populated, where the underlying economies are dominated by trade and services. Totally, five separate KGFS institutions are working in very different regions of the country and serve a total of 200,000 clients. Three core operating principles differentiate the KGFS model: (*a*) complete coverage of the population in a focused geographic area, (*b*) customized client wealth management services, and (*c*) a broad range of products. These three core elements are standard across all KGFS institutions; however, serving diverse geographic regions has enabled KGFS to learn, adapt, and apply the learnings to new KGFS institutions.

The KGFS approach is still fairly new, though it has moved beyond being a small experiment. The oldest KGFS has been in operation since June 2008, and the most recent commenced operations in February 2012. At the end of 2011, KGFS institutions had 110 branches and managed a loan portfolio of US$10 million. Some branches of these institutions have become profitable, though none of the five KGFS institutions has broken even yet on a consolidated basis. Early client response to these institutions shows a significant proportion of households, over 50 per cent, enrol within the first 18 months of a KGFS branch opening nearby. The model's mass customized wealth management approach starts with identifying household needs and goals to provide services centered on client needs and without biases to sell one product or another. Clients have begun to use multiple financial services centered on client needs from KGFS institutions, especially insurance and pensions. More than 60 per cent of enrolled clients across all KGFS institutions use insurance services; 22 per cent use only insurance. At the same time, credit remains important, with slightly more than 55 per cent accessing a loan product. The ultimate aim is meaningful improvement in the financial well-being of households, an outcome KGFS is evaluating with external research help. Initial experience shows that clients are increasingly responding to the KGFS approach, operational challenges can be overcome, and financial viability is within reach. Client acceptance is reflected in the high enrolment and take-up rates across multiple products, especially in the significant demand for insurance and pensions. Operational challenges presented by using the intensive wealth management approach and the partnership model have largely been overcome. Wholesale funding from domestic financial institutions is being developed to finance expansion. The process of adapting to new geographies will remain an ongoing challenge as KGFS institutions open across India. The commitment to work with the entire population of a small geographic area should be possible in other environments. The coverage area of one institution may need to be expanded or contracted, depending on the population density of the area covered and how varied the area is economically and linguistically. Branch service areas and regional coverage will have to be adjusted to ensure viability while not losing the emphasis on deep local knowledge. The wealth management principle is predicated on solid information and good advice that enables clients to properly use a full range of financial services. The demands of the wealth management approach have required persistence and patience besides staff and client training. It is also worth considering whether a balance of staff training and client training might be more feasible and lead to better outcomes than the current KGFS approach of primarily focusing on staff capability to provide good financial advice.

Under the KGFS model a branch is expected to achieve operational efficiency in around eight months and break even in 20 months. The depth of penetration in a single local area enables KGFS branches to reach scale in a relatively small geography. It is projected that the Tamil Nadu KGFS institution (Pudhuaaru KGFS) will achieve full profitability during 2012, based on depth of penetration and the increasing maturation of its 66 branches. This matches KGFS's initial expectations, which took a four to five year view on what is required to achieve deep financial inclusion.

To enhance the reach and to expand to wider geographies, the operation model of KGFS has undergone a strategic change from a balance sheet origination model to a predominantly direct origination model (DO). For direct origination model, IFMR Rural Channels would partner with a bank as their business correspondent (BC) or with an NBFC, offering an array of products. The implication of this model for the customers is paramount for attaining financial inclusion in remote rural areas.

Post the Andhra crisis, all financial institutions including MFI's catering to the rural market have been facing an uphill task in raising funds both debt and equity. IFMR Rural Channels Pvt. Ltd, the investment and distribution company, which is also the licensee of KGFS raised its first external equity from Lok Capital and Proparco of France, in March 2012.

The KGFS model demonstrates how a business model can be reconfigured to pursue complete financial inclusion, committing to reach as many households as possible in a service area, putting client needs at the center, and offering a wide range of needed services. However, the effectiveness of the wealth management approach at client level needs to be assessed in detail before expansion of the model. IFMR has already launched an evaluation study focusing on the impact of the model both at institutional as well as client perspective covering social and economic aspects and the results are expected in 2012–15. This model, being commercial in nature, the financial feasibility and pricing of products assumes greater significance for future expansion.

FINANCIAL INCLUSION—ISSUES AND CHALLENGES

Financial inclusion means much more than simply having or not having a bank account: it goes beyond the mere *availability* of services to their a*doption and usage*. A majority of the clients with formal accounts makes one to two withdrawals or deposits a month, while 10 per cent of formal accounts are inactive. In a study covering four microfinance providers, CGAP observed that a staggering 70 per cent of cell phone banking accounts is currently inactive. While this is an old issue in microcredit, it seems to have re-emerged with a new buzz. The implicit argument was that lower-than-expected retention rates reflected client failure to see the value of the product, rather than a provider's failure to appreciate their market.

Many microfinance providers assume that consumers, once enrolled, will use their financial products forever. Yet, just like providers, clients take their time in testing out the added value of new microfinance products—not just loans, savings and insurance, but also smart cards and cell phone banking—as they come on the market. It has to be noted that frequency of use is not synonymous with continuous use. The Findex data show that incomes in the lower quintiles are often too small and too variable to permit continuous use of all types of financial services. For the consumer, these choices are trade-offs; by contrast, providers tend to view products in silos.

Information on micro-level issues such as how clients prioritize and in what order they use financial services are important, which need to be carefully studied. For poor people, building financial assets is hard. Savings are usually earmarked for meeting financial goals and are reluctantly redirected to other uses, including health emergencies, the death of a loved one, crop loss or theft, and fire. Households faced with a sudden shock such as these, take their first stop towards borrowing from relatives, friends and associates, while credit from formal financial service providers is used least. But it is worth noting that accessing formal credit is rarely timely, especially when the situation is urgent.

Financial inclusion is a challenging task as it has to facilitate access, ensure adoption and sustained use of financial products and services, which requires behavioural changes on the part of the users. However, changing patterns of financial behavior is not easy. Most risk-mitigation strategies have evolved over time. Behavioural shifts will require a strategy that affects changes in consumer knowledge, skills and attitudes, at the same time as triggering new product offerings and/or delivery methods by financial service providers. This is no small challenge, since financial service providers and their clients often perceive the same situation very differently. The goal must be to diminish the perception gap between the users and the providers, moving each toward a point where their gains are optimized. There is a need for a more level playing field, one where clients have the resources and confidence to negotiate in their self-interest. Financial education, with its emphasis on building new knowledge, skills and attitudes, can change behavior and increase consumer capability to assess the financial products available to them and providers of financial services all along the value chain should make it a priority to gain a much richer understanding of the dynamic behaviors within their market segments if they are to maximize the adoption and usage of their service offerings.

SUMMING UP

Despite the laudable achievements in the field of rural banking, issues such as slow progress in increasing the share of institutional credit, high dependence of on non-institutional sources, skewed nature of access to credit between developed regions and less developed regions loom larger than ever before.[27] Financial inclusion has remained a supply side initiative, and the nature of demand has not been fully internalized while designing the inclusions strategy. Therefore, the key issue now is to ensure that credit from institutional sources achieves wider coverage and expands financial inclusion. If PACS and MFIs already have a network then why not make use of the same instead of creating parallel high cost networks

For achieving comprehensive financial inclusion, though, earlier the focus was in credit and savings inclusion, broad-based demand driven innovative financial products with cost effective delivery mechanism assumes greater significance for future strategies. Technology failure in the field making the BC services unreliable—without fixing this no point in going for even better technologies.

What is important is achieving the larger objective: financial inclusion should lead to financial security for the poor and the vulnerable. That is, at some stage, the focus is bound to shift to the quality and not the quantity of inclusion.[28]

Microfinance being a sector that serves a very large number of small clients distributed over a wide geographical area could be a highly cost-intensive proposition. The adoption of appropriate technological solutions both in hardware and software platforms will ensure that the cost remains within the reasonable limits. This further enhances the value proposition for banks, BCs and, above all, customers. Better integration of platforms and technology deployed for Financial Inclusion purposes with those for mainstream banking is essential to fully reap the benefits of BCs as a new channel. The customers especially from the poor and vulnerable groups for whom the institutional credit structure was inaccessible till recently are willing to pay for the better services. Hence there is a greater scope for the BC model, which is emerging as a strong intermediary between the customers and banks in the financial inclusion strategy, to reinvent more players including MFIs and SHG federations.

ANNEX 4.1[1]
Sustainability of BC Network Managers (BCNMs) in India: Analysis on the pricing structures[29]

INTRODUCTION

Business correspondent network managers (BCNM) have a very vital role in making electronic/mobile banking (e/m-banking) a success. However their earnings and sustainability have been a constant and unaddressed challenge.[30] They must achieve basic economic thresholds of meeting expenses and earning a reasonable return; yet they are often squeezed and dwarfed by large players such as banks, telecoms, technology service providers (TSP) and government agencies during pricing discussions and negotiations. BCNMs must cross two independent break-even points (first, by earning revenue through enrolment commissions and second, through transaction commissions) before they achieve sustained profitability.[31]

PRODUCT REVENUE DRIVERS

The most common revenue drivers for a variety of BC channels in India are described below.

Account opening: Since the first step of financial inclusion is opening an account for the un-banked population, all banks in India remunerate BCNMs for opening accounts. However, BCNMs cannot become too dependent on this commission as high rates of account opening cannot be sustained indefinitely.

Deposit and withdrawal facilitation: Not all banks remunerate BCNMs for facilitating deposit and withdrawal transactions. Some banks pay a commission for facilitating either deposits or withdrawals; while some pay for both.

Money transfers/remittances/P2P transfers: The success of SBI's *tatkaal* product, which allows deposits into remote accounts, highlights the demand for remittances in India.[32] In India, banks offer money transfer facilities both 'within' the BCNM's customers for that bank and 'outside' the BCNM's network to any account of the same bank, such as those typically serviced at branches. However, the latter option is still rare compared to the former. Among banks that offer both types of transfers, the commission for outside network transfers is higher than for within network transfers. Inter-bank money transfer is still not very common in the Indian branchless banking landscape, but is being slowly rolled-out by the major banks.

Balance maintenance: Though not as prevalent as other schemes, some banks also pay BCNMs for the balances maintained in the accounts operated through the BCNM's network, as banks ultimately earn revenue using depositors' money. The payment calculation for balance maintenance is generally performed on a quarterly basis. However, most banks do not offer balance based commissions and few BCNMs take a long-term, balance-focused view to promote it.

Account maintenance: Some banks, especially those that do not pay for transaction facilitation, pay BCNMs for the accounts that are active during a specific period. Most banks take a one-year period with at least one transaction to consider an account active. By paying an account maintenance fee, banks compel BCNMs to encourage transactions in order to keep the accounts active, even though they are not remunerated for transaction facilitation.

COMMISSION CALCULATION METHODS

In order to assess the different methods of calculating BCNM commissions, *MicroSave* analyzed the financial results of an Indian BCNM based on six different types of commission structures offered by three

[1]The author gratefully acknowledges the support provided by Dr Manoj K. Sharma, Director, MicroSave and his team in preparing the Annexure.

major banks in India over the course of 12 months. The dynamics of broadly used commission calculation methods in India are presented below.

Percentage vs. flat: The overall results indicate that remuneration for facilitating a transaction is generally maximized for BCNMs when the commission payable is calculated as a percentage of the value of transaction. However, flat fees help cover fixed operational and financial costs incurred on low value transactions. For a BCNM that facilitates a large number of small value transactions (perhaps in the early roll-out period), a flat fee-based commission system would be more financially beneficial. However, of course, as the transaction size grows, percentage based commissions become more rewarding.

Tier-based/hybrid pricing: Tier-based/hybrid fee structures perhaps have the best features of both flat and percentage based commissions. In this scheme, low value transactions that fall under the lowest tier are paid on a nominal flat fee basis, and subsequent higher value transactions are paid either on a percentage basis or a higher flat fee basis. While these structures were not prevalent in earlier years, both are becoming more common with Indian banks. Below is an example of tier-based pricing.

Tier-based pricing model example

Range	Floor (₹)	Cap (₹)	Fee
Range I	1	499	2.00
Range II	500	2,499	5.00
Range III	2,500	10,000	10.00

Of late, some customers are also given the option to choose their pricing plans (though giving a choice is less common). The BCNM's commission is calculated based on the customer's choice of pricing plans. The following are two commonly offered pricing plans.

Pay-per-use pricing plans: Under the pay-per-use pricing method, the customer pays for every transaction that he/she performs, and BCNMs are compensated for every transaction that is facilitated through a combination of the calculation methods above. Pay-per-use pricing is generally the preferred plan for poor customers.

Subscription plans: When customers opt for subscription plans, they pay an additional fee that entitles them to a certain number of 'free' transactions for a specific period. For every active customer who opts for a subscription plan, the bank will share a part of the subscription fee paid by these customers with the BCNM, and they do not pay commissions to the BCNM for facilitating individual transactions. *MicroSave's* analysis indicates that even when 50 per cent of customers opt for subscriptions plan, both pay per use plans and yearly subscription plans yield about the same revenue for the BCNM, based on actual customer behaviours for one BCNM.[33] Most banks do not provide this choice to customers and generally offer only pay-per-use plans.

REVENUES TO THE BCNM

Having discussed each revenue driver individually, the commission structure is now analyzed in its entirety. The graph beside shows revenue that a BCNM has earned from one agent in one month, on average, analyzed over a period of one year.[34] It is quite clear that the remuneration from Bank A is the highest! Yet before drawing the conclusion that Bank A's structure is most promising, it is important to analyze the revenue break-up and to understand which commission structure is more stable and sustainable.

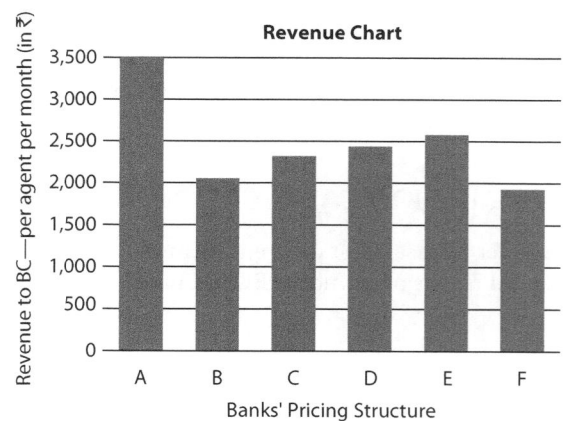

REVENUE CONTRIBUTION[35]

From the graph below, it is evident that each bank and its commission structure favour a 'primary product' and not all favour the same products equally. For instance, commission structures A, B and C target transfers outside network by heavily incentivizing BCNMs for facilitating transfers outside network (and due to demand). As mentioned earlier, option A yielded the most per agent per month with this focus but also with a smaller but significant balance of fees from deposits (15 per cent) and withdrawals (16 per cent). Structure C also focuses on out of network transfers, but also has a significant percentage of its revenues from account opening (13.5 per cent) and withdrawals (11 per cent).

Unlike other commission structures, commission structure F's revenues are equally split between account opening, deposits and withdrawals in the ratio of 30 per cent, 34 per cent and 34 per cent respectively. Commission structures D and E on the other hand target account opening. This focus on account opening seems to be an old practice due to RBI mandates to open accounts that are slowly being phased out by Indian banks after many mishaps and distortions. Even though options D and E seem to be the second and third most lucrative option respectively, they are likely not sustainable in the long run as new account opening growth will slow.

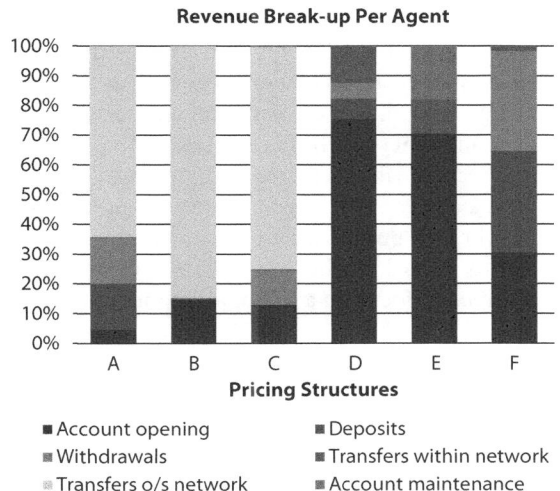

COST SAVINGS FOR BANK

Outsourcing low-value transactions to BC channel not only results in cost savings but also helps to build efficiency in the bank branch operation. Thus, the efficiency built can be utilized to increase the business by channelizing it on high net worth transaction. A significant amount of time is spent in opening accounts and servicing deposits account (accepting deposits and facilitating withdrawals). In a typical rural branch, which has five to seven staff members, 39 per cent of the time is spent in opening and serving deposits accounts. This provides a clear case for banks to develop the business correspondent and use it for opening and servicing deposit accounts, thus utilizing the time saved for developing other remunerative product lines such as big ticket size agriculture loans, trade financing etc.

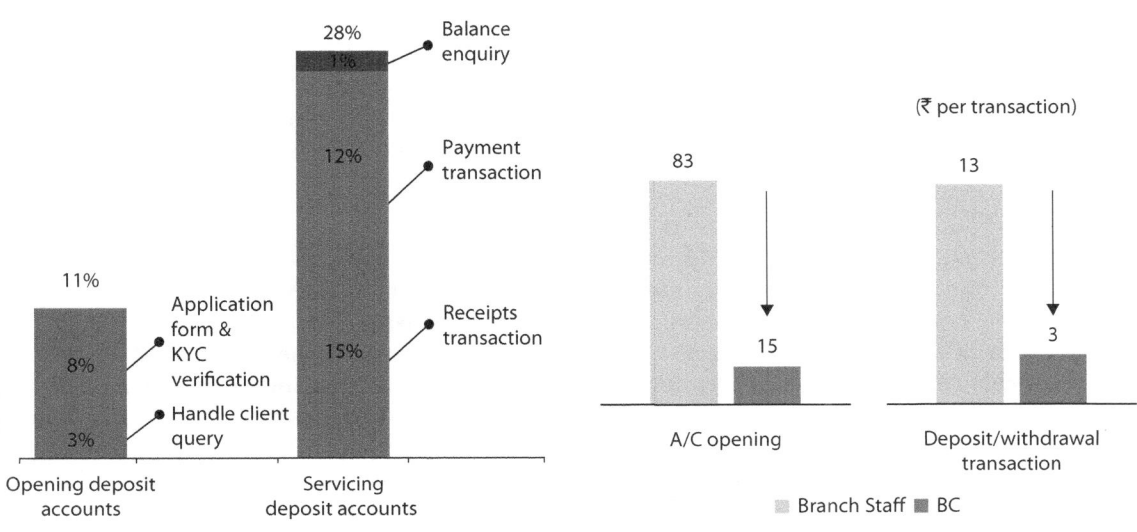

MicroSave's activity based costing implementation at selected four rural branches of a client bank shows that every account opened in the branch costs ₹83 whereas it costs ₹15 if the account is opened through the BC channel. This includes the commission paid to the BCNM and other overheads involved in managing the channel. Similarly, every deposit or a withdrawal transaction performed in the bank branch costs ₹13 per transaction whereas it cost only ₹3 per transaction when performed through BC channel.

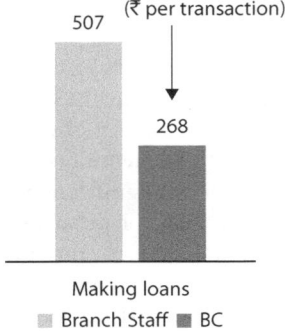

The study also indicates that offering loans through the BC channel can help the bank to reduce up to 50 per cent of the cost of making loans. The study shows that on an average a branch staff spends seven per cent of his/her working hours in handling customer loan enquiries, pre-sanctions and performing loan application and KYC verification, and it costs ₹507 that includes staff cost and all pertinent branch overheads. These are activities that can be efficiently handled by BC personnel. If these activities are performed through BC channel, it would cost ₹268 that includes BCNM and other overheads involved in managing the channel.

In a branch, where all credit and savings products were being delivered through the BCNMs, there was not just an increase in business due to what was directly brought in by the BCNMs, but even an increase in regular branch business. The graphs below display this phenomenon clearly. This is perhaps due to decongestion of bank branches as BCNMs help to ease the transaction pressure and improve efficiency of staff that helped to focus on additional business generation.

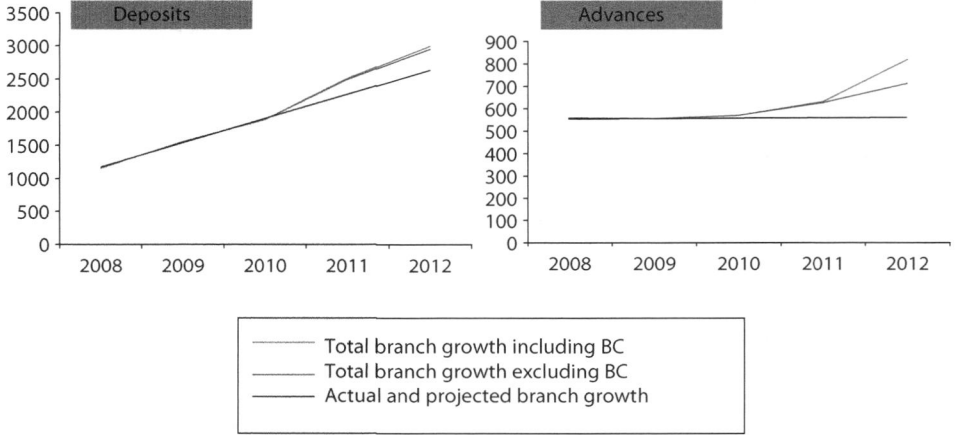

Thus, the ability of the business correspondent model to reduce costs not only helps banks to sustainably serve the low balance no-frill accounts, but also provides a compelling business case for banks to develop the business correspondent channel as an extension of banking halls. Developing the business correspondent model as a full service channel will result in multiple benefits to banks—reduction in costs, increased efficiency, increase in branch profitability, ultimately resulting in *real* financial inclusion.

CONCLUSION

Easy and quick returns are from account openings, however BCNMs should remember that sustained earnings are from transaction-based revenues. Offering balance or account maintenance-based commissions could be in the best interest of banks and BCNMs. However this needs a longer-term outlook by both. Though earlier either flat or percentage fees were offered by the banks, it now appears that tiered and hybrid pricing (a combination of both flat and percentage) is becoming more common. Interestingly, in most of the commission structures discussed, the contribution of revenues is skewed towards one revenue driver. While it does appear that money transfer/remittance is the key to revenue maximization, it is also important to have a portfolio of other products. With evolving and newly emerging business models, rapid technological innovations, state initiatives and more players entering the market, competition will play an influential role through new product features, convenience and commissions. In this scenario, major dependence on one product could be a risky strategy.

To ensure the success of branchless banking and financial inclusion initiatives, banks need to offer a diversified commission structure, such as the emerging tiered commission structures. By pushing one product, banks risk wrongly incentivizing BCNMs to focus only on the most lucrative ones, while ignoring other products. BCNMs could also tie-up with more than one bank to diversify the risk as well as to cater to a wider customer base. BCNMs would also do well by enhancing the depth of products offered by partnering with multiple service providers. Services like merchant payments, airtime top-ups, international remittances and social security payments can ensure revenue diversity and stability for BCNMs. Additional banking services being carried out by business facilitators like loan sourcing and repayments could add to the earnings and have not been extensively explored.

NOTES AND REFERENCES

The author gratefully acknowledges the support provided by Dr Manoj K. Sharma, Director MicroSave and his team in preparing the Annexure.

1. NABARD. 2010. 'Microfinance—Overview', Occasional Paper, Mumbai: National Bank for Agriculture and Rural Development.

2. *Promoting Financial Inclusion*. 2012. New Delhi: FICCI report, http://www.m-cril.com/BackEnd/ModulesFiles/Publication/Report-on-Promoting-Financial-Inclusion.pdf

3. Demirguc-Kunt, Asli, and LeoraKlapper. 2012. 'Measuring Financial Inclusion: The Global Findex Database'. Policy Research Working Paper 6025, Washington: World Bank.

4. Rangarajan, C. 2006. Committee on Financial Inclusion, Government of India.

5. Raguraman Committe Planning Commission. 2008. 'A hundred small steps: Report of the Committee on Financial Sector Reforms' Available at; www.planningcommission.gov.in/reports/genrep/report_fr.htm

6. 2012. *The Little Data Book on Financial Inclusion*. The World Bank, p. 74.

7. While financing through SHGs increased access to finance for the poor, the RBI still does not consider membership in SHG as financial inclusion.

8. RBI Monetary Policy 2012–13, Mumbai: The Reserve Bank of India.

9. Reddy, D.R.K. 2012. 'Financial Inclusion: Road Ahead, Bankquest', *The Journal of Indian Institute of Banking & Finance*, 83(2): 40–46.

10. 2012. Budget Speech by Finance Minister, Union Budget presentation in Parliament.

11. Graham A.N. Wright, Mukesh Sadana, Puneet Chopra and Manoj Sharma. 2011. http://www.microsave.org/sites/default/files/research_papers/Why_EM_Banking_Will_Soon_Reach_Scale_in_India.pdf

12. See *MicroSave* Policy Brief. Forthcoming. 'Is the Business Correspondent Model in Policy Paralysis?'

13. See *MicroSave* Case Study on FINO's Electronic Benefit Transfer System for *Tendu* Leaf Collectors. 2011. http://www.microsave.org/sites/default/files/research_papers/Case_Study_FINO_EBT_System_for_Tendu_Leaf_Collectors.pdf

14. See *MicroSave*, 2011. Review of MMT Payments to Accredited Social Health Activists (ASHAs) in Sheikhpura, Bihar. http://www.microsave.org/briefing_notes/review-of-mmt-payments-to-accredited-social-health-activists-ashas-in-sheikhpura-biha

15. 2012. 'Financial Inclusion: A study on the Efficacy of Banking Correspondent Model,' Study conducted by SaDhan and City Foundation.

16. N. Srinivasan, L. M. Ganesan Aimthy Thoumoung. 2012. 'Functionality and Sustainability of Customer Service Points', Survey conducted by CAB and CGAP (Report to be published by CAB is expected to be in the public domain shortly).

17. http://microfinance.cgap.org/2012/05/18/india%e2%80%99s-mobile-banking-ekosystem/. Accessed in July 2012.

18. http://technology.cgap.org/2012/03/13/eko%e2%80%99s-mobile-banking-demonstrating-the-power-of-a-basic-payments-product/. Accessed in July 2012.

19. http://technology.cgap.org/2012/02/09/an-optimistic-picture-of-branchless-banking-from-india-interview-with-microsave/. Accessed in July 2012.

20. http://microfinance.cgap.org/2012/05/18/india%e2%80%99s-mobile-banking-ekosystem/. Accessed in July 2012.

21. http://finmin.nic.in/reports/Report_Task_Force_Aadhaar_PaymentInfra.pdf. Accessed in July 2012.

22. http://microfinance.cgap.org/2012/03/26/the-biggest-social-experiment-on-the-planet%e2%80%94-is-unique-id-a-unique-opportunity-for-india%e2%80%99s-poor/. Accessed in July 2012.

23. http://technology.cgap.org/2012/03/29/branchless-banking-in-india-3-more-reasons-for-optimism/#more-5685. Accessed in July 2012.

24. Data on state wise distribution of SBLP clients collected from NABARD. Though the region wise MFI client's information is available in the SaDhan

publication, the state wise data is not made available. Hence the same has been worked out based on the proportion as in the previous year.

25. http://www.microsave.net/sites/files/technical-Briefs/indiaFocusNotes/IFN_67_ Clients_Willingness_ to_Pay_Reasonable_Fee_for_BC_Services.pdf. Accessed in July 2012.

26. Ananth Bindu, Gregory Chen and Staphen Rasmussen. 2012. 'The Pursuit of Complete Financial Inclusion: The KGFS Model in India'. Available at http://www.cgap.org/gm/document-1.9.57523/Forum4.pdf.

27. Puhazhendhi, V. 2012. 'Financial Inclusion—Forward step for Microfinance Sector, Bank Quest', *The Journal of Indian Institute of Banking and Finance*, 83(2): 5.

28. Bakshi Prakash. 2012. 'Financial Inclusion—BC/BF Model—What New, Bank Quest', *The Journal of Indian Institute of Banking and Finance*, 83(2): 30.

29. Compiled from *MicroSave* India Focus Notes 71, 'Sustainability of BC Network Managers (BCNMs) in India—How are BCNMs Paid?', 72 'Sustainability of BC Network Managers (BCNMs)—Review of Commission Structures' and 73 'Sustainability of BC Network Managers (BCNMs)—Business Scenarios and its Effects'. It should be noted that this note focuses exclusively on top-line revenue for BCNMs and does not take into account the relationship revenue maximizing has with costs.

30. Please note that the price that a customer pays does not directly reach BCNMs in India, as BCNMs are not allowed to charge customers directly. The revenue earned by the BCNM is totally dependent on the commission paid by banks. For more information, see: 2009. 'Financial Inclusion by Extension of Banking Services—Use of Business Correspondents (BCs), RBI Circular No. RBI/2009–10/238, Reserve Bank of India.

31. See *MicroSave* India Focus Note 24, 'Making Business Correspondence Work in India'.

32. See *MicroSave,* India Focus Note 68 'SBI *Tatkal*-From Cash to Cash Cow'.

33. A subscription plan yielded four per cent higher revenue than a pay-per-use plan, with transaction levels kept constant.

34. Other than commission structures, all other variables were held constant, such as transaction volumes and number of accounts.

Microfinance—beyond credit

Traditionally, microcredit is viewed as a mechanism for credit delivery to rural poor, in order to enable them taking up income-generating activities to support their livelihood. However, in several instances, microcredit clients used the credit availed for various kinds of consumption purposes. In recent times, microcredit clients are provided with diverse set of special purpose loans and services such as savings, health, insurance and pension, water supply and sanitation, housing as well as financial literacy. There is increasing evidence that providing client-responsive financial services can both serve the needs of poor people while maintaining or in-fact improving the sustainability and profitablility of MFIs. The major financial institutions such as banks and insurance companies are providing a bundle of products and services to serve a host of customer needs. These products are not only necessary to attract a diverse range of customers, but also to reduce the operating costs through economies of scale and scope. The same logic could be extended to microfinance institutions and other operators in the microcredit and insurance industries to justify their role as providers of range of products and services apart from microcredit. Many MFIs and public sector as well as private sector insurance companies have already forayed into the business of microinsurance and micro pension. Similarly, a number of MFIs are providing other products and services such as savings, health and housing loans, loans for water supply and sanitation, etc. For the purpose of this chapter, microfinance products such as savings, microinsurance, micropension and credit support for other than income generation and consumption are defined as beyond credit innovation. This chapter provides an overview of these products including a brief description of their performance, along with a description of specific programmes implemented by various agencies.

SAVINGS

Savings have been an integral part of budgeting in all households, as insurance against emergencies, for religious and social obligations, and for investment and for future consumption. However, even though the poor are inclined to save, they often do so by informal mechanisms that fail to meet their needs in a convenient, cost-effective and secure manner resulting in the loss or misuse of their hard earned savings. The poor look for some system to provide the security and accessibility necessary for them to save. Therefore, when they are given an opportunity to save in a safe and secure manner, their commitment to saving is remarkable. Several studies have highlighted the need for savings services to the poor for two distinct needs such as planned expenditures intended to meet lifecycle events; as well as cash flow management so as to meet regular expenses or emergencies, given the uneven and irregular income streams.

Past studies in MFIs show that only a small percentage of delayed payments of loans were in the nature of willful default, the rest occurring due to immediate cash requirements of the households, which could have been serviced by appropriate savings options, if available. This is also obvious from the fact that household savings were cited as the most commonly used avenue by households to repay loans in lean periods and loans falling towards delinquency. Another point that came to the fore was the need for structured savings options to service lifecycle needs. Many respondents have cited lifecycle events as a significant contributor to financial stress; the five most stressful events cited being marriage, education, setting up a business, house construction and festivals.

From an organizational perspective, provision of savings services brings some important advantages for the institution:

1. Competitive edge as a one stop shop for all financial needs;
2. Product diversification, thereby providing for an alternate source of income which would not require the level of capitalization required by a credit product;
3. Improvement in the loan portfolio quality, since the clients would have access to a reserve to turn to in case of shortfalls;
4. Better outreach by enabling the organization to serve clients who may not be interested in/require credit;
5. Enhanced client loyalty which can be crucial in ensuring retention given the trust element that typically accompanies savings;
6. Increased operational efficiency through leveraging existing branch infrastructure and human resources to deliver a wider range of services; and
7. Additional possibility to bring cash transactions like loan repayments and disbursements by linking client's savings accounts through a mobile platform with the MFI's account, resulting in reduced risk and increased operational cost efficiency.
8. Therefore, it is very essential for an MFI to do the following before finalising savings products:

   - Understand the features of product offerings of different savings options and make an objective comparison of the advantages and disadvantages of each; and
   - Assess the fit of different savings options suited to the MFI under the criteria of client demand, institutional capacity, governance requirements and external checks.

A study by the Institute for Financial Management and Research revealed that saving was common among the majority of the clients.[1] It was found that a staggering 75 per cent of interviewed clients saved in at least one form in the three months prior to the survey. SHGs (40 per cent of 115 clients) were the most popular form of savings in Maharashtra, whereas National Banks were used by West Bengal clients (40 per cent of 200 clients), Karnataka (46 per cent of 202 clients) and UP (21 per cent of 204 clients). 80 per cent of 205 clients from urban areas of Chennai, Tamil Nadu were using local NGO/MFI service as one of the savings avenue. Non-routine expenditures such as marriages, festival and funeral were overwhelmingly financed through savings.

CATEGORIZATION OF SAVINGS OPTIONS

Regulatory requirements mandate that NBFCs have to depend largely on vending of third party products so as to provide savings options to their clients. The other option is to provide quasi-savings products like gold acquisition loans, which could be delivered by the NBFC itself as its own proprietary product. In both these cases, the opportunity for the organization to mobilize funds would be non-existent and the financial incentive to the organization would be in terms of revenue from fee income or interest spread.

Saving options

1. Bank Led Savings Options
   Business Correspondent (BC) model has been used by commercial banks to provide savings as well as term deposits to end-clients where branch infrastructure is limited or absent. The RBI has been encouraging the model which depends on third party agents to provide the service. There have been many initiatives involving the electronic and mobile banking solutions within the BC model so as to enable efficient delivery of customer solutions. The model typically focused on providing no-frills accounts; but lately some banks have also started delivering normal savings accounts, recurring deposits and term deposits also using the BC channel.

2. Proprietary Options
   The most prominent proprietary savings option seen in India has been the Gold Acquisition Loan which is a quasi-savings instrument working on the principle of reverse savings. Some prominent MFIs as well as NBFCs primarily working in South India have been offering gold acquisition loans to their clients so as to enable a build-up of savings balances in the form of gold.

3. Mutual Fund Products
   Money market mutual funds are in general considered to be relatively stable, highly liquid instruments since they focus on investing in debt (largely government debt of short duration like T Bills) and since they have historically shown very little day to day fluctuation in their Net Asset Values (NAV). Some organizations have adapted

money market instruments to provide a savings bank account proxy for their clients.

4. Pension Products

Pension products which provide a regular income post retirement have been in vogue for a long time in India. But most of the pension schemes have been directed at the organized sector and generally directed at middle—higher income groups. Recently, there have been several voluntary pension products oriented at the bottom-of-the-pyramid customers and delivered through channel partners including MFIs. Government of India's New Pension Scheme (NPS) which also has a voluntary nature as well as a provision for periodical withdrawals is an interesting option, which can combine the attributes of a voluntary savings product into a pension product. The government is also considering the introduction of an option for unorganized workers under the NPS.

5. Insurance Products

Insurance products combining the features of life insurance as well as term savings are another option available to MFIs for exploration. ULIPs are one option available for further exploration. Another route to take would be to offer endowment policies in partnership with life insurance companies.

Comparison of savings options on specific attributes

1. Cost to customer: There were several costs to be incurred by the customer in availing the different savings options available. These included both charges payable to the service provider as well as other transactional expenses incurred indirectly by the customer. Many options did not have an upfront registration fee other than pension schemes, which charged registration fees and some gold loan schemes, which levied a processing fee. Transaction fees were charged largely in insurance and pension fund schemes, while gold loan schemes charged a straight interest rate on the loan. In pension schemes, transaction fees as well as registration charges are regulated by the Pension Fund Regulatory and Development Authority. Other transaction costs incurred by clients indirectly involved being subject to market risks, costs of technology like GPRS, SMS cost, travelling costs and loss of value of investment on surrender of insurance policies before maturity.

2. Returns to the clients: The returns to the clients were generally variable in nature due to the fact that returns were, in general, market linked. The type and range of returns expected varied widely based on the savings instrument used. Notable exceptions were no frills accounts and term-life insurance schemes, which offered guaranteed returns. Some of the savings options provided additional benefits in the form of insurance cover, tax benefits etc. In gold loans, the returns were essentially linked to expected appreciation in gold prices.

3. Primary utility of the product: Of the savings options studied, the primary utility of most schemes were for the longer term, with strong disincentives for withdrawal before maturity (e.g., comparatively low surrender value of life insurance policies). Exceptions were no frills accounts delivered by the BC model and MMMF, which were essentially designed to be instruments to manage short term cash flow smoothening. Gold loans were interesting since, though it was primarily designed for long term usage, it provided limited short term liquidity by an option to pledge the gold.

4. Security aspects: Trust in the organization is crucial where the customers are investing their money. In most of the options studied, the association with a respected and well known financial service provider provided the element of trust. This was reinforced by physical evidence like transaction receipts. In many cases, the client is also exposed to market risks.

5. Cost to the organization: The costs incurred by organizations introducing savings options include the cost of identifying and entering into partnerships with other third parties like banks, insurance firms, mutual funds and pension funds. They also incur considerable expenses towards promotion as well as training of staff/agents.

6. Returns to the organization: Returns to the organization were in the nature of commissions in general (other than in the case of gold acquisition loans where the income was from the interest rate spread). The returns varied widely on product to product and from the partnering organization.

7. Regulatory aspects: Entering into partnerships with other players would necessitate being subject to additional regulation by regulators like the Reserve Bank of India, the Securities Exchange Board of India, Insurance Regulatory and Development Authority and Pension Fund Regulatory and Development Authority (PFRDA). Gold acquisition loans were the only option where the

requirement for additional regulatory compliance was minimal.

8. Need for partnerships: Almost all options required partnerships in one way or the other. In most options the primary product was owned by the partner, while the field-level organization functioned primarily as a delivery channel.

HEALTHCARE AND SANITATION INITIATIVES

One of the important issues in livelihood development and poverty alleviation is tackling malnutrition and health problems faced by the poor in both rural and urban areas. Poverty and poor health are often entangled in a vicious cycle, and the problem of breaking this cycle is likely to become worsened as a result of mounting costs of health care. Consequently, poverty alleviation and universal health care have become the twin goals of the development policy in recent years. Recent studies on the economic costs of illness stress the detrimental effect of health shocks on rural households, which results not only in direct financial and time costs but also causes indirect costs of illness such as a reduction in labour supply.[2]

India's share of public expenditure in total health outlay has been increasing steadily. This trend is very encouraging and needs to continue because greater reliance on private spending on healthcare infrastructure and service may lead to inadequate provision of healthcare. The increasing importance given to universal health care is evident from the fact that the share of Government spending on public health is poised to nearly double from 1.4 to 2.5 per cent of GDP by the end of the Twelfth Five Year Plan (2017). This increased spending will provide support towards a vision of universal health care, which will enable every citizen to access preventive, diagnostic, therapeutic and rehabilitative services. To accomplish this, India embarked on the National Rural Health Mission in 2005, an extraordinary effort to strengthen the health systems.

The need for publicly-funded universal health coverage is beyond argument. At present, private out-of-pocket health expenditure constitutes 3.3 per cent of GDP, or around 67 per cent of the total spending. Moving towards universalization of healthcare can cut it to about 33 per cent by 2022.[3] The High Level Expert Group of the Planning Commission has provided a road map that envisages setting up of public health cadres for services and management at the national and state levels, standard setting, and a timeline for merger of existing government-led health insurance schemes such as the Rashtriya Swasthya Bima Yojana and those operating at the State level. An increase in outlay on medicines from 0.1 per cent of GDP to 0.5 per cent for public procurement can ensure free universal access to essential drugs. However, this has to be supplemented with appropriate health insurance programmes so as to ensure a reduction in out-of-pocket expenditure.

Recent estimates suggest that the role of health expenditure of households has increased substantially in the most recent period. According to the Report of the National Commission on Macroeconomics and Health, 2005, households undertook nearly three-fourth of all the health spending in the country. Public spending was only 22 per cent, and all other sources accounted for less than 5 per cent. Further, there is a trend of gradually increasing household expenditure on health care, even as a share of household budgets. Households are found spending increasing amounts on private health services as the quality of public health services is deteriorating by the day.[4] Therefore, providing healthcare services in rural areas at lower costs assumes enormous significance in achieving the development goals.

Microfinance in healthcare

There are two important justifications for microfinance institutions to include health services in their agenda of activities: health services are a natural extension of their mission of financial security and social protection of the client, and healthier clients better serve the microfinance institutions' goals of growth and long-term viability. Clients are not the only beneficiary; when a family member is ill, it affects productivity. Thus access to health-related programmes and services generally includes the household, not just the client.[5] Provision of credit alone is not sufficient to address the multi-dimensional challenges posed by poverty. As ill-health and poverty are closely linked to each other, ensuring timely and cost-effective delivery of health-related services is of paramount importance not only in eradicating poverty but also in protecting households from falling into poverty. As microfinance institutions work with the poor and have long-term relationship with their clients, mostly women, they offer a unique opportunity to employ their vast infrastructure for delivery of health-related services to those most in need.

As a crucial means of women empowerment, microcredit programme could act as an important vehicle through which, not only the health-related awareness can be created but also the health service products could be delivered to rural poor at lower costs. Lack of health knowledge among rural poor especially among women, lack of physical and financial access to quality healthcare, and the importance of women's role in overall household health and nutritional status are the important reasons for a number of microfinance institutions to include health services in their agenda. Further, as demonstrated by many studies, health status of the family is one of the important determinants of labour supply decisions, and hence the income of the households and the loan repayment are closely linked with health status of client households. This provides another important rationale for microfinance institutions' interest in healthcare services, and there are significant economies of scale and scope when microfinance institutions are involved in these tasks rather than a separate agency for healthcare services.

Studies have shown that MFIs could provide health services to rural poor at lower marginal costs,[6,7] in view of their large and growing network. In view of its greater outreach among poor in rural and remote areas, microfinance institutions and self-help groups could play a complementary role in delivering health services where public health system is underperforming its job. A number of studies have reported significant positive impact of health services extended by microfinance institutions or self-help groups especially in the areas of maternal and infant mortality.[8]

Healthcare initiatives by MFIs

A number of MFIs and SHGs are providing one or more health services to their clients. An analysis of 134 MFIs in India shows that approximately 25 per cent had provided some type of health services to clients.[9] A survey by Freedom from Hunger, the Indian Institute of Public Health at Ghandinagar, and the Microcredit Summit Campaign of 19 self-identified MFIs and SHPIs providing health services in 2011, provides an overview of the types of organizations that are engaged in linking microfinance and health, client needs, the types of services provided and some approximations of costs.[10] The details of these health programs, their locations, total active borrowers and reach of the health program[11] are provided in Table 5.1.

Table 5.1 MFIs reporting active health programmes (2011)

MFI	Registered office	MFI est.	Active borrowers	Health program est.	Access to a health programme
Bandhan	West Bengal	2002	3,227,864	2007	345,750
BWDA	Tamil Nadu	2003	159,684	2003	400,000*
Cashpor	Uttar Pradesh	1997	377,987	2010	45,000
Community Development Society	Maharashtra	1988	5,720	1996	12,000*
ESAF	Kerala	1995	295,270	1995	200,000
Equitas	Tamil Nadu	2007	1,300,000	2007	700,000
Gram Utthan	Odisha	1990	53,142	2004	25,000
Gram Vidiyal	Tamil Nadu	2003	1,046,497	2008	68,933
Kajila Janakalyan Samiti	West Bengal	2000	8,255	2007	5,000
Kotalipara Development Society	West Bengal	1992	60,648	1992	NA
Mahasemam Trust	Tamil Nadu	1999	102,345	2002	200,000*
NEED	Uttar Pradesh	1995	30,751	1997	20,000
Nidan	Bihar	2009	4,614	1997	25,000*
OAZOANE	Tamil Nadu	1998	6,398	1997	3,000
PioneerTrad	Tamil Nadu	1993	22,000	2006	NA
PMD	Tamil Nadu	1975	NA	2009	5,300
SERP	Andhra Pradesh	2000	8,000,000	2005	100,000
SKDRDP	Karnataka	1995	1,400,000	2004	1,690,000*
Star Youth Association	Andhra Pradesh	1997	25,499	2007	6,430
Total			16,126,674		3,851,413

Note: NA – Data not available.

*Reporting reaching community members with health programmes beyond their clients.

The primary health needs addressed by the MFIs in India are maternal care and childhood illnesses, followed by malnutrition, HIV/AIDS, and hygiene and sanitation. The MFIs provide a combination of approaches to address these needs. While health education was the most commonly reported intervention, MFIs are also venturing into the provision of health services through health camps, linkages to health providers and the direct provision of services through clinics and health product distribution. Some of the MFIs are also providing health loans, health savings and health microinsurance.

Though most of the MFIs in the country across the regions are implementing several innovative healthcare and sanitation programmes, as a sample, some selected successful programmes undertaken by MFIs are presented in the Annexure. The case studies include tie-up with the hospitals, efforts to reduce infant and maternal mortality, preventive measures such as water treatment and construction of toilets, etc.

All the programmes discussed are innovative on its own way and the experiences and lessens drawn will certainly provide greater scope for expansion and replication in other areas with in-depth benefit realization. Appropriate integration of the health programmes with other developmental and credit activities assumes greater importance for the success of the health initiatives. Limited evidence is available on what specific elements of integrated programs have been successful. It may be helpful to explore these issues more critically for future plan. Some of the key questions to be answered for further shaping up the opportunities include delivery infrastructure, funding support to reach the vulnerable, capacity of the organizations and supportive institutional arrangements.

Watsan loan

The role of safe drinking water and sanitation (Watsan) in improving health of poor and reducing incidence of diseases is well known. While public and grant funding is able to reach a part of the needy population, suitable financial products can facilitate access to water and sanitation by many other poor. For some time now international NGOs, NGOs, NGO-MFIs and MFIs operating in the country have been convincing government agencies, bankers, policy makers and others about the logic of saving money for poor households through microfinance interventions in water and sanitation. It may not be income generating but it is income saving. Organizations across the world working with poor communities have evolved techniques for arriving at methods to show how individual families in communities have stood to gain economically by taking up Watsan loans. At the current population level of 1,220 million there would be 271.2 million of households (worked out @4.5 persons per household as per the NSSO survey 2010). Of this 65 per cent households are in need of piped connections and that works to 176.3 million of households. Presuming that even 50 per cent of these households would come under any of the central or state interventions, 88.2 million families are in need of financial assistance to get individual drinking water connections. At an average loan size of ₹5,000 the microfinance needed would be ₹4,400 billion for getting individual pipe water connections for 88.2 million families. Similarly at an average loan size of ₹15,000 the microfinance needed for construction of individual toilets for 54.2 million households would be another ₹820 billion

International institutions like water.org, WaterAid, Water for People, Arhgym, Plan India, and others have been playing a crucial role in the Watsan sector across the country. Of all the interventions, the WaterCredit of water.org makes it unique among the lot and can be rightly called the main accelerator of Watsan loans in the country. Recognizing the value of access to potable water and proper sanitation, Hand in Hand India implemented a project in Kancheepuram in Tamil Nadu state. The first phase of the project was implemented by Hand in Hand with the support of water.org during the period December 2008 to May 2011 with the objective to provide access to clean and protected water through private water taps and improve sanitation facilities to the poor. The Hand in Hand watsan loans comprised the ₹6,000 toilet loan and the ₹6,000 and ₹3,000 loans for setting up a water connection in urban and rural areas, respectively. Both the loans were repayable over a period of 10 months. During the project period, Hand in Hand covered five blocks in Kancheepuram district where 3,225 loans totaling ₹20.1 million were given for the construction of toilets and 4,422 loans totaling ₹14.0 million were given for water tap connections. Hand in Hand took feedback from its clients to continuously refine the loan product and make it client centric. The watsan loan programme proved to be very successful; the main reason being the innovative packaging with adequate training, cost effective construction design for reduced investment cost and easy maintenance.

The Watsan loan programme was successful in bringing about a perceptible change in the health behaviour of targeted families. The major impacts of the programme are given below:

1. The end line survey conducted at the end of the Phase I of the project indicated that 24 per cent

of member households in the project area use private toilets against 5 per cent of member households using toilets in the pre-project period.

2. The end line survey further revealed that access to private water tap connections has improved with 70 per cent of member households having access at the end of the project period as compared to 66 per cent in the pre-project period.

3. Water collection time came down by 1 to 2 hours and now lesser physical effort was needed to walk long distances to fetch water. This time and energy saved can be spent productively either at home or at work.

4. There were fewer quarrels at the public tap during water collection.

5. Member households that availed watsan loans reported lower incidence of water borne diseases that could be attributed to their access to protected water and improved sanitation.

6. Panchayat revenues have gone up as people pay the required deposit of ₹1,000 and taxes of ₹360 for taking new water tap connections.

7. It is a huge relief for adolescent girls, elderly persons and the differently-abled, as open defecation was a difficult option for them. It is now convenient for other members also, especially during the rains and after dark.

8. There is enhanced self-esteem among members due to having a toilet in their home.

9. Overall health has improved and out-of-pocket health expenses are lower because of reduction in the occurrence of water borne diseases.

10. Better health has meant more and productive working days, especially for the rural people who depend largely on physical labour to earn their livelihood.

There are, however, a few challenges and limitations of the financing to watsan products through microfinance approaches. Primarily, assessing the demand is a difficult task and this product may not withstand as a stand-alone product due to an income generating nature. However, packaging watsan with another set of services will have better impact. Further government support along with subsidy needs to be adequately integrated for greater success of this product.

MICROINSURANCE

Microinsurance in India has broadly developed as a sub-sector of the insurance industry. India is among the few countries to draft and implement specific microinsurance regulations. However, rural and social sector insurance and microinsurance have always been considered similar by the regulator. The regulator has, so far, counted the rural and social insurance and microinsurance numbers interchangeably.

The Rural and Social Sector Obligation (2002)[12] and the Microinsurance Regulations (2005) have helped the growth of regulated microinsurance in India. According to the IRDA Annual Report, 2010–11, about 3.65 million microinsurance policies were sold in India in the year 2010–11 covering lives of 18.9 million people. The cumulative premium collected from microinsurance was ₹2.86 billion. Hence, microinsurance constituted 4.59 per cent of the total lives covered, 7.6 per cent of total number of policies sold and 0.23 per cent of premium collected by the insurance industry of India. However, these numbers constitute only the policies sold by the insurance companies (Box 5.1).

Box 5.1 Goat insurance

Goat has been one of preferred livelihoods source for rural poor across the nation. However, financial services like credit and insurance accessibility has been a critical constraint to upscale and improve this reliable business of the poor. On livestock insurance, the problems are seen both at demand side (complex registration process, complicated and long formats, low awareness on livestock insurance products, high cost of claim settlements) as well as supply side (low premium size, remoteness, and difficulty in claim verification). Hence, for occupation like goat farming by poor families, community insurance seems only feasible option to enhance insurance literacy, enhance social capital and mitigate risk through community initiatives. The Goat Trust[13] and its partners have taken up the task of providing community insurance for goat farming in one of the poverty pockets and semi-arid regions of the country (Bundelkhand). Under a project supported by Sir Dorabji Tata Trust (SDTT).

As a first part of risk mitigation in goat farming, services of Livestock Nurses (trained semi-literate village women—as per standardised process developed by Goat Trust with 300 such Livestock nurses) had been made available at each hamlet/village level with 50 to 70 goat farmers and 200 goats. A trained Community Livestock Manager (a term used by Goat Trust for trained youth with having basic skills of goat management, effective rural communication and first aid services) has been provided at each cluster of 10 villages to support Livestock Nurses and conduct capacity building training for Goat Farmers. As per community based risk assessment, the three major risks covered under the present insurance scheme are: (*a*) Mortality—100 per cent of sum insured; (*b*) Infertility—40 per cent of sum insured; (*c*) Paralysis of back part—50 per cent of sum insured. Free services include vaccinations, two de-worming, training and regular visit by livestock nurse. The premium is fixed based on live body weight estimation and pricing of goats/kids and bucks are evaluated. Ten per cent of sum assured is taken as premium and a maximum of 50 per cent of market value is covered by the product. For average price of ₹3,000 in the area, a premium of ₹150 is deposited by goat farmer in the fund.

This project is implemented since December 2011 and so far 1,019 goats have been covered under community insurance. In the last five months a total of 24 claims were settled by the claim committee. The average time taken in settlement is less than 20 days. Payment has been received in cash and given by community themselves with a minimum level of paper formalities. Within the limited experiences, this has promoted both a sense of social/mutual help and pro-poor risk management services. Up to December, around 5,000 goats shall be covered under the project meant for goat farmers and whole process shall be managed by community themselves.

Some of the trends clearly visible in the regulated microinsurance sector in India are:

- With a premium collection of ₹2.61 billion, the public insurer (LIC of India) is the market leader. LIC's microinsurance business is generated through 9,724 microinsurance agents (MIA).

- The regulators assumed that the 'rural and social sector obligation' would drive microinsurance innovation by the insurance companies. However, a comparison of number of policies (NoP) sold in rural areas (by private players) with the total number of policies sold reveals that most insurers, adopt a 'just achieve target' approach in microinsurance, so that they only achieve the mandatory number.

- Though every life and general insurance company needs to fulfil their mandatory rural and social sector obligation, only 14 private companies (of a total of 47 private companies) have registered microinsurance products with IRDA. Of these, only seven companies have actually sold microinsurance products in 2010–11. However, except for one, none has under-achieved the rural and social sector obligation. While all the market players have achieved their rural sector targets, very few have sold microinsurance products to do this. Clearly, the insurers do not depend on microinsurance products to achieve the mandatory number anymore. The influence of the mandatory rural targets, which was responsible for the growth of microinsurance in India, has reduced over the years.[14]

- The Microinsurance Regulations of IRDA (2005) proposed specialized distribution channel for microinsurance through the microinsurance agents (MIA). However, only eight insurance companies have actually registered MIAs in last five years. Some private players have even decreased the number of their MIAs in recent years.

Government sponsored microinsurance

Insurance for the low income population is closely linked with the concept of social security. Hence, government sponsorship in microinsurance is to be expected. *Rashtriya Swasthya Bima Yojana* (RSBY) is the flagship health insurance scheme of the Government of India targeted at BPL families. Recently, MGNREGS beneficiaries have been brought under this programme. RSBY is spread over 27 states of India. Enrolment of beneficiaries has been completed in 225 districts in these states and enrolment is getting carried out in 160 districts. The scheme potentially aims to cover 422 districts of the country and 56.56 million families. As on 22 June, 2012, nearly 29 million families have been covered under this scheme. The premium (a national average of ₹530/family) is paid in the ratio of 75 per cent–25 per cent by the central and the respective state government. This dependence on fiscal funding is pivotal to the long term sustainability of the scheme. While the estimated annual fiscal expenditure stands at ₹24.65 billion to ₹33.53 billion)[15] (0.2–0.3 per cent of total budget), the budgetary allocation (in 2012–13) is only ₹10.96 billion for the scheme (0.037 per cent of the total budget). Clearly, the scheme is far behind the target of universal coverage. The claim ratio of RSBY for 2009–10 is 80 per cent,[16] which is less as compared to the other publicly funded, private or community based health insurance schemes in India. However, the claim ratio and burn-out ratio[17] is highly state specific. The burn-out ratio varies from as low as 27 per cent in Assam to as high as 136 per cent in Nagaland.

Community-based microinsurance

In a strictly regulated insurance industry in India, cooperative insurers (a common term for community-based insurers) enjoy a 'benign neglect' from the IRDA. Currently there are nearly 50 insurance schemes (most covering life and health risks) initiated by NGOs and cooperatives and run with or without any partnership of insurance companies. Most of these schemes depend heavily on government or donor funding for survival. For example, *Yeshasvini* receives a constant funding of ₹300 million annually from the Karnataka Government. Being largely localized experiments, the outreach of these programmes is limited to one or two states only (barring some schemes like *Yeshasvini* that have crossed more than 3 million members. Successful integration with the state government's cooperative structure has helped them achieve such high numbers).[18] Because of their social focus, most of these schemes are also designed towards women specific risks. In *Vimo SEWA*, *Yeshasvini* and *Karuna* Trust, nearly 40–50 per cent of the lives covered are women.

Challenges of microinsurance

Despite impressive growth, microinsurance sector in India has its fair share of challenges. While the government and community based schemes are constrained by the sustainability issue, the insurer initiated schemes are struggling with strategic incongruence, lack of product innovation, distribution dis-stability and lack of insurance awareness. The challenges can be categorized as:[19]

Strategic positioning issue

Neither the insurers nor their channel partners (mostly MFIs) are sure whether microinsurance can be an independent revenue generator, or provide value addition over their existing services. As a consequence, the insurer conceives only simple term-life product, which results in less interest from the MFIs, since these products neither respond to their clients' needs nor generate major revenue for them.

Product innovation issue

The lack of interest of the insurers and MFIs is coupled with lack of actuarial data on the low income population, a reason for limited innovation in the microinsurance space. Insurers have already suffered huge losses by designing innovative products for the low income segment without adequate actuarial analysis. Due to the transient nature of aggregator-client relationship and highly migratory nature of many of the low income clientele, long term products are also not a high priority for insurers.

Distribution issue

The regulation is fully biased towards the partner-agent model of microinsurance, which is a costly model from a transaction and acquisition cost point of view. The high costs of partner acquisition, distribution and logistics explain, in no small measure, why insurers prefer not to enter the domain seriously. The community based model, though scores high on service quality, these are constrained by their outreach, which is limited to one or two states only.

Micro pension products

Pension, as a social security instrument, is closely linked with insurance. India has 786[20] microcredit institutions and over 125[21] microinsurance schemes that cater to needs of the low-income segment. However, 28 per cent of the salaried workforce and approximately 340[22] to 393[23] million workers of the unorganized sector are excluded from any form of pension. India's ageing population is also expected to rise from 87.5 million in 2005 to nearly 200 million by 2030,[24] which will further add to the pressure on old age social security. The government's proposed National Social Security Scheme[25] has excluded a vast section of the low income unorganized workforce, probably because of its anticipated burden on the exchequer.[26] Contributory pension schemes, therefore, are the only option left for unorganized workers. It is estimated that the potential for such Micro Pension savings in India is approximately ₹201.3 billion per year.[27] Currently there are three prominent models of Micro Pension in India: the NPS-Lite, the Invest India Micro Pension (IIMPS) and the *Abhaya Hastham* schemes.

NPS-Lite is conceived by the Pension Fund Regulatory Development Authority (PFRDA) for the unorganized workforce under India's pension sector reforms initiative. This is primarily a self-contributory pension scheme with the option of linkage with the co-contributory *Swabalamban* Scheme. It is argued that the growth of this scheme can only be attributed to the government's generous co-contribution. Till May 2011, approximately 0.6 million NPS-Lite accounts have been opened. Invest India Micro Pension (IIMPS) is another contributory pension scheme for low income unorganized workers. This was borne out of a pilot scheme between UTI-MF and SEWA bank in 2005-06. Currently IIMPS delivers a combined pension product of UTI-MF and NPS-Lite. The aggregators of the pension are MFIs, NGOs, auto-driver's association, NABARD command areas, etc.

Abhaya Hastham is a co-contributory pension[28] scheme for the women of Andhra Pradesh delivered through the Self Help Groups (SHGs) of SERP, the government sponsored NGO. Members of the SHG and the Government co-contribute ₹1 per day, deposited with LIC of India on an annual basis. A minimum pension of ₹500 can be drawn from the age of 60, if the member has contributed for 10 years. The pension comes along with a life insurance cover of ₹30,000 and a scholarship of ₹1,200 per month for children of the clients. To date, nearly 4.6 million members have enrolled for the pension scheme. Though demonstrating good outreach, this scheme is highly dependent on the government subsidy and is expected to be nearly self-sufficient only by the year 2045.[29]

HOUSING MICROFINANCE—A NICHE PRODUCT

Housing Microfinance is defined as the provision of small sized loans to low-income households for a wide range of housing needs, including for repair, renovation, rehabilitation, improvements to existing structures, purchase of land and new construction. One of the key issues with the current housing finance market in India is that it is not reaching low income group in both rural and urban areas poor.

As the demand for housing remains high with limited or no financing options, the low income group usually explores other available credit options, such as moneylenders, relatives, friends, etc. Many a times these options may not work in favour of such borrowers, but they cannot ignore expenditure on housing. In this scenario, with the promulgation of microfinance across the world, and more successfully in the Indian subcontinent, it has been posited that microfinance can become an innovative and sustainable channel to provide low-income groups with access to finance for their housing needs. Housing microfinance (HMF) could be an important alternative for poor and low-income groups for financing their housing needs.

It has been posited that poor families build their houses through a process referred to as 'incremental housing' or 'progressive build,' implying that they build gradually and incrementally a new room or do repairs or home improvement, at a time. Thus, microfinance loans would appear to be compatible with this form of housing finance since finance for 'progressive build' can be dispensed in the form of small loans with shorter tenure. Housing microfinance is a specific form of unsecured end-user finance that leverages the savings and, more often, the sweat equity of the homeowner beneficiary. Credit assessment for these loans is similar to the same cash flow and character analysis process applicable to individual lending, but often includes some documentation to verify the proof of property ownership. *Micro-mortgages* are small housing loans with shorter loan tenures than a typical mortgage, but require title to the property, which will be mortgaged as security for the loan. In India, Housing Finance Companies (HFCs), such as the Micro Housing Finance Company Ltd, specifically focus on delivering micro-mortgage products and eventually micro mortgage will serve to pave the way for affordable housing.

There are noteworthy differences between housing microfinance loans and the standard microfinance loans. Housing microfinance loans are larger in size with a longer repayment tenure; not easily fungible; usually offered as individual loans with or without security and the affordability assessed based on current income.

Housing microfinance market in India

The demand for housing microfinance is high. Indeed, MFIs say that clients already channel a good portion of microenterprise loans to house construction and repairs. It is estimated that 20–40 per cent of total microfinance loan disbursements are used by end-clients for housing purposes.[30] As discussed elsewhere, India's housing shortage of around 69 million units and more than 90 per cent of this shortage is in economically weaker sections and low income groups. With government and philanthropic organizations offering free or subsidized housing schemes in the country, a conservative estimate of even 50 per cent of the shortage as demand for housing microfinance would result in over 30 million units. With an average loan size of ₹50,000, the demand for housing microfinance is estimated to be to the tune of ₹1500 billion. If this huge market for housing microfinance in the country gets the right impetus it deserves, it would help the economy to grow beyond the current GDP levels. This would also pave the way for employment opportunities and business at the local level and eventually reflect on the macroeconomic stability of the country as the housing sector is inextricably linked to it. As per the World Bank report, for every rupee invested in housing in India, ₹0.78 gets added to the national GDP.

At existing levels, housing microfinance could be interpolated between microfinance and traditional mortgages. The average loan size of micro-lending by banks and MFIs may be between ₹7,000–9,000. The category of housing loans between ₹30,000 to ₹150,000 can hold a promise of new business for MFIs, while HFCs could look at the next segment of housing loans between ₹150,000 and ₹300,000. The upper income category of households usually qualifies for a mortgage, while those with moderate income and those formally employed with legal title qualify for micro-mortgage. The bottom layer represents primarily very poor or ultra poor households who cannot afford credit, but are often targeted by Government and social NGOs for providing free or highly subsidized housing funding.

The market segment of near-poor urban households, who derive their incomes primarily from formal employment, and who also reside on formally titled land, often have access to consumer credit companies, housing cooperatives and some banks.

This segment poses potential credit risk as these households are more prone to over-indebtedness. Therefore, MFIs have to be especially adept at cash flow analysis for this segment and not simply rely on payroll or salary deduction. There also those who are formally employed but have no formal title to land. This segment may be a target group for housing microfinance but they may also be over-indebted if they have signed up for payroll deductible loans. An important and under-served market segment with which many MFIs are very familiar is those households which derive their income from predominantly informal sources, e.g., micro-entrepreneurs. Some of these households may have formal title, but many possess informally recognized documented rights to their land like patta, property tax receipts, etc. They may have no legal titles, but have informal rights to the land on which they reside and feel sufficiently secure to invest their time, sweat equity and savings to build and improve their housing. The typical market segments targeted for housing microfinance lies within the broad middle to low income range with a family income of around ₹10,000 to ₹20,000 per month.

Challenges and opportunities to housing microfinance

For MFIs, housing microfinance offers great value in terms of product diversification and cross-subsidization of products. Offering housing microfinance also allows MFIs to improve client satisfaction and retention; maintain longer relationships and loyalty with their existing clients; and also attract newer clients. However, in spite of these advantages, there are some challenges that MFIs must overcome to be able to provide housing microfinance products and services. Some of the major challenges they face include lack of access to long term funding, the absence of land titles and collateral for many poor households, lack of awareness amongst clientele, and the institutional adjustments required to design and deliver HMF products and services, which are different from the traditional microfinance operations and management.

Despite various issues impeding housing microfinance, several important new trends have emerged, which promise a more facilitating environment for housing microfinance. Allowing External Commercial Borrowing (ECB) for low cost housing; creation of Indian Mortgage Guarantee Company by NHB and establishment of MicroBuild India by Habitat for Humanity to provide wholesale funding to MFIs for housing microfinance are some of the recent developments which encourage MFIs to venture into housing microfinance. Similarly, International Finance Corporation (IFC), the National Housing Bank (NHB) and the Rajasthan government are coming together to establish a housing finance company to provide home loans to low-income households in the state. As microfinance continues to evolve, and the market adapts to emerging demand and external capital support, housing microfinance will play a more prominent role in diversifying larger MFIs' portfolios. Nevertheless, the housing microfinance product itself will likely remain an important niche product.

FINANCIAL LITERACY

Financial literacy is the ability to understand financial matters including financial planning and financial management. Financial awareness/literacy may be defined as the knowledge of fundamental principles of personal financial planning and budgeting, the need for savings and financial risk mitigation measures.

Financial education becomes more vital in the lives of the poor, who have limited and mostly irregular income and are more vulnerable to shocks. The poor also have similar financial needs like people from other economic strata such as meeting their daily needs, planning for the future with respect to children's education, wedding and funeral ceremonies, etc., building assets if possible and securing their families from exigencies. Hence, managing money, which includes choosing appropriate financial products and services and, in the best manner, gains importance in this scenario.

Despite several initiatives, the task of providing financial literacy remains challenging and requires concerted efforts from all stakeholders. Recent report by Visa [Global Financial Literacy Barometer, 2012], India ranked 23rd among the 28 surveyed countries on financial literacy.[31]

A wide spectrum of institutions is involved in financial literacy initiatives, which include: (*a*) apex organizations such as the Reserve Bank of India and NABARD; (*b*) research/professional institutions such as Indian Institute of Banking and Finance and the Indian School of Microfinance for Women; (*c*) regulatory bodies such as the Securities and Exchange Board of India individual banks; (*d*) NGOs; (*e*) microfinance institutions; and (*f*) financial service providers and financial advisory service providers. Besides these, financial literacy is also a part of several government programmes and implementing agencies such as Kudumbshree, Kerala Swabhiman campaign and Doordarshan, etc.

The role of MFIs and SHGs in providing financial literacy to the poor and underprivileged people need not be overemphasized. As a part of their microcredit programme and in view of their wider reach and accessibility to the poor people in both rural and urban areas, the MFIs and SHGs could play a key role in providing financial literacy to the poor. In fact, the process of becoming financially literate becomes much easier for the poor when they learn through their own involvement in and experience with microcredit activities. Imparting financial literacy to enable microcredit clients will not only help them make informed decisions on their financial matters, but also provide significant unintended benefits to the society at large through its multiplier effect on others in the group/community. Informal and need-based learning through experience makes the process easier and more relevant for poor people. It makes the small borrowers understand purposeful borrowing especially for productive purposes, options available for borrowing, repayment options and the associated terms and conditions, interest rate differences and its implications, etc.

Financial literacy by MFIs—some cases

The Andhra Pradesh Mahila Abhivruddhi Society (APMAS) is providing financial literacy to SHs and federations as a component of its pilot project on self-regulation. This programme is limited to awareness creation on savings and wise use of credit. The other minor components are bookkeeping, interest calculation and auditing. The programme is currently being implemented in one block of Andhra Pradesh.

Agricultural Finance Corporation Limited, in partnership with NABARD, has been conducting a Financial Literacy Programme in Murshidabad district in West Bengal focused on rural adults, especially women. The programme is aimed at providing awareness about money management, cash flow, basic economic and financial concepts and thrift and savings to the members of self-help groups and farmers' clubs.

Parinaam Foundation—in collaboration with its sister organization, Ujjiwan Financial Services, an MFI in operation in 20 states—is providing holistic financial literacy to educate customers on financial management. The programme is implemented through documentary films and structured training modules. The feedback from the beneficiaries reveals that about 80 per cent of them have opened savings bank account after attending the training programme. In-depth training is imparted to enable clients to learn numerical skills using calculators, to maintain household cash flow using financial diaries,

and to understand their debt servicing capacities and various savings options.

SEWA Bank was the pioneer of financial literacy training to clients and was instrumental in establishing Indian School of Microfinance for Women (ISMW) and setting up the National Alliance for Financial Inclusion and Literacy (NAFIL) to continue this work. SEWA had already designed modules on financial literacy and passed on this expertise and materials to ISMW. The main objective of SEWA's financial literacy programme is to make poor women understand the basic concepts of financial planning and motivate them to plan for their future. The SEWA Bank's training modules cover aspects such as evolution of money, money management, importance of financial planning, savings, consumption, borrowings, investments, insurance and financial planning. The training is delivered through lectures with examples, stories, role plays, games and discussions.

Suryodaya, an MFI based out of Maharashtra, uses an innovative way to educate its clients on social and financial issues. It chooses a topic (education of kids, savings, health etc.) and develops a script for the same. It is then recorded in local language using an audio device. This recorded message is played in the weekly meeting of the client. This attracts more attention of the beneficiaries, and they retain it for a longer time. The process keeps the message standardized for all clients across different states and can be adopted by developers and implementers of Financial Literacy Training Programmes.

Kudumbashree introduced a financial literacy campaign to build knowledge about banking procedures, interest rates and awareness about various products and services through banks among the Neighbourhood Group (NHG) members. The first phase of the campaign was launched in 2010–11. It focused on Kudumbashree schemes related to microfinance, proper book keeping and banking procedures, services etc. Presently, Kudumbashree is in the process of developing the second phase of its Financial Literacy Campaign.

Impacts

Since the formal financial literacy programmes are mostly in their nascent stage, not much information is available on achievements and impacts. Very studies have documented the scope, methods used and impacts of financial literacy programmes offered by a diverse set of organizations. A recent study by IFMR[32] reveals that almost all the organizations include savings and borrowing as one of the components of their financial literacy programme. Besides this, some of the other important components include interest rates, budgeting and financial planning, while topics like pensions, insurance and numeracy are not very popular. As regards the impact of financial literacy on beneficiaries, the study revealed that the financial literacy programme has yielded significant benefits in terms improving the perceived capability as well as the actual behaviour and/or performance. Though the perceived level of people's capability has increased after receiving training across all the important segments of financial literacy, there has been a marked improvement in the way people understand savings after the training. The percentage of women interviewed who used to save was only 21 per cent before the training but the percentage increased to 90 per cent after the training. As much as 68 per cent of people have started practicing the concepts of borrowing. Although the concept of insurance is more complex than saving and borrowing, the percentage of people having insurance increased from 16 per cent to 60 per cent. It is encouraging to know that people maintain household budgets, if not using the financial diaries (that they were given during the training), in some other way of their own.

SUMMING UP

MFIs in India have historically displayed mixed enthusiasm in experimenting with new products on account of their own imperatives as well as regulatory limitations. While many of the products showed the success for replication, still there are several unresolved issues which need to be appropriately considered while up scaling these innovations. Some of the insurance products can be inappropriate for the poor. Health mutual unless managed across widely different geographies can run in to covariant risks. In Watsan examples, The NGOs may help people to make their own water filters and also repair them without the need for external service. Alternatively one can go for proprietary products requiring change of filters, batteries, etc., from a company. The preference of the approaches may be depending on the client as well as BGO profile. Housing loans bundled with low cost appropriate tech on good house construction will be very helpful compared to vanilla loans. Some housing loans are given for three years at 26 per cent—whether this is a workable product—the point is that we should provide insights in to some of these efforts—while they are desirable, the actual product and delivery process should be engineered to deliver benefits and not inflict costs. In savings the functionality of SHGs should be covered—and SHG2's potential contribution with some desirable changes could be introduced.

Despite these, many institutions innovated in product design within the regulatory ambit to offer enterprise loans, asset creation loans, loans for sanitation and non-financial services. The AP crisis and renewed focus on clients would ideally have served as a platform for more innovation, but while the RBI regulations and proposed Microfinance Bill have recognized MFIs role in the financial inclusion landscape of the country, regulatory restrictions also have the potential to hamper freedom to design appropriate products. How MFIs will reinvent themselves to recover from the painful past events whilst conforming to constraints of the guidelines remains to be seen. It is hoped that, once the effects of the crisis have passed, regulation will become less restrictive and MFIs and their clients will be able to continue in a symbiotic spirit of mutual trust and cooperation.

ANNEX 5.1
Selected case studies on healthcare and sanitation initiatives by microfinance institutions

TELEMEDICINE PROGRAMME OF APOLLO HOSPITALS AND EQUITAS

Equitas, an MFI based in Chennai has tied up with Apollo Hospitals, Chennai to provide telemedicine facilities to urban slum dwellers, and Equitas plans to extend this facility to its other centres to cover one million poor people. These telemedicine centres are equipped with medical testing equipments and a laptop with video-conferencing facilities and are staffed with nurses trained in telemedicine protocols including computerized medical records and medical information systems.

WOMEN EMPOWERMENT TO REDUCE INFANT AND MATERNAL MORTALITY: THE EKJUT EXPERIMENT

Ekjut is an NGO based in Jharkand and Odisha, which trains SHG women members to reduce infant and maternal mortality. To improve maternal and infant health, Ekjut community facilitators conduct meetings/trainings with SHGs to help the women identify their health problems, the causes thereof and measures to improve their health conditions. It was found that about there was 32 per cent reduction of neonatal mortality rate and a 57 per cent reduction in postnatal maternal depression (see note 7). Ekjut has replicated this intervention in new areas and is now evaluating a possible replication through Accredited Social Health Activists (ASHA) in five more districts.

COMMUNITY-BASED HEALTH EDUCATION: THE BANDHAN CASE

The Bandhan Health Programme was initiated in 2007 in collaboration with Freedom from Hunger (initial funding support) in some of the most socially and economically backward villages in West Bengal. The Bandhan Health Programme works with women, children and adolescents. The health programme is comprised of health education (health forums facilitated by Bandhan's Health Community Organizer), health product distribution (via health kits provided to the health volunteers) and providing linkages/referrals to public health centres.

The goal of the Bandhan Health Programme is to create health awareness among mothers and adolescent girls, to ensure easy accessibility to health services available at the government and non-government level in a sustainable level. In addition, the programme works to reduce health expenditure of poor families, as well as to develop health entrepreneurs/volunteers. The monthly health forums are conducted in an interactive and participatory manner. An array of topics such as diarrhoea, care of pregnant women, quality health care, pneumonia, water and sanitation, neonatal care and others are covered during these forums. In a short span of four years after the launch of the programme, the number of branches covered under the programme increased from five in 2008–09 to 51 in 2011–12, and the number of villages covered increased from 37,500 to 382,500 during this period. A study conducted on the impact of Bandhan programmes revealed that the percentage of respondents who reported breastfeeding an infant within one hour of birth increased from 61 to 96 per cent, and the impacts extended beyond just the Bandhan clients, as the number of women who reported providing advice to others regarding breastfeeding and malnutrition also increased substantially (Metcalfe, 2012).

HOLISTIC HEALTHCARE SERVICES IN RURAL AREAS: ICTPH—SUGHAVAZHVU HEALTH CARE PROGRAMME

The IKP Centre for Technologies in Public Health (ICTPH) and partner Sughavazhvu Health Care are demonstrating an innovative managed healthcare model designed to provide high-quality, cohesive and low-cost health services to rural populations. SughaVazhvu Health Care Pvt. Ltd. is a wholly owned subsidiary of IKP Trust. It comprises a team of doctors, nurses and field coordinators who work as a team in trying to make access to healthcare a reality for rural populations through the use of innovations in public health with improved preventive and primary care. The programme operates six village-based Rural Micro Health Centres (RMHC) in Thanjavur district of Tamil Nadu that provide access to primary medical care and diagnostic services, dental care, eye exams and eyeglass-dispensing to 15,000 families.

The RMHCs are staffed by nurses, community health workers, and locally hired doctors with undergraduate degrees in Ayurveda, Unani, or Siddha systems of medicine. The doctors are trained and recertified in an ICTPH year-long programme. Delivering standardized evidence based care to remote rural population is the main objective of the programme. A village-based physician-managed Rural Micro Health Centre (RMCH) provides access to primary care services to 10,000 rural Indian residents. With a vision of creating Disease Free villages in Rural Thanjavur district, Sugavazhvu Healthcare today serves a population of 50,000 people. The AYUSH physician and the Health Extension Worker primarily based at the RMCH manage both acute walk-in patients along with carefully following up identified high risk individuals through activities such as Rapid Risk Assessment (RRA). RRA is a systematic assessment of adult health risk factors through mobile-based household health screening protocol.

ICTPH and Sughavazhvu are working with IFMR Rural Finance, the **Kshetriya Gramin Financial Services** (KGFS) network of small branch-based village banks and insurance partners, to design and market a product that will couple fixed-price, pre-paid primary care and insurance mechanisms to pool risk for secondary and tertiary care.[33] The goal is to demonstrate an affordable, fully integrated healthcare model to enable the poor to reduce the impact of high out-of-pocket spending and the risk of catastrophic healthcare needs. Although still evolving, the Sughavazhu model is an innovative and comprehensive approach that, if replicated, will offer opportunities for linkages with MFIs and SHGs seeking to improve access to quality care in rural communities.

SPANDANA-PATH WATER PURIFIER PROJECT

PATH, an international non-profit organization has launched several pilot projects in India to test whether collaborations between microfinance institutions (MFIs) and manufacturing companies can result in better market penetration of household water treatment and safe storage (HWTS) devices among poor households. Spandana, a large microfinance institution, has partnered with Hindustan Lever and Path in the Spandana Jaldhara Project so that the safe drinking water is available to the low income households. Spandana facilitates distribution of water purifier at affordable rates along with funding and service support to clients.

Both MFI loan officers and manufacturers promote the product. The MFI offers financing, and the manufacturer is responsible for delivering the product and training customers on proper use and handling. The Spandana-Path team has tested different loan terms in the state of Tamil Nadu. In two centers, customers pay a little less than ₹50 (US$1) per week, for about 50 weeks. In two other centers, customers pay a little less than ₹100 (US$2) per week for about 25 weeks, and it was found that members preferred longer repayment schedule. HUL has achieved double-digit market penetration among low-income consumers. For these pilots, Spandana has also modified the types of loans it typically offers, growing its business practices from its traditional role as a microfinance institution to that of a micro-creditor as well. Most importantly, households that could not afford home water treatment products are now using them to clean and filter their water.

BISWA's INSECTICIDE TREATED MOSQUITO NET PROJECT IN ODISHA

BISWA (Bharat Integrated Social Welfare Agency) is a rural micro-lending and development organization that provides a range of integrated financial and non-financial services since 1994, covering close to 1 million people. It is providing where existing markets and public distribution had not been successful in achieving widespread coverage of insecticide-treated bed nets (ITNs) to prevent malaria. From 2007 to 2008, BISWA was involved in a randomized control trial to evaluate the extent to which loans provided by the MFI would increase ownership of ITNs among poor households. The provision of MFI loans to purchase ITNs at market rates was compared to both free distribution and a control group (with no interventions). Education was provided to all clients about the use of ITNs to prevent malaria and to encourage regular retreatment of nets. The ownership of ITNs increased substantially in the group that had microloans for net purchase, with 52 per cent of the sample households purchasing at least one net. The increased ownership was also associated with large increases in use.[34]

These findings add to those from the PATH-Spandana initiative and support the importance of the role that MFI financing may have to increase uptake and use of higher-priced health-protection products and interventions with proven health benefits.

SERP: HEALTH SAVINGS, LOANS AND MICROINSURANCE

Working through networks of SHGs and their federations, SERP programmes reach 3 million poor households. Health improvement is a primary component of SERP's holistic approach to community development and poverty alleviation as it strives to break the link between poverty and poor health and reduce the use of SHG member loans to cover health expenses. SERP provides health education, operates child feeding and maternal health centers, and has established health savings and a low-interest loan that aim to provide financial support for health emergencies and assist clients to save ahead and prepare for health needs. SHG members save ₹10–30 (US$ 0.20–0.60) per month and after six months of savings may access health loans at 6 to 12 per cent interest with flexible repayment terms. SERP also provides a community managed insurance product called Sanjeevani that works with public and private hospitals and interfaces with the Andhra Pradesh Aarogyasri public insurance scheme. As of July 2011, about 253,000 SHG members had established health savings accounts and about 38,000 had availed loans through the health-risk product. As of March 2011, about 70,000 SHG members had been enrolled.

RURAL SANITATION PROGRAMME BY NAGESHWARA CHARITABLE TRUST

Nageshwara Charitable trust (NCT) known as 'Arogyalay Yojana' is promoting SHGs since 2001 for NABARD and DRDAs. The SHG movement started by NABARD has created a visible awareness with respect to health and sanitation in rural areas. NCT has taken up sanitation and plantation of trees as main social activities through SHGs since 2003. NCT conducted a survey of its 8,600 SHGs during 2007 and found that 87 per cent of SHG members do not own a toilet, and they are eager to build one, if the required money is made available. The main reason for not owning a toilet was lack of resources, and the construction of a toilet is not their priority with the existing source of income. Almost every woman member of SHGs demanded low cost, affordable loan for this specific purpose as they are the worst effected by not having a toilet. NABARD's positive response, encouraged NCT to approach it for support to 1,000 SHG members. During March 2009, NABARD sanctioned ₹1 million at 6 per cent interest under its Rural Innovation Fund (RIF) for supporting 100 SHG members. Loans were given to 115 members (loan amount between ₹8,000 to ₹9,000, and the balance was contributed as SHG members share). Though NCT suggested that, if the toilets are constructed in clusters, by their own engineers, the cost would be much lower than construction of individual toilets, the SHG members wanted to construct as per their need. Consequently, NCT dropped the plan of construction by the Trust and released loan to SHG members. As a pilot, 115 toilets were constructed. Considering the demand NABARD sanctioned ₹5 million as second loan for 500 SHG members in Nagpur, Wardha and Amravati districts. NCT has also trained over 160 masons in low cost toilet construction. By the end of June 2010, NCT released were loans to all 500 members and NABARD has enhanced its support by ₹20 million (₹10 million each for Maharashtra and Madhya Pradesh). By the end of June 2012, 2,874 units were constructed as against the target of 2,600 units. The highly positive aspect of the story is that 100 per cent of members are repaying the loan regularly in EMIs and 100 per cent toilets are being used by the families. NCT would like to support all its (around 60,000) SHG members who are in need of such type of sanitation loan, in the next five years. NCT is looking for more support from NABARD to enhance the loan to ₹720 million supporting 5,000 SHG members in Nagpur, Wardha and Amravati district of Vidarbha Region.

NOTES AND REFERENCES

1. Deepti, K.C. 2012. 'Rethinking Reserve Bank of India (RBI) Regulations for MFIs', Center for Microfinance IFMR. Chennai.

2. Asfaw, A., A. Admassie, J. von Braun, and J. Jütting. 2004. 'New Dimensions in Measuring Economic Costs of Illness: The Case of Rural Ethiopia', *Quarterly Journal of International Agriculture*, 43(3): 247–66.

3. Selvaraj, S. and A.K. Karan. 2009. 'Deepening Health Insecurity in India: Evidence from National Sample Surveys since 1980s', *Economic Political Weekly*, 44(40): 55–60.

4. Reddy, V. Ratna and S. Galab. 2006. 'Agrarian Crisis: Looking beyond the Debt Trap', *Economic and Political Weekly*, XLI(19): 1838–41.

5. Leatherman, S. and C. Dunford. 2010. 'Linking Health to Microfinance to Reach the Poor', *Bulletin of the World Health Organization*, 88(6): 470–71.

6. Reinsch, M, C. Dunford and M. Metcalfe. 2011. 'Costs and Benefits of Microfinance Institutions Offering Health Protection Services to Clients', *Enterprise Development and Microfinance*, 22(3): 241–58.

7. Metcalfe, M., S. Leatherman with C. Dunford, B. Gray, M. Gash, M. Reinsch and C. Chandler. 2010. 'Health and Microfinance: Leveraging the Strengths of Two Sectors to Alleviate Poverty', *Freedom from Hunger Research Paper No. 9*, 27 pp. Davis, CA: Freedom from Hunger.

8. Tripathy, P., N. Nair, S. Barnett, R. Mahapatra et al. 2010. 'Effect of a Participatory Intervention with Women's Groups on Birth Outcomes and Maternal Depression in Jharkhand and Odisha, India: A Cluster-Randomised Controlled Trial', *The Lancet*, 375(9721): 1182–92.

9. Saha, S. 2011. 'Provision of Health Services for Microfinance Clients: Analysis of Evidence from India, *Int. J. Med. Public Health*, 1(1): 1–6.

10. Reed, L.R. 2011. *State of the Microcredit Summit Campaign Report 2011*. Washington, DC: Microcredit Summit Campaign (MCS).

11. Metcalfe. 2012. *Integrated Health and Microfinance in India: Harnessing the Strengths of Two Sectors to Improve Health and Alleviate Poverty, State of the Field of Integrated Health and Microfinance in India.* Freedom from Hunger and the Micro Credit Summit Campaign.

12. The Rural and Social Sector Obligation necessitates every insurance company to sell a certain number of their policy in the rural and social sector. Later, microinsurance regulation has built upon this guideline, where any microinsurance policy necessarily qualifies to be counted for rural and social numbers.

13. Goat Trust is an innovative experiment/success story of financial inclusion in the area of integrated services and risk management financial services for goat farming. The Goat Trust along with its partner in Bundelkhand and eastern Uttar Pradesh has facilitated Goat farmers-led community insurance named as Samudai Suraksha Yojana (SSY) to provide integrated services and risk management financial services for goat farming. More details please see ftp://ftp.solutionexchange.net.in/public/mf/cr/res21061203.pdf

14. Please see MicroSave India Focus Note 87 "Microfinance in India: Evolution of Market Trends" for detail of the reasons for such trend.

15. David, M. Dror and Sukumar Vellakkal. 2012. *Indian Journal of Medical Research*, January 135(1): 56–63.

16. 2010. *A Critical Assessment of the Existing Health Insurance Models in India*, PHFI.

17. RSBY uses Burnout Ratio instead of Claim Ratio to convey the scheme's overall sustainability. The Burnout ratio is defined as the outgo from an Insurance Company in terms of percentage of expenditure incurred in payments made to the hospitals, smart card cost and service tax as against the total premium received. It does not contain the other administrative expenditure.

18. For more details on the *Yeshasvini* programme, refer to CGAP Working Group on Microinsurance, Good and Bad Practices; Yeshasvini Trust, Karnataka [http://www.microinsurancenetwork.org/publication/fichier/_Yeshasvini_Trust_Case_Study_20.pdf] and GDN Working Paper Series, Impact Evaluation of India's Yeashasvini Community Based Health Insurance Programme http://depot.gdnet.org/newkb/submissions/Health%20project_India_Aggarwal_2.pdf

19. Source: MicroSave India Focus Note 86: Challenges of Microinsurance in India.

20. According to NABARD 2009–10.

21. For details of all the microinsurance product types in India, see *MicroSave* IFN86: Microinsurance Product types of India.

22. According to the National Commission for Enterprise in the Unorganized Sector (NCEUS) report, 2006.

23. National Sample Survey, 2004–05.

24. Asher Mukul G. and Savita Shankar. 2007. *Time to Mainstream Micro-pension in India*. In: Working Papers. *RePEc:ess:wpaper:id:964*.

25. Unorganized Sector Workers' Social Security Act, 2008.

26. The Scheme proposes expenditure of nearly 0.5 per cent of the GDP in the scheme, according the NCEUS.

27. 2006 and 2008. 'Pension Reforms for Unorganised Sector', ADB. IIMS DataWorks Survey.

28. Members of the SHG and the Government co-contribute ₹1 per day, deposited with LIC of India on an annual basis. Pensions (minimum ₹500 or US$11.21 per month) can be drawn from the age of 60, if the member contributed for 10 years.

29. According to various projection reports by SERP.

30. Inputs provided by Milroy Paul, Housing Microfinance Habitat for Humanity India, Chennai is gratefully acknowledged.

31. http://www.practicalmoneyskills.com/resources/barometer.php

32. Umapathy, D., P. Agarwal and S. Sadhu. 2012. *Evaluation of Financial Literacy Training Programmes in India: A Scoping Study*. Chennai: Institute for Financial Management and Research.

33. Srinivasan, N. 2012. *Microfinance India: State of the Sector Report 2011*. New Delhi, India: Access Development Services, SAGE Publications India, 1–46.

34. Tarozzi, A., A. Mahajan, B. Blackburn, D. Kopf et al. (2011). 'Micro-Loans, Insecticide-Treated Bednets and Malaria: Evidence from a Randomized Controlled Trial in Odisha (India).' *Economic Research Initiatives at Duke (ERID) Working Paper No. 104*.

Policy environment and regulation—signs of reign

The year 2011–12 has experienced a series of significant developments in the regulation of microfinance sector. The Indian microfinance sector has been pushed to 22nd rank[1] globally with respect to regulation initiatives during the year 2011 from the 14th rank in the previous year by the Economic Intelligence Unit (EIU) assessment, which emphasized the need for greater attention in regulation and related issues in India. Recognizing the wide negative fallout of this on the sector and vulnerability of customers, the policy establishment took several initiatives that resulted in positive regulatory developments. During the last year, the RBI has issued a series of guidelines, notifications and directives, starting with the creation of a separate category of NBFC-MFIs. The regulatory guidance extends to capital requirement, qualifying asset category, asset classification and provisioning norms, pricing of credit, fair lending practices, transparency and disclosure in interest rate, avoidance of multiple lending and excessive debt, recovery practices, corporate governance and improvement in efficiency through information technology.

CURRENT POLICY DEVELOPMENTS

Priority sector lending is a policy initiative, which requires banks to allocate a percentage of their portfolios to investment in specified priority sectors at a reduced interest rate. Currently, the loans from microfinance institutions registered as NBFC-MFIs are designated as a priority sector. In order to register as an NBFC-MFI, an institution must meet requirements specified by the RBI. The RBI requires that a minimum of 75 per cent of NBFC-MFIs' loan portfolio must have been directed towards income-generating activities.[2] Additionally, an NBFC-MFI must have 85 per cent of its total assets (excluding cash, balances with banks and financial institutions, government securities and money market institutions) as qualifying assets. A qualifying asset is a loan, which meets different criteria such as (*a*) given to rural borrowers with an annual household income of not exceeding ₹60,000 or less and to urban borrowers with an annual household income of ₹120,000 or less, (*b*) loan size limited to ₹35,000 (first cycle) and ₹50,000 (subsequent cycles) with a maximum total indebtedness of ₹50,000 per borrower, a minimum tenure of 24 months when loan exceeds ₹15,000, no prepayment penalties, no collateral and flexible repayment schedule of weekly, fortnightly or monthly instalments at the choice of the borrowers. An NBFC-MFI must also adhere to the pricing requirements such as margin cap of 12 per cent, interest rate cap of 26 per cent, with the maximum processing fee of one per cent without security deposit or margin. Now the margin cap has been fixed at 10 per cent for large micro-lenders and retained at 12 per cent for other microfinance companies. Banks are responsible for ensuring that the institutions receiving priority sector funds adhere to these requirements, with verification through a quarterly Chartered Accountant's Certificate. Securitized assets may also qualify as priority sector assets if an institution meets these requirements. The current regulation stipulates that only NBFCs and cooperatives are permitted to accept deposits, though NBFCs must adhere to additional stringent regulations and cooperatives are only permitted to accept deposits from their members, not from the general public. The deposits limit for NBFCs is linked to the size of an institution's Net Owned Fund (NOF). No microfinance institution registered as an NBFC currently accepts deposits because regulation requires that institutions must obtain an investment grade rating, which no microfinance institution has yet obtained. The Malegam Committee made no recommendations regarding deposit-taking, thus RBI is not expected to address this issue for NBFC-MFIs in the near future.

The banking fraternity, in a significant move, concluded the corporate debt restructuring package with MFIs in respect of bank loans to the tune of over ₹80,000 million. Earlier the regulator had allowed banks to recast the debt of MFIs without lowering the asset quality, as a one-time measure. In December 2011, the RBI opened up the external commercial borrowings (ECBs) channel to NBFC-MFIs, something that was previously open only to non-profit MFIs, and they raised the limit for borrowing from ₹249 million (US$5 million) to ₹490 million (US$9.8 million), opening new alternative sources of funding for MFIs. Access to capital is determined primarily by an institution's registration status. MFIs with certain types of registration are better suited to access traditional financing, such as bank lending, equity, and more sophisticated financial products, while others obtain funds through donations, grants, or subscriptions paid by members. NBFCs can receive both equity and debt investments. NBFCs can raise foreign equity investment, though a minimum investment US$500,000 restriction applies, which cannot result in more than a 51 per cent stake in the institution. Grants and subsidized on-lending funds from domestic and foreign sources are not restricted, provided that the foreign grants do not exceed the ceiling of US$5 million per year. The Foreign Investment Promotion Board (FIPB) has mandated the foreign direct investment (FDI) for NBFCs with maximum 51 per cent FDI for companies with capitalization of US$500,000 or less and a maximum 75 per cent FDI for companies with capitalization US$500,000 to US$50 million. There is no maximum FDI for companies with a capitalization greater than US$50 million. Investors of foreign origin fall under the above restrictions for foreign capital, even if funds are channeled through local semi-independent funds. Two of the main sources for domestic capital are currently SIDBI and NABARD, and emerging local microfinance-focused funds such as Bellwether Microfinance Fund and Aavishkaar Goodwell. NBFCs are also the only entities that attract more sophisticated financial options, such as securitization or non-convertible debentures, where additional RBI guidelines apply. The RBI has not addressed any investment regulation regarding NBFC-MFIs, so, at this point,

we presume that these institutions must adhere to the same requirements as NBFCs. The future of Section 25 companies have difficulty attracting equity investments as they do not offer dividends and exit opportunities is difficult to predict. They can access External Commercial Borrowing (ECB) up to US$5 million, though many Section 25 companies end up borrowing significantly less than the US$5 million limit due to leverage limitations. Other MFI forms cannot accept equity investments.

The RBI recently relaxed provisioning norms for microfinance institutions that have significant exposure to small borrowers in Andhra Pradesh, allowing them to set aside money for bad loans over a period of five years.[3] The earlier deadline set for making such provisions for bad loans was 31 March 2013. Had the regulator stuck to the original deadline, this would have eroded the capital of many MFIs that have piled up massive bad loans, with a bulk of the borrowers in the southern state turning defaulters. They need to set aside money or make provisions for loans where borrowers have not paid for three to six months. The revised provision norms stipulate that micro-lenders will have to make the required provisioning as on 31 March, but this amount can be used for the purpose of calculating their capital adequacy. The RBI statement specifies that '...the provisioning made towards AP portfolio shall be notionally reckoned as part of NOF (net owned funds) and there shall be progressive reduction in such recognition of the provisions for AP portfolio equally over a period of five years.' Accordingly, if an MFI makes a 100 per cent provision for the Andhra Pradesh portfolio as on 31 March 2013, this will be added back notionally to the NOF for capital adequacy purposes as on that date. The RBI statement adds that this add-back will be progressively reduced by 20 per cent each year up to March 2017. MFIs are required to keep a 15 per cent capital adequacy. This means that for every ₹100 loan, they need a capital of ₹15. MFIs lend small loans to low-income borrowers at 24–36 per cent and source money mainly from banks, to do the business.

The RBI has now relaxed the earlier condition and allowed MFIs to consider only assets originated after January 2012 to comply with the qualifying assets criteria. According to RBI norms, not less than 85 per cent of the total loans of any MFI should count as qualified assets that are necessary for them to qualify for the status of a non-banking financial company (NBFC) MFI. Also, MFIs can lend at least 70 per cent of their loans for income-generating activities against 75 per cent earlier, the RBI said. This will enable micro-lenders to lend the remaining 30 per cent for other purposes such as house repairs, education, medical and other emergencies. Further, all new MFIs will require minimum funds of ₹50 million, while existing companies will have to achieve ₹50 million net owned funds by 31 March 2014. Now, the RBI has come up with a decision to defer the implementation of asset classification and provisioning norms for NBFC-MFIs to 1 April 2013, as intimated by its notification dated 20 March 2012. However, other regulations are to be complied with effect from 1 April 2012, and no relaxation has been granted here.

An NBFC-ND would be categorized as an NBFC-MFI that has a Minimum Net Owned Fund of ₹50 million (except for MFIs in the North East for which the requirement is ₹20 million) and not less than 85 per cent of the net assets would be in the nature of qualifying assets. As discussed by Sinha, the implications of these provisions were many—MFIs are into the business of small lending, there are several such MFIs that have a very small capital base, not sure how they would raise their capital levels to ₹50 million (₹20 million for MFIs in North East) to get the NBFC-MFIs status. If companies are unable to raise their capital levels and do not get the NBFC-MFI status, this would mean a non-NBFC-MFI cannot extend more than 10 per cent of its total assets to the microfinance sector; banks may not see any incentive in extending funds to such companies as priority sector norms would not be applicable to such non-NBFC-MFIs. This would strangulate their flow on funds and financing options and ultimately push them out of business altogether, as per these directions. This means that big would become bigger, and small would be ugly and pushed out of the sector.[4]

POLICY DEVELOPMENTS: NEW CHALLENGES

Though the newly developed set of regulations has given greater legitimacy to the sector, it has also created new challenges for the MFIs, leading them to change their business strategies and scale down their expansion plan to newer geographical territories. As funding support has become scarce and costlier, MFIs have become selective in the way they conduct their business within the existing regulations, restricting their operations to existing locations, and not expanding to new and remote areas. Managing margins within the cap of 10 per cent and 12 per cent for larger and smaller MFIs respectively

has been difficult for MFIs, which already face increased cost of operations on account of shrinking portfolio and higher finance costs. Expansion to new locations requires investment costs, which are even more difficult to absorb in the current environment. This is a perverse development, as poorer and remote areas that badly need services of microfinance will be denied the same on account of a regulation that seeks to protect customers.

Compliance with RBI guidelines

An analysis made by Sa-Dhan related to compliance on RBI guidelines collected from a sample of 50 organizations across 11 states representing different legal forms viz. NBFC, Section 25 companies, Societies and Cooperatives brought out the following issues:[5]

1. To ascertain household income in rural and urban areas, MFIs have adopted the practice of self declaration supported by house to house surveys, contact/group member information. While more than 66 per cent of the MFIs comply with the limit of ₹60,000 and ₹120,000 in rural and urban areas, MFIs have to leave unserved many borrowers who are outside the limit.
2. Within the limit of a loan amount not exceeding ₹35,000 in the first cycle and ₹50,000 in the subsequent cycles, the level of compliance was as high as 84 per cent among the MFIs, though it was felt that upper household income ceiling should be raised for repeat borrowers.
3. On the guideline of a total indebtedness of clients not exceeding ₹50,000, the MFIs have used various ways like credit bureau, member filled information in KYC form and self attested information, no objection and present loan outstanding certificate, checking with institutions not part of the bureau. Sixty-eight per cent of the sample MFIs complied with this. A limited number of MFIs contributing to the credit bureau constrains the effectiveness of the information.
4. On a tenure of loan not less than 24 months for loans in excess of ₹15,000, about 64 per cent of the sample MFIs complied. In the case of crop loans, loan period beyond nine months amounts to a mismatch of cash flows, and hence could result in problems to the client. As a result, MFIs are restricted to limit crop loans to ₹15,000, which is a serious limitation.
5. Ninety-two per cent of the sample MFIs provided loans without collateral as prescribed in the

RBI guidelines. In the case of housing loans out of the funds from National Housing Bank (NHB), mortgage of the house is a precondition.

6. On the RBI guideline that 75 per cent of the aggregate loan amount should be for income generating purpose, 92 per cent of the sample MFIs complied. This is also verified through loan utilization check after disbursement of loan.

7. With regard to loan repayment periodicity at the convenience of clients, 68 per cent of the sample MFIs complied with this guideline. These decisions are taken at a group-level meeting.

8. As much as 88 per cent of the sample MFIs have complied with the norm that the margin cap should be maintained at 12 per cent. However, the increasing cost of bank loans has made it difficult for MFIs to realize the permitted margin. This will require frequent change in product and any small change in product or process becomes a hazard for field-level communication. The exact methodology for calculation of the margin cap is also unclear; a clear example from the RBI would be very helpful.

9. No penalty for delayed payment: 96 per cent of the sample MFIs complied with this. MFIs train their field staff and are conducting village level meetings and orientation programs to encourage clients to deposit repayments on time. However, with no penalty, the clients do not have any disincentive to make late repayments.

Limitations of the current regulation

One of the major limitations of the current regulation is the lack of clarity regarding central and state regulatory jurisdiction. During late 2010 and early 2011, both Andhra Pradesh and Gujarat have passed legislation barring specific microfinance practices within the state, requiring specific consumer protection policies and capping interest rates.[6] States currently seem to have great discretionary power as to how to interpret the Money Lending Act. Stability and confidence will elude the sector until this regulatory ambiguity is resolved. A second limitation is the implementation of the new RBI requirements regarding priority sector lending, particularly with regard to borrower income and borrower indebtedness. Since there are no tax filings or credit reports for the majority of microfinance customers, the income related information is mostly self reported by the customer. Thus, customers have an incentive to misrepresent their income and indebtedness in order to qualify for a loan. Without a functioning credit bureau, these customer characteristic requirements are impossible to accurately enforce.

Another limitation is the universal margin and interest rate cap, which could be detrimental for the sector, since it would most likely result in the reduction of financial services in various areas and populations where returns would not justify the operating costs. Interest rate cap should factor in aspects influencing cost of operation such as area of operation, average loan amount, legal form, and size of the microfinance institution. When interest rate caps have been implemented on microfinance services in other countries, microfinance institutions have pulled out of rural areas, stopped serving the poorest of the poor, increased the average loan size, and have had difficulty remaining solvent. Lack of diversification of funding sources is also problematic for microfinance institutions due to the current regulation regarding access to capital. Microfinance institutions are highly dependent on lending from Indian banks with over 70 per cent of MFI loan portfolio getting funding through bank borrowings,[7] which was problematic when all of the banks stopped finding microfinance institutions to be during the AP crisis. Though microfinance institutions may diversify lending amongst Indian banks, these banks tend to view the microfinance sector very similarly, resulting in a lack of diversification benefits. Finally, allowing microfinance institutions to accept public deposits would help fund diversification and benefit the customer. Customers may also be able to do better consumption smoothening and resist the temptation to spend if they have access to a savings product. Regulations should permit institutions that meet reasonable prudential qualifications to accept public deposits.

MFI response to new RBI regulations

The Centre for Microfinance interviewed over 30 MFIs in the summer of 2011, about their response to the recent regulation and their perspectives on the sector in general. Overall, the surveyed MFIs reported that national regulation has been needed for a long time. They feel that the new RBI regulations are not clear or well communicated, and the banks that previously acted as sources of funding are more cautious and selective in offering financial support. However, MFIs felt that the RBI regulation could protect MFIs against the implementation of restrictive state legislation. Further, the uniform policy would be more difficult for smaller MFIs to adapt and adhere to if applied to all, resulting in smaller institutions being pushed out of the market by larger, more resourceful organizations. There is also a question on how difficult it will be for new start-up microfinance organizations to meet the demands of the market. Several MFIs have also expressed concern over the requirement that a minimum of NBFC-MFI's loan portfolio must be used for income-generating activities since they have recognized that a large proportion of clients use loans for consumption, rather than productive purposes. The MFIs had a mixed response with regard to the interest rate and margin cap. While many institutions described the margin as reasonable, one MFI reported that these new restrictions on margins and interest rates are too stringent, and they will limit product innovation. Additionally, operating costs vary across regions, and these caps may not be high enough to support initiatives in remote areas. Another institution stated that the margin cap would act as an incentive for MFIs to scale up at a greater rate. One aspect of the regulation to which all MFIs responded positively was the recommendation for the creation of a credit bureau and the mandatory membership of all MFIs. Currently, appraisal of a client's credit-worthiness is expensive, time-consuming and often inaccurate. Many MFIs felt that a credit bureau could serve as a more accurate tool for reviewing indebtedness and repayment history.

Microfinancial Institutions (Development and Regulation) Bill 2011

The much-awaited Microfinance Institutions (Development and Regulation) Bill, 2012 was tabled in the Indian Parliament in May 2012 and is being referred to the Parliamentary standing committee on finance. The Bill has been modified, but only slightly, from the draft Microfinance Bill posted by the Ministry of Finance, Government of India on its website on July 2011. The draft Bill was widely welcomed by industry observers as a major step forward in the government's engagement with the microfinance sector. The tabling of this Bill in Parliament furthers the process of rounding out the regulatory framework for microfinance that has been evolving since the outbreak of the microfinance crisis in India in October 2010. This Bill views microfinance institutions as 'extended arms of banks and financial services. It proposes to: (*a*) Create advisory councils to guide the development of the industry, (*b*) Place registration and micro prudential regulatory functions upon the RBI and (*c*) Create a new redressal mechanism for handling consumer grievances. The preamble introduces the purpose of the Bill as providing access to financial services for the rural and urban poor and similar disadvantaged sections of people through microfinance institutions.

M-CRIL welcomed the Bill and opined that, if this Bill is passed by Parliament in its present form, it should signal the beginning of the end of the Indian microfinance crisis.[8] However, there are views that, if the sole objective of the Bill is to preclude an Andhra Pradesh-type State operation, then there are better ways to achieve that. One must admit that the crisis reflects the collective inaction, and the Bill is an opportunity to provide remedy and equalize the power relationship between the micro-lender and the poor. Focusing on bringing regulation focusing on the growth of the sector, signalling unqualified bias in favour of consumer protection, social accountability and grievance redressal systems are the positive aspects of the Bill. However, raising the credit ceiling to ₹0.5 million from ₹50,000 and a further increase to ₹1 million is viewed as a last minute change and has surprised microfinance industry as well as banks. The draft Bill's recommended limit has the backing of the Malegam Committee. The concern raised by the industry stakeholders is that, by increasing the credit limit, there is every possibility that the original targeted segments of the poor may be further excluded. Micro-lenders extend small loans to poor at about 26 per cent interest. If the proposed higher loan ceiling is accepted, it will expand the universe of borrowers for MFIs. The Bill also proposes that district-level committees, headed by the collector or another officer not below the rank of additional collector, be set up. Their meetings, to be held every three months, will be attended by representatives from the local lead bank, NABARD, local MFIs and their clients. This committee will report any violations to the RBI. However, it is not certain if these measures suffice. Further, explicit mention of state jurisdictions is a conspicuous omission in the present form of the Bill. If State Governments start enacting their own legislations to regulate microfinance institutions (MFIs), including the ones regulated by the Reserve Bank of India, there will be a plurality of regulations leaving scope for regulatory arbitrage, says the report on 'Trend and Progress of Banking in India 2011–12.' 'If other States also come out with legislations similar to those of the AP Government, it will raise concerns not only about multiple regulations but also about client protection, as borrowers would then be subject to different regulations,' says the report. Still there is a long way to go to get real benefit of the Bill, either by the delivery institutions or the clients. However, the first positive sign that the Bill will be considered on merit came through the message from Yashwant Sinha Chairman, Parliamentary Standing Committee on Finance (Box 6.1).

Box 6.1 Message from Chairman, Parliamentary Standing Committee on Finance

The Bill is currently under examination of the Standing Committee, and in due course, we will start oral hearings of stakeholders. In the meantime, the Committee would welcome concrete suggestions from experts/stakeholders to make the provisions of the Bill more coherent and effective with a view to fulfilling the aims and objectives of the Bill. The Standing Committee would seek to examine the different provisions in all its ramifications in order to further the national agenda of financial inclusion and inclusive growth. Lacunae, if any, will be addressed constructively, so that the Bill truly emerges as a comprehensive piece of legislation on microfinance and the issues related thereto.

Source: Message from Yashwant Sinha Member of Parliament, Chairman, Standing Committee on Finance of Parliament for MFIN—MEDC Colloquium held on 25 Augest at Mumbai.

MFIs, especially smaller and medium ones, suffering from liquidity problems hope for early relief, once the bill is approved by the Parliament.

THE FUTURE OF REGULATION

The latter quarter of 2012 will be critical for the future of the microfinance regulatory regime as the RBI further clarifies the acceptance of the Malegam Report and its role with regards to microfinance institutions operating as NGO-MFIs, Cooperatives, and Section 25 companies. Regulation will surely be refined as microfinance institutions implement the new requirements and consumers and regulators see a theoretical framework put into practice. There is an expectation that, as the sector returns to a state of normalcy, some of the more restrictive requirements will be relaxed or removed. The priority sector classification, which always brings controversies is well recognized by the regulating authorities, and there is an open minded approach towards the suggestion emerging from different segments of the MF sector. The new norms mandated a higher priority sector lending target for foreign banks, with more than 20 branches in India. Further, the RBI recognizes that there are still some issues on priority sector lending of which some are quite reasonable. Further dialogue and reconsideration may certainly lead to positive contribution of regulatory initiatives for the microfinance sector as a whole.

The Reserve Bank of India (RBI) has already relaxed some of the norms pertaining to microfinance institutions' net worth, capital adequacy and provisioning needs.[9]

The roll-out of the new regulatory regime has run into some bottlenecks. Some MFIs are unable to comply with the qualifying asset criterion for registering as non-banking finance company-MFIs and, therefore, banks are reluctant to make fresh loans to them, as such loans do not qualify as priority sector lending.

RBI Governor Dr Subbarao said, at an event organized by the Indian Overseas Bank. He further added that,

Small MFIs are also not able to meet the ₹50 million entry point capital to be eligible to register as an NBFC-MFI. In particular, Andhra Pradesh-based MFIs, saddled with huge losses, large NPAs (non-performing assets) and eroded capital, are facing an especially acute problem in complying with the capital and provisioning norms. RBI is working on resolving these issues, so that MFI operations can get back on track.

In the meantime, the issue arises whether the present regulatory environment is in favour of bigger MFIs that can adapt to the changes more easily due to economies of scale, advanced MIS systems, and higher operational efficiencies. However, the recent restriction of 10 per cent margin cap to MFIs with more than ₹1,000 million of loan portfolio is still viewed as restriction in the sector. The unchanged margin cap of 12 per cent to smaller MFIs may be an indication of explaining concerns of the RBI towards the viability of this segment of the sector. The great benefit of the Andhra Pradesh crisis and the resulting call for regulation is that the Indian microfinance sector has heightened its focus on providing services that meet the needs of customers. Institutions, investors and regulators agree that microfinance services aim to improve the status and livelihood of the poor. As the sector develops, regulators must be sure to address the issues that this report has highlighted: implementation of priority sector lending requirements, diversification of funding and acceptance of public deposits. As we move forward, regulators will ensure that microfinance institutions' operations and objectives are ultimately to serve and benefit the customer.

RESPONSE OF THE SECTOR TO THE POLICY DEVELOPMENTS

The microfinance community has also responded to the situation with appropriate measures, bringing in changes to their business practices, redesigning their products and services and their process and communication strategies to align themselves with the changing circumstances. The synergy that had been missing among stakeholders during the accelerated growth stage due to competition is now in place, with much wider participation in sharing information on their practices, lending rates, and customer data. Microfinance credit bureaus have been operational, and are successfully helping the MFIs in screening multiple borrowing by customers from MFIs. The network organizations, support institutions, research and policy advocacy groups have been working to bring microfinance back to track and prepare it for orderly and responsible growth. The lead initiative taken by SIDBI towards carrying out the Code of Conduct Assessments of MFIs has helped pave the way for ensuring effective client protection principles in the operations.

Microfinance institution self-regulation

Microfinance institutions in India often voluntarily join an industry association, which acts as a commitment and guide for self-regulation. Microfinance industry associations have been developed to have better discussion with policy makers, improve capacity building, and identify minimum standards of performance through institutional collaboration and commitment. An industry association will identify a code of conduct for its members, which will focus on fair practices with borrowers and among member organizations. This code of conduct will address lending methods, collection practices, institutional transparency, and training practices for member institutions. Often, institutions will be required to develop their own code of conduct as well, which would more specifically address how the institution will uphold the fair practices outlined by the industry association. Currently, the two biggest industry associations in India are Sa-dhan and the Microfinance Institutions Network (MFIN), the latter having membership of NBFC MFIs only. Both of these associations offer a great deal of resources, guidance, and forums for inter-institutional discussions so that the most pressing issues facing the industry can be collectively addressed. The International Network of Alternative Financial Institutions (INAFI) with the membership of 17 MFIs has been working towards promoting professionalism in microfinance programmes, besides focusing on self regulation.

THE WAY FORWARD

It is widely recognized that banks have not yet been able to reach the remote pockets, and therefore MFIs still have scope and space for furthering the financial inclusion agenda. Towards forging this partnership between the banks and the MFIs, many suggestions have been made to create an environment where banks feel more comfortable in lending to the sector. It was suggested that as the sector is moving towards a regulated form, it would take time for both banks and MFIs to understand each other within the contours of the regulation, till a comfort level is achieved. In this context, it is important that RBI provides a 'transition time' for the sector to comply with the new regulation in its true spirit. A strategy needs to be formulated on adherence to the guidelines.

The RBI may consider MFIs as an integral part of the mechanism through which financial inclusion is achieved. Going forward, one of the key investments that will be required is on technology. This is the only way through which the operational cost of MFIs could be brought down in the scenario of increasing interest rates from banks to MFIs and eroding margins on account of a cap on lending to clients. It is also suggested that banks may take more interest in the governance aspect of MFIs, boards, organizational structure, etc. The sector has initiated the work on compliance with the code of conduct, and it is hoped that it is a long term initiative. It was also shared by banks that business correspondent outlets had been opened in great numbers. However, the quality and delivery of services is a question. As MFIs are based in deep pockets of the rural areas, their staff can also make regular visits to these outlets. This could be a major area of work for the MFIs. Also, the sector needs to communicate the good work that it is doing. There is a need for close interaction between banks and MFIs. Banks also need to realize their social obligation and choose all channels available to fulfil these obligations, which include lending to MFIs for on-lending to marginalized sections of society. The State of the Sector Report 2011 expressed concern on the hard times ahead for the regulatory environments in the Indian Microfinance sector.[10] However, this year, happenings in the sector indicate signs of better footing with regulatory norms in place. The enforcement of new regulations and the concerted efforts of MFIs in complying with the regulatory and client protection norms and bank continued patronage will go a long way for sustainable growth of the Indian Microfinance sector.

VILLAGE FINANCIAL SERVICES LTD (VFSL)

Village Financial Services have operated as an NBFC since 2006. The institution focuses its services in West Bengal and Bihar, reaching 222,357 clients. Clients are limited to women, who have a maximum monthly income of ₹4,000 in rural areas and ₹5,000 in urban areas. The institution uses a joint lending model. Since the introduction of the Malegam Committee Recommendations, VFSL reports that repayment has dropped from 99 per cent to 96–97 per cent. The NBFC attributes these changes to clients' growing uncertainty about the microfinance sector. Borrowers are delaying their last repayment instalments because they lack assurance that they will have continued access to new loans. Furthermore, the institution says that it is currently waiting for bank funding, and loans are being dispersed to clients on a highly selective basis. Clients are receiving false hope and are subjected to extensive waiting periods. The representative from VFSL notes that larger MFIs have additional funding sources, so they are able to better withstand the delay in bank funding. However, smaller regional MFIs are experiencing the impact more acutely. VFSL also expressed concern over the interest and margin caps, describing the measure as a negative step. VFSL states that in the past their funding costs were 10-11 per cent, but their funding costs have increased to 14–15 per cent in the recent months due to the RBI revisions of the base rate. The issue is further aggravated by the lack of regulation on interest rates charged on priority sector lending by banks. In the light of these challenges, the NBFC has stated that it is exploring other ways to minimize their costs. VFSL also expressed concern over the two-year loan tenure for loans above ₹15,000. It fears that the increase in loan tenure will result in dampened liquidity and increased risk. VFSL also expressed apprehensions regarding verification of client income. In order to determine client income, VFSL uses ration cards of prospective clients, as other methods are too expensive and timely. The NBFC noted that the RBI guidelines lack clarity over what will happen if a regular MFI client has an increase in income while availing micro-financial services.

AROHAN FINANCIAL SERVICES PVT. LTD (AFSL)

Arohan Financial Services Pvt. Ltd is an NFBC operating in 23 districts across West Bengal, Assam and Bihar. The institution has been in service since 2006, currently serving 214,059 clients. Arohan uses a joint lending group model, and it has ₹90 million in outstanding loans as of March 2011. A representative from Arohan reports that the institution is concerned over the lack of regulation regarding an interest rate cap on how much MFIs can be charged by banks. The representative stated that there are likely to be cases in which banks charge 14 per cent interest rates, thus reducing the profit margin for MFIs which is financially unsustainable for MFIs.

Yet, Arohan reports that, in the long run, the new RBI regulations will give banks greater confidence in the microfinance sector, but banks are not ready to begin funding. The Arohan representative stated that banks do not feel compelled to lend to MFIs and predicted that, in the future, an MFI's overall performance, credibility, accountability and personal relations will be the determinants of available funding opportunities. The Arohan representative explained that the institution is currently experiencing a shortage of funds, which is affecting timely loan disbursals to clients.

TRIDENT MICROFINANCE

Trident Microfinance is a Non-Banking Financial Company (NBFC), which has been operating in Andhra Pradesh, Madhya Pradesh and Uttar Pradesh since 2007. Trident utilizes a joint lending group operational model to serve 254,000 clients. As of the end of March 2011, the NBFC had ₹1,500 million in outstanding loans. A representative from Trident reported that, overall the institution believes that the Malegam Committee's recommendations are a positive addition to the microfinance sector. However, Trident had to take certain steps to ensure the survival of the institution following the AP crisis and subsequent Committee recommendations, such as the laying off of staff and closing down of MFI branches. As of the end of September 2010, Trident had 109 branches, which has since been reduced to 84. Currently, the institution is in the process of further reducing the number of branches to around 50. Branches were primarily eliminated from urban areas, particularly in Hyderabad. The representative from Trident Microfinance expressed concern over several of the RBI regulatory changes. The representative reported that the 26 per cent interest rate cap was 'not encouraging,' and Trident's clients had rarely reported problems with the interest rate in the past. However, as of present, it appears unlikely that the interest rate cap will affect the institution. Trident Microfinance also believes that the 12 per cent margin cap proposed by the RBI is unreasonable, and it should be removed from the recommendations.

In response to the new RBI rule that borrowers' indebtedness cannot exceed ₹50,000, Trident stated that it would be likely that borrowers could easily misstate details regarding their debt. However, the institution expressed faith that a microfinance credit bureau would be able to adequately address the problem of concealed indebtedness. While the Malegam Report has recommended that a common credit bureau be created, Trident reports that MFIs are reluctant to join.

NOTES AND REFERENCES

The Author gratefully acknowledges the support extended by Satadarshan and his team in the Centre for Microfinance, IFMR Chennai by providing inputs for this chapter.

1. Global Social Research, 2 May 2012, available at https://groups.google.com/group/casei3students/browse_thread/thread/38f137785b1b028b and accessed in July 2012.

2. Kenny, Kline and Santadarshan Sadhu. 'Microfinance in India: A New Regulatory Structure', Centre for Microfinance, IFMR, Chennai.

3. http://www.livemint.com/2012/08/03222804/Norms-for-AP-microlenders-ease.html?atype=tp accessed in August 2012.

4. http://www.microfinancefocus.com/mffnews/rbi-gives-breather-ailing-mfis-deferral-asset-classification-and-provisioning-norms accessed in August 2012.

5. Proceedings of the Roundtable on 'Fund Flow from Banks to the Microfinance Sector: Issues, Challenges and Way forward' on 14 June 2012 organized by Access Development Services at IIBF Leadership Centre, Mumbai.

6. Sriram, M. 'Microfinance: A Fairy Tale Turns into a Nightmare', *Economic and Political Weekly*, Vol. 45, No. 43, October 23 2010.

7. 'Microfinance-Growing Against All Odds', *The Bharat Microfinance Quick Report 2012*, Sa -dhan Publication, New Delhi.

8. www.m cril.com accessed in August 2012.

9. Business Standard http://www.business-standard.com/india/news/rbi-may-relax-nbfc-mfi-norms/479443/ accessed in August 2012.

10. Srinivasan, N., 'State of the Sector Report Microfinance 2011' SAGE Publications Pvt. Ltd, New Delhi.

11. Kenny, Kline and Santadarshan Sahu 'Microfinance In India—New Regulatory Structure', Centre for Micro Finance, IFMR Research, Chennai.

National Rural Livelihoods Mission

The Government of India has restructured its flagship programme for poverty reduction. Swarnajayanti Gram Swarozgar Yojana (SGSY),[1] and National Rural Livelihoods Mission (NRLM) seek to build on these successes and scale it across the country to cover all 350 million rural poor households in a time-bound manner (Annexure 7.1). This will be one of the world's largest initiatives to improve the livelihoods of poor rural people and boost the rural economy. Further, this programme focused on social and economic empowerment of rural women and based on past experience is expected to have transformational impact in terms of MDGs on nutrition, gender and poverty.

It can therefore be seen that NRLM constitutes a significant departure from the 'financial services approach' of SGSY to a more comprehensive 'livelihoods approach'. The single point focus on income generation activities and the one-off assetization in productive assets under SGSY have been considerably expanded to address multiple dimensions of poverty including assets, skills, incomes, consumption and risks (including food and health risks) under NRLM. Convergence with other poverty reduction programmes, social security schemes and safety nets are particularly encouraged. Second, the platform of aggregate institutions is brought into the program design in the form of SHG federations and producer collectives that will allow poor accessing higher order support services in the last mile particularly for risk management, productivity enhancement and systematic participation in value chains and formal markets.

KEY FEATURES OF NRLM

NRLM is being rolled out in all districts and blocks of the country. The first pillar of program strategy, referred to as '**intensive block strategy**', is key to the programme's mandate of saturated coverage of all poor households and of providing them continuous handholding support till they come out of poverty. This strategy will be implemented in a phased manner. During the first phase this strategy will be rolled out in 600 blocks in 150 districts, including Left Wing Extremism (LWE) districts. All blocks in the country will be covered in seven years, and all villages are expected to be covered within 10 years. The intensive block strategy of NRLM will create a favorable ecosystem for empowering the poorest households to create and harness growth opportunities (Box 7.1):

1. **Social inclusion** through saturated mobilization of all poor households into good quality grassroots institutions (SHGs, SHGs Federations, Producers Collectives)
2. **Financial inclusion** through savings and credit promotion, investment planning, risk management, financial counselling services and linkages with formal financial institutions.
3. **Economic inclusion** through intensive support in key livelihood sectors like agriculture, livestock, Non-Timber Forest Produce (NTFP), fisheries, non-farm sector, micro-enterprise development, skills development and jobs, etc.
4. **Social Security** through effective last mile delivery of public services, social safety nets and other entitlement programmes.

Box 7.1 NRLM: Key features

1. **Goal**: Poverty elimination in rural areas through building and nurturing institutions of the poor, with a focus on women SHGs and their federations.
2. **Target**: Reaching 70 million rural poor households in the next 10 years.

---

3. **Core assumption**: It takes six to eight years for a poor household to come out of income poverty provided they are organized, supported and nurtured by their own institutions, and are enabled to access at least ₹100,000 from external sources (banks) through repeat loans. With this kind of long-term nurturing, annual household incomes of ₹50,000 per annum from two to three livelihoods can be ensured.

4. **Coverage**: Phased coverage of villages in the country over a period of 10 years.

5. **Comprehensive livelihoods promotion**

   - Overcoming shocks—Food security credit, health risk fund, usurious debt swapping fund, etc.
   - Strengthening existing livelihoods—Agriculture, livestock, NTFP, fishery, weaving, etc.
   - Skilling and placing youth from rural poor households.
   - Micro-enterprise development: EDP trainings, skilling, apprenticeship and handholding.
   - Risk management: Life, health, assets and livelihoods risks.

6. **Required investment**: During the intensive phase (first six years), an investment of ₹9,000 per household is required. Subsequently, during the maintenance phase (four years), an investment of ₹3,000 per household is needed.

7. **Financial inclusion**: Full range of financial services made available to the poor. SHG-bank linkage as main source of institutional finance. Leveraging credit 1:8 times the scheme investment per household.

8. **Anticipated Outcomes in Intensive Blocks over five years**

   - 80% poor households mobilized into SHGs.
   - 80% of SHGs rated as good quality.
   - 80% of SHGs are credit linked.
   - 70% of villages have nested federations of SHGs.
   - 70% poor households have food security.
   - Jobs for 10 million youth from poor households.

Source: Ministry of Rural Development, Government of India.

In the remaining blocks of the country, until they are covered as intensive blocks, the interventions will center round capacity building of all existing SHGs in the area and support for SHG-bank linkage. Further value chain linkages will be facilitated in select livelihood clusters, besides micro-enterprise development support through Rural Self Employment and Training Institutes (RSETIs) and opportunities for placement linked skill development programs will be pursued.

IMPLEMENTATION ARRANGEMENTS

The NRLM is embedded within the Ministry of Rural Development (MoRD), Government of India. The World Bank is extending International Development Association (IDA) credit of US$1 billion to strengthen the implementation of NRLM. The project is designed to create an enabling environment and develop institutional capacities of the center and the states that will allow NRLM to produce significantly higher outcomes (Annexure 7.2). The National Mission Management Unit (NMMU), comprising a multi-disciplinary team of professionals drawn from government, banks and market has been set up at the center. The main focus of the NMMU is to provide technical assistance to the states in their implementation of the NRLM. States will be required to create separate autonomous implementation structures as State Rural Livelihood Missions (SRLMs). Similarly, district and block units will be set up for implementing NRLM activities. In order for the states to access funds under NRLM, they have to comply with the following three conditions:

1. Set up dedicated and autonomous program implementation structure at SRLM;
2. Trained professionals to implement NRLM activities at district/sub-district level are in place; and
3. State Perspective and Implementation Plan (SPIP) reflecting the local poverty context is prepared.

CURRENT STATUS

SRLMs have been set up in 20 States and one Union Territory in the country. Implementation entities managing World Bank supported Rural Livelihoods Projects in Bihar, Madhya Pradesh, Odisha, Rajasthan and Tamil Nadu will be subsumed into or re-designated as State Rural Livelihoods Missions. Similarly, all blocks in Andhra Pradesh and Kerala covered by 'Indira Kranthi Patham' and 'Kudumbashree' programmes will also be considered as 'intensive blocks'. As a result of these, an intensive block strategy is under implementation in 825 blocks in about 135 districts. The overall social mobilization supported by NRLM during 2011–12 covered 5.21 million SHGs and credit mobilization during the year stood at ₹137.269 billion. State-wise details of the outreach and credit mobilization during 2011–12 are given in Annexure 7.3.

FINANCIAL INCLUSION UNDER NRLM

NRLM will work with the mainstream financial institutions seeking to ensure affordable and reliable access to a full suite of financial services to the targeted rural poor households from a delivery point within a distance of 5 km from each habitation. The suite of financial services will include financial advice and counselling services, savings, both individual and SHG levels, credit, both individual and SHG levels, payments, including cash transfers and private remittances, microinsurance and micro pensions.

Targeted investments of ₹100,000 per poor household translate into a market opportunity worth ₹7,000 billion for formal financial institutions over the next 10 years. This will achieve substantial gains in poverty reduction covering the bulk of the rural poor households. Making the poor the preferred clients of the banking system and mobilizing bank credit are core to the NRLM financial inclusion and investment strategy. SHG-bank linkage will be the main source of institutional finance. Leveraging institutional credit of 1:8 times or more than the scheme investment is the aim of NRLM. The financial assistance package to SHGs and their federations is therefore aimed to strengthen their institutional and financial management capacity and build their track record to attract mainstream financial institutions (Box 7.2).

> **Box 7.2 Financial assistance package under NRLM and role of subsidy**
>
> Subsidy is to be seen as seed capital and as a means to capitalize SHGs and their federations and is a resource in perpetuity for them and not a 'viability gap funding' for individual households or their projects. The provision of these funds is expected to strengthen their institutional and financial management capacity and build their track record to attract mainstream bank finance. This takes the following forms in 'intensive blocks':
>
> 1. **Revolving Fund (RF)** support to the SHGs as corpus, with a minimum of ₹10,000 and up to a maximum of ₹15,000 per SHG. The RF support, besides meeting consumption and initial production credit needs, also builds institutional capacities of SHGs in managing loans and funds.
> 2. **Capital Subsidy (CS)** is provided to SHGs or their federation based on the institutional quality, track record in thrift and credit management and household level micro investment plans. This also helps member SHGs develop a track record for attracting mainstream financing from banks. CS fund mainly aims to inject financial resources into the institutions of the poor and catalyze investments for strengthening the livelihoods of the poor.
> 3. **Direct Bank Finance** will take two forms. First and foremost is financing SHGs or their federations for their consolidated micro investment plans under SHG-Bank Linkage Programme. Second, they could also be financed for specific economic activities on cluster basis.
> 4. **Interest Subsidy** can be arranged by the states with a view to provide access to credit at an affordable rate of interest of 7 per cent per annum to those rural poor households who are regular in loan repayment. This performance-linked incentive is available to SHGs till their cumulative loaning, over several doses, reaches ₹100,000 per household.

Source: Adapted from NRLM—Framework of Implementation, MoRD, Government of India.

RISK MANAGEMENT SOLUTIONS

Climatic risks, economic fluctuations, and a large number of individual-specific shocks like death of the bread winner, food shock, and health risks, etc., leave poor households vulnerable to severe hardship. The result is that risk is an important constraint on broad-based growth in living standards in many developing countries. NRLM will therefore work with insurance companies to ensure universal coverage of microinsurance services, particularly to cover life, health and asset risks of the poor households.

MICROINSURANCE

A few SRLMs, which are implementing World Bank supported projects have worked in convergence with a few insurance schemes launched by the Government of India like 'Aam Admi Bima Yojana', 'Jan Shree Bima Yojana', 'Rashtriya Swasthya Bima Yojana' and other agriculture and livestock insurance schemes. These initiatives will be scaled up across the States over a period of time. The present coverage of microinsurance schemes under these select SRLMs is presented in Table 7.1.

Table 7.1 **Coverage of microinsurance schemes**

States	Life insurance	Health insurance
Andhra Pradesh	9,669,452	–
Bihar	218,490	–
Odisha	202,267	–
Madhya Pradesh	16,340	–
Tamil Nadu	65,397	82,095
Total	10,155,606	82,095

Source: WB supported Rural Livelihoods Projects.

These projects have invested in building a cadre of community professionals who are trained on various aspects of insurance products and services including member enrolment, claims documentation and claims processing. In addition, they have invested in putting in place insurance call centers and developing web-portals for all insurance transaction processing. This has ensured providing a better last mile service delivery model and in ensuring seamless claims processing wherein the turn-around-time in insurance claims settlement has been brought down from an average of four-six months to three-four weeks.

SAFETY NETS AND MICRO PENSIONS

Old-age provisions in the form of pensions are an effective way of reducing income poverty. Safety net mechanisms like old age pensions, disability pensions and widow pensions increase poor older people's access to services, particularly health care. The support of micro pensions not only provides income security to the vulnerable but also helps in reducing their dependency. SRLMs will partner with other Government departments to ensure convergent provision of the safety nets to the members of the SHG and their federations in an efficient and predictable manner.

Complementing this effort is to dovetail other contributory pension mechanisms that allow the poor to safely accumulate, grow, and protect wealth in the old age. Society for Elimination of Rural Poverty (SERP) the designated SRLM in Andhra Pradesh is implementing a 'Abhaya Astham' scheme that bundles Janashree Bima Yojana of LIC with State run co-contributory pension scheme/National Pension Scheme-Lite (NPS-Lite) into one product. About 4,089,746 rural women are participating under the scheme and death claims have been settled for 13,350.

FINANCIAL INNOVATIONS

Various important lessons have been learned and incorporated in the design of the NRLM to ensure that financial inclusion of the poor is achieved in a sustainable and responsible manner. Efforts made by large scale rural livelihood initiatives in Andhra Pradesh, Bihar and Tamil Nadu have resulted in formal financial institutions committing larger resources for financing rural poor households. NRLM will therefore collaborate with mainstream financial institutions to coordinate supply side response in the form of product innovations, technology-led channel innovations and alternate business solutions. Some of the financial innovations leveraging SHG-based institutional platforms that will be scaled up under NRLM include:

INNOVATIONS FOR IMPROVING FINANCIAL CAPABILITIES OF THE POOR

1. Financial literacy and debt counselling services: Financial literacy and business education modules have been embedded in the basic trainings of SHGs in Andhra Pradesh, Bihar and Odisha. A cadre of community-based debt counselors are being prepared to provide face-to-face counselling services for helping the poor households choose appropriate financial products, decide investment priorities and educate them on responsible borrowing.
2. Electronic bookkeeping: The NRLM will invest in strong and automated financial management and accounting system at SHG/federations through e-booking using different front-end devices, including net books, mobile phones and tablets for improving financial management and accounting systems in SHGs/Federations. E-booking is being pursued in nearly 15,000 village level federations of SHGs in Andhra Pradesh and another 1200 in Tamil Nadu. Similarly pilots are underway in Bihar and Odisha.

PRODUCT INNOVATIONS ENHANCING HUMAN DEVELOPMENT OUTCOMES

1. Health Savings and Health Risk Fund: The poor are very vulnerable to health shocks when they resort to borrowing from informal sources at usury interest rates. About 2.2 million women in village level federations of SHGs in Andhra Pradesh and Bihar make dedicated health savings and

participate in health risk fund (HRF) model, which encourages the poor to save on a regular basis during good times and borrowing for health needs (including emergencies) from the health risk fund at nominal interest rate and easy instalments. The HRF is capitalized by a revolving fund for health.

2. Food Security Fund: About 3.5 million households in Andhra Pradesh, Bihar and Tamil Nadu participated in food security initiatives, such as the collective purchase of rice and other food commodities, access to public distribution system, and food credit facilities. These activities made food affordable and resulted in savings for poor households. Food assurance also reduced the proportion of indebted households and increased the daily wage rate by 30 per cent in Andhra Pradesh due to the enhanced bargaining power of the poor farmers.

3. Nutrition Credit: Community managed Nutrition-Cum-Day Care Centres (NDCCs) set up to tackle maternal and child health outcomes in about 4250 villages in Andhra Pradesh and Bihar provide pregnant and lactating women and their children under two with three cooked, balanced, nutritious meals a day. These meals taken over a one year period (from the second trimester into pregnancy to six months after child birth) are combined with entitlement schemes and credit making nutrition affordable to the poor households. The credit component is repaid over an 18–36 months period. This initiative reaching some 222,000 women and young children have consistently shown newborns with a birth weight of more than two and a half kgs and very low infant and maternal mortality rates compared to the state average.

INNOVATIONS IN LAST MILE DELIVERY OF FINANCIAL SERVICES

1. SHG federations as banking correspondents/CSPs: Several SHG federations at the village/Panchayat level in Andhra Pradesh and Tamil Nadu are functioning either as banking correspondents or their Customer Service Providers (CSPs). Effectively combining the strengths of information technology with community-managed financial systems in the last mile, the branchless banking initiative can radically transform the manner in which rural financial services are produced and delivered for the poor. The 'smart card banking' initiative jointly by the Government of Andhra Pradesh and the commercial banks helped them in increasing their presence by five times i.e., from 4,487 rural and semi-urban branches to 20,979 villages in the State.

2. Bank Mitra: A Bank Mitra is a community professional who runs a help desk at a bank branch is trained to act as 'client relationship manager' for women SHGs and other poor clients of the bank. Around 5,000 Bank Mitras in Andhra Pradesh and Bihar are providing business facilitation and counselling services to the poor clients. This includes opening of bank accounts, facilitating deposit and payment transactions, loan documentation, monitoring of credit linkage, etc. At present, Andhra Pradesh has around 4,000 Bank Mitras, with nearly one-third of them being paid by the Banks. Bihar, on the other hand, has 271 Bank Mitras across nine districts, all of whom are paid by the community.

3. Bima Mitra: A Bima Mitra is a community professional appointed by SHG federations for promoting awareness on microinsurance programmes and servicing microinsurance clients. There are about 1,100 Bima Mitras in Andhra Pradesh who provide last mile connectivity for community based microinsurance management architecture. Hall mark of this arrangement is that within four hours from receipt of information on death at the call center, Bima Mitra will handover solatium to the bereaved household. She will also help the client household to document the claim and follow-up with local authorities for death certificate and other documents, opening of account, etc., till the claim is fully settled with the insurance company.

IMPACT OF RURAL LIVELIHOODS INITIATIVES

The program draws on the lessons learnt over the last ten years from World Bank supported rural livelihood projects in seven states of India where nearly 13 million women were organized into affinity based self help groups managing own savings of ₹60 billion leveraging nearly ₹425 billion loans from commercial banks, helping poor invest in food security, commodity marketing and several other community enterprises. Youth belonging to poor households have been able to access education and skill development opportunities resulting in the creation of half a million jobs in services, retail and other growth sectors of the economy. External evaluation has shown that sustained investments for poverty reduction in AP over a period of the last 10 years has reduced poverty incidence among poor households from 29.2 per cent to 17.6 per cent in the State. An increase in net income per household from 50 per cent to 115 per cent has been reported in AP, Rajasthan and Madhya Pradesh, with significant income improvement also in Tamil Nadu. More recently, similar investment in Bihar over three years has shown interesting trends with 48.5 per cent of the households have cleared old high cost debts and 90 per cent of the households reporting improvement in food availability. Similarly, these projects facilitated land access of 875,000 by the poor, adoption of sustainable agricultural practices and improved cropping technologies over 1.4 million acres, milk production of nearly 2.8 million litres resulting in significant increase in food security and nutrition indicators. Another significant impact has been in terms achievement of MDG indicators (peri-natal and neo-natal mortality) and significant reduction in malnutrition in about 4,200 villages through setting up of community managed doorstep nutrition and day care centers. These projects have had a substantial impact on rural poverty, the main reason for NRLM to be designed on their lines.

CHALLENGES FOR NRLM

1. Quality of the groups formed under SGSY: Second, a significant number of the groups under earlier SGSY programme is weak. There is a need to develop a dedicated strategy to build their capacity and improve the quality of these groups. NRLM is contemplating strategic partnerships with NGOs, resource agencies, training institutions, etc. to support the states in this endeavour.

2. Banking footprint and response: The trends in banking sector development in lagging regions show low rural branch footprint, abysmally low credit deposit ratios and huge disparity in performance under SHG-bank linkage programme. These are symptomatic of problems in delivering financial services in the last mile. The rural branch organization of banks in the current form is not geared to deal with the special needs of the rural poor households, thereby lowering potential impacts of anti-poverty efforts. This is exacerbated by lack of appropriate products meeting the lifecycle and livelihoods needs of the poor.

   i. NRLM will develop strategic partnerships with major commercial banks and insurance companies at various levels. It invests in creating enabling conditions for both the banks/ insurance companies and the poor for a mutually rewarding relationship.

   ii. NRLM will partner with specialized financial institutions like NABFINs, Thrift and Credit Cooperatives, MFIs, etc., to develop financial products and innovative delivery channels that help them reach affordable and reliable financial services to poor households, SHGs and their federations in challenging areas.

   iii. NRLM will support large scale branchless banking pilots to demonstrate models for effective financial inclusion.

3. Risk Sharing Products: Risk aversion abounds in the banking structure, particularly at the branch level in the lagging regions. NRLM will invest in piloting financial products in partnership with mainstream financial institutions to develop, which could be an alternate to the livelihood grants provided to SHGs. The new financial products could take the shape of partial risk guarantee for lending by commercial banks to SHGs and higher level institutions like Producer Groups/ collectives/companies (PC).

4. Trained and sensitive HR: Another key constraint for expansion of financial inclusion initiatives under NRLM is availability of trained manpower with appropriate skills and attitude. There are just not enough academic and training institutions to produce quality programmes for training and upgrading skills in this sector. The formal financial institutions would need to add an estimated 1000 senior/middle level managers, 6,000 junior executives and 200,000 financial inclusion agents to realize full potential of various financial inclusion and branchless banking initiatives[2] in the country. Similarly, it is estimated that the MFI sector needs another 20,000 middle level managers and 150,000 loan officers in the country to serve 50 million clients. HR practices in the financial services industry have undergone sea change and HRD strategies relying up on *in-situ* learning systems alone will only deliver sub-optimal results. NRLM will arrange technical assistance to banking training institutes and management schools in curriculum design, training pedagogy and development of course materials/packs for both short term and long term courses on financial inclusion. These institutions can then partner with SRLMs to offer specialized courses for producing financial inclusion professionals and train staff of SRLMs, partner financial institutions, etc.

5. Client protection systems: Large scale overlap of the client base of SHGs and other microfinance

initiatives resulting in multiple loans to the same households without proper due-diligence by lenders led to unsustainable debt burden for these households. (*a*) intensifying financial literacy/credit counselling services to promote responsible borrowing, (*b*) promoting strong savings focus in SHGs, (*c*) building robust MIS and information bureau with geo-mapping capability to track multiple borrowings, (*d*) data sharing with formal financial institutions, and (*e*) activating community-based recovery mechanisms ensure prompt repayment of loans. In addition, it will support client feedback mechanisms along-side effective and transparent third party verification process to enforce responsible microfinance practices. This will help in objectively dealing with client grievances, particularly in the areas of service deficiencies, pricing disclosure, and non-compliance with the responsible microfinance practices.

SUMMING UP

The major strength of NRLM is that its design evolved based on the successful experiences of large scale State level livelihoods initiatives and those of

SGSY and keeping it flexible and dynamic suiting local context throughout the project cycle.[3] NRLM seeks to promote inclusive growth in India by mobilizing the rural poor and enabling them to save, build productive assets and enterprises, access financial, livelihood, educational, health and nutrition services and entitlements, negotiate better terms for their products and services and provide rural youth with skills and opportunities to secure jobs in India's mainstream economy. The World Bank support will therefore create enabling environment and develop institutional capacities of the center and the states that will allow NRLM to produce significantly higher outcomes. NRLM initiatives will significantly contribute to the institutional development of the client's progress both in terms of economic and human development indices.

NOTES AND REFERENCES

This chapter is adapted from an unpublished note on 'National Rural Livelihoods Mission: Financial Inclusion Strategies' by *Sitaramachandra Machiraju,* Senior Rural Development Specialist, The World Bank, New Delhi. Assistance provided by Aarti Dayal, Bhanu Shyam Nakka and Charulata Sharma with data assistance and review of this document is also acknowledged.

NOTES

1. Swarnajayanti Gram Swarozgar Yojana is a rural self-employment programme for poor families that was introduced in 1999 by the Government of India.
2. Guess estimates to cover dedicated staff for channel management, product development and management, back office processing, data warehousing, technology support and risk management services, etc.
3. Refer Interview with Mr Vijay Kumar Joint Secretary, Ministry of Rural Development, Government of India, *State of the Sector Report 2011.*
4. Source: Ministry of Rural Development, Government of India & WB supported projects in AP, Bihar, MP, Odisha and Tamil Nadu.

ANNEX 7.1
Transition from SGSY to NRLM

The Government of India introduced the Swarnajayanti Gram Swarozgar Yojana (SGSY) programme in April 1999, with the objective of bringing poor households out of poverty by providing productive assets that generate sustainable income. The basic financial instrument in the programme was a government subsidy (grant), linked to bank credit using the institutional mechanism of Self-Help Groups. An overview of program implementation showed mixed results. About 25 million poor households have been organized into SHGs but only 22 per cent of the groups were able to access bank credit. This also brought into focus important shortcomings like vast regional variations in mobilization of rural poor and quality of the SHGs and insufficient capacity building of beneficiaries resulted in lack of building necessary absorption capacity among rural poor. Furthermore, several states have not been able to fully utilize the funds received under SGSY indicating a lack of appropriate delivery systems. Based on the recommendations of the 'Committee on credit related issues under SGSY', Government decided to restructure SGSY and implement the programme in mission mode under National Rural Livelihoods Mission largely drawing upon the successes of livelihood initiatives in Andhra Pradesh, Kerala and Tamil Nadu. Significant transformational changes that were brought in SGSY are discussed below:

PROGRAMME RELATED

The single point focus of the programme on income generation activity and one-off assetization in productive assets under SGSY is considerably expanded to address multiple dimensions of poverty including assets, skills, incomes, consumption and risks (including food and health risks). Convergence with other poverty reduction programmes, social security schemes and safety nets are particularly encouraged. Second, platform of aggregate institutions is brought into the programme design in the form of SHG federations and producer collectives that will allow poor accessing higher order support services in the last mile particularly for risk management, productivity enhancement and systematic participation in value chains and formal markets.

IMPLEMENTATION RELATED

The District Rural Development Agency (DRDAs) was mandated to anchor SGSY implementation with a very limited role for state governments. DRDAs are overburdened with implementation of multiplicity of other government schemes with limited staff resources that often lack skills to nurture institutions of the poor. NRLM envisages a lead role for state governments in developing poverty reduction strategies and creating professionally competent State Rural Livelihood Missions (SRLM) as dedicated support organizations with reach up to the community level, to nurture and support community institutions in a process intensive manner. It recognizes the need for multi-stakeholder engagement positioning and has built collaborative arrangements with innovators, social entrepreneurs, civil society, public and private sectors in the programme. NRLM will also invest in high quality technical assistance architecture to support SRLMs and partner agencies.

POLICY RELATED

Moving away from entitlement-based fund allocations made on year-on-year basis, NRLM subscribes to programme-based financing of perspective plans for poverty reduction plans prepared by states. This is effectively complemented by an emphasis on evidence-based policy impact analysis rather than an expenditure-focused scheme management.

ANNEX 7.2
National Rural Livelihoods Project

The World Bank is extending International Development Association (IDA) credit of US$1 billion to strengthen the implementation of NRLM. The National Rural Livelihoods Project (NRLP) is designed to create an enabling environment and develop institutional capacities of the center and the states that will allow NRLM to produce significantly higher outcomes. This is sought to be achieved by creating '*professionally competent and dedicated implementation structures*' at all levels and transform MoRD as a provider of '*high quality technical assistance and hand-holding support*' to the States for effective implementation of poverty reduction programmes. The proposed project will also help NRLM establish '*national programme management systems*' and make '*targeted livelihood investments*' that will provide large scale 'proof of concept to states joining the project and support '*innovation forums*' that will bring together innovators, social entrepreneurs, public and private sectors to engage with institutional platforms of the poor. The project will be implemented in 13 high poverty states accounting for 87 per cent of the poor in the country. Out of these, intensive livelihood investments will be made in 100 districts and 400 blocks.

NRLP will invest intensively in the high priority states to create best practice sites to develop them as local immersion locations and generate a critical pool of social capital for catalyzing social mobilization of the poor and building quality institutions of the poor. In other words, NRLP will prime the transformational process of MORD and strengthen the NRLM and SRLMs. The project will help set up national systems for ICT-enabled MIS and service delivery; monitoring and evaluation; financial management and audit; and procurement management. This will also help NRLP to deliver high quality TA to states taking advantage of advancements in knowledge, technologies and management practices in the external environment. The project will also provide TA to partner agencies to create a large pool of service providers, particularly at the community level to ensure continuity and sustainability of service delivery in the last mile. Finally, NRLP will also facilitate partnerships with public, private and social enterprise sectors to delivery programme-related services in the last mile.

ANNEX 7.3[4]
NRLM: Outreach and credit mobilization during 2011–12

State	Groups supported by 2011–12 (Number)	Credit provided during 2011–12 (₹ in millions)
Andhra Pradesh	1,309,269	82,254.3
Arunachal Pradesh	681	3.3
Assam	246,815	2,218.4
Bihar	269,290	2,535.3
Chhattisgarh	74,388	1,295.9
Goa	1,169	8.4
Gujarat	122,284	651.9
Haryana	29,433	976.1
Himachal Pradesh	11,713	424.8
Jammu & Kashmir	10,870	131.6
Jharkhand	80,917	986.4
Karnataka	82,453	2,091.7
Kerala	287,649	2,206.9
Madhya Pradesh	403,895	3,437.8
Maharashtra	265,055	3,629.1
Manipur	3,238	0.00
Meghalaya	11,824	24.5
Mizoram	2,616	25.8
Nagaland	5,749	13.1
Odisha	297,587	7,052.2
Punjab	8,818	352.5
Rajasthan	213,550	2,591.9
Sikkim	2,512	19.9
Tamil Nadu	460,346	12,290.0
Tripura	38,311	268.8
Uttar Pradesh	575,699	9,999.8
Uttarakhand	39,994	555.6
West Bengal	359,861	1,178.0
A&N Islands	599	0.90
Daman & Diu	0	0.00
D&N Haveli	16	0.00
Lakshadweep	21	0.00
Pondicherry	2,320	36.2
Total	**5,218,942**	**137,269.0**

Investment climate—faltering, but hope remains

8

Chapter

The crisis in Andhra Pradesh (AP) had significant impact on the investment climate of the sector. The uncertainty introduced by the AP developments and possibility of competitive regulation by other states hit the investment sentiment and made the equity investors wary. The post-Malegam Committee regulatory initiatives by the RBI brought some sense of confidence to investors. An attempt has been made in this chapter to highlights the developments in the MFI investment climate in the country during the year 2011–12.

Access to equity capital remains difficult for MFIs even two years after the Andhra Pradesh crisis, which induced a drastic drop in repayment rates from 99.5 per cent to 5 per cent and halted new loans from MFIs. The PAR-30, according to reports from MIX market, is at 10.52 per cent,[1] far from an optimal value of being below 1 per cent, highlighting the plight MFIs continue to face in procuring loan repayments. The Bharat Microfinance Quick Report 2012 has indicated that the PAR 60 days of non-AP MFIs stands at 0.84 per cent and for AP based MFIs it stands at 31.86 per cent. Moreover, investor confidence in the sector, including that of banks, continues to be tenuous, but the recent cautious optimism outside of AP shows promise.

New MFIs outside of the state are doing well and expanding their portfolios. The deadline for 100 per cent loan provisioning norms on loan instalments overdue for 180 days was extended from April 2012 to April 2013, as it was impossible for AP-based MFIs to meet these provisioning requirements. However, even with this revised schedule, many MFIs in Andhra Pradesh remain concerned about meeting the provisioning requirements. The net worth of most AP-based MFIs stand technically eroded and would be formally recognized when they apply provisioning requirements next year as per the RBI dead line.

EQUITY FUNDING

Despite such an uncertain climate, private equity investments almost doubled in the 2011 fiscal year from the previous year (Table 8.1). In Andhra Pradesh, the state hit hardest by governmental regulations on MFIs, the fiscal year closed with 19 deals of private equity worth US$88 million compared to 10 deals worth US$44 million in the 2010 fiscal year.[2] Initially, between October 2010 and May 2011, investment amounts were considerably small; the two main investments in this period amounted to roughly ₹100 million and ₹130 million, respectively. Investor confidence in the climate increased

Table 8.1 Selected equity investments 2011–12[3]

Investor	Investee(s)	Amount (₹ million)	Date
BlueOrchard	Svasti Microfinance	45	May 2011
Citi-Venture Capital International	Janalakshmi Financial Services	650	June 2011
Sequoia, Lok, Unitus Equity, India Fin. Incl. Fund and SIDBI	Ujjivan	940	June 2011
Norwegian Microfinance Initiative	Utkarsh Microfinance Pvt. Ltd	410	September 2011
International Finance Corporation	Bandhan Financial Services	1,350	September 2011
Incofin	Arman	150	November 2011
Netherlands Development Finance Company *and* WCP Mauritius Holdings III	Ujjivan	1,279	1, February 2012
International Finance Corporation	Equitas Holdings Pvt. Ltd	1,000	May 2012
International Finance Corporation	Ujjivan	500	May 2012

dramatically with the Reserve Bank of India's recognition of the existence of NBFC-MFIs at the end of 2011, leading a more robust equity investment outlook in 2012. In the FY 2011–12, there were eight major equity investments in MFIs.[4]

Mid-2012 heralded the launch of the long-awaited 'Indian Microfinance Equity Fund' a government-run fund through SIDBI with ₹1,000 million.[5] The fund is designed for smaller MFIs that have a more difficult time than larger MFIs in attracting equity finance. SIDBI had made investments out of this fund to the tune of ₹790 million in 24 small and medium MFIs.

RECENT TRENDS AND PREDICTIONS

The Governor of the Reserve Bank of India stated in July 2012 that he believes investors are looking at the MFI market with positive sentiments.[6] Recent trends in the equity front have been very promising. Compared to the climate in late 2010 and early 2011, when investments were rare and few, investments have picked up both in size and frequency (Table 8.2). Investor confidence in the sector has been at least partially restored on account of the certainty on regulatory aspects brought in by guidelines of the RBI. The ratings upgrades of non-AP MFIs also lifted the market sentiment.

Table 8.2 Selected equity investments in the latest quarter of 2012[7]

Investor	Investee(s)	Amount (₹ million)	Period
Accion	Saija	122.6	June 2012
India Financial Inclusion Fund *and* GAWA Microfinance Fund	Janalakshmi Financial Services	800	July 2012

SKS, after its IPO, started faltering; there is an extensive debate about the initiatives of the IPO by profit making MFIs and investors. SKS continues to maintain multiple branches in AP, but hopes its transition to Maharashtra will ease its investment climate. The SKS experience does not entirely rule out entering MFIs entering the capital markets in search of equity. Chandra Sekhar Ghosh, Founder of Bandhan, the now largest MFI in India by loan portfolio size, believes that an IPO route is an eventual possibility but articulates his sentiments that the market should be left to determine valuations as compared to artificially raising valuations.[8]

A qualified institutional placement (QIP) is a capital raising tool listed MFIs can use to raise equity from a select group of investors. MFIs can use this tool to issue debentures and securities convertible to equity shares. This tool was set up for public companies in India in 2006 to prevent dependence of Indian MFIs on foreign capital in the form of securitization deals. In addition, QIPs have several advantages including increasing transaction efficiency and decreasing the cost and time involved in transactions. In July 2012, SKS Microfinance launched a qualified institutional placement, the first-ever made by an MFI, which was oversubscribed, with ₹2,300 million raised.[9] The QIP issue confirmed the fact that MFIs find the climate outside of Andhra Pradesh much more suitable to expanding a portfolio.

The proposal of treating any excess of the fair market as income to be taxed, as indicated in the Finance Bill of 2012, may hurt the startups, especially among smaller MFIs because their valuations are not fully defined in the beginning phases, and there is not enough cash among startups to begin with to make a proper valuation. New MFIs in India will have to turn to foreign venture capital to avoid this, as foreign venture capital funds will not fall under the provisions of Indian Regulations (Table 8.3).[10] For reasons other than taxation issues, many small MFIs may have to be consolidated to meet capital requirements,[11] a point made by Mr N.K. Maini, Deputy Managing Director of SIDBI.

Smaller MFIs are more at risk than are larger MFIs for multiple reasons. Primarily, smaller MFIs are more concentrated in small geographies than larger MFIs, which makes them all the more susceptible to market failures in a particular local area. For instance, many of the Andhra Pradesh based small MFIs including Dovefin and CRESA have as much as 70 per cent of operations located inside the state, subject to governmental pressure, in comparison to larger MFIs that have much more flexibility in shifting operations and headquarters geographically. Further, smaller MFIs face significantly more risk in the current investment climate as they often cannot engage in debt restructuring, which is offered only

Table 8.3 Selected recent venture capital transactions[12]

Date	Buyer	Target	Amount (₹ in million)
January 2012	Acumen	GUARDIAN	52
June 2012	Incofin	Annapurna	130
June 2012	Pragati	Saija	128.2

to larger MFIs.[13] Accordingly, MFIs such as Bandhan, Ujjivan, and Janalaskhmi are taking over the industry as Andhra Pradesh companies such as SKS and Spandana falter.[14]

Borrowings

One of the major sources of raising debt fund for MFIs is commercial banks. The crisis situation had a negative impact of the debt flow from commercial banks to MFIs during 2011–12. The MFIs reported that they received ₹72 billion as debt fund during the year 2011–12, which was only 71 per cent of funding during the previous year.[15] The bank loan extended to MFIs during the same period was ₹67 billion. The MFIs that depended on bank borrowings took most of the financial hit once the MFI sector buckled-under in 2010, as the majority of the capital for MFIs has been from debt. Until September 2011, loan growth to MFIs had decreased 16.4 per cent, compared with a 7.5 per cent growth in loans in the first half of 2010.[16] Moreover, in early 2012 banks raised their interest rates to MFIs from a previous rate of 12–14 per cent to a rate ranging from 15.5–18 per cent, and additionally started charging a processing fee and requiring a cash collateral in transactions with MFIs.[17] In the wake of this, interest rates for MFIs have remained steady as there is an upward cap on their rates to meet consumer demand of loan products, nullifying the previous benefits of debt financing. In light of this, in an industry once heavily weighted towards debt, with an all-industry debt to equity ratio of 4.65 in 2010, this ratio has greatly decreased in the past few years. In 2011, the Debt Equity ratio decreased to 3.58.[18] This highlights the plight of MFIs taking loans from banks, which currently rest on the whims of bank rates. Moreover, overall, banks greatly reduced lending outside of Andhra Pradesh and completely stopped in the state.[19] With equity investments recently on the rise, and bank loans still slogging, the debt-to-equity ratio continues to fall, with a current ratio of 3.26.[20]

According to Puli Kishore Kumar, CEO of Trident Microfin, '*The bankers are not able to digest the impact of the crisis. They believe that uncertainty continues in the sector and refrain from lending to us... the authorities need to convince boards of commercial banks about the need to lend to MFIs*.'[21] However, P.H. Ravikumar, interim non-executive chairman of SKS Microfinance Ltd, articulated in June 2012 that lending from banks looked promising recently—*in fiscal 2011–12, except for the last three months, bank disbursements, vital for MFIs to disburse new loans and build-up new clientele, dried up. It was only in the last quarter of FY12 that the bank disbursements were available.*[22] He refers to a recent increase in bank loans in the May and June 2012 months.

The roundtable on 'Fund Flow from Banks to the Microfinance Sector: Issues, Challenges and Way forward'[23] has brought out the following issues:

1. The problem in one state should not be allowed to influence and affect 30 million clients across the country. In the wake of the Andhra Pradesh situation, the sector still faces a political risk.
2. Restricted fund flows to MFIs would be a setback for the banks' drive on 'Responsible Finance.'
3. In case liquidity issues are not addressed quickly, the MFIs might lose good and potential clients, as they have suffered in the post crisis period. There is a huge concern on clients going back to the moneylenders.
4. MFIs require a continuous stream of funds for on-lending throughout the year, whereas banks usually wait till fag end of the financial year to lend.
5. It would be good for banks to consider a Tier II capital structure for MFIs.
6. Banks also ask for personal guarantees from members of top management of MFIs.
7. When the regulation has become stronger, why banks are holding back on lending is not clear.
8. The cost of compliance with RBI guidelines is huge. Various Auditors' certificates on RBI compliance are being asked by banks every now and then, which has a cost involved, and ultimately this cost would pass on to the borrower.
9. Banks do not lend unless MFIs have capital. For smaller MFIs, raising capital is difficult as they do not even reach the break even level of business due to crisis.
10. The challenge is to lend to the poor, the lender being sustainable despite the higher risks.
11. Delinquencies have increased manifold and are becoming an increasing proportion of the continuously shrinking portfolios.
12. Banks should give some incentive (lower interest rates) to MFIs that do well on social performance and responsible finance.
13. There is a need to form some kind of partnership, either of banks and MFIs or Lenders' Forum and MFIs.
14. The sector has been demonstrating enhanced transparency and focus on client centric practices.

The general feeling was that there was no justification for continued constraint on funds to MFIs from the banking system. The sector has responded well to the requirements of responsible finance, customer protection and RBI regulations. Many MFIs with business outside AP have been able to maintain portfolio quality and continued servicing of bank loans. RBI regulations clearly lay down norms for operations of MFIs, and it is a tacit recognition by RBI that the sector is legitimately pursuing financial services business focused on vulnerable people. There is an urgent need on the part of banks to reappraise their risk perceptions and resume funding to the deserving MFIs, instead of keeping themselves away from the entire sector.

Issues of Smaller MFIs (Section 25 Companies, Trusts, Societies) distinctly differ from larger MFIs in every respect. The key concern is the liquidity crunch arising from reduced fund flows. The break in fund flows from the banks has lead to a substantial shrinkage in the portfolio of MFIs. Besides the decrease in the portfolio, the crucial impact has been the delinquencies in the field. A study conducted by the CGAP and M-CRIL shows that the Indian Microfinance industry is the largest but the worst in terms of portfolio quality.[24] The Government of India is also trying hard to safeguard the small institutions under the financial inclusion drive and is in dialogue with the Andhra Pradesh government on the Andhra Pradesh Act pertaining to microfinance.

Debt-restructuring

The RBI permitted banks to retain the asset classification after restructuring. Five different MFIs wanted to procure debt-restructuring in 2012, as listed in Table 8.4, but faced high provisioning rates before they could be accepted. After the successful restructuring in June 2011 of (*a*) Spandana Spoorthy, (*b*) Asmitha Microfin, (*c*) Trident Microfin, (*d*) Future Financial Services and (*e*) SHARE in 2011, Basix was included in the second round of proposals for CDR. In July 2012, Basix, one of India's oldest MFIs, was attempting to negotiate further NCD deals with a group of banks as a last resort as the MFI started to shut-down.

Ratings

Ratings for securitization deals for MFIs are showing the upgrading trend. For instance, in February 2012, one of the main rating agencies in India, CRISIL, upgraded the rating of MFIs including Equitas (upgraded from BBB-/positive to BBB/stable), Ujjivan (upgraded to BBB/stable from BBB-/stable), and Janalakshmi (upgraded to positive).[25] These upgraded ratings perhaps were mirrored in

the fact that recent equity investments in both Equitas and Ujjivan picked up at a substantial rate. The positive correlation between equity investment and ratings validates the ratings for these particular MFIs (Table 8.4).

Table 8.4 Selected ratings for MFIs as of June 2012[26]

Rating agency	MFI	Rating 2010–11	Rating 2011–12
CARE, CRISIL	SKS	CRISIL P1	CARE: A1
ICRA	Utkarsh Micro Finance Private Ltd	M3+	M2
CRISIL	Equitas	BBB-/Positive	BBB/Stable
CRISIL	Ujjivan	BBB-/Stable	BBB/Stable

Non-convertible debentures

Because debt sources have been difficult for MFIs to come by, many MFIs have been turning to Non-Convertible Debentures (NCDs). In December 2011, the RBI issued a release stating several NBFCs had violated maturity guidelines by issuing NCDs with a maturity of less than 90 days, a provision set up in 2010 to protect interests of both lenders and borrowers.[27] MFIs in Andhra Pradesh since 2010 find it difficult to issue NCDs, on account of their low rating.

MFIs continue to look towards NCDs as viable alternatives to access credit (Table 8.5). Mr Udaya Kumar, CEO of Grameen Financial Services articulated the importance of his company's June NCD deal—'... *is very important and stabilizes our liquidity position due to the nature of the transaction. With support from domestic banks and institutions, we will be able to consolidate* ...'

Table 8.5 Major NCD deals[28]

Company	Amount (₹ million)	Date
Grameen Koota	250	June 2012
Sahayata (purchased by DWM Cyprus)	195	April 2012
Satin Creditcare Network Limited (Advised by Unitus Capital)	120	March 2011
Ujjivan	290	January 2012
Ujjivan	320	August 2011
Bandhan	280	November 2011
Equitas	500	June 2011

There are also further developments on the NCD front. IFMR Capital placed its first two NCDs, the first in December 2011, and the second in June 2012, invested by FMO, a Dutch Development Bank. Great promise NCDs have attracted investor and institutional attention and have become an important resource mobilization tool for MFIs.

Securitization

As of April 2012, MFIs had sold ₹30 billion of loans through securitization deals, an amount close to double the amount of such deals carried out during the previous year.[29] Banks are turning to securitization of MFI portfolios to meet their priority sector portfolio needs (Table 8.6). The RBI regulations in December 2011 capping interest rates at 26 per cent, have helped increase banks' confidence in the sector and bolstered the market for securitization deals. Securitized loan portfolios have had significant advantages for MFIs, including freeing up equity by providing some sort of immediate liquidity for MFIs to invest.

Table 8.6 Major securitization deals in 2012[30]

Originator	Amount (₹ million)	Time period
SKS	10,000	January–March 2012
Bandhan Financial Services Pvt. Ltd	5,000	February 2012
Grameen Financial Services	249.5	2012
GramaVidiyal	279.2	2012
Annapurna	331.43	2012
Grameen Financial Services	188.3	2012
Satin Creditcare Network Limited	197.4	2012
GramaVidiyal	225.2	2012
Annapurna, Asirvad, Disha, Fusion, Mimoza, Satin, S.M.I.L.E., Suryoday, SVCL	443.6	2012

In 2010, IFMR Capital proposed the new idea, called a multi-originator securitization, which helps in reducing investor's risk across geographic regions and across multiple MFIs rather than only one MFI. In September 2011, IFMR Capital reached a ₹511 million multi-originator loan from 49,881 microloans from a number of MFIs, the largest such transaction.[31] One sign of how MFIs are doing financially is

their loan books, which are correlated with two main factors: (*a*) shares of equity and debt finance and (*b*) regulations placed on lending by the RBI. Overall, MFIs in states other than Andhra Pradesh increased their loan portfolios by 22 per cent, whereas MFIs in Andhra Pradesh shrunk by 38 per cent, giving an average total of 15 per cent shrinkage in loan portfolios in the entire country.[32]

It is evident the earlier discussions in Chapter 3 that growth rate in gross loan portfolio of MFIs outside AP continues to remain encouraging. However, because AP makes up such a large proportion of the total loan portfolios nationwide, the overall focus remains on this market. The emerging question is whether MFIs in Andhra Pradesh will be able to meet capital and provisioning requirements to regain a proper footing in the industry, or whether they will have to diversify the operations for existence.

SUMMING UP

Consequent to the crisis in the sector, the investment climate in India seems more dynamic than ever before. Despite a dearth of debt financing, the equity front looks promising. MFIs and capital-infusing institutions have turned their attention with new found rigor to new forms of capital flows including securitizations, multi-originator securitizations, NCDs, and qualified institutional placements. In the meantime, the Indian government continues to unfold small-scale programmes designed to help smaller MFIs including the Indian Microfinance Equity Fund. With the positive responses from the sector in terms of an improved regulatory environment and responsible financing by the MFIs, the equity flow is expected to be encouraging for all MFIs more particularly to smaller and medium sized ones, and hence, despite flattering performance, hope remains.

NOTES AND REFERENCES

Extensive work on this chapter was carried out and an initial draft provided by Keshav Garud, intern with CMF IFMR, Chennai. The author is gratefully acknowledging the excellent work.

1. MIX Market weighted average of reported PAR-30 values.
2. http://www.business-standard.com/india/news/development-financial-entities-fuel-mfi-growth/478040/ accessed in June 2012.
3. Referred to the VCCircle deal database for most of the equity deals, and performed back-checks with following sources (some of which were my primary source) In order from the top down:

http://www.grameencapital.in/images/pdf/Svasti_May2011.pdf accessed in June 2012.

http://www.msdf.org/about-us/newsroom/press-releases/2011/06/06/ujjivan-raises-$19.6-million-of-equity-capital accessed in June 2012.

http://www.dealcurry.com/20120629-Incofin-Invests-In-Annapurna-Microfinance.htm accessed in June 2012.

http://business-standard.com/india/news/mfi-saija-finance-gets-45-mn-investment/477408/ accessed in June 2012.

http://www.business-standard.com/india/news/ifc-to-make-rs-150-cr-equity-investment-in-equitasujjivan-mfis/473631/ accessed in June 2012.

http://www.indiaprwire.com/pressrelease/financial-services/20120201110761.htm

http://www business-standard.com/india/news/development-financial-entities-fuel-mfi-growth/478040/ accessed in June 2012.

http://videos.livemint.com/2012/07/16215213/Janlakshmi-raises-₹-1450million-crore.html?h=B accessed in June 2012.

4. http://www.ifmr.co.in/blog/2012/05/04/funding-to-the-microfinance-sector-review-of-options/ accessed in June 2012.

5. The government may consider replenishing this fund at a future date. http://articles.economictimes.indiatimes.com/2012-05-26/news/31861006_1_nbfc-mfis-sidbi-small-industries-development-bank accessed in June 2012.

6. http://www thehindubusinessline.com/industry-and-economy/banking/article3602865.ece accessed in June 2012.

7. Source is as indicated in note 6.

8. http://wrd.mydigitalfc.com/news/ipo-route-mfi-growth-not-bad-valuations-worry-754 accessed in June 2012.

9. http://videos.livemint.com/2012/07/17202103/SKS-Microfinance-raises-230-c.html?atype=tp accessed in June 2012.

10. http://www.darashaw.com/uploads/resource-center/reports/darashaw-552.pdf accessed in June 2012.

11. http://www thehindubusinessline.com/industry-and-economy/banking/article3573631.ece?homepage=true&ref=wl_home accessed in June 2012.

12. http://www.dealcurry.com/2012079-SKS-Micro-To-Raise-Funds-For-Expansion.htm
http://www.vccircle.com/news/micro-finance/2012/01/17/acumen-fund-invests-1m-microfinance-firm-guardian accessed in June 2012.

13. http://www.business-standard.com/india/news/small-mfis-facing-bankruptcy/433231/ accessed in June 2012.

14. http://www.business-standard.com/india/news/a-brave-new-worldmicrofinance/466274/ accessed in June 2012.

15. Microfinance—Growing Against All Odds, The Bharat Microfinance Quick Report 2012, Sa-Dhan Publication.

16. http://www.livemint.com/2011/11/01233122/Sharp-drop-in-bank-loans-to-MF.html accessed in June 2012.

17. http://www.livemint.com/2012/02/10000307/Banks-raise-loan-costs-for-MFI.html accessed in June 2012.

18. MIX Market Debt to Equity Ratio, Weighted Average.

19. http://www.livemint.com/2012/02/10000307/Banks-raise-loan-costs-for-MFI.html accessed in June 2012.

20. MIX Market Debt to Equity Ratio, Weighted Average.

21. http://www.livemint.com/2011/11/01233122/Sharp-drop-in-bank-loans-to-MF.html accessed in June 2012.

22. http://www.moneycontrol.com/news/business/-act-will-aid-recovery-expect-no-murmursap-govt-sks_717395.html accessed in June 2012.

23. Proceedings of the Roundtable on 'Fund Flow from Banks to the Microfinance Sector: Issues, Challenges and Way forward' on 14 June 2012 organized by Access development Services at IIBF Leadership centre, Mumbai.

24. M-CRIL Microfinance Review 2011, Anatomy of crisis, http://www.m-cril.com/BackEnd/Modules-Files/Publication/Executive-Summary-Review-2011.pdf. accessed in June 2012.

25. http://www.indianexpress.com/news/crisil-ups-ratings-of-three-mfis/917856/1 accessed in June 2012.

26. In order from the top down:
http://www.dealcurry.com/20120629-Incofin-Invests-In-Annapurna-Microfinance.htm accessed in June 2012.
http://business-standard.com/india/news/mfi-saija-finance-gets-45-mn-investment/477408/ accessed in June 2012.
http://www.crisil.com/Ratings/RatingList/RatingDocs/sks-microfinance_24sep10.htm accessed in June 2012.
http://www.sksindia.com/credit_rating.php accessed in June 2012.
http://www.microfinancefocus.com/mffnews/utkarsh-mfi-grading-upgraded-m2-m3-icra accessed in June 2012.

27. http://www.rbi.org.in/scripts/BS_NBFCNotificationView.aspx?Id=6913 accessed in June 2012.

28. In order from the top down:
http://www.thehindubusinessline.com/industry-and-economy/economy/article3554726.ece?homepage=true&ref=wl_home accessed in June 2012.
http://www.ifmr.co.in/blog/tag/ncd/ accessed in June 2012.
http://unitus.com/updates/unitus-capital-raises-11-7-million-for-india-mfi-satin/ accessed in June 2012.

http://www.business-standard.com/india/news/ mfi-ujjivan-raises-rs-290-million-through-ncds/ 462800/ accessed in June 2012.

http://business-standard.com/india/news/top-mfis- look-at-ncds-to-raise-funds/441584/ accessed in June 2012.

http://www.vccircle.com/finance-microfinance? page=1 accessed in June 2012.

http://www.microfinancefocus.com/crisil-revises- equitas-microfinance-ncd's-rating-positive accessed in June 2012.

29. http://www.livemint.com/2012/04/01184327/MFIs- see-sharp-rise-in-securit.html accessed in June 2012.

30. <http://capital.ifmr.co.in/deal-portal (Most of these securitization deals were found from the IFMR Cap- ital Deal Portal.)

http://www.livemint.com/2012/04/01184327/MFIs- see-sharp-rise-in-securit.html> accessed in June 2012.

31. http://www.ifmr.co.in/blog/2011/09/21/ifmr-capi- tal-completes-its-largest-multi-originator-securiti- sation-transaction/ accessed in June 2012.

32. Data extracted from first edition of Micrometer published by Sa-Dhan 2012.

Global trends in microfinance

Microfinance as a part of financial sector is expected to be influenced directly or indirectly by the positive or negative changes that take place in the global economy or the regional financial markets. Understanding the trend and progress of global microfinance assumes greater importance in the present day context in view of its significant influence on the Indian microfinance sector. The Economist Intelligence Unit (EIU) has brought out a report entitled Global Microscope on the MFI sector for the year 2011.[1] The study covered 55 countries. The countries had been ranked on the basis of various revised parameters, which include overall microfinance business environment, regulatory framework and practices, and supporting institutional framework and stability. The study concluded that, in the aftermath of the global financial crisis, microfinance has begun to enter a more mature and sustainable growth phase. After years of rapid expansion, the focus has turned to accelerating the improvements already underway in corporate governance, responsible finance practices and regulatory capacity and risk management. Further, risk management, which has become a post-crisis priority for all financial institutions, has improved considerably in the microfinance sector, which is essential, given that it is offering an increasingly diversified range of innovative financial services to the poor.

The ranking of the top 10 countries in microfinance revealed that Peru continued to top the list with the highest score followed by Bolivia and Pakistan. India and Ghana, which were in the list of the top 10 countries during the year 2010 could not retain their positions in 2011 and hence got dropped from the list (Table 9.1). On the other hand, countries such as Uganda, Mexico and Panama have gained entry into the list of the top 10 countries. Uganda, which was displaced from the list last year, regained entry into the list in the ninth position, while its co-entrants, Mexico and Panama, have occupied the

tenth position. On the whole, all the top-ranking countries, with the exception of Kenya, have declined in terms of their score as compared to their score in the preceding year. Under the overall business category, Bangladesh—the land of microfinance origin has been ranked 43rd, and Vietnam was in the last place.

Pakistan, Philippines and Uganda shared the first place in regulatory framework and practices, while Trinidad and Tobago have occupied the lowermost position in the list. Bolivia and Peru shared first rank in Supporting Institutional framework followed by Columbia and Armenia. Costa Rica has topped the list in terms of stability factor followed by South American countries viz., Uruguay and Chile. As in the overall business category, Vietnam was in the bottommost position in terms of supporting institutional framework.

Peru had an excellent record of legal framework, sophisticated regulators and government commitment, which purely focused on making the unbanked

Table 9.1 Ranking of the top 10 countries in microfinance in 2011

Rank	Country	Score in 2011	Change from 2010
1.	Peru	67.8	−6.5
2.	Bolivia	64.7	−4.9
3.	Pakistan	62.8	−2
4.	Kenya	60.3	5.3
5.	El Salvador	58.8	−2.5
6.	Philippines	58.5	−13.3
7.	Colombia	56.0	−0.8
8.	Ecuador	55.1	−6.2
9.	Uganda	53.7	New entrant
10.	Mexico and Panama	53.6	New entrant

Source: Global Microscope on the Microfinance Business Environment, 2009–11, Economic Intelligence Unit Ltd (www.eiu.com).

bankable. Bolivia had better price transparency and disclosure rules. Pakistan, placed in the third position, had a separate legal framework for microfinance banks and good networking. The Kyrgyz Republic has stepped down from the 12th position to the 21st rank globally. This is due to a change in the political regime, which halted regulatory overhaul. Latin America and the Caribbean have the largest number of top performing countries in the Global Microscope. The region has eight countries in the top 12 global positions. In addition, the first two places are occupied by Peru and Bolivia respectively. This had been possible mainly because of their very strong position in supporting institutional framework, even though these countries are not very strong in regulatory framework and practices.

The Middle East and North African countries have faced political unrest earlier this year, which seriously handicapped the functioning of the microfinance industry. Yemen is one of the most affected countries, which slid from the 27th to the 44th place. This instability has caused many MFIs to reduce their scale of operations, ending up with closure of banks too. Kenya is one of the strongest and most stable countries in this region. Kenya is placed in the fourth place and Uganda in the ninth place in the global list. But Uganda finds itself in the first place globally in terms of regulatory framework and practices. Clients are benefitted with active microfinance markets.

India has been pushed to the 27th rank with a score of 43.1 in the overall microfinance business environment. It occupied the 22nd rank in regulatory framework and practices, the 20th place in supporting institutional framework and the 40th rank in terms of stability. The Government of India had strongly promoted the Self-Help Group model through the National Rural Livelihood Mission by offering cheap funding and also restricted market-based lending. In a study carried out by Microrate MIV survey 2011,[2] Latin American and the Caribbean (LAC) countries and Europe and Central Asia continue to account for the majority of microfinance investments receiving a combined total of 73 per cent of all microfinance investments in 2010.[3] JP Morgan's CGAP Global Equity Valuation Survey 2012 has reported that the LAC region had more than half of the investment followed by Asia.[3] India is the major contributor with more than 92 per cent of Asia's investment levels.

REGION-WISE PERFORMANCE OF MFIs IN THE WORLD

The growth and performance of microfinance sector at global level during the recent years has shown significant differences across regions. With a view to capture the direction of movement of the sector among the regions, a comparative analysis of the performance of the sector in regions like Africa, East Asia and Pacific, Eastern Europe, Central Asia, Latin America, Caribbean, Middle East and North Africa and South Asia is attempted in this section. The data from Mix Market for the period 2003–10 has been the basis for this analysis.[4]

The number of MFIs had, by and large, shown an upward trend in almost all the regions up to the year 2007 and 2008, after which the numbers have started dwindling in all the regions. In all the regions of the world, the number of MFIs has decreased during the year 2011 as compared to the previous year, except in East Asia and the Pacific, where the number remained unchanged (Figure 9.1). The decrease in the number of MFIs has ranged from about 10 per cent

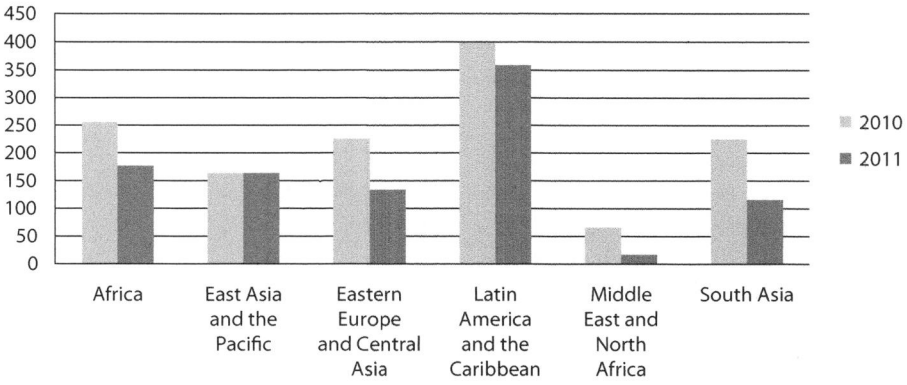

Figure 9.1 Number of MFIs in different regions

Source: http://www.microrate.com/media/downloads/2012/04/The-State-of-Microfinance-Investment-2011-MicroRate.pdf accessed in June 2012.

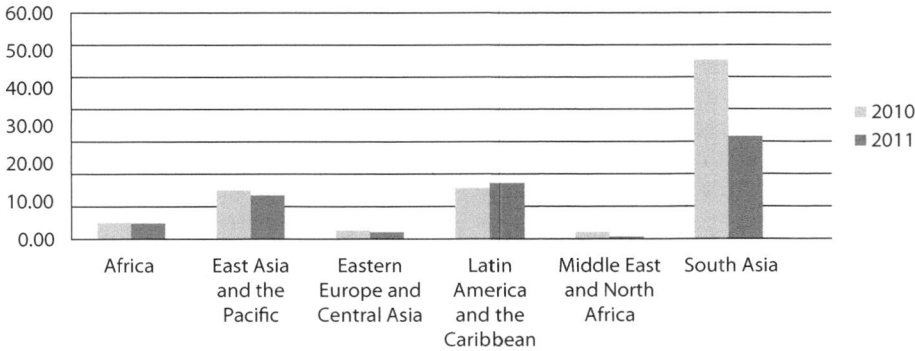

Figure 9.2 Number of active borrowers (in million)

Source: http://www.microrate.com/media/downloads/2012/04/The-State-of-Microfinance-Investment-2011-MicroRate.pdf accessed in June 2012.

in LAC countries to close to 75 per cent in the Middle East and the North African region. In South Asian countries the decline in the MFI count was about 50 per cent. This is probably due to the overall economic situation as the world was experiencing severe economic recession during this period.

The number of active borrowers during the year 2011 has declined in most regions of the world as compared to the preceding year, with the exception of LAC countries where there was a marginal increase in the number (Figure 9.2). The decline in the number of active borrowers was the highest in MENA countries where the decline was about 70 per cent between the years 2010 and 2011, while it was more than 40 per cent in South Asian countries. The decline in active borrowers has reflected in reduction of deposits too.

The trend in the number of depositors shows a disheartening trend in most parts of the world with a decline in their numbers in recent years (Figure 9.3). By the year 2010, the South Asia region had the highest number of depositors (23.73 million), though it declined by about 50 per cent to about 12 million in the year 2011. Consequently, the African countries accounted for the highest number of depositors in the year 2011, with 16.25 million depositors though with a marginal decline from about 17 million in the preceding year. Middle and North African countries had the lowest number of depositors (0.1 million) in 2010, and this too had declined by 63 per cent in 2011, thus making it negligible as compared to the other regions of the world. East Asian countries have recorded the highest year-on-year growth in the number of depositors, from about 6 million in 2010 to 7.73 million in 2011, while the LAC countries have maintained

their number around 15.50 million in both the years. In the world as a whole the total number of depositors declined from more than 65 million to about 54 million between the years 2010 and 2011, thus recording a decline of 17.50 per cent.

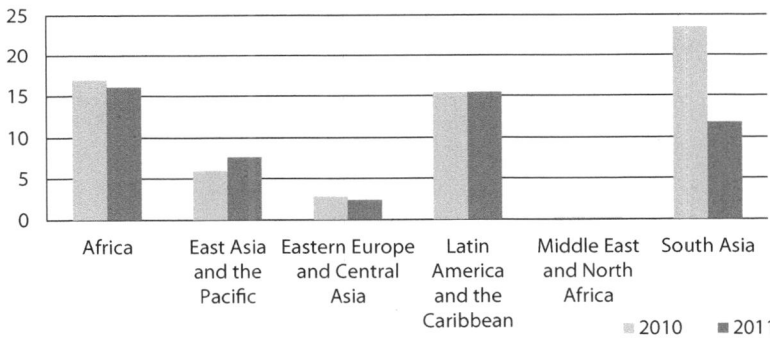

Figure 9.3 Number of depositors (in million)

Source: http://www.microrate.com/media/downloads/2012/04/The-State-of-Microfinance-Investment-2011-MicroRate.pdf accessed in June 2012.

Due to the decline or stagnation in the number of deposits in most of the regions, there has been a marginal to steep decline in the deposit amounts between the years 2010 and 2011 in all the regions except in Latin American and Caribbean countries and the African region where there was an increase in the deposit amount (Figure 9.4). The decline in the deposit amount was the steepest in East Asia and the Pacific region where the deposits registered a fall of 80 per cent from about US$31 billion to 6 billion. In South Asia, a 50 per cent decline in number of depositors has resulted in more than 80 per cent decline in the deposit amount.

The MENA region has recorded the highest fall of about 95 per cent in the deposit amount as a consequence of more than 60 per cent decline in the number of depositors. Due to the moderate to steep decline in deposit amounts in most of the regions, the deposit amount at a global level has recorded a 40 per cent decline from US$63 billion to US$37.5 billion.

The gross loan portfolio has shown an increasing trend in all the regions of the world during the period 2009–10 (Figure 9.4). In Eastern Europe and Central Asia, the increase was more pronounced with an increase of 60 per cent, while it was around 20 per cent in Africa, and East Asia and the Pacific, while the increase in other regions falling in between these two extremes.

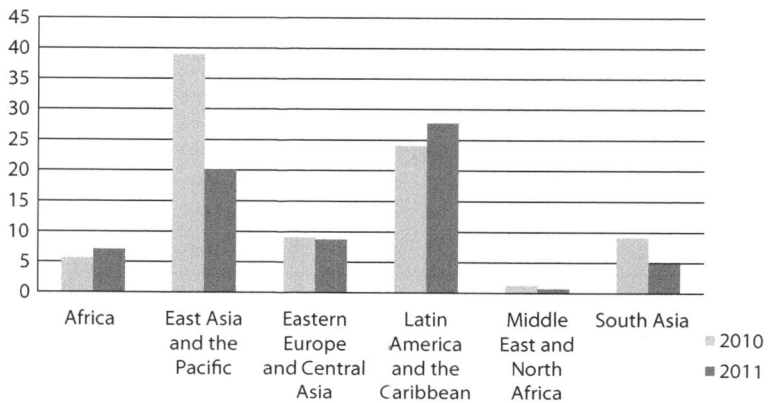

Figure 9.4 Gross loan portfolio (Sum) (in billion US$)

Source: http://www.microrate.com/media/downloads/2012/04/The-State-of-Micro-finance-Investment-2011-MicroRate.pdf accessed in June 2012.

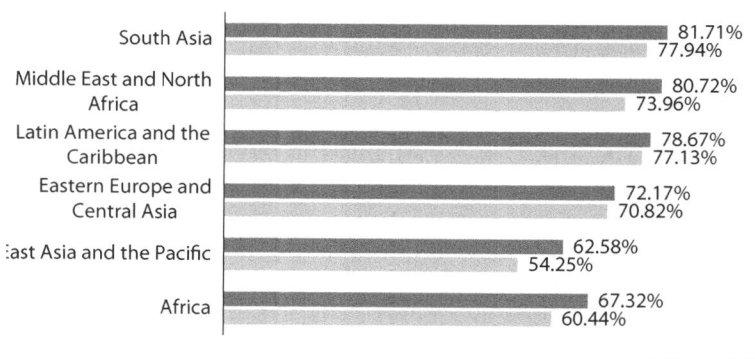

Figure 9.5 Gross loan portfolio to total assets

Source: http://www.microrate.com/media/cownloads/2012/04/The-State-of-Microfi-nance-Investment-2011-MicroRate.pdf accessed in June 2012.

Though the sector seems to have achieved a positive growth in gross loan portfolio/total assets for almost all the countries during 2011 over the year 2010, it has shown a mixed trend during the period 2003–11 in most of the regions (Figure 9.5). The ratio of gross loan portfolio to total assets was the lowest in East Asia and the Pacific countries, among all the regions of the world though this region has increased it from 54 per cent to 62 per cent between the years 2010 and 2011. African countries have also recorded a similar increase in their gross loan portfolio to total assets ratio. The Middle East and the North Africa region closely follows the South Asian countries in terms of their gross loan portfolio/total assets during the year 2011.

A country-wise analysis for South Asia reveals that the total assets in 2011 have declined for most of the countries as compared to the corresponding figures in the previous year. Attrition in total assets is found to be the highest in Bangladesh and Sri Lanka where the assets declined by about 97 in 2011 as compared to the previous year. Though India's assets declined by 50 per cent between the years 2010 and 2011, India continued to top the list of South Asian countries in terms of total assets, with a total asset value of about US$2.90 billion. In terms of the median asset value, Bhutan topped the list of South Asian countries during the year 2010, with a median asset value of about US$95 million, though the figures of Bhutan are not available for the year 2011. The median asset values have increased for all the countries in South Asia during the year 2011 as compared to the previous year, though with wide differences across nations. Bangladesh topped the list of South Asian countries in terms of median asset value in 2011 (US$506 million), followed by Pakistan (US$56 million).

PORTFOLIO AT RISK (90 DAYS)

The portfolio at risk has been showing a mixed trend across different regions over the period 2003–11. Though the portfolio at risk for the African region has been fluctuating during this period, the PAR has decreased from 5.3 per cent in 2003 to 3.36 per cent in 2011. A similar kind of fluctuating trend was observed in East Asia and the Pacific nations, but there has been a perceptible decrease in PAR from 3.89 per cent in 2003 to less than one percent in 2011. East Europe and Central Asia have shown an increasing trend in recent years though the PAR in 2011 has decreased to 2.47 per cent from 6.73 per cent in 2010. In the case of Latin

American countries, the PAR has been fluctuating around 4–5 per cent over the period from 2003 to 2011, while in the MENA countries, the PAR was smaller than most of the other regions with minor fluctuations over the years. In South Asian countries, though the PAR has been showing a declining trend from 2003 to 2009, from more than 4 per cent in 2003 to 2.76 per cent in 2009, it has made a sudden spurt in the recent years with 14.13 per cent in 2010 and 19 per cent in 2011. However, South Asian countries had the lowest risk coverage 20 per cent in 2010 and 5 per cent in 2011, while all other regions had the risk coverage of more than 60 per cent in the year 2011.

The loan loss rate is found to have made a sudden spurt in the year 2011 in MENA, which was 6.38 per cent, up from less than one per cent during all previous years. In spite of having a large loan portfolio, LAC had a a loan loss rate of only 1.83 per cent, thus promoting additional portfolio growth. The other regions of the world such as Africa, East Asia and the Pacific and Eastern European and Central Asian countries have all had a loan loss rate of less than one per cent in all the years.

Though all the regions have reported an operational self-sufficiency (OSS) ratio of more than 100 per cent since 2005 until 2011, indicating that the sector is self-sufficient, the OSS for South Asian countries has suddenly slumped to 64 per cent in 2011 from 115 per cent in the previous year. African countries and the East and Pacific region have recorded a very high OSS of about 128 per cent in the year 2011. For East Asia and the Pacific region, this is a remarkable recovery from its previous year OSS ratio of just above 100 per cent.

The percentage of operating costs to total assets was the highest in Africa at 18 and 19 per cent respectively during 2009 and 2010, closely followed by Latin American countries with 17 per cent in both the years (Figure 9.6). It was the lowest at 11 and 12 per cent respectively in South Asia, and East European and Central Asian countries during both 2009 and 2010.

Yield on gross portfolio was the highest at 25 per cent for Latin American countries closely followed by East Asia and the Pacific region at 24 per cent. It was the lowest at 13 per cent for South Asia and higher than 20 per cent in all other regions.

The Return on Assets (RoA) of the African region has shown steady progress from 1.65 per cent in 2001 to 4.21 per cent in 2011, though it was fluctuating around less than 1 per cent till 2010, before recording a spurt in 2011. Similarly, East Asian and Pacific nations recorded a fluctuating trend around less than

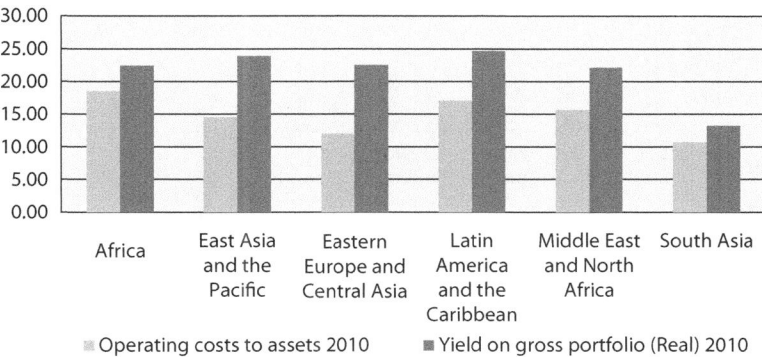

Figure 9.6 Operating costs and yield on gross portfolio (%)

Source: http://www.microrate.com/media/downloads/2012/04/The-State-of-Microfinance-Investment-2011-MicroRate.pdf accessed in June 2012.

1 per cent until 2010, and recorded a significant rise in 2011 to reach 2.3 per cent, in spite of the steep fall in their gross loan portfolio. Though LAC countries had a higher gross loan portfolio, it has achieved a very low RoA of only 2.92 per cent (2011) though it has marginally improved its performance over the previous year. The RoA of LAC had not been impressive with respect to its portfolio size.

The African region outperformed all other regions in terms of the RoA, RoE as well as profit margin during the year 2011. Both EAP and EECA regions have achieved an impressive growth in all the three indicators viz., profit margin, RoA and RoE as compared to their corresponding figures in the previous year. LAC countries however made a tardy progress in all these parameters. The most disheartening trend is noticed in the case of South Asia where there has been a strong negative growth in all the three indicators. The MENA region has witnessed a fall in profit margin while RoA and RoE have not recorded any noticeable change between 2010 and 2011.

The profit margin slumped from about 13 per cent in 2010 to as low as –56 per cent in 2011, while the RoA slipped from 2.2 per cent to –9.5 per cent and RoE declined from about 11 per cent in 2010 to –38 per cent in 2011 (Figure 9.7). The main reason for the sharp fall in profit margin in the South Asia region is the manifold fall in profit margin in Afghanistan probably due to the prevailing political instability and its socio-economic fallouts. Surprisingly, Bangladesh, the homeland of microfinance as well as India, have also witnessed a sharp downturn in profit margin, RoA as well as RoE in the year 2011 as compared to the previous year and all these figures have become negative in the year 2011. Not

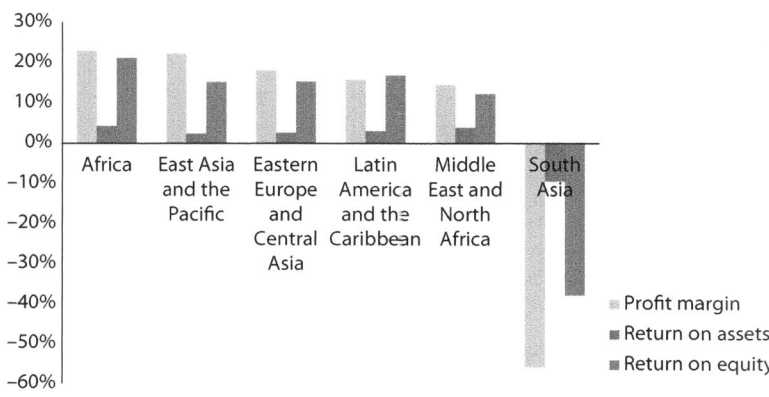

Figure 9.7 Rate of return and profit margin, 2011 (weighted averages)

Source: http://www.microrate.com/media/downloads/2012/04/The-State-of-Microfinance-Investment-2011-MicroRate.pdf accessed in June 2012.

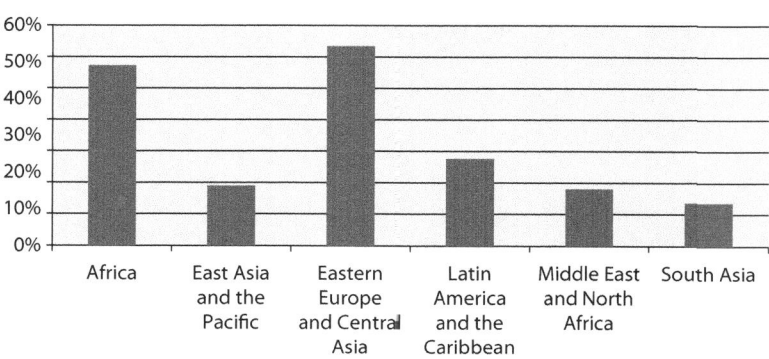

Figure 9.8 Average outstanding balance/GNI per capita

Source: http://www.microrate.com/media/downloads/2012/04/The-State-of-Microfinance-Investment-2011-MicroRate.pdf accessed in June 2012.

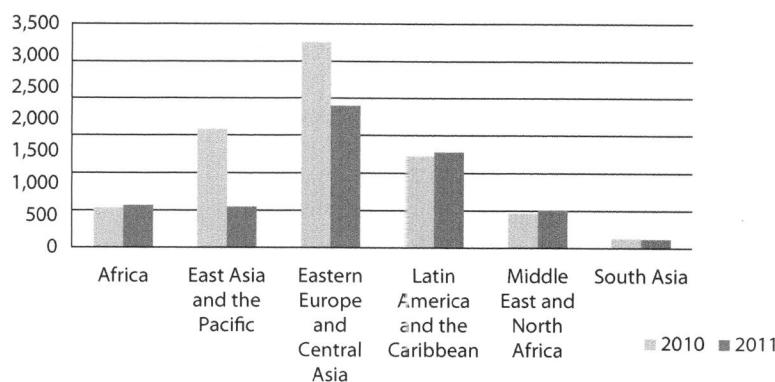

Figure 9.9 Average loan balance per borrower (weighted average US$)

Source: http://www.microrate.com/media/downloads/2012/04/The-State-of-Microfinance-Investment-2011-MicroRate.pdf accessed in June 2012.

much change has happened in the case of Pakistan, except for an increase in profit margin from –2 per cent in 2010 to 3 per cent in 2011.

LOAN OUTSTANDING

The total number of loans outstanding in South Asian regions was found to have reached a peak of more than 180 million in 2010 and slipped steeply to 36 million in 2011. Eastern Europe and Central Asia and East Asia and the Pacific regions have recorded a marginal decline in their total number of loans outstanding between the years 2010 and 2011, while African countries and Latin American and the Caribbean countries have recorded a marginal increase in the number of loan outstandings. The countries in the MENA region have reduced their loans outstanding in recent years though it has been increasing till 2008. The most noticeable feature is that MENA countries have reduced their outstanding loans with less operating expenses.

The average outstanding balance as percentage to gross national income per capita (median) provided in Figure 9.8 reveals that the median outstanding balance as percentage to per capita gross national income was more than 50 per cent in the case of Eastern European and Central Asian countries, closely followed by African countries. All the other regions have this ratio between 12 and 25 per cent with the Asian countries falling in the lower end of the range.

The average loan per borrower has, by and large, exhibited an upward trend in almost all the regions up to 2007 and 2008, after which it started declining (Figure 9.9). The steepest fall in the average loan size between the years 2010 and 2011 was observed in the case of East Asia and the Pacific Region, where it declined from US$1,844 to US$647. However, during the year 2011 the African, LAC and MENA regions have seen a marginal increase in the average loan size. A cross-regional comparison of the average loan size during the year 2011 suggests that the average loan per borrower was the highest in East European and Central Asian countries (US$2,214), followed by Latin American and Caribbean countries (US$1,500). The average loan size is found to be the lowest in South Asian countries in almost all the years, and it was very meager at around US$150 during 2011.

The proportion of the average salary of MFI staff to the per capital gross national income of the regions shows that, barring Africa, in all other regions, the average staff salary was about two to five times the per capita gross national income of the respective regions, whereas in Africa it was more than nine times, probably because of the very low per capita gross national incomes of many of the African countries (Table 9.2). The ratio of average staff salary to per capita gross national income was the lowest at 2.70 in MENA countries. The number of borrowers per staff member was the lowest at Eastern Europe and Central Asia (61 borrowers per staff), followed by 113 in Africa, while it was the highest in South Asia with 231 borrowers per staff.

Table 9.2 Proportion of average staff salary to GNI per capita and number of borrowers per staff (2011)

Region	Average salary/GNI per capita (weighted average)	Borrowers per staff member (weighted average)
Africa	9.38	113
East Asia and the Pacific	4.77	244
Eastern Europe and Central Asia	3.92	61
Latin America and the Caribbean	3.46	135
Middle East and North Africa	2.68	152
South Asia	2.79	231

Source: http://www.microrate.com/media/downloads/2012/04/The-State-of-Microfinance-Investment-2011-MicroRate.pdf accessed in June 2012.

The administrative expense as a percentage of total assets (weighted average) has shown mixed trends across regions between the years 2010 and 2011 (Figure 9.10). It was the highest at 8 per cent in Africa during the year 2010, which has decreased significantly to less than 6 per cent in 2011. Quite the contrary happened in the South Asian countries where the administrative costs as a percentage to total assets increased significantly from 3 per cent in 2010 to close to 6 per cent during 2011. In the case of the East Asian and Pacific region also, the percentage has doubled from 1.23 to about 2.50 per cent between the years 2010 and 2011. However, in the case of East Europe and Central Asia and the Latin American and Caribbean region, this percentage has almost remained stagnant during the two periods. In the MENA region, the percentage of administrative costs to total assets has showed an increase from 3.87 to 5.13.

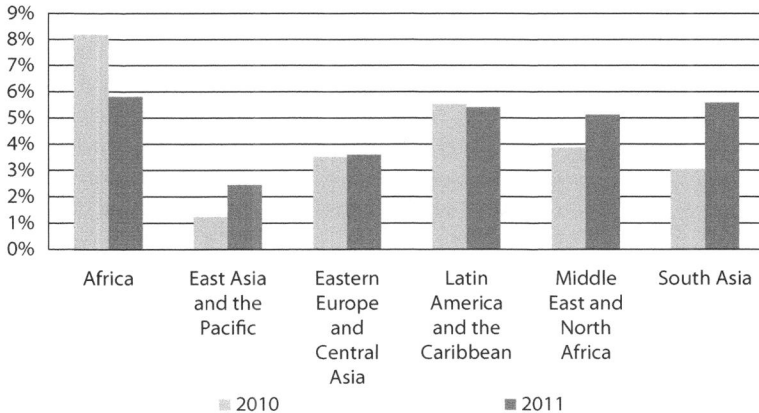

Figure 9.10 Administrative expenses/total assets (%)

Source: http://www.microrate.com/media/downloads/2012/04/The-State-of-Microfinance-Investment-2011-MicroRate.pdf accessed in June 2012.

The average loan balance per borrower during the year 2011 was the highest at more than US$1,700 in Eastern Europe and Central Asia, followed by Latin American and Caribbean countries with US$1,033, and MENA region with about US$600. It was the smallest in South Asia (US$155). The cost per borrower was also the lowest in South Asia (US$20 per borrower), and the highest in Eastern Europe and Central Asia (US$290 per borrower) (Figure 9.11).

The cost per borrower and the cost per loan have increased by almost two-fold for LAC countries during 2011 as compared to its 2010 figures, though the costs recorded very small increases during the

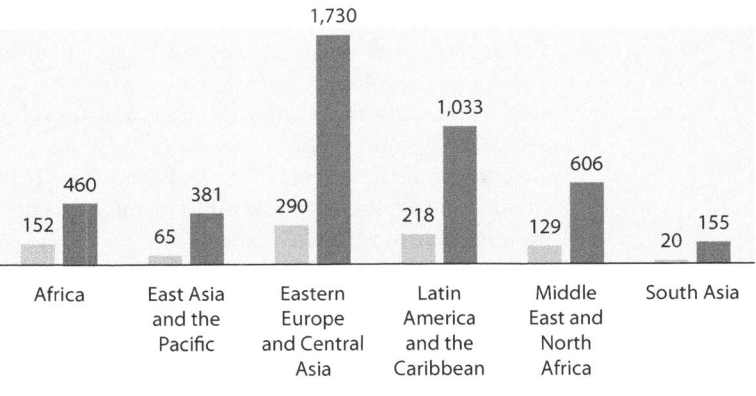

Figure 9.11 Loan balance and cost per borrower

Source: http://www.microrate.com/media/downloads/2012/04/The-State-of-Microfinance-Investment-2011-MicroRate.pdf accessed in June 2012.

previous years. During the year 2010, for which the cost data are available for all the regions, both the cost per loan and the cost per borrower were the highest in the EECA region, followed by LAC countries. The MENA region has experienced significant inflation in cost per loan. But African and AEP regions have recorded a dip in costs due to a large decline in their active borrowers.

THE BANANA SKIN SURVEY

The Banana Skin Survey for the year 2012[5] reveals that, globally, over-indebtedness is the topmost risk in the year 2012, in contrast to the credit risk topping the list in the previous year, which has now moved down to the fourth position in the list of global risk factors. Corporate governance and management quality are ranked as the second and third most dominant risks. Management quality appears to be gaining prominence as it moved from the seventh position in 2011 to the third position during 2012. Political interference continues to be in the fifth position as in the last year, which is probably due to the political apprehensions about overcharging, and use of unethical lending and recovery practices by MFIs. The risk of competition, which occupied the third position during 2011, has moved down to the eighth rank during the latest year. The quality of risk management and client management, which did not find a place in the list of global risk factors during 2011, have come to occupy sixth and seventh positions respectively, during 2012. The Survey states that, of the top 12 risks, eight are 'institutional risks,' i.e., ones that are internal to the MFIs themselves—such as the strength of leadership, the quality of the loan book and the effectiveness of internal controls. The others are external risks such as political interference and regulation, but even these risks are, to some extent, internal as they represent reactions by the external world to the behaviour of MFIs. Therefore, many of the important risks facing the MFIs could be made more manageable through greater professionalism within MFIs.

Microfinance practitioners are more concerned about over-indebtedness, credit risk as well as competition, while non-practitioners such as investors, regulators and observers place more importance on risks of management and governance issues. The MFI practitioners attribute the credit risks, both to the internal elements such as their control weaknesses as well as to external factors like increasing competition and political interference. Managerial and governance issues are the other important risk factors perceived by practitioners. The risk perception of deposit-seeking MFIs is very similar to the perception of MFIs in general. Investors in MFIs regard both managerial quality and corporate governance issues in addition to over-indebtedness as the most important risks. The quality of risk management is also a critical risk factor as perceived by MFI investors, while political interference and regulation are also perceived to be important risk factors by investors.

Regulators, consisting of government officials, regard institutional weaknesses such as corporate governance and managerial quality as the most important risk factors besides credit risk and indebtedness. Similar to MFI investors, the observers consisting mainly of consultants and analysts perceive management quality and corporate governance, besides over-indebtedness as important risk factors. Client management and risk management are seen to be the other important risks by the observers. Over-indebtedness and credit risks are the most important risk factors in most regions of the world with the exception of Asia where, political controversies in the aftermath of the Andhra Pradesh crisis, and the consequent tougher regulations dominate the microfinance sector, and hence political interference is seen as one of the important risk factors in the MFI. While liquidity topped the list of risk categories in Asia, corporate governance and management quality issues remain high priority issues in reviving the reputation of MFIs. In contrast to most other regions of the world, credit risk and over-indebtedness are much lower in the rank list of risk factors faced by MFIs in Asia.

Many respondents of the Banana Skin Survey, 2012 reported that over-indebtedness is a consequence of the absence of centralized lending data such as credit reference bureau that would enable MFIs to assess the borrowing capacity of potential clients. However, many commentators also pointed to the increasing multiple lending as the primary cause of over-indebtedness, which cannot be solely addressed by the credit reference bureau. Overall, the institutional risks relating to management and governance issues dominated the ranking list of MFI risks, and this calls for radical improvement management skills, managerial quality and client management aspects.

SUMMING UP

Overall, the global scenario is not promising for the MFI industry as such. Though some economies have booked portfolio, it is found that they are struggling hard to manage their expenses. State of the Microcredit Summit Campaign Report 2012 has argued that a number of initiatives like values of responsibility, corporate ethics and social performance management have emerged to address the key challenges faced by the sector.[6] MFIs have to adopt new strategies to bring back their clients as well as to reduce their operating and administrative expenses.

NOTES AND REFERENCES

Support provided by Deepak Goswami Access Assist in data processing from Mix Market is gratefully acknowledged.

1. Source: Global Microscope on the Microfinance Business Environment 2009–2011, Economic Intelligence Unit Ltd (www.eiu.com).

2. MicroRate, The State of Microfinance Investment 2011 MicroRate, available at http://www.microrate.com/media/downloads/2012/04/The-State-of-Microfinance-Investment-2011-MicroRate.pdf accessed in June 2012.

3. http://www.jpmorganchase.com/corporate/socialfinance/document/DiscoveringLimits_GlobalMicrofinanceValuationSurvey2011.pdf accessed in June 2012.

4. The data were sourced from MIX Market website using their excellent Data Analysis tool. The data relates to the quarter end period based on the dates MFIs close their books during the year 2011.

5. Centre for Study of Financial Innovation, Microfinance Banana Skins Survey, 2012, New York.

6. http://www.microcreditsummit.org/pubs/reports/socr/2012/WEB_SOCR-2012_English.pdf accessed in June 2012.

Future—forward looking

The Indian microfinance sector has been showing a mild sign of recovery from the crisis. Bringing the sector on the fast track growth trajectory is the responsibility of all the stakeholders, representing areas like policy formulation and enforcement, regulation, funding and delivery mechanism. Though the different players in the sector have their own set of missions and objectives, the past experiences prove that these are individualistic ones without the needed coordination and synergy. Hence, it is necessary to focus the future outlook through the lens of retrospection of the rights and wrongs of the past. Let us start with the wrongs first.

WHAT WENT WRONG?

The first and foremost issue is related to the shift in basic approaches and strategies. When microfinance was conceptualized and implemented, two decades ago, the focus was on empowering rural women through the Self-Help Group mechanism. Social considerations were given greater attention with saving as a fundamental strength. Credit and other financial products were subsequently introduced with a broader objective of overall development of the rural families. Initially, the progress was slow as expected since the process of developing cohesiveness in the group approach was certainly time-consuming. Besides, the socio-economic conditions of the poor further also did not enable speedy progress of such programmes. Widely shared understanding is that the microfinance movement took root under social considerations. However, certain impatient players resorted to fast growth strategies along with commercial considerations, which had a severe negative impact on the sector, as a whole.

The second issue relates to the targeted segment. There are several different models of service delivery within the microfinance sector, and these have varied impacts on the poor. The evidence from existing studies on the impact of microfinance on the poor provides mixed results, ranging from substantial positive impacts to negligible effects. This is partly attributable to the fact that research findings and their conclusions depend on the analytical methods used. In brief, MFIs generally reach a combination of poor and non-poor people. The fungible nature of microcredit also helps the poor women to utilize the loan based on their priority, which normally for the best purpose. However, bundling of different segment of the customers characterized by varied income levels (from the poorest of the poor to non-poor), location (rural and urban), nature of occupation (labourers and small/micro-entrepreneurs), and skill levels (skilled and unskilled), and targeting all the customers with uniform financial products are the major constraining factors in achieving the objective of microfinance. This has been due to the lack of existence of differentiated products suiting to the clients preferences.

The third issue is the treatment of clients by the MFIs, especially profit oriented ones, as well as their field staff. The performance incentives used by many MFIs exert undue pressure on field staff to achieve financial targets and ignore their social performance—the ways in which they relate to clients. Previous years' reports have brought to light the role of unofficial microfinance intermediaries in the sector, who provide an easy entry for new MFIs setting up operations in an area. Most of these MFIs have concentrated around the same operational area and often compete with each other and serve the same set of households, encouraging multiple loans. With such high levels of commercialization, it is only to be expected that some staff are encouraged to push their financial performance. They tend to target more and bigger loans to clients irrespective of the repayment capacity of the borrowers. Recent evidences suggests that MFIs have moved in the right direction to set right past flaws in processes and staff incentives.

The fifth issue is the high interest rates that prevailed till recently to microfinance customers. Recently, the regulatory intervention fixed the cap on interest rate. While MF practitioners justify the need for higher interest rate considering the cost of fund as well as high cost of servicing smaller loans, there is an argument that the customers may not be convinced as the interest rate charged by the formal sector remains much lower than they pay. Some experts argue that MFIs are no way better than money lender in terms of high interest rate and fixing terms of lending. While the money lender lends out of his owned money, MFIs are actually borrowing from banks and on-lending the money, and hence, MFIs are leveraged money lenders. Charging high interest rate in the initial periods of the microfinance movement was not taken seriously as the size of the loans was very small, and the benefit of interest rate recovery was shared by all the members. However, as the average loan amount per borrower increased, the interest burden was viewed seriously. In addition, the lack of transparency among MFI lending has compounded the negative impact of microfinance norms.

The sixth and final issue, common to all lending operations, is that when the volume of microfinance lending expands rapidly, excess and easy credit would tempt the borrowers to borrow beyond their capacity. Thus, client's capacity to absorb the credit and other financial products was not adequately assessed by the target minded suppliers deteriorating the credit discipline in the market.

WHAT WENT RIGHT?

The long journey of the microfinance sector with both ups and downs, several noteworthy and positive happenings provide greater hope of success in the future. Obviously, microfinance initiatives have certainly widened the choices that millions of near-poor and poor people have access to basic financial services such as loans, savings and insurance. This choice, when exercised judiciously without resorting to over borrowing, helped them to manage their finances more effectively. In terms of outreach, microfinance facilitated greater penetration of financial services to unreached areas. Particularly, Bandhan's effort in reaching out to the poor in the North Eastern region is worth mentioning here. Similarly,

Ujjevan, Equitas, CASPHOR and other MFIs provide ample evidence of clients enjoying social and economic benefits. Microfinance innovations discussed in this report has wider scope for replication. Effective microfinance players provide valuable services to clients and contribute to the vibrancy of local economy. The sector has a long way to go before reaching out and meeting the needs of the needy.

Different successful microfinance models harbinger good prospects ahead. Multiple approaches shown under models like cooperatives or local area bank or NGO promoted SHGs MFI, NABARD sponsored institutions (NABFINS) provide robust micro financial infrastructure in India. Each model demonstrated success in its own way. The development professionals and the govrment have wide choice to choose from to adopt a model best suited to local socio-economic conditions.

Government initiatives have provided the much needed impetus to the microfinance movement across the country. SGSY and its current avatar, NRLM has become the national movement focusing on poverty alleviation. Learning from the successes and failures of SGSY and incorporating the insights into the NRLM hold the key for giving the flagship programme a new vigour. The present microfinance crisis may be viewed as serendipity and offered opportunities to reconfigure the microfinance operations in the country in the light of the new regulation.

The financial inclusion agenda pursued by the government and RBI offers greater scope for microfinance sector. The agenda drives the banks and civil society organizations to reach out to the unreached through SHGs, digital technology etc. Banking Correspondents (BCs) as an effective intermediary between the banks and the clients, will have critical role in financial inclusion. As Raguram Rajan Committee recommended, there is greater scope for MFIs to undertake the role of BCs paving way for synergy between the resource potential of banks and community rapport of MFIs resulting in better financial inclusion.

Finally, the unsavoury developments in the sector have amplified the importance of responsible finance through client protection and social performance.

THE WAY FORWARD

The 25-year-old microfinance market which is dynamic in nature has undergone drastic changes. While the changes in the last five years have seen the sector expanding, attracting a lot of commercial attention, the last two years have seen changes towards customer protection and responsible finance Coordinated initiatives from different stakeholders of the microfinance sector are necessary at this juncture to ensure balance focus on social and financial perspectives of the customers.

The space provided by SBLP due to its relatively slow progress led to the emergence of MFIs as a significant player in the microfinance sector. Recognizing the increased demand and potential of reaching the poor, the SBLP model should strive for may initiate a proactive role for greater outreach with increased penetration in underserved areas without compromising the quality of lending. There is a need for clear distinction in the mechanism of undertaking a financial and non-financial role with the promoters of the groups. The potential for federal structure as an institutional arrangement for SHGs to facilitate banklending to SHGs through bulk loans. NRLM implementation likely to introduce a new dimension in the SHG movement, and the emergence of the federations as interlinking institutional arrangements for the forthcoming government programmes would go a long way in reaching the poor with a well-established institutional structure under the microfinance fold. Further bringing SHGs and their federations under more specific customer protection regulation is needed to have streamlined process of member's welfare. More dialogue on federations of SHGs and the need for NABARD and NRLM to align their approaches in the interest of the poor are the essential elements for drawing future strategies on SBLP.

Expectation in SHG 2 is what it can achieve in the coming years and greater emphasis on voluntary savings may facilitate effective financial inclusion. With the advantage of technology the members may have easy access to the banks. Converting the NFA in to basic saving bank deposit account by RBI is an appropriate move through which the members may prompted to activate the NFA accounts and avail better banking facilities.

The future journey of the MFIs calls for balancing approach of customers' interests and sustainability. Recognizing the need for customer centric approach, there is a need to understand the clients more closely in terms of their preparedness to use the provided financial services and the desirable level of credit use. Broader approach of livelihood initiatives is more relevant in this context rather than focusing on any specific product such as credit, insurance, etc. Greater attention is required on capacity building of the clients through appropriate skill development along with providing needed infrastructure support, including marketing arrangement.

MFIs which have already established as strong entities in the rural financial market need to engage closely with the mainstream banking. MFIs need to go beyond the regulatory guidelines in dealing with customers and should introduce low-cost systems using appropriate technology so as to reduce the cost and prevent likelihood of client abuse through good monitoring. In recent times MFIs across the country are showing greater commitment towards transparency and accountability, with a growing number reporting on the social benefits of their activities through innovative approaches and initiatives. MFIs need to examine the ways in which they assess field staff performance and reform them, so that field staff understands that the quality of their relationships with clients is as important as achieving financial targets. More action is expected from sector associations in disciplining member MFIs.

The review of the policy initiatives in an earlier chapter clearly brings out the fact that RBI is in favour of ensuring regulatory norms with the protection of clients in focus. Several relaxations provided after issuing the direction reemphasize the concern of RBI for the MFIs, particularly for smaller MFIs.

Tabling the long-awaited Microfinance Institutions (Development and Regulation) Bill has given the greater scope for microfinance practitioners, and almost all the stakeholders are anxiously waiting for the approval by the Parliament. Many of the microfinance experts expressed a positive opinion of impact of the bill even though there is a debate on some of the clauses in the bill.

Consequent up on the impact of crisis, there is resurgence in funding and equity. As a result it is expected that some of the bigger MFIs show growth and consolidation. Sa-Dhan quick report already points out closure of branches and reducing staff. Merger and sale of business might be more common place in the next 18 months. There will be a reaction from MFIs to the excessive focus on social performance, responsible finance agenda driven from well meaning donors and service providers. New product development and livelihoods based financing might be the next new normal among MFIs. After passing of MF bill, one can expect easing of the regulatory rigour and SROs might get up and the industry associations asked by RBI to become responsible. The efforts of revival of the MFIs and bring back the growth and performances will succeed only when the problem of fundings is addressed. Creation of an exclusive *equity funding* would provide greater relief to MFIs in general and smaller and medium MFIs in particular. Mainstreaming of the MFIs are feasible if there is a provision for MFIs act as BCs and hence any action in this direction would certainly improve the role and participation of MFIs in financial inclusion agenda. Ultimately the need of level playing field for MFIs should be ensured through routing government programmes on the same terms as that with banks.

Another priority that needs greater attention is the credit information sharing through appropriate credit bureau arrangements. Appropriate incentives with adequate funding arrangement will certainly improve the quality of the existing services and also will achieve greater participation by many MFIs.

Even though the sector has witnessed a downward trend in the growth performance parameters in recent years, there are positive signals from different directions. Efforts in bringing the sector under the regulatory regime will certainly improve the confidence among different stakeholders, which will certainly bring back growth and sustainability. Recognizing the microfinance sector as a strategic partner in financial inclusion strategies and providing greater emphasis in social performance are the needed future steps. MFIs, being partners in the main stream banking and actively integrated with the banking system, will provide greater leverage for the microfinance sector in the years ahead. Effective co-ordination among stake holders will facilitate healthy competition, thereby reducing overlapping of activities and aligning the quality and performance of the sector with overall banking expectations.

The performance objectives of the microfinance sector should take in to account the programme of central and States. *As long as the ultimate focus of microfinance initiatives are towards the poor and their livelihood improvement, microfinance will survive, sustain and grow. The only relevant expectation that it should strive to meet is that of the vulnerable customers.*

Appendix

Appendix A.1 Bank Loans Provided to MFIs and their Non-performing Assets (NPAs) and Recovery Performance—2011–12

(Amount ₹ million)

Sl. no.	Name of the bank	Loan disbursed by banks to MFIs No. of MFIs	Amount disbursed	Outstanding bank loans against MFIs as on 31 March 2012 No. of MFIs	Amount	Gross NPAs of bank loans to MFIs Amount	No. of MFIs	% to total outstand-ing loans	Percent-age of recovery to demand of bank loan to MFIs
A	**Commercial Banks—Public Sector Banks**								
1	Allahabad Bank	1	400.00	11	972.68	0.00	0	0	100
2	Andhra Bank	16	1,770.00	16	3,681.89	NA	NA	NA	NA
3	Bank of Baroda	0	0.00	0	0.00	0.00	0	0	0
4	Bank of India	3	94.00	19	2,499.64	16.45	1	0.66	NA
5	Bank of Maharashtra	7	915.00	7	253.28	0.00	0	0	100
6	Canara Bank	9	1,899.45	91	3,083.25	25.51	6	0.83	NA
7	Central Bank of India	NA	NA	NA	NA	NA	NA	NA	NA
8	Corporation Bank	11	2,587.50	45	6,821.52	16.38	3	0.24	NA
9	Dena Bank	13	4,341.00	19	4,997.50	37.70	1	0.75	NA
10	IDBI Bank	32	13,355.76	48	17,885.95	87.88	3	0.49	NA
11	Indian Bank	3	52.60	41	579.00	11.80	5	2.04	NA
12	Indian Overseas Bank	36	1,493.50	123	4,923.50	NA	NA	NA	NA
13	Oriental Bank of Commerce	1	5.60	7	79.11	0.04	1	0.05	NA
14	Punjab & Sind Bank	2	1,150.00	7	1,824.28	0.00	0	0	100
15	Punjab National Bank	3	150.00	182	957.87	0.00	0	0	100
16	State Bank of Bikaner and Jaipur	0	0.00	0	0.00	0.00	0	0	0
17	State Bank of Hyderabad	NA	NA	2	230.72	0.00	0	0	100
18	State Bank of India	66	5,158.70	220	9,267.90	323.30	25	3.49	92
19	State Bank of Mysore	0	0.00	1	24.23	0.00	0	0	100
20	State Bank of Patiala	NA	NA	NA	NA	NA	NA	NA	NA
20	State Bank of Travancore	1	50.00	9	728.69	91.67	1	12.58	20
21	Syndicate Bank	6	925.00	291	1,828.28	0.00	0	0	100
22	UCO Bank	11	1.07	69	30.79	0.00	0	0	NA
23	United Bank of India	1	1,850.00	21	2,243.40	3.04	1	0.14	80
24	Vijaya Bank	3	1,040.00	15	2,518.32	0.00	0	0	100
	Sub total—Public Sector Banks	**225**	**37,239.19**	**1,244**	**65,431.78**	**613.77**	**47**	**0.94**	**76.3**
B	**Commercial Banks—Private Sector**								
1	Axis Bank	14	1,735.00	51	5,916.99	365.32	15	6.17	NA
2	Capital Local Area Bank	1	1.72	1	1.58	NA	NA	NA	100
3	City Union Bank	4	163.51	8	159.73	0.47	NA	0.29	99.8
4	Dhanalakshmi Bank	56	408.61	145	660.18	41.40	12	6.27	80
6	HDFC Bank	4	620.00	57	2,445.60	70.33	10	2.88	98
7	ICICI Bank	0	0.00	43	5,286.62	NA	NA	NA	97

(Continued)

Continued)

Sl. no.	Name of the bank	Loan disbursed by banks to MFIs		Outstanding bank loans against MFIs as on 31 March 2012		Gross NPAs of bank loans to MFIs			Percentage of recovery to demand of bank loan to MFIs
		No. of MFIs	Amount disbursed	No. of MFIs	Amount	Amount	No. of MFIs	% to total outstanding loans	
8	Indusland Bank	1	25.00	5	511.50	0.00	0	0	100
9	ING-Vysya Bank	0	0.00	31	779.50	NA	NA	NA	NA
10	Jammu & Kashmir Bank	0	0.00	6	2,237.42	0.00	0	0	100
14	Karnataka Bank	16	1,453.60	34	3,367.96	842.17	11	25.01	57.2
15	Kotak Mahindra Bank	5	7,263.14	5	7,263.14	NA	NA	NA	NA
16	South Indian Bank	10	600.00	36	2,025.02	184.40	8	9.11	80.5
17	Tamilnad Mercentile Bank	NA	NA	4	3.55	NA	NA	NA	100
18	The catholic Syrian Bank Ltd.	0	0.00	9	123.36	6.32	NA	5.12	75
	Sub total—Private Sector Banks	**111**	**12,270.58**	**435**	**30,782.14**	**1,510.40**	**56**	**4.91**	**89.8**
	Commercial Banks—Foreign Banks								
	Citi Bank	0	0.00	5	1,895.89	**NA**	**NA**	**NA**	**NA**
	Sub total—Foreign Banks	**0**	**0.00**	**5**	**1,895.89**	**NA**	**NA**	**NA**	**NA**
	Total—All Commercial Banks	**336**	**49,509.77**	**1,684**	**98,109.81**	**2,124.17**	**103**	**2.17**	**82.5**
	Regional Rural Banks								
1	Allahabad UP Gramin Bank	0	0.00	1	5.05	0.00	0	0	100
2	Andhra Pragati Gramin Bank	0	0.00	6	1.67	0.00	0	0	0
3	Assam Gramin Vikas Bank	1	60.00	14	104.00	0.00	0	0	80
4	Bangiya Gramin Bank	95	58.64	NA	NA	NA	NA	NA	NA
5	Hadoti Kshetriya Gramin Bank	NA	NA	11	50.90	NA	NA	NA	NA
6	Kalinga Gramy Bank	1	3.00	2	7.72	0.00	0	0	10
7	Karnataka Vikas Grameena Bank	0	0.00	3	103.83	NA	NA	NA	NA
8	Manipur Rural Bank	0	0.00	2	2.51	1.51	1	60.22	40
9	North Malbar Gramin Bank	1	1.10	4	4.25	1.85	2	43.44	65
10	Pallavan Gramin Bank	1	5.09	1	6.99	0.00	0	0	98
11	Pandya Gramin Bank	2	1.99	14	10.39	0.00	0	0	98
12	Rushikiya Gramya Bank	5	1.26	5	3.26	0.51	3	15.63	62
13	South Malbar Gramin Bank	7	1.76	41	69.87	5.39	13	7.71	79
14	Utkal Gramya Bank	0	0.00	24	4.64	4.07	24	87.57	12
	Sub total—Regional Rural Banks	**113**	**132.83**	**128**	**375.09**	**13.33**	**43**	**3.55**	**58.5**
	Cooperative Banks								
	Assam Cooperative Apex Bank	3	14.82	18	46.44	19.16	12	41.25	38.7
	South Canara DCCB	1	1.26	1	1.03	0.00	0	0	100
	Sub total—Cooperative Banks	**4**	**16.08**	**19**	**47.47**	**19.16**	**12**	**40.36**	**69.3**
	Total (Com. Banks [Public, Pvt., & Foregin]+RRBs+Coops.)	**453**	**49,658.68**	**1,831**	**98,532.38**	**2,156.66**	**158**	**2.19**	**74.7**
	Financial Institutions								
	SIDBI	12	2,394.20	129	15,971.12	386.75	21	2.42	99
	Grand Total of Lending to MFIs	**465**	**52,052.88**	**1,960**	**114,503.49**	**2,543.41**	**179**	**2.22**	**75.3**

NA: Not available/Not reported.

Appendix A.2 Financing Joint Liability Groups

(Amount ₹ million)

Sl. no.	Name of the regional office	As on March 2011		As on March 2012		As on March 2012	
		No. of JLGs	Loans disbursed	No. of JLGs	Loans disbursed	Cumulative no. of JLGs	Cumulative loans disbursed
	Northern Region						
1	Punjab	23	NA	856	69.77	879	69.77
2	Haryana	1,395	338.20	1,303	155.23	2,698	493.43
3	New Delhi	0	0.00	26	3.27	26	3.27
4	Himachal Pradesh	185	13.63	640	126.99	825	140.62
5	Jammu & Kashmir	0	0.00	0	0.00	0	0.00
6	Rajasthan	0	0.00	3,185	390.74	3,185	390.74
	Sub total	**1,603**	**351.83**	**6,010**	**745.99**	**7,613**	**1,097.82**
	North Eastern Region						
1	Tripura	11	0.48	0	0.00	11	0.48
2	Assam	7,113	298.44	9,140	262.54	16,253	560.98
3	Meghalaya	31	1.87	33	4.50	64	6.37
4	Mizoram	4	2.58	73	2.24	77	4.82
5	Arunachal Pradesh	4	0.23	0	0.00	4	0.23
6	Sikkim	52	6.39	13	5.84	65	12.23
	Sub total	**7,215**	**309.98**	**9,259**	**275.13**	**16,474**	**585.11**
	Eastern Region						
1	Bihar	1,614	102.78	19,325	1,114.34	20,939	1,217.12
2	Jharkhand	0	0.00	175	6.13	175	6.13
3	Odisha	32,146	1,237.15	21,116	1,079.00	53,262	2,316.15
4	West Bengal	20,860	1,324.81	27,864	9.11	48,724	1,333.92
5	Andaman & Nicobar	0	0.00	32	4.04	32	4.04
	Sub total	**54,620**	**2,664.75**	**68,512**	**2,212.62**	**123,132**	**4,877.37**
	Central Region						
1	Madhya Pradesh	3,683	135.70	3,603	96.06	7,286	231.76
2	Chhattisgarh	475	17.58	1,385	122.06	1,860	139.64
3	Uttar Pradesh	13,207	164.71	7,106	881.13	20,313	1,045.84
4	Uttaranchal	236	5.72	1,541	236.59	1,777	242.31
	Sub total	**17,601**	**323.71**	**13,635**	**1,335.83**	**31,236**	**1,659.54**
	Western Region						
1	Goa	0	0.00	259	30.32	259	30.32
2	Gujarat	260	0.32	2,209	200.98	2,469	201.30
3	Maharashtra	726	48.99	2,679	297.09	3,405	346.08
	Sub total	**986**	**49.31**	**5,147**	**528.38**	**6,133**	**577.69**
	Southern Region						
1	Karnataka	4,145	366.40	31,786	2,583.75	35,931	2,950.16
2	Andhra Pradesh	0	0.00	35,773	5,221.90	35,773	5,221.90
3	Tamil Nadu	52,734	7,026.15	16,516	3,425.04	69,250	10,451.19
4	Kerala	2,141	360.82	5,024	675.27	7,165	1,036.08
	Sub total	**59,020**	**7,753.37**	**89,099**	**11,905.95**	**148,119**	**19,659.32**
	Grand Total	**141,045**	**11,452.95**	**191,662**	**17,003.91**	**332,707**	**28,456.85**

Appendix A.3 **UN Solution Exchange Initiatives—State of the Sector Report**

Like in the past, the UN Solution Exchange played a proactive role during this year also in making the State of the Sector Report more relevant through seeking opinions from different sections of the sector through posting two queries to have an e-discussion as well as a round table discussion to give deeper insight into the themes and issues of MF involving leading practitioners of Microfinance.

QUERY ON STATE OF THE SECTOR REPORT—PHASE I: STRUCTURE OF THE REPORT, PRODUCTS AND SERVICES AND MICROFINANCE PROGRAMMES AND PROJECTS

Query on the structure of the report

In response to the query posted by the author on the structure of the report with specific reference to design and structure of the report, products and services to be discussed and views on microfinance programmes and projects, 23 members enthusiastically participated and the consolidated responses are presented below:

Compiled by: Navin Anand, Resource Person & Moderator, and Monika Khanna, Research Associate, MF CoP, Solution Exchange, United Nations

Contributors: Daniel Lazar, Deepti George, D.S.K. Rao, E. Varathkanth, GirijaSrinivasan, Hemantha Kumar Pamarthy, Jaipal Singh, M. Chidambaranathan, Mani A. Nandhi, Milroy Paul, Mohammad Azahar, Monika Khanna, N. Jeyaseelan, Navin Anand, P.S.M. Rao, Prasenjit Sen, Ritesh Dwivedi, Sandhya Suresh, Savita Shankar, Subrata Sarkar, VandanaSethi and Veerashekharappa

SUMMARY OF RESPONSES

Members recognized that the state of the sector is an authentic and excellent document as it provides a good overview of the Microfinance (MF) sector. The report was found to be useful for MFIs, policy makers, researchers, economists and all those who are associated with microfinance. Giving their initial remarks, members suggested identifying relevant issues and some common parameters for tracking progress of the sector every year and providing an analysis of the same in the report. Further, it will be useful to give a glimpse of the important events in a particular year, important circulars affecting the MF sector and regional analysis of outreach of Community-based Microfinance Institutions (CBMFIs) and MFIs in the SOS report. The issues of Microfinance Institutions, Non-Banking Financial Companies (NBFCs) and Community-based Microfinance Institutions could be segregated, and equal weightage to each type of institution in SOS needs to be given.

SUGGESTIONS ON THEMATIC AREAS

Policy and regulatory environment for Microfinance: Key features of the MF Bill, MF and Cooperative Acts, RBI/NABARD Regulations on savings, the Nair Committee recommendations, Malegam Committee recommendations, securitization guidelines from RBI financing and IRDA regulations on Micro-insurance.

Geographical coverage of Microfinance: Rural, semi-urban and urban; slum areas, mountain and remote areas, tribal areas, extremist affected areas; and a brief on MF status in every state and UT.

Microfinance through different legal entities: NBFCs (for-profit institutions), NGOs-MFIs (not-for-profit institutions), Cooperatives/Mutual Benefit organizations and Banks (Commercial banks, Regional Rural Banks, Local Area Banks and Cooperative Banks); a comparative Analysis of MF through different legal entities.

Various models of microfinancing: Various Group-based financing models as well as individual financing models.

Microfinancing for different segments of people: Economically poor people i.e., Ultra poor and BPL including women, People with disabilities (PwDs), youth, older Persons (OPs), marginal and small farmers, migrants and labourers.

Microfinancing for various livelihood and subsector: MF for Farm (Agriculture and Agriculture-Allied) and Non-Farm sector (Manufacturing, Vending and Trading and services).

Coverage of government programmes: Flagship programmes like National Rural Livelihood Mission, Mahila Kisan Sashaktikaran Pariyojna, MGNREGA (Payments issues). Initiatives by the State Governments (directly or through partnership with NGOs), MF strategy adopted by them and challenges faced and the impact realized. Examples of the states and case studies of some states that are taking major measures for improving financial inclusion.

Microfinance plus activities: Non-financial services especially health protection services—health education, providing access to health products and services and health related financial products, such as, health loans, health savings and health insurance. (Reference—workshop on linking health with microfinance in India organized by Microcredit Summit Campaign [MCS], Freedom From Hunger [FFH] and Indian Institute of Public Health, Gandhinagar.)

Leveraging funds—debt, equity and grants: Coverage on new funding opportunities—new funding opportunities such as NCDs, ECB access and FII licences etc.; Statistics, Government/RBI guidelines and information on sources of funds.

Design and management of microfinance programmes and project—innovative systems, procedures and technology: MIS, Monitoring and Evaluation, Value Chain Management in Microfinance services, Mobile Phone banking, Internet banking and other innovative technologies for management of MF activities within the projects and programmes and also for providing MF services.

SUGGESTIONS ON OTHER MF SUBSECTORS

Urban microfinance: Members recommended including a separate chapter on urban microfinance. This chapter may provide information on growth and spread of microfinance in urban area, client outreach, loans outstanding, average loan size, savings, housing finance, insurance, and remittances. It should also provide information on support systems, financial institutions and various support organizations.

Housing microfinance: Keeping in view the growing demand of affordable housing in rural and urban areas and more and more MFIs diversifying their products to housing, members categorically recommended including a chapter on 'Housing Microfinance'. The chapter may cover regulations and best practices in Housing Microfinance drawn from India and other countries.

MF through CBMFIs including cooperatives: Referring to various successful examples of SHG-cooperatives identified in the evaluation studies, members suggested for including a chapter on Community-based MFI (CBMFIs) covering SHG cooperatives models as it gives women both leadership and ownership.

Suitable microfinance services for migrant workers: Informal sector workers, who are mostly migrants of varying duration, face innumerable hardships in their money management practices, and it is imperative to address what has been the role of MFIs so far in urban areas for this huge segment of population. There is a need to design suitable/innovative products for urban migrants in the informal sector.

SUGGESTIONS ON OTHER ISSUES

Impact of MF and consumer protection: The report could focus on consumer protection in microfinance and how institutions are handling this. The Report may include an assessment of 'impact' of financial service providers at the bottom of pyramid. Inclusion of case studies from the field or even the excerpts of the interviews with clients will reveal the impact of Financial Inclusion. The initiatives taken by NGOs/MFIs on transparency issues may also be included in the report.

Credit bureaus: Since Credit Bureaus are gaining prominence as a means to reduce information asymmetries, NBFC-MFIs have now begun participating in the sector-level credit bureau. Therefore an analysis of credit bureaus in the report could be a useful input.

Clarity on effective rate of interest: Highlighting the low level of clarity on the meaning of effective rate of interest, members gave reference of RBI's Circular on interest rates and clarified that there are three components for pricing the micro loans viz. interest, processing fee and insurance and therefore effective rate of interest incorporates all the three components. They informed that some practitioners do not take insurance into account while calculating effective rates of interest. Members recommended bringing out more clarity on this through SOS 2012 report.

Learning from the failures: Members referred to two publications that had captured the learning from failures in Latin America as well as in other parts of the world and suggested for having a chapter on Learning from the failures.

Perspective of the community: Mentioning the AP crisis and its impact on microfinance, members suggested covering perspectives of community through Focus Group Discussions (FGDs). They suggested including some studies on the impact of implementation of the Andhra regulation on Microfinance Services and case studies on the barriers of RBI guidelines. A 'White Paper on Microfinance' can also be thought of as an additional booklet or a portion of report.

SHG bank linkage programme: The aspect of sustainability of SHGs and SHG-SBLP-2 initiated recently by NABARD could be covered in the chapter on SHG-Bank linkage programme. Interviews of Lead Bank managers and NABARD District managers will be useful to know the realities in SHG-Bank linkage.

Career in MF and role of educational institutions: In the last few years several educational institutions in India have added the subject of Microfinance in their curriculum/syllabus or started exclusive courses on MF, and the whole effect was very positive. Exclusive placement services were pressed into, and aspirants could make decent careers. Micro-Education Loans are also becoming more and more popular in some parts of the country. The SOS report can cover the aspect of careers in microfinance and the role of educational institutions.

Special focus on HR: Many MFIs/NGOs face higher turnover of staff due to various reasons. The SoS report can document national and international best practices adopted in the field to manage this problem. The HR-centric schemes of various NGOs/MFIs may also be highlighted in the report.

Microfinance products and services: Members suggested introducing a separate chapter covering innovative savings, credit, microinsurance/micro pensions, transfer of money and micro leasing products and services.

Overall, members examined the structure of tprevious reports and suggested a new composition of the report focusing more on client's perspective and recommended many new subsectors and issues that need to be incorporated in the State of the Sector Report 2012.

QUERY ON STATE OF THE SECTOR REPORT—PHASE II: POLICY AND REGULATORY ENVIRONMENT, SOCIAL AND FINANCIAL PERFORMANCE MANAGEMENT AND INNOVATIVE EXPERIMENTS/SUCCESS STORIES OF FINANCIAL INCLUSION

In response to the second phase of query posted by the author, 21 members of MF CoP enthusiastically participated in the discussion. Thesummary of the discussion is presented below:

CONTRIBUTORS

Aloysius P. Fernandez, Navin Anand, R. Sunil, Subhash C. Wadhwa, Hemantha Kumar Pamarthy, Tara Nair, Madhurima Jaiswal, D. Lazar, Resham Singh, Usha Gopinath, Sandhya Suresh, Sashi Kumar, Sanjeev Kumar, Madhu Sharan, Sachin Kumar, Alka Parikh, Rangan Varadan, Usha Gopinath, L. Ajimon Veerashekharappa, Rajesh Verma

Compiled by: Navin Anand, Resource Person & Moderator, MF CoP, Solution Exchange, United Nations

SUMMARY OF RESPONSES

In the second phase of discussion on State of the Sector report, the focus has been on policy and regulatory environment, social and financial performance management and innovative experiments/success stories of financial inclusion.

In context of the coverage, members highlighted the importance of three environments that exist in the microfinance sector—macro/external, intermediary or meso-level and micro environment. Members also find it rational to classify these three environments as—policy environment, provider environment and user environment. While members stressed on appraising the sector from users' perspective, they appreciated the importance of technology as a facilitator to achieve the desired goals.

Social and Financial Performance Management: Emphasizing on the importance of covering social and financial performance management (SPM) in the report, members felt that a right blend of SPM cannot be achieved unless the senior management is keen to support social performance management in the way as they support financial performance management. Members appreciated the initiatives of socially committed MFIs that focus on socio-economic growth of the clients. Such initiatives add to the retention rates of the clients.

Members suggested MF stakeholders to accept the globally established 'universal standards of social performance' and recommended for acknowledging and rewarding practitioners who adhere to the standards. MFIs should also be supported with some grants to develop SPM systems. Members also felt that social performance without financial performance is not sustainable however it is important that MFIs avoid exploiting the poor when they are trying to become financially sustainable. The only way to have a balance between financial and social performance would be to encourage more and more social funding, stipulating a blend of realistic and sustainable social and financial terms and conditions.

Customer Service and Code of Conduct: Members quoted examples of MFIs such as Ujjivan, Grameen Financial Services, Arohan etc., that have institutionalized industry code of conduct as well as RBI's fair practice code into their day-to-day operations and staff training modules. Many MFIs have even incorporated client protection and service guidelines into their monitoring and internal audit functions. The staff members who violate code of conduct and client protection guidelines have to bear penalties and other career related disadvantages. Through different networks, some institutions are sharing the names of the staff terminated due to fraud or violation of code of conduct. Few organizations also run staff refresher training to reiterate the importance of customer service and code of conduct. MFIs have even formulated and implemented whistle blowers policy to keep the employees' identity confidential who reports the improper behaviour of staff in violation of code of conduct and customer service.

Policy and Regulatory Environment for Microfinance: RBI has been playing a lead role in regulating and supervising the MF sector. Some of the recent initiatives of RBI include—categorizing NBFC engaged in micro financing as NBFC-MFIs and attaching importance of priority lending with this category; defining target clientele, extending the facility of RTGS or NEFT to all the rural cooperatives/bank branches through its nodal clearance house at Mumbai; responding to the AP crisis by submitting affidavit in the AP High Court against the act of AP government; and setting guidelines on multiple borrowing etc. Members suggested that in order to make improvements in the circulars related to MF, RBI may seek feedback from MF associations and networks.

Members recognize that a good MF Act will impact financial inclusion goals and will boost the lenders and equity investors to revive the stagnancy in the sector. Government has recognized the role of MFIs in financial inclusion space, however, Micro Finance Institutions (Development and Regulation) Bill, 2012 is yet to be cleared.

Regulations and Community Based MFIs: Discussing about the impact of regulations on community based microfinance institutions (CBMFIs), members shared that the decrease in Banks' financial exposure towards Microfinance sector has also affected CBMFIs as they also depend on formal financial services.

Microfinance for Street Vendors: Members mentioned about an earlier discussion on street vendors in Solution Exchange wherein microfinance issues related to street vendors were covered. The issues covered under the discussion incorporates savings services for street vendors especially system of daily collection; loan schemes, including innovative example of daily loan scheme; possibilities of micro leasing; Mobile phone banking arrangements; strengthening BC model for providing better services to street vendors; feasibility of promoting Joint liability groups for street vendors; possibilities of forming cooperative bank of vendors; and microinsurance as well as micro pensions needs and initiatives for street vendors.

Innovative Experiments/Success Stories of Financial Inclusion

Successful cases of Business Correspondent model: There have been many innovations in the field of credit offerings for small business and micro-enterprises. Besides there have been umpteen efforts by the Banking Correspondents and MFIs to offer money transfer, pension services to their target clientele i.e. mainly organised sector workers and self-employed low income population. BCs such as FINO, EKO, ALW, Oxigen have been using innovative models and technologies to offer money transfer services. It would be good to incorporate few case studies on viable BC Models.

Equity Based Models: Members shared innovative equity based models like—'MicroVenture investment model' initiated by MicroGraam. Equity based models provide solutions to a number of problems that loan-based programmes are having such as loan defaults due to decline in the business, stress of high rates of interest on clients and problems of cash flows faced by micro-entrepreneurs due to strictly structured loan repayment schedules etc. The role of micro-venture capital provider is not limited to providing equity financing but also giving professional advice and mentoring to the micro-entrepreneur.

Micro Pensions: In the pension domain, members mentioned about IIMPS that exclusively works to offer micropension for the working poor in South Asia. It has been able to subscribe lakhs of unorganized sector workers, small and micro-entrepreneurs through SHG and JLG models managed by SHPIs, NGOs and MFIs.

Microfinance Services to the Rickshaw Pullers: Members shared an innovative microfinance-centric social entrepreneurship project "Life on Wheels" which aims at financial inclusion and overall upliftment of rickshaw pullers. The microfinance model is based on the concept of Joint Liability. Linkages are created with a nationalized bank to provide loans to the rickshaw pullers under a specially designed 'Jan Mitra scheme', wherein the poor can open no frills savings accounts. While financial literacy is an important component of the project, life insurance of the rickshaw pullers is done through JanshreeBimaYojna of LIC and asset insurance is provided through Oriental Insurance Company.

Livestock Risk Management and Insurance: Members shared an innovative experiment of financial inclusion in the area of integrated services and risk management financial services for goat farming. The experiment supported by Sir Dorabji Tata Trust (SDTT) is done by 'The Goat Trust' along with its five partners in Bundelkhand and eastern Uttar Pradesh. They have facilitated a Goat farmers led community insurance named as Samudai Suraksha Yojana (SSY) to provide integrated financial services. Some of the distinct features of present services are—No indirect cost of insurance access and claim settlement; Door step registration, claim verification and payment; complementary services of vaccination, de-worming and regular health checkup of goats; free training on membership, claim process and improved goat management.

Coverage of Regional Rural Banks: While members suggested for including a separate chapter or a section on Regional Rural Banks in SOS 2012, members also shared key outputs of a discussion held on RRBs in Solution Exchange—

- RRBs are better placed to provide customized financial services to the rural people by evolving innovative financial products and mechanisms such as—engaging local youth as agents, opting for BCs or adopting technology based options like mobile phone banking, biometric cards etc.
- RRBs can also play pivotal role in facilitating Flagship programmes by undertaking financial literacy initiatives as well as facilitating in transfer of money

Focus on Financial Literacy: Quoting examples of various studies done on financial literacy including OECD survey study carried out across 13 countries, members highlighted the low level of financial literacy and suggested for a comprehensive research on financial literacy in India. They also suggested for collection of empirical evidences that shows the impact of financial literacy programs. Referring to the financial bulletin of RBI, members also stressed on the need of addressing the issue of non-availability of standardized material of financial literacy.

Members shared two innovative experiments of Accion pertaining to client education—Business training through dialogue for building business skills of micro-entrepreneurs; and financial literacy to help low-income clients to better manage their personal and household finances and become informed and effective consumers of financial services. Members also highlighted successful partnerships with CSR wings or foundations of various companies for financial literacy initiatives.

Giving the example of NABFINS, members felt that microfinance can be sustainable and continue to be poor friendly. It gives practical approach to microfinance without sacrificing the main mission statement of most of the MFIs i.e., helping and empowering the poor. Further, members recognized the importance of 'Microfinance Plus' activities for better productivity of credit and empowerment of poor. Members recommended NABFINS experiment of sustainable Resource centers for studying and adopting by others with need based variations.

Besides specific suggestions, members also suggested the following—

- A compilation of the results of the studies carried out on microfinance to indicate the impact on the members of the saving groups and other benefits generated.
- Cover savings led MF models and the best practices adopted for sustainability.
- Come out with a comprehensive report once in three years by engaging some eminent scholars.
- A five-year comparative analysis on the status and functioning of CBMFIs.
- Provide a critical reflection on the broad trends and patterns observed over the past 20 years.
- Include innovative success stories of women's entrepreneurship and empowerment.

In the nutshell, members shared innovative experiments related to financial inclusion and suggested measures for strengthening policy and regulatory environment as well as systems for social and financial performance management.

REPORT OF THE ROUNDTABLE ON *STATE OF THE SECTOR REPORT 2012*—MICROFINANCE

Besides conducting two e-discussions, the Microfinance Community also took the initiative of organizing a round table on SOS 2012 with the support of UNDP. While e-discussions have their own relevance as practitioners from various parts of the country give their inputs in various forms by sharing views, documents, reports and case studies, the Roundtable on SoS provides a chance to go deeper into the themes and issues of MF involving leading practitioners of Microfinance. The objectives of conducting a roundtable on SoS 2012 were—

- To strengthen the coverage of the report by getting first-hand information from practitioners, professional, researchers and policy makers;
- To enhance the ownership of the report amongst Government, RBI/NABARD, UN agencies and other international organizations, NGO/MFIs, various networks, federations, independent thinkers and promoters of MF; and
- To strengthen the structure of the *State of the Sector Report 2012* through a consultative process.

The SOS—Roundtable 2012 witnessed the presence of a good mix of members representing NGOs, MFIs, UNDP, Training and Research Institutions, Government and MF promoting institutions. Besides representatives of a range of organizations, individual experts and practitioners of the microfinance sector have also participated in the roundtable. In total 35 members participated in the roundtable. The programme was moderated by Mr V. Puhazhendhi, Lead Author of the *State of the Sector Report 2012—Microfinance* and anchored by Navin Anand, Resource Person and Moderator, Microfinance Community, Solution Exchange.

While giving the opening remarks, Mr Brij Mohan, Chairman Access Development Services stressed the need to cover various issues like the response of the sector after AP crisis, impact of MF initiatives on clients, comparative assessment of various models etc. The report needs to focus on forward-looking initiatives and discuss issues on small, medium and large MFIs.

The author of the report gave a presentation on the structure of the SoS 2012 report and shared the proposed chapter plan with the participants. Though the proposed chapters are tentative, the author is proposing to bring out the sector report more usefully and make it more user friendly. While the previous year's *State of the Sector Report* gave an account of the recent crisis and its impact on the sector entirety, the *2012 Report* covers many of the promising developments in providing products and services beyond credit by the Microfinance sector and financial inclusion.

VIEWS AND SUGGESTIONS OF THE PARTICIPANTS—

i. There is a need to have a well-defined framework and structure focusing on trends in MF sector, interdependence, competition, innovations and standardizations etc.
ii. Greater importance of discussion on financial inclusion with critical analysis on the priorities and initiatives.
iii. Understand the targeted beneficiaries of the report and redesign the content of the report accordingly. The report is being used by different people, for different purposes, at different points of time. So the report needs to balance several contradictory and conflicting demands, and we have to put sufficient amount of data to fulfill the demand of different stakeholders.
iv. Sustainability issues in the sector need to be analyzed in depth and the linkage MF growth and livelihoods must be discussed in depth.
v. Reliable secondary data must be analyzed for the report and primary data analysis may be considered where ever feasible.
vi. There is a need for an in-depth analysis from the angle of different stakeholders like SHGs, MFIs and even private equity players, venture capitalists and the corporate sector.
vii. Microfinance institutions need a comprehensive governance structure, therefore the report may cover initiatives of good governance.
viii. Need for greater emphasis on client protection issues in a separate chapter and the report must bring out an essence of the real issues from members' perspective.

ix. While coverage of SHG bank linkage programme is important in the report, it will also be worthwhile to do a critical review of the two decades of SHG bank linkage programme.

x. The report may discuss more on equity-based products, its role and issues in sectoral growth.

xi. Analysis of the BC model in financial inclusion in terms of its use. Coverage cost and sustainability.

xii. Impact of women empowerment among the poor due to microfinance interventions needs to be analyzed and documented with case studies.

xiii. Coverage of MF issues in underserved areas is very important due to the fact that besides NRLM, UN and many donor agencies are having huge livelihood programmes in these underserved areas.

xiv. Urban poverty issues need to be covered in the report. If there is a huge urban poverty alleviation programme coming up, then it will be prudent to include a chapter on urban poverty and study urban poverty alleviation initiatives.

xv. The dynamic nature of the regulatory issues in the sector and its impact on institution as well as customer perspective needs to be analyzed in the report. Customer protection and self regulation by MFIs need to be discussed in the present day context.

xvi. Housing Microfinance is slowly gaining momentum, because of the huge demand for 'affordable' housing from the rural and urban poor in India. There is a need to have a chapter on 'Opportunities and Challenges of Housing Microfinance in India'.

xvii. The report may devote a special chapter on learning from the failures. There are examples of documenting and disseminating such failures in Latin America as well as in other parts of the world. The report may also devote some part on the initiatives that were started but not taken up further, such as innovations in sectors like insurance, remittances, branchless banking, MIS, development of multiple software etc. So there are some cracks that can be captured in the report.

xviii. Some of the state governments have taken up innovative and very positive initiatives. There could be some initiatives that have not given good results so both positive and negative initiatives of state governments needs to be captured in the report.

xix. In terms of coverage of people, there are subsets of people like extremely poor, migrants etc. that sometimes we miss out completely. There can be coverage of these people in the context of MF.

xx. Comparative studies comparing the MF sector of our country with other countries could be done as there are good things about India whereas there are few areas in which we need improvement. The success stories of other countries can be adopted.

xxi. Current liquidity issues due to the crisis and potential flow of capital infusion need to be analyzed in the report.

xxii. Keeping in view the importance of Community-based institutions in the present context, it will be good to have a chapter on 'Cooperatives and Financial Inclusion or Cooperatives and MF. It is logical to have a chapter on cooperatives as this year is declared by the UN as an 'international year of cooperatives'.

The roundtable ended with concluding remarks from the lead author.

LIST OF PARTICIPANTS

Arindom Datta, Rabo India Finance Ltd, Gurgaon, Arpita Sen, Bandhan, Kolkota, Brij Mohan, ACCESS Development Services, New Delhi, C.P. Mohan, NABARD Financial Services Ltd, Bangalore, C.S. Reddy, APMAS, Hyderabad, Chandni Ohri, Grameen Foundation, New Delhi, Dilip Kumar Mishra, NABARD, Mumbai, EituVij Chopra, Hand in Hand India, New Delhi, Harish Chotani, Resource Consultant—Microfinance and Livelihood Promotion, Gurgaon, Harsh Singh, Independent Consultant, New Delhi, Hema Bansal, Smart Campaign, Bangalore, Jui Gupta, Trickle Up, Kolkata, K. Martina Rani, Vignana Jyothi Institute of Management, Hyderabad, Madhu Saran, Independent Consultant, New Delhi, Manoj Sharma, Microsave, Lucknow, Meena Negi, UNDP-India, New Delhi, Milroy Paul, Housing Microfinance, Habitat for Humanity India, Chennai, Mukul Jaiswal, CASHPOR MICRO CREDIT, Varanasi, N. Jeyaseelan, Hand in Hand India, Chennai, N. Srinivasan, Independent Consultant, Pune, Navin Anand, Microfinance Community, Solution Exchange, New Delhi, Nirupama Soundararajan, Financial Sector and Corporate law division, FICCI, New Delhi, Prema Gera, UNDP—India, New Delhi, Rajen Vardha, technology for the people, Karnataka, Rangan Varadan, MicroGraam Marketplace Pvt. Ltd, Bangalore,

Ratnesh, UNDP—India, New Delhi, Resham Singh, Punjab Gramin Bank, Punjab, Sachin Kumar, IIMPS, Noida, Smita Premchander, SAMPARK, Bangalore, Tara S. Nair, Gujarat Institute of Development Research, Ahmedabad, Thangaperumal, terre des hommes-netherlands, India Programme, V. Puhazhendhi, Lead author, *State of the Sector Report Microfinance—2012*, Vijayalakshmi Das, ANANYA Finance for Inclusive growth, Ahmedabad, Vipin Sharma, ACCESS Development Services, New Delhi, Y.C. Nanda, former Chairman of NABARD, Gurgaon.

ACKNOWLEDGEMENTS

The proceedings of the roundtable are prepared by Navin Anand Resource Person and Moderator, United Nations Solution Exchange—Microfinance Community whose contribution is gratefully acknowledged. Detailed summary of responses and the proceedings of the roundtable may be seen from UN Solution Exchange—Microfinance community link.The author is grateful to UNSE and all contributors and participants in the roundtable discussion.

Bibliography

Asfaw, A., A. Admassie, J. Von Braun, and J. Jutting. 2004. 'New Dimensions in Measuring Economic Costs of Illness: The Case of Rural Ethiopia. *Quarterly Journal of International Agriculture*, 43(3): 247–266.

Bakshi Prakash. 2012. 'Financial Inclusion—BC/BF Model—What New', Bank Quest, *The Journal of Indian Institute of Banking and Finance*. 83(2), April—June, Mumbai.

Bindu, Ananth, Gregory Chen and Staphen Rasmussen. 2012. *The Pursuit of Complete Financial Inclusion: The KGFS Model in India*. Research Report, CGAP.

Cheston, Susy. 2006. *Just the Facts, Ma'am: Gender Stories from Unexpected Sources with Morals for Microfinance*. Micro-credit Summit Campaign, Washington DC.

Chowbey, Manesh and Mishra, Babu Lal. 2011. *Scope of Promoting Micro-enterprises through SHGs—A Study in Select Districts of Uttar Pradesh and Bihar*. Patna: Sub-centre of Centre for Microfinance Research Centre.

Daniel Rozas. 2011. *The State of the Practice, 2011. A Report from the Smart Campaign*. Center for Financial Inclusion Publication No. 14.

David M. Dror and Sukumar Vellakkal. 2012. *Indian Journal of Medical Research*, January 135(1): 5–63.

De, Sudipta and D. Sarker. 2010. 'Impact of Micro-credit Programmes on Women Empowerment: An Empirical Study in West Bengal', *The Microfinance Review*, 2(1): 46–67. Lucknow: Bankers Institute of Rural Development.

Deepti, K.C. 2012. *Rethinking Reserve Bank of India (RBI) Regulations for MFIs*, Chennai: Center for Microfinance, IFMR.

Dhanya, M.B. and P. Sivakumar. 2010. 'Microfinance, Women Empowerment and Banking Habit: Perspectives on Kerala', *The Microfinance Review*, 2(1): 97–109. Lucknow: Bankers Institute of Rural Development.

Economic Intelligence Unit. 2012. *Global Microscope on the Microfinance Business Environment 2009–2011*. New York, USA: Economic Intelligence Unit Ltd.

Eversole, Robyn. 2003. 'Help, Risk, and Deceit: Micro-entrepreneurs Talk about Microfinance', *Journal of International Development*, 15, 179–188.

GOI. 2012. *The Union Budget*. Ministry of Finance, Government of India, New Delhi.

GOI. 2012. *The Economic Survey 2012*. Ministry of Finance, Government of India, New Delhi.

Government of India. 2011. *Faster, Sustainable and more Inclusive Growth- Approach Paper to the 12th Five Year Plan*. October. Planning Commission, Government of India, New Delhi.

Graham, A.N. Wright, Mukesh Sadana, Puneet Chopra and Manoj Sharma. 2011. *Why EM Banking will Soon Reach Scale in India*. Research Report, MicroSave, December 2011.

Gyanendra, Mani and T. Sudheer. 2012. 'Two Decades of SHG Bank Linkage Programme: Different Facets', *The Microfinance Review*, IV(1), January—June, Bankers Institute of Rural Development, Lucknow.

Harper, Malcolm, 2012. 'Self Help Group 2 Vs MFIs—Competing to Serve the Poor', *The Micro Finance Review*, Centre for Microfinance Research, 4(1), Lucknow: Bankers Institute for Rural development.

Heijden, Jael van der. 2006. *Sustainability and Empowerment through SHG Federations—A Study in East Uttar Pradesh, India*. Thesis submitted for the Masters Program in International Development Studies (IDS), University of Amsterdam, The Hague, Netherlands.

IMF, 2012. *World Economic Outlook Update, April 2012.* International Monetary Fund, Washington DC, USA.

Kenny, Kline and Santadarshan Sahu, 2011. *Microfinance In India—New Regulatory Structure.* Centre for Micro Finance, IFMR research, Chennai.

Kumar, Pankaj and Ramesh Golait. 2009. *Bank Penetration and SHG Bank Linkage Programme: A Critique.* Reserve Bank of India Occasional Papers, Vol. 29(3), Mumbai.

Kumar, S. 2010. *Study on SHG Federations—Challenges and Opportunities.* Lucknow: Centre for Microfinance Research, Bankers Institute for Rural Development.

Leatherman, S. and C. Dunford. 2009. 'Linking Health to Microfinance to Reach the Poor', *Bulletin of the World Health Organization*, 2010; 88(6): 470–471.

Mahajan, R.K. and D. Bansal. 2009. 'Microfinance and Women Empowerment: A Case Study of Punjab', *The Microfinance Review*, 1(1): 84–104. Lucknow: Bankers Institute for Rural Development.

Metcalfe, M., S. Leatherman with C. Dunford, B. Gray, M. Gash, M. Reinsch and C. Chandler. 2010. 'Health and Microfinance: Leveraging the Strengths of Two Sectors to Alleviate Poverty', Freedom from Hunger Research Paper No. 9, p. 27.

Metcalfe. 2012. *Integrated Health and Microfinance in India: Harnessing the Strengths of Two Sectors to Improve Health and Alleviate Poverty, State of the Field of Integrated Health and Microfinance in India, 2012.* Freedom from Hunger and the Micro Credit Summit Campaign.

MicroSave. 2011. *SBI Tatkal—From Cash to Cash Cow.* India Focus Note 68, MicroSave, India.

MicroSave. 2011. *Micro insurance in India: Evolution of Market Trends.* India Focus Note 87, MicroSave, India.

MicroSave. 2011. *Making Business Correspondence Work in India.* India Focus Note 22, MicroSave, India.

NABARD. 2012. *Annual Report 2011–12.* National Bank for Agriculture and Rural Development, Mumbai,

Nair, A. 2005. *Sustainability of Microfinance Self Help Groups in India: Would Federating Help?* World Bank Policy Research Working Paper 3516, The World Bank, Washington DC, USA.

Niels, Hermes and Aljar Meesters. 2011. 'The Performance of Microfinance Institutions: Do Macro conditions Matter?' *The Handbook of Microfinance*, World Scientific, 2011.

Panda, D.K. and H. Atibudhi. 2009. 'Impact of Group Based Microfinance on Rural Household Savings: Empirical Findings from India', *The Microfinance Review*, 1(1): 54–68, Lucknow: Bankers Institute of Rural Development.

Puhazhendhi, V. 2012. 'Financial Inclusion—Forward step for Microfinance Sector', Bank Quest, *The Journal of Indian Institute of Banking and Finance.* 83(2), April–June, Mumbai.

RBI. 2012. *Mid-Quarter Monetary Policy Review—June 2012.* Reserve Bank of India, Mumbai.

RBI, 2012. *Annual Report 2011–12.* Reserve Bank of India, Mumbai.

Reddy, V. Ratna and S. Galab. 2010. 'Agrarian Crisis: Looking beyond the Debt Trap'. *Economic and Political Weekly*, XLI(19): 1838–1841.

Reed, L.R. 2011. *State of the Microcredit Summit Campaign Report 2011.* Washington, DC: Microcredit Summit Campaign (MCS).

Reinsch, M. C. Dunford and M. Metcalfe. 2011. *Costs and Benefits of Microfinance Institutions Offering Health Protection Services to Clients.* Enterprise Development and Microfinance, 22(3): 241–258.

Sa-Dhan. 2012. *The Bharat Microfinance Quick Report.* Sa-Dhan Publication, New Delhi.

Sa-Dhan. 2012. 'Microfinance—Growing Against All Odds', *The Bharat Microfinance Quick Report 2012.* New Delhi: Sa-dhan Publication.

Saha, S. 2011. 'Provision of Health Services for Microfinance Clients: Analysis of Evidence from India', *International Journal of Medical Public Health*, 1(1), 1–6.

Sahu, Gagan Bihari. 2012. *Loan Defaults by SHGs in Odisha and Madhya Pradesh*. IDS, Jaipur Sub-centre of Centre for Microfinance Research, Lucknow: Bankers Institute of Rural Development.

Selvaraj, S. and A.K. Karan. 2009. 'Deepening Health Insecurity in India: Evidence from National Sample Surveys since 1980s', *Economic and Political Weekly*, 44(40), 55–60.

Sharma, Abhijit. 2011. *Delinquencies by SHGs in North East*. IIBM, Guwahati, Sub-centre of Centre for Microfinance Research, Lucknow: Bankers Institute of Rural development.

Singh, Surjit and Gagan Bihari Sahu, 2011. *SHG Bank Linkages in North West India—Experiences and Challenges in Financial Access and Poverty Alleviation*. IDS, Jaipur, Sub-centre of Centre for Microfinance Research, Lucknow: Bankers Institute of Rural Development.

Srinivasan, N. 2009. *Microfinance India: State of the Sector Report 2009*. Access Development Services, New Delhi: SAGE Publications.

Srinivasan, N. 2010. *Microfinance India: State of the Sector Report 2010*. Access Development Services, New Delhi: SAGE Publications.

Srinivasan, N. 2011. *Microfinance India: State of the Sector Report 2011*. Access Development Services, New Delhi: SAGE Publications.

Srinivasan, Girija and Ajay Tankha. 2010. *SHG Federations: Development Costs and Dustainability*. New Delhi: Access Development Services.

Sriram, M. 2010. 'Microfinance: A Fairy Tale Turns into a Nightmare', *Economic and Political Weekly*, Vol. 43, 23, October.

Srinivasan. Girija, 2012. *Microfinance Social Performance Report 2012*. Access Development Services, New Delhi: SAGE Publications.

Tankha, Ajay. 2012. *Banking on Self Help Groups—Twenty Years on*. New Delhi: SAGE Publications.

Tarozzi, A., A. Mahajan, B. Blackburn and D. Kopf. 2011. *Micro-Loans, Insecticide-Treated Bednets and Malaria: Evidence from a Randomized Controlled Trial in Odisha (India)*. Economic Research Initiatives at Duke (ERID) Working Paper No. 104.

Tripathi, Ashutosh. 2012. *Life Cycle of SHGs—What are the Critical Interventions Required in the Life Cycle of a SHG*. Centre for Microfinance Research, Lucknow: Bankers Institute of Rural development (on-going study).

Tripathy, P., N. Nair, S. Barnett and R. Mahapatra. 2010. 'Effect of a Participatory Intervention with Women's Groups on Birth Outcomes and Maternal Depression in Jharkhand and Orissa, India: A Cluster-Randomised Controlled Trial', *The Lancet*, 375(9721), 1182–1192.

Umapathy, D., P. Agarwal and S. Sadhu. 2012. *Evaluation of Financial Literacy Training Programmes in India: A Scoping Study*. Chennai: Institute for Financial Management and Research.

Index

Knowledge Partner

Solution Exchange, launched at the beginning of 2005, is a unique initiative experiment of the United Nations that provides an impartial platform for exchange of knowledge and ideas among development practitioners in key thematic areas relevant for achieving under the framework of the Millennium Development Goals (MDGs). The UN serves as a catalyst and plays a facilitation role. The project has various Communities of Practice around different domains related to the MDGs. Solution Exchange brings together practitioners cutting across institutional boundaries to share knowledge, ideas, information and experiences.

Technical Partners

Centre for Micro Finance (CMF) at IFMR Research, Chennai was established in 2005 to conduct rigorous research in topics related to financial inclusion for the poor in India to improve access to and quality of financial services through knowledge dissemination and evidence-based policy outreach. Since its inception, CMF has conducted over 65 research studies that are completed or are currently being implemented in different regions of India. CMF works with many prominent national financial-service providers, researchers, policy makers and regulators, in addition to internationally renowned universities and organizations.

MicroSave is a consultancy firm and training provider that focuses on the needs of financial institutions targeting under- and unserved populations and enterprises. We also assist institutions such as telecom operators, technology service providers, fast-moving consumer goods companies, livelihood institutions and development agencies serving the bottom of the pyramid. We have nearly 80 financial services professionals assisting our clients to achieve their business objectives with practical, market-led solutions.

MIX is the premier source for objective, qualified and relevant microfinance performance data and analysis. Committed to strengthening financial inclusion and the microfinance sector by promoting transparency, MIX provides performance information on microfinance institutions (MFIs), funders, networks and service providers dedicated to serving the financial sector needs for low-income clients. MIX fulfils its mission through a variety of platforms.

On MIX Market (www.mixmarket.org), we provide instant access to financial and social performance information covering approximately 2,000 MFIs around the world. Our publications, *MicroBanking Bulletin* and *MIX Microfinance World*, feature thorough and timely analysis based on qualified data and research. Incorporated in 2002, MIX is a non-profit organization headquartered in Washington DC with regional offices in Azerbaijan, India, Morocco and Peru.

About the Author

Venugopalan Puhazhendhi has been involved with microfinance research for three decades. He has been providing professional support to the committee on 'Financial Inclusion', headed by Dr C. Rangarajan, and the committee on 'Agricultural Indebtedness', headed by Dr Radhakrishna constituted by the Government of India. The study report authored by him on 'Impact evaluation of Self Help Group Bank Linkage Programme in India' published by NABARD is one of the widely referred reports in the microfinance sector. He has published five research papers in international journals and about 30 research articles in leading Indian journals. He also undertook consultancy assignments with IFAD, UNDP and others.

He has two decades of research experience in the field of programme evaluation and microfinance in NABARD as agricultural economist. Till recently, he was teaching Agricultural Economics to management students in Konkuk University, Seoul, South Korea, for four years. Presently, he is an independent consultant in Development Economics.